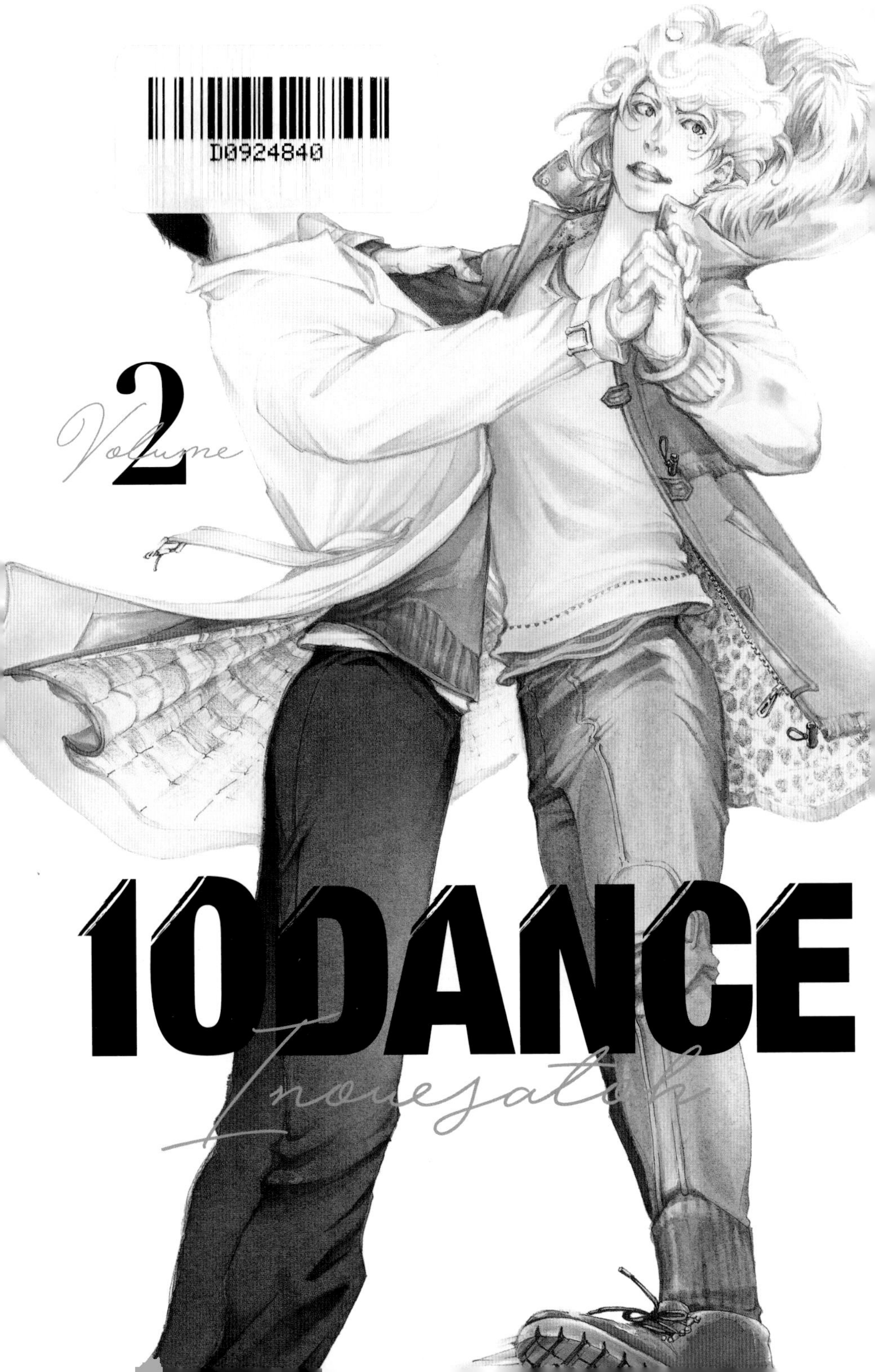
Volume
2
10DANCE
Inouesatoh

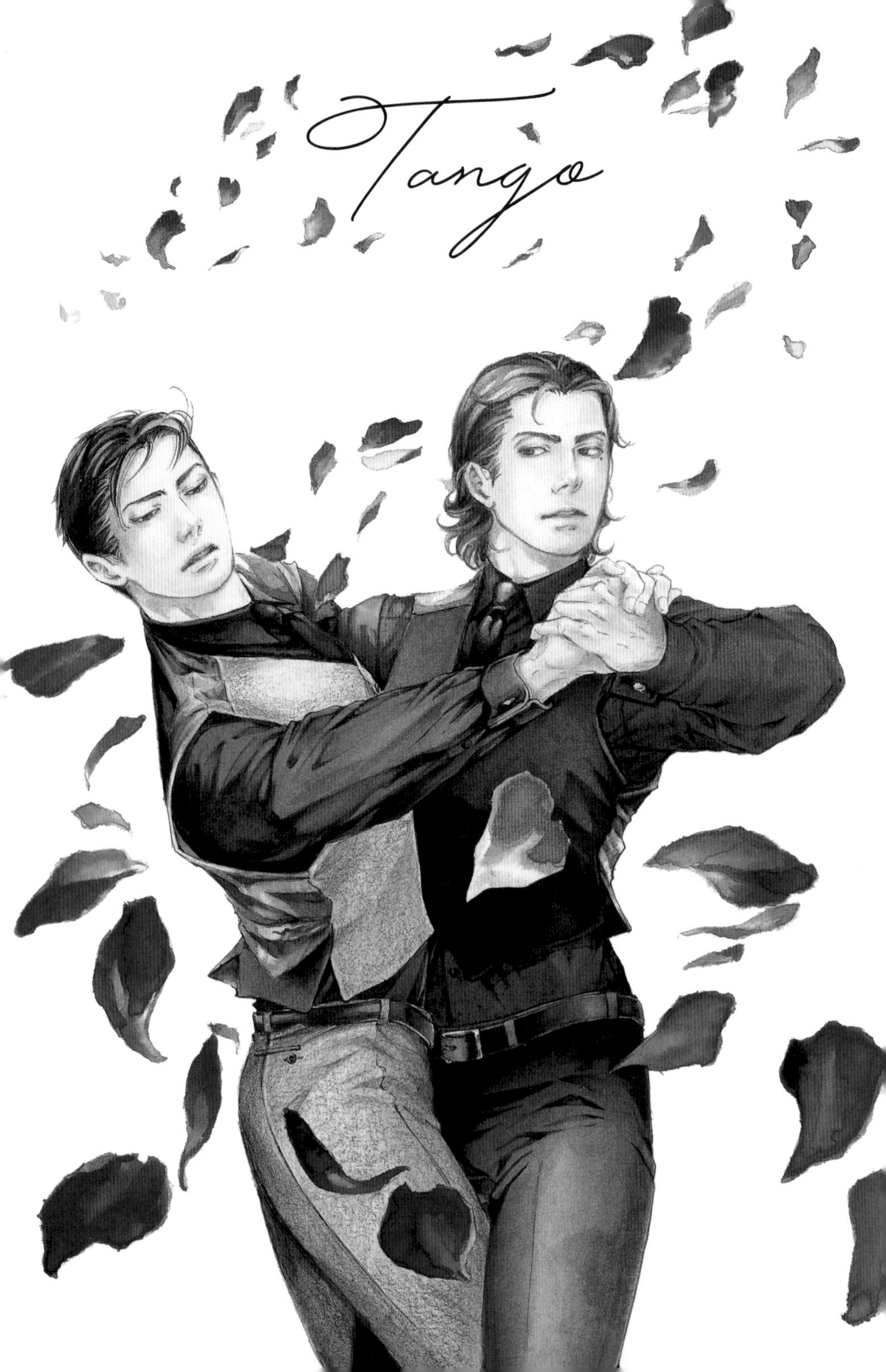
Tango

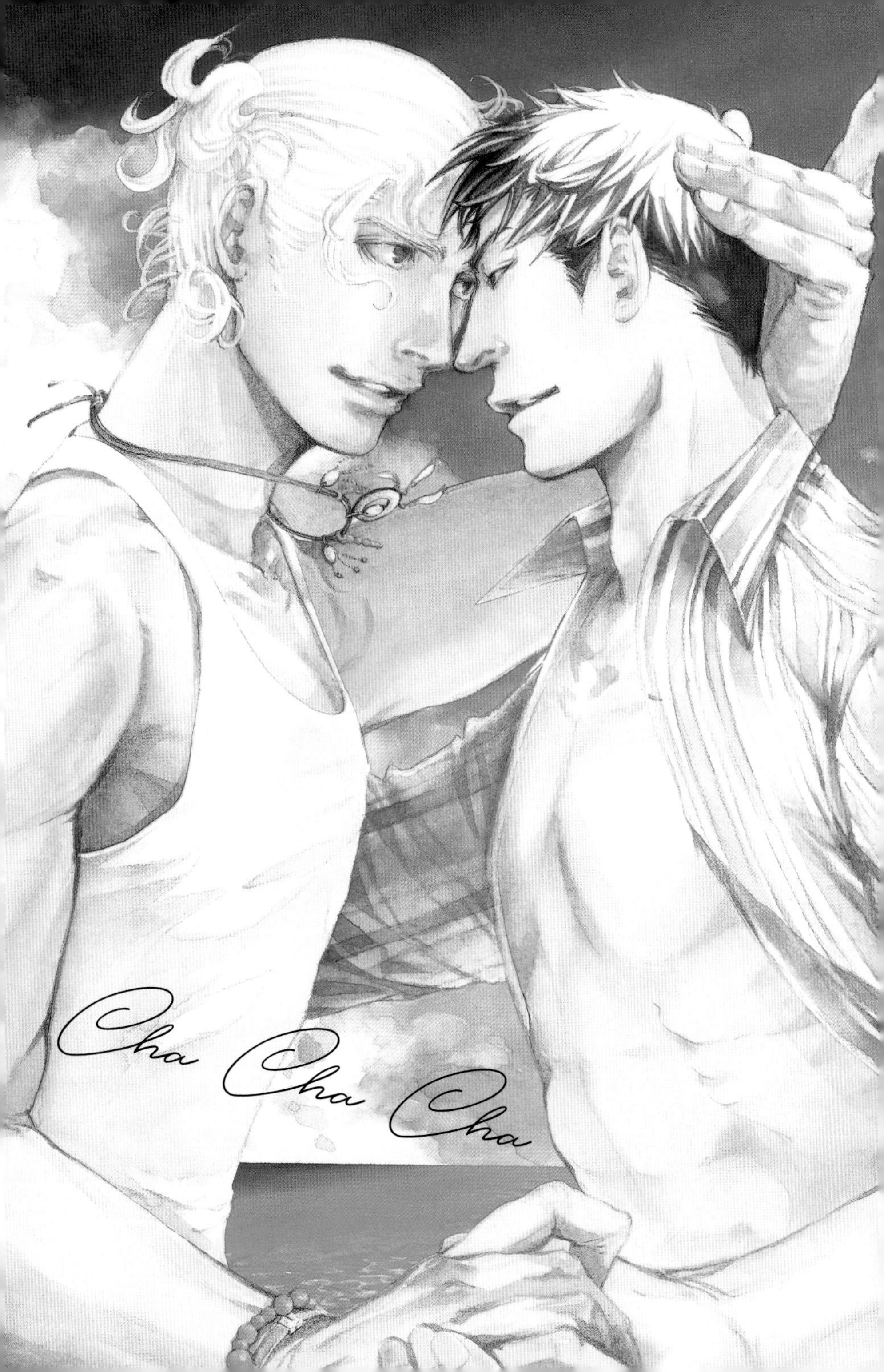
Cha Cha Cha

Contents

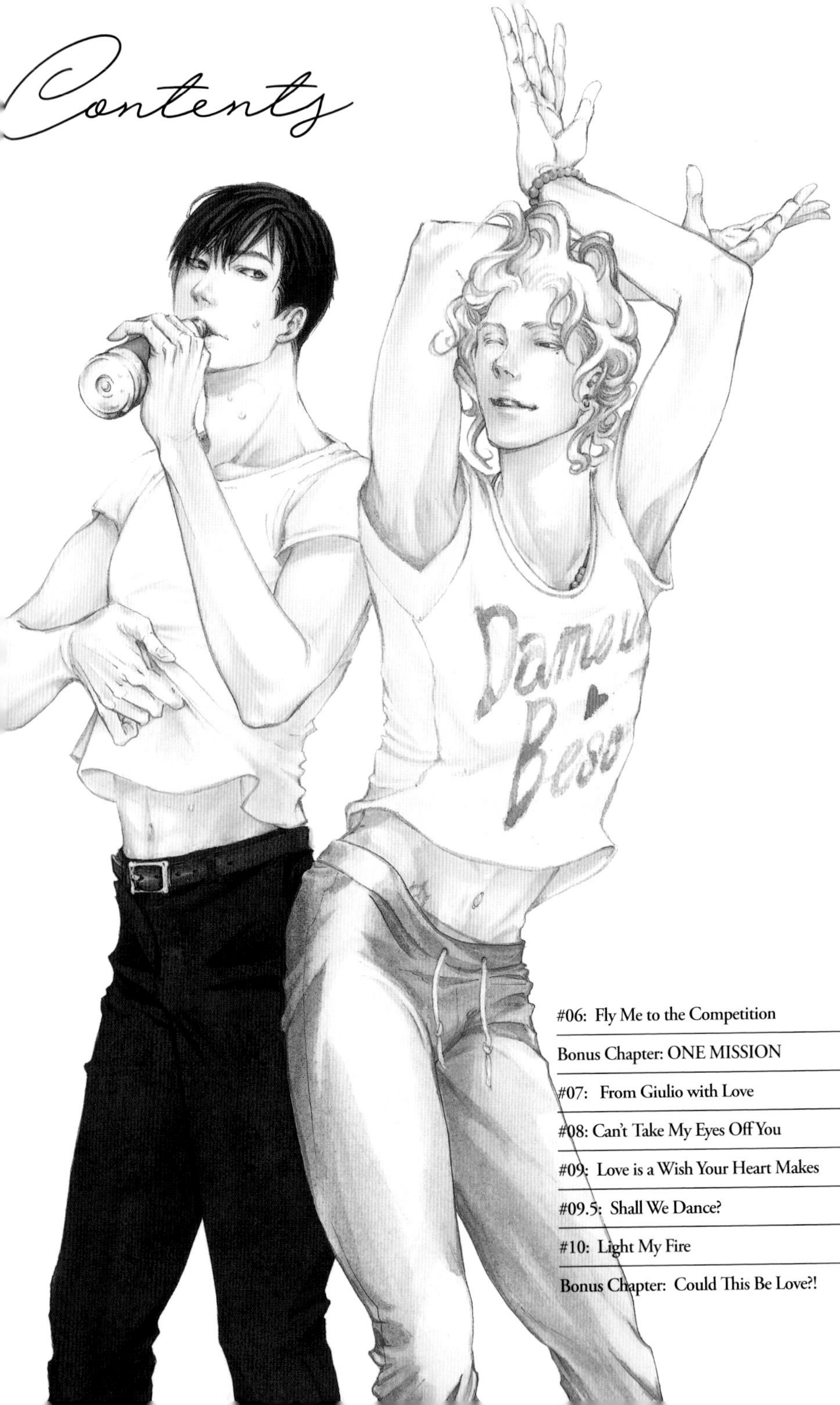

#06

FLY ME TO THE COMPETITION

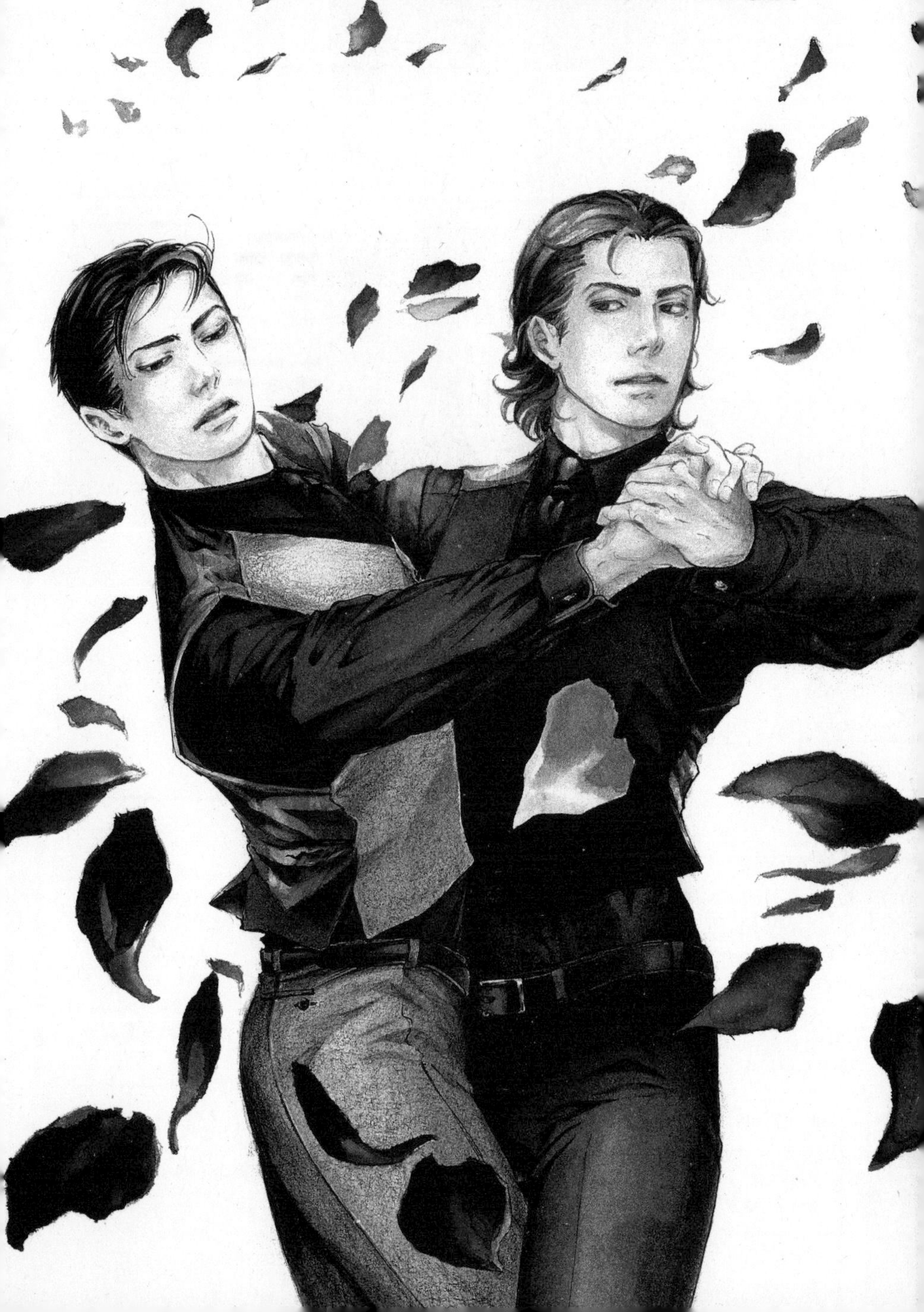

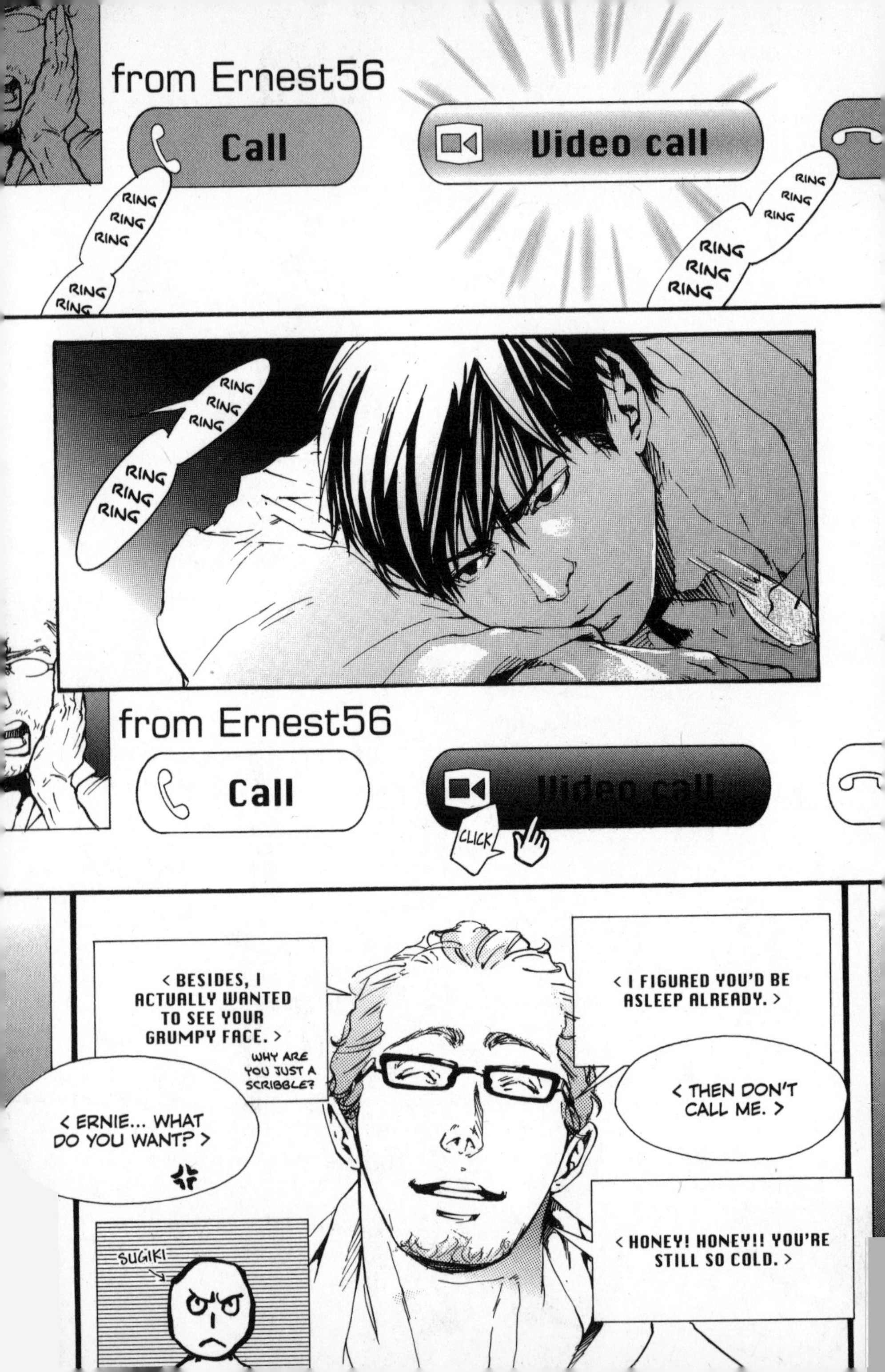
RING
RING
RING
RING
RING
RING
Video call
Call
from Ernest56
RING
RING
RING
RING
RING
RING
RING
RING
RING
RING
RING
from Ernest56
Call
Video call
CLICK
< I FIGURED YOU'D BE ASLEEP ALREADY. >
< THEN DON'T CALL ME. >
< HONEY! HONEY!! YOU'RE STILL SO COLD. >
< BESIDES, I ACTUALLY WANTED TO SEE YOUR GRUMPY FACE. >
WHY ARE YOU JUST A SCRIBBLE?
< ERNIE... WHAT DO YOU WANT? >
SUGIKI

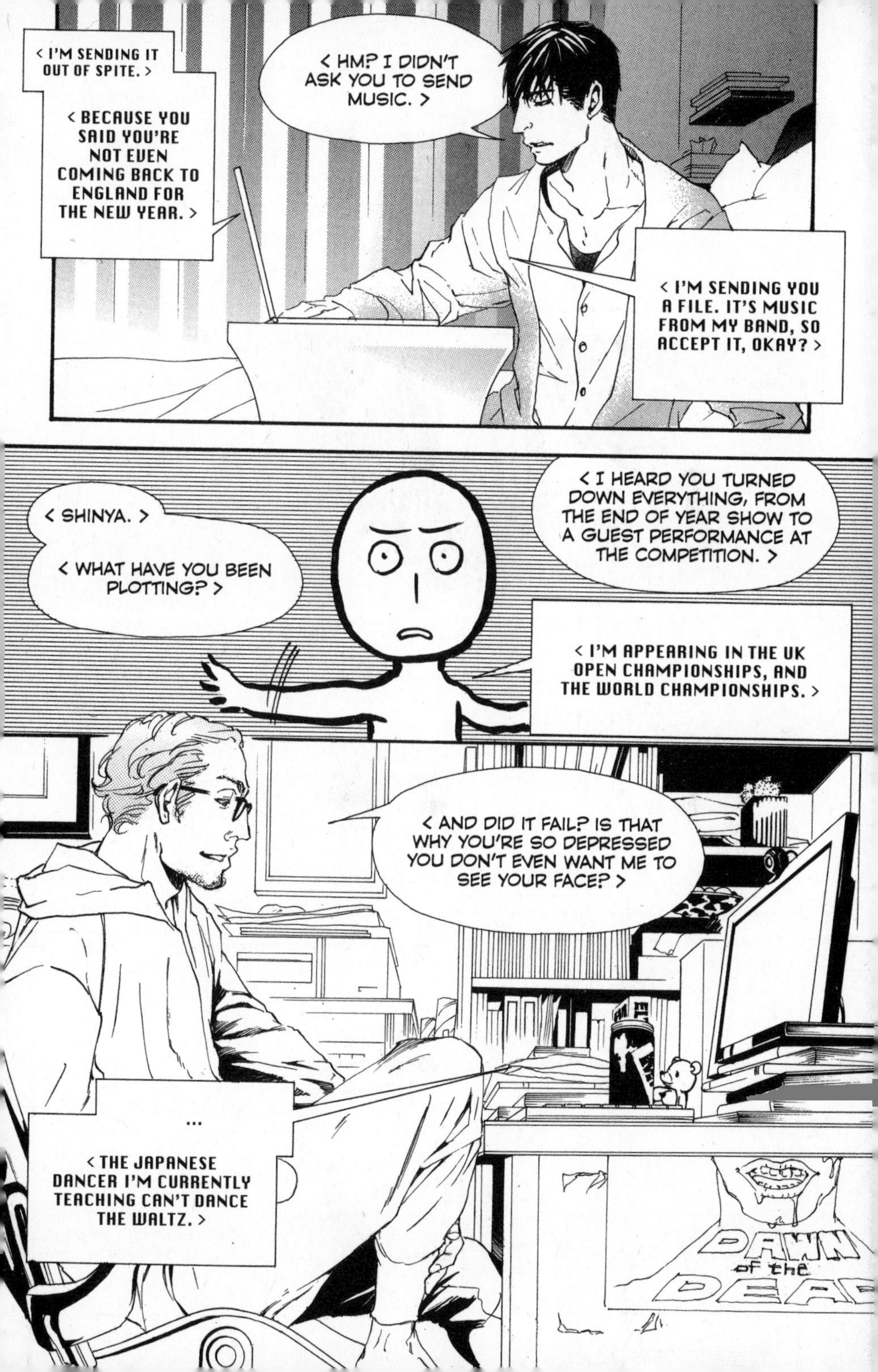
< I'M SENDING YOU A FILE. IT'S MUSIC FROM MY BAND, SO ACCEPT IT, OKAY? >
< HM? I DIDN'T ASK YOU TO SEND MUSIC. >
< I'M SENDING IT OUT OF SPITE. >
< BECAUSE YOU SAID YOU'RE NOT EVEN COMING BACK TO ENGLAND FOR THE NEW YEAR. >
< I HEARD YOU TURNED DOWN EVERYTHING, FROM THE END OF YEAR SHOW TO A GUEST PERFORMANCE AT THE COMPETITION. >
< SHINYA. >
< WHAT HAVE YOU BEEN PLOTTING? >
< I'M APPEARING IN THE UK OPEN CHAMPIONSHIPS, AND THE WORLD CHAMPIONSHIPS. >
< AND DID IT FAIL? IS THAT WHY YOU'RE SO DEPRESSED YOU DON'T EVEN WANT ME TO SEE YOUR FACE? >
...
< THE JAPANESE DANCER I'M CURRENTLY TEACHING CAN'T DANCE THE WALTZ. >
of the

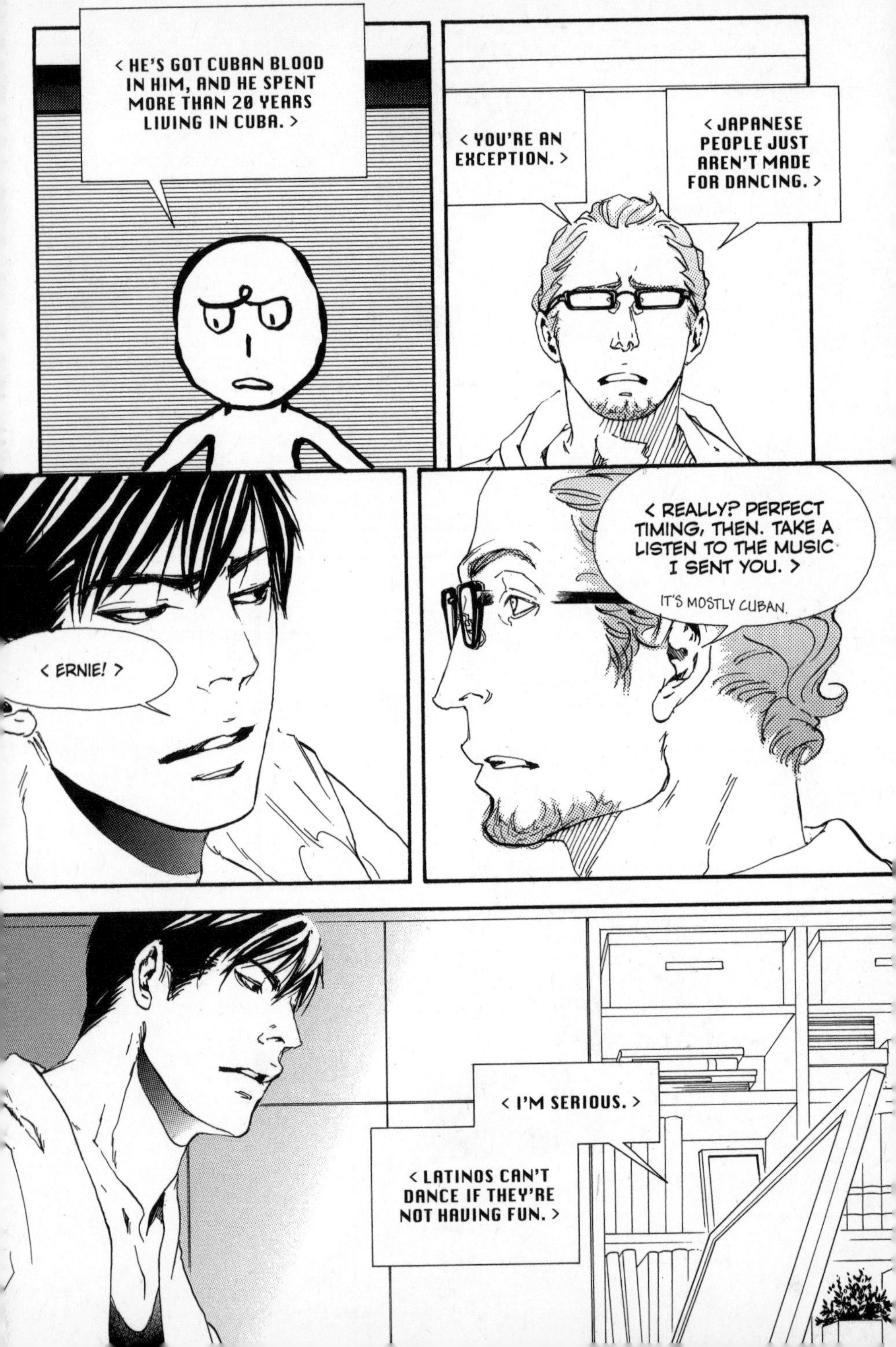
< JAPANESE PEOPLE JUST AREN'T MADE FOR DANCING. >
< YOU'RE AN EXCEPTION. >
< HE'S GOT CUBAN BLOOD IN HIM, AND HE SPENT MORE THAN 20 YEARS LIVING IN CUBA. >
< REALLY? PERFECT TIMING, THEN. TAKE A LISTEN TO THE MUSIC I SENT YOU. >
IT'S MOSTLY CUBAN.
< ERNIE! >
< I'M SERIOUS. >
< LATINOS CAN'T DANCE IF THEY'RE NOT HAVING FUN. >

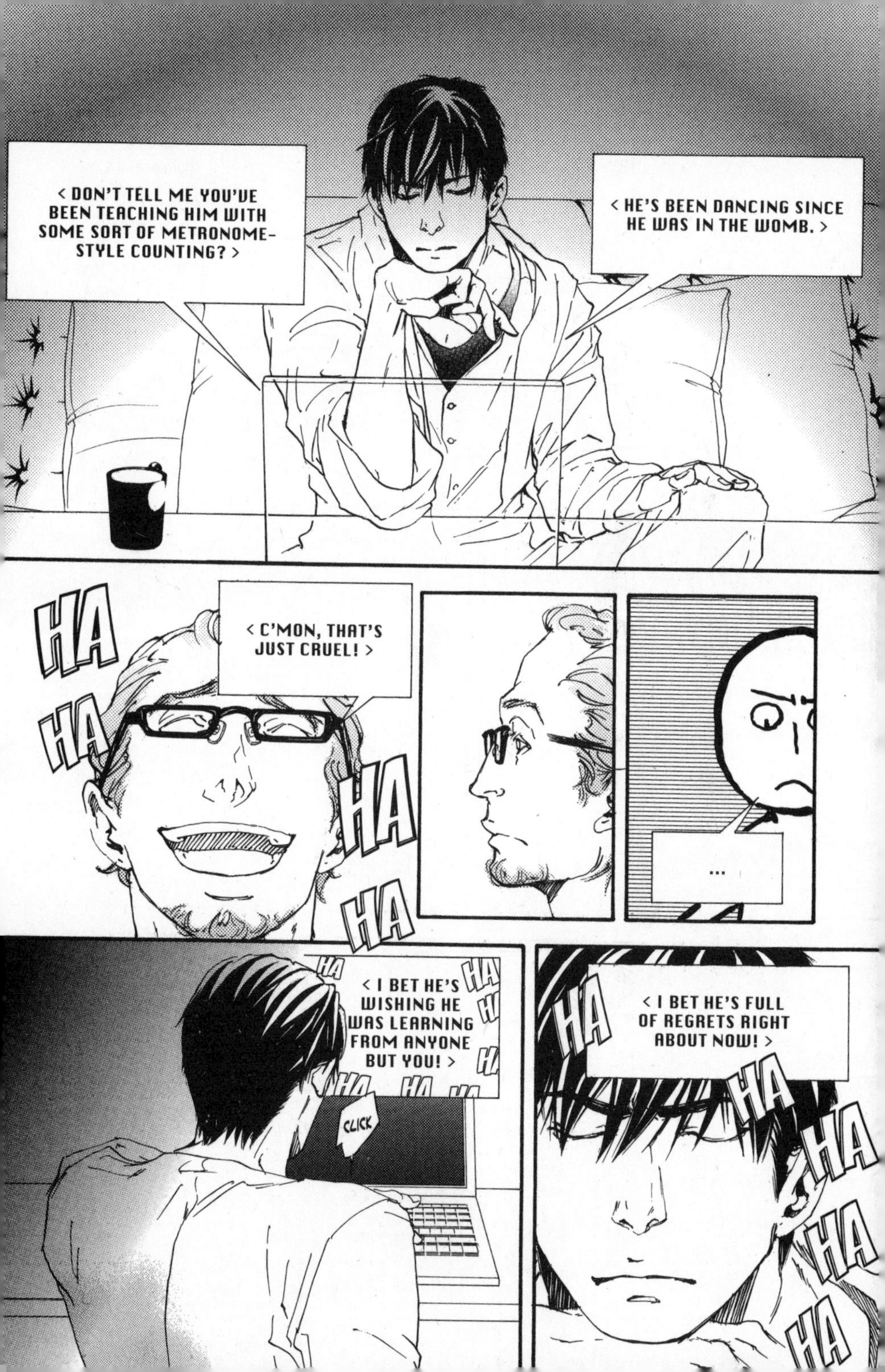
< HE'S BEEN DANCING SINCE HE WAS IN THE WOMB. >
< DON'T TELL ME YOU'VE BEEN TEACHING HIM WITH SOME SORT OF METRONOME-STYLE COUNTING? >
...
< C'MON, THAT'S JUST CRUEL! >
HA HA HA HA
< I BET HE'S FULL OF REGRETS RIGHT ABOUT NOW! >
HA HA HA HA HA
< I BET HE'S WISHING HE WAS LEARNING FROM ANYONE BUT YOU! >
HA HA HA HA HA HA HA
CLICK

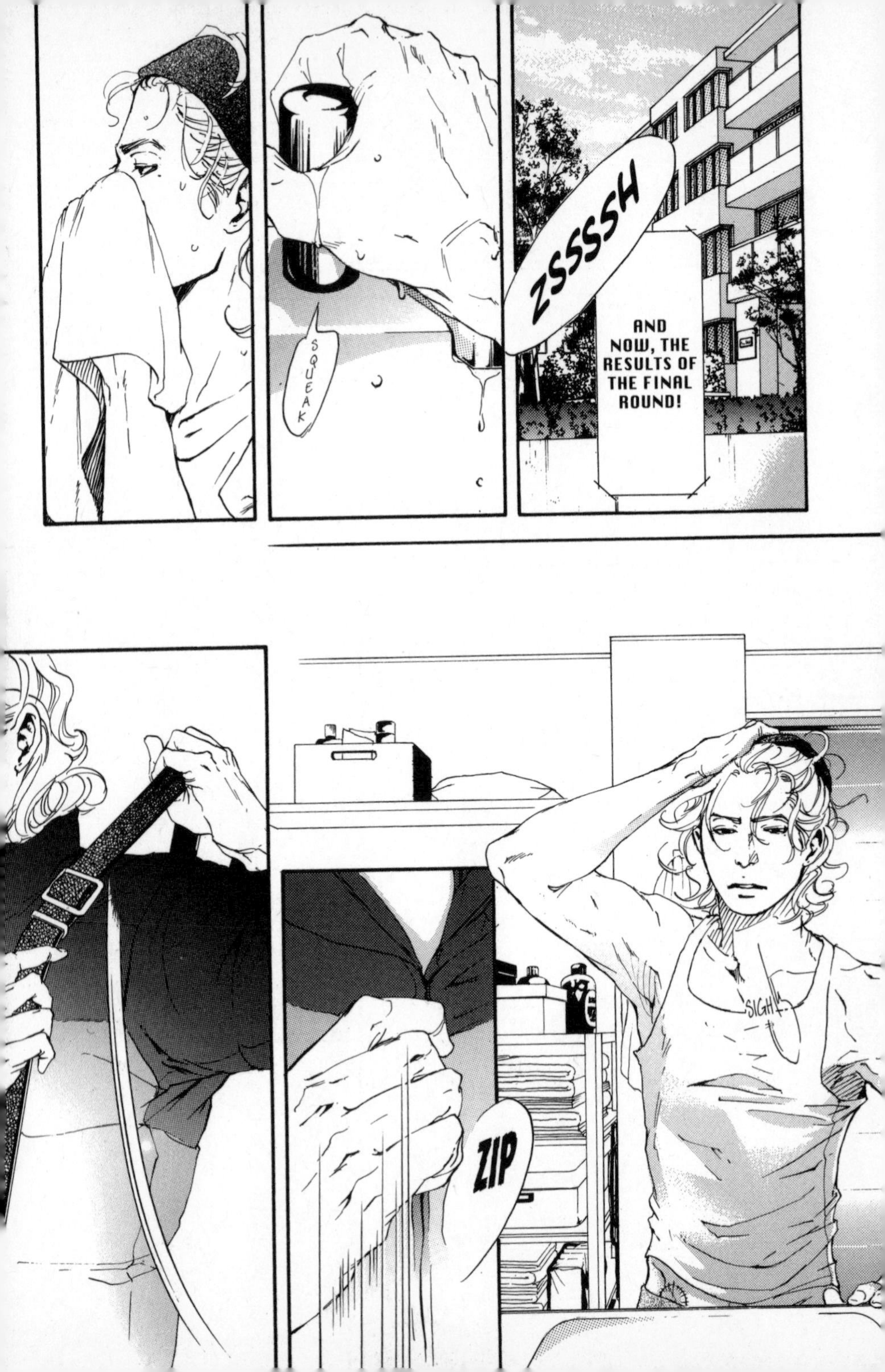
ZSSSSH
AND NOW, THE RESULTS OF THE FINAL ROUND!
SQUEAK
SIGH
ZIP

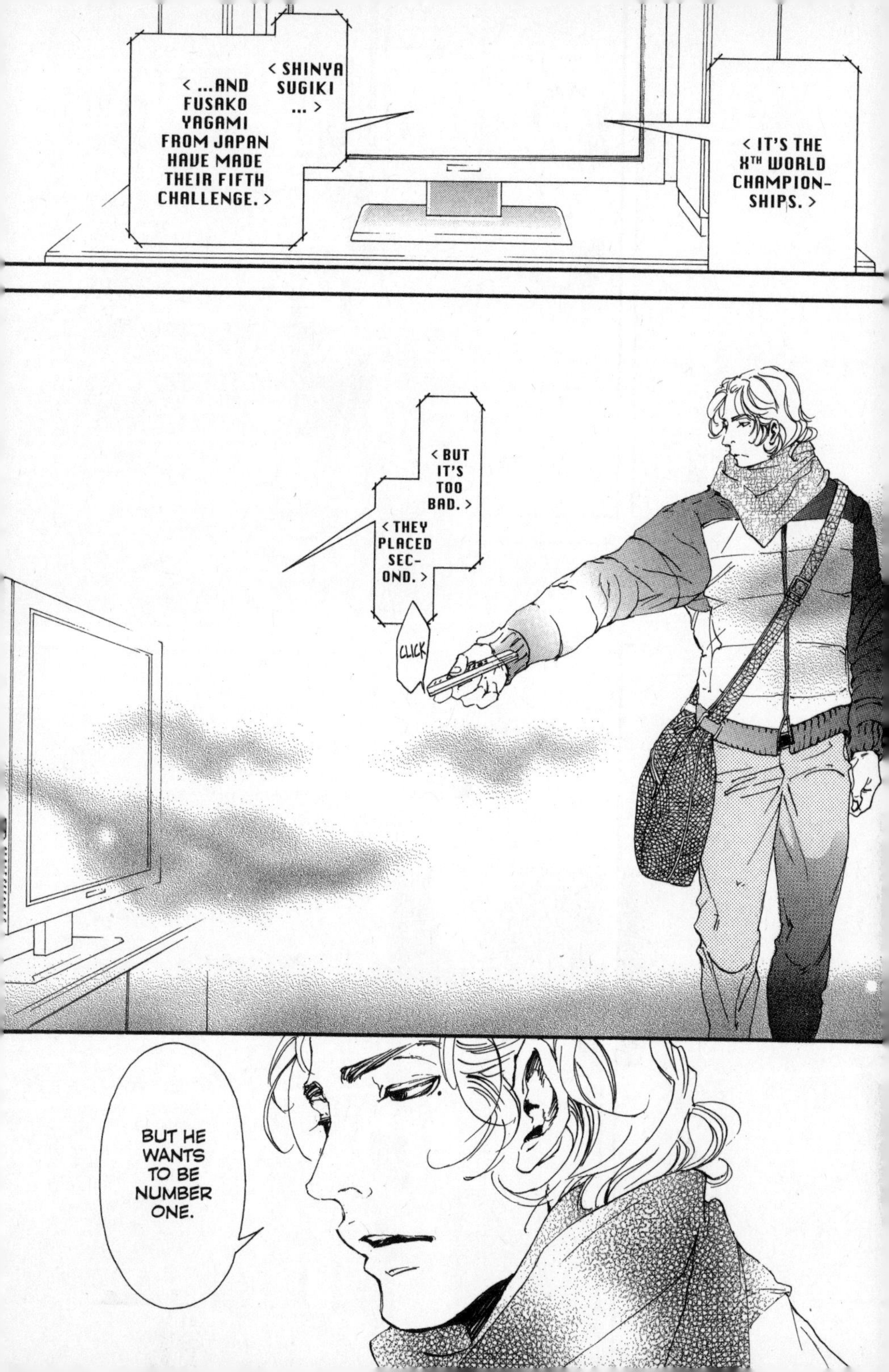
< IT'S THE Xth WORLD CHAMPIONSHIPS. >
< SHINYA SUGIKI ... >
< ...AND FUSAKO YAGAMI FROM JAPAN HAVE MADE THEIR FIFTH CHALLENGE. >
< BUT IT'S TOO BAD. >
< THEY PLACED SEC-OND. >
CLICK
BUT HE WANTS TO BE NUMBER ONE.

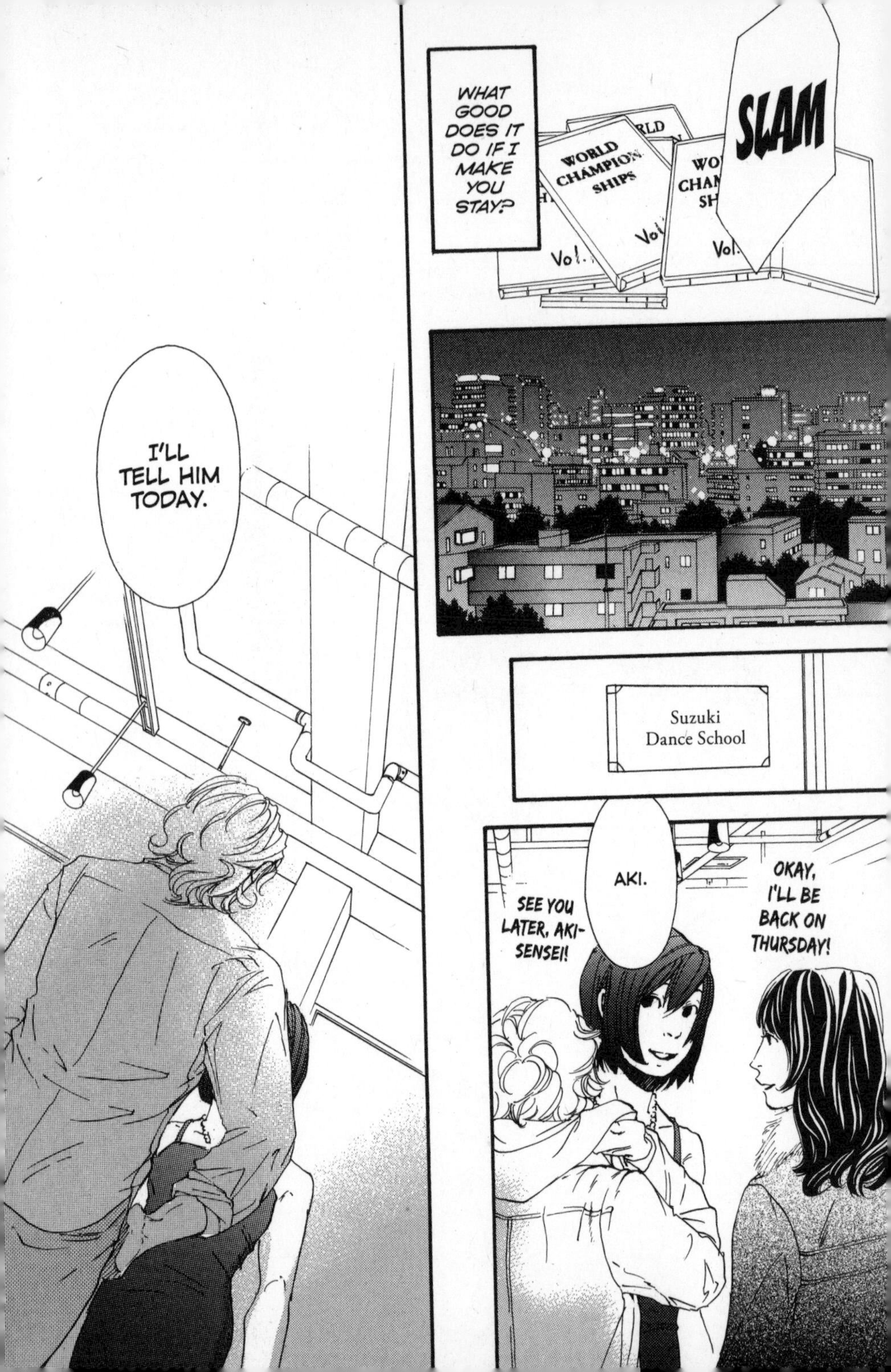
SLAM
WORLD CHAMPIONSHIPS Vol.
WHAT GOOD DOES IT DO IF I MAKE YOU STAY?
Suzuki Dance School
OKAY, I'LL BE BACK ON THURSDAY!
AKI.
SEE YOU LATER, AKI-SENSEI!
I'LL TELL HIM TODAY.

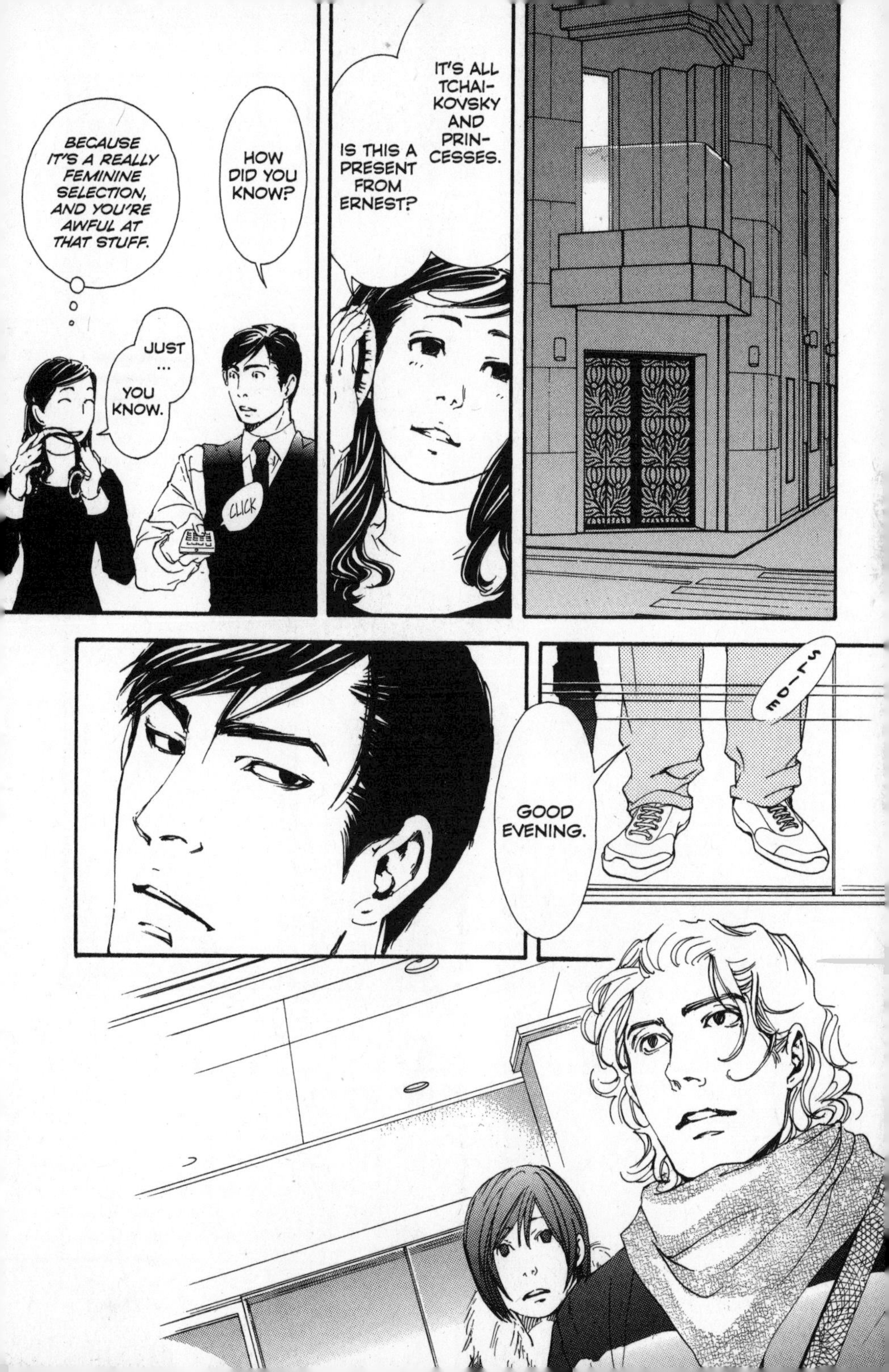
IT'S ALL TCHAIKOVSKY AND PRINCESSES.
IS THIS A PRESENT FROM ERNEST?
HOW DID YOU KNOW?
BECAUSE IT'S A REALLY FEMININE SELECTION, AND YOU'RE AWFUL AT THAT STUFF.
JUST ... YOU KNOW.
CLICK
SLIDE
GOOD EVENING.

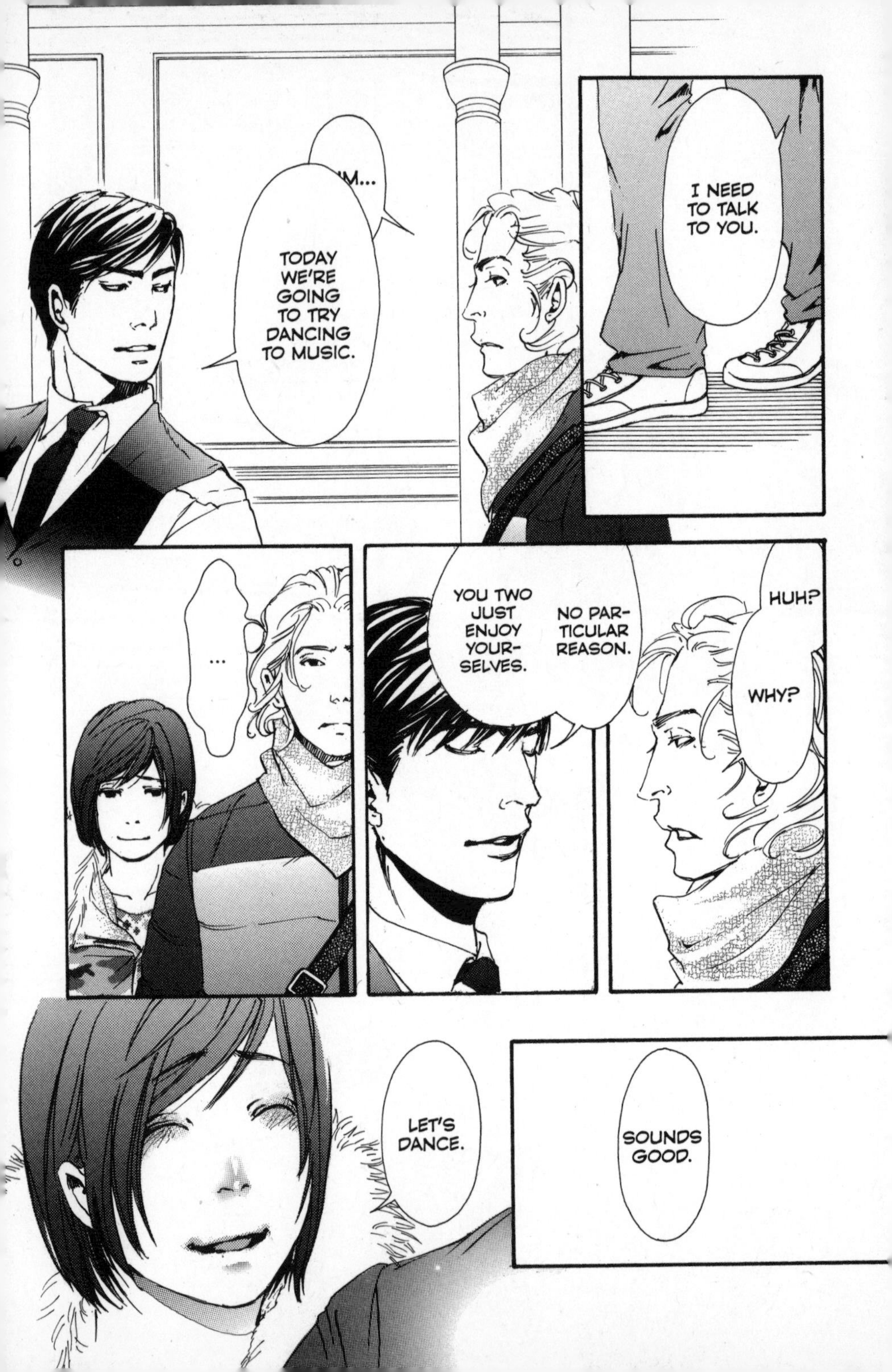
I NEED TO TALK TO YOU.
M...
TODAY WE'RE GOING TO TRY DANCING TO MUSIC.
HUH?
WHY?
NO PAR-TICULAR REASON.
YOU TWO JUST ENJOY YOUR-SELVES.
...
SOUNDS GOOD.
LET'S DANCE.

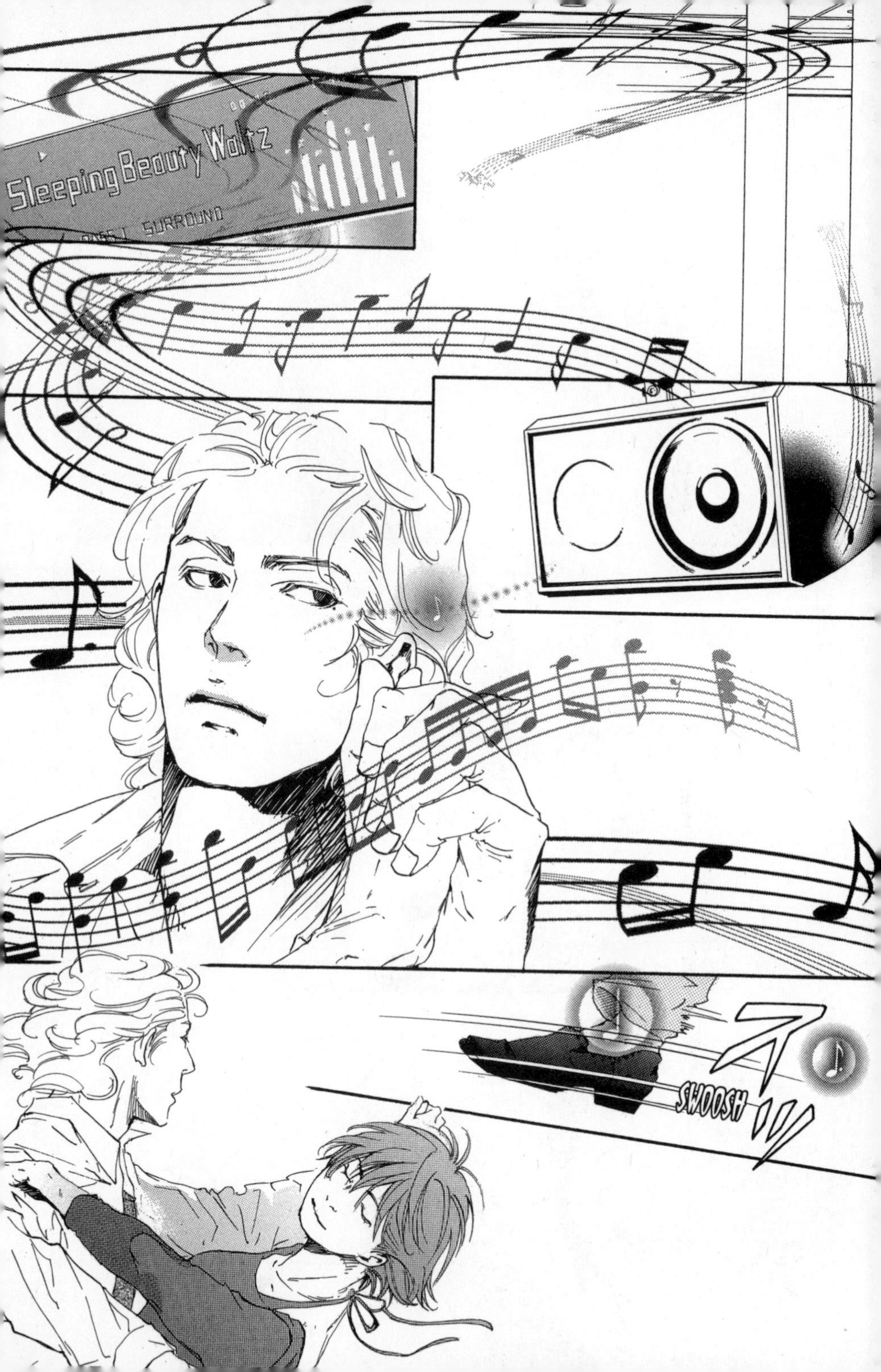
Sleeping Beauty Waltz
SURROUND
SWOOSH

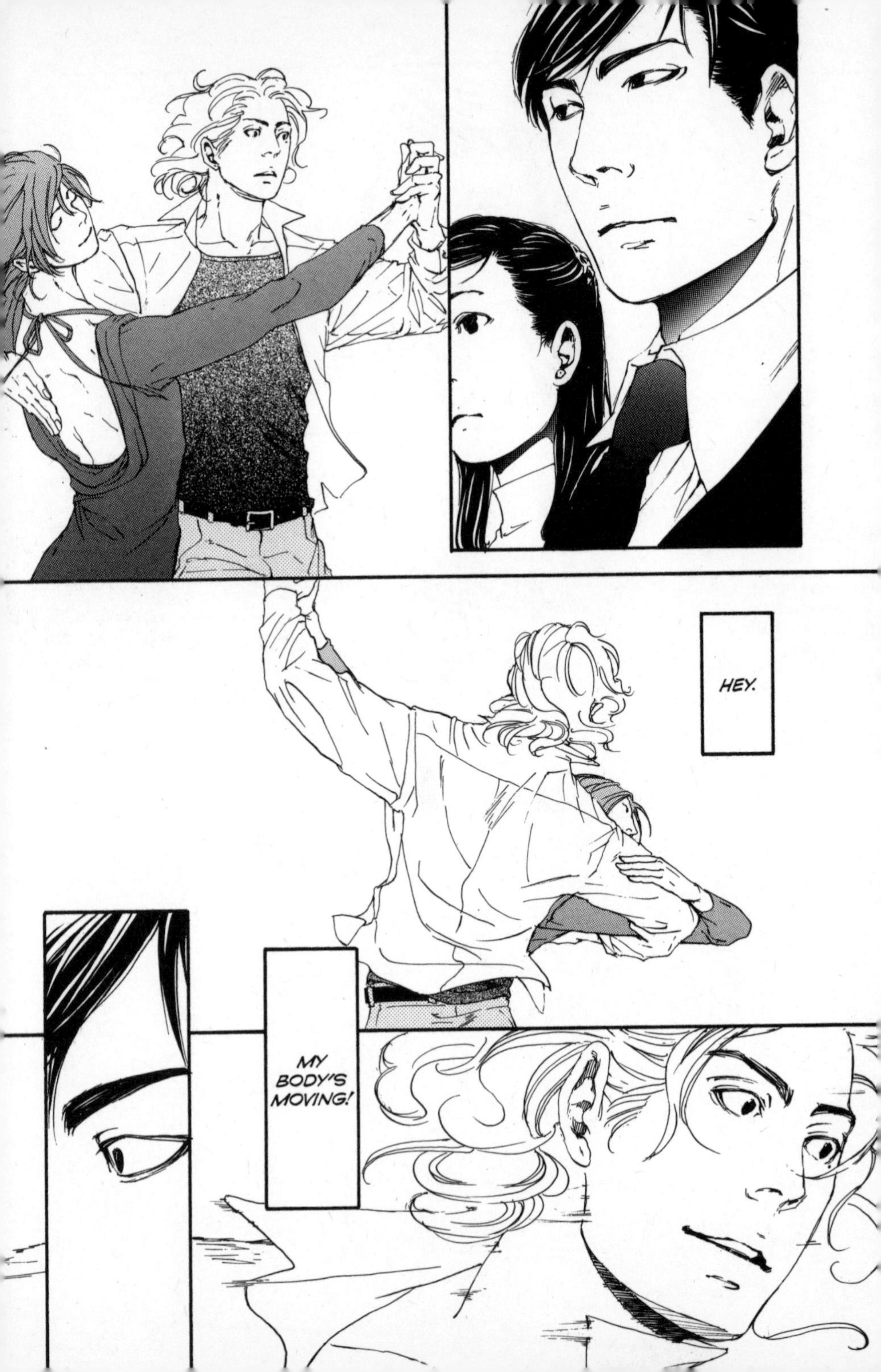
HEY.
MY BODY'S MOVING!

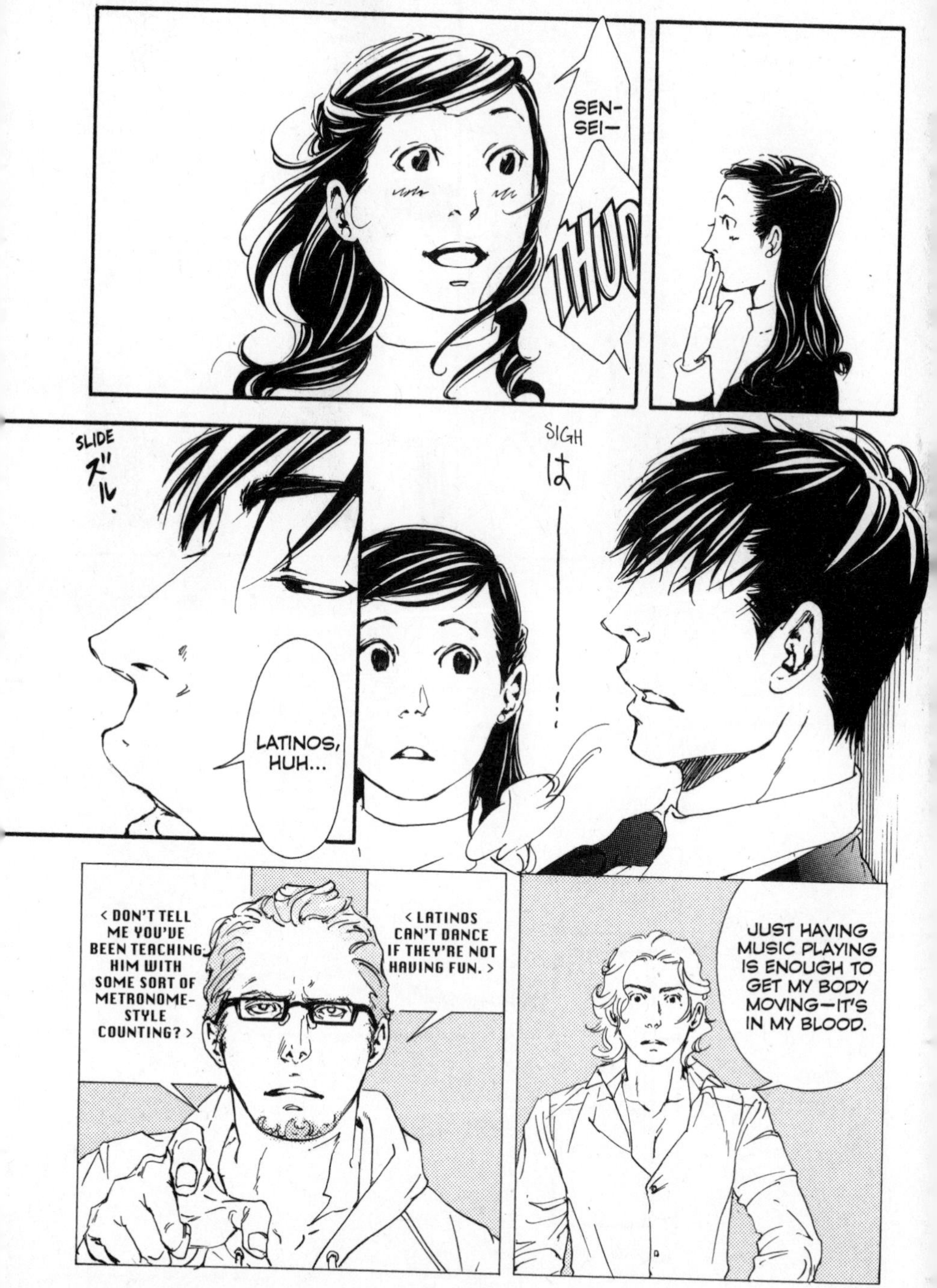
SEN-SEI—
THUD
SIGH
は
SLIDE
ズル
LATINOS, HUH...
JUST HAVING MUSIC PLAYING IS ENOUGH TO GET MY BODY MOVING—IT'S IN MY BLOOD.
< LATINOS CAN'T DANCE IF THEY'RE NOT HAVING FUN. >
< DON'T TELL ME YOU'VE BEEN TEACHING HIM WITH SOME SORT OF METRONOME-STYLE COUNTING? >

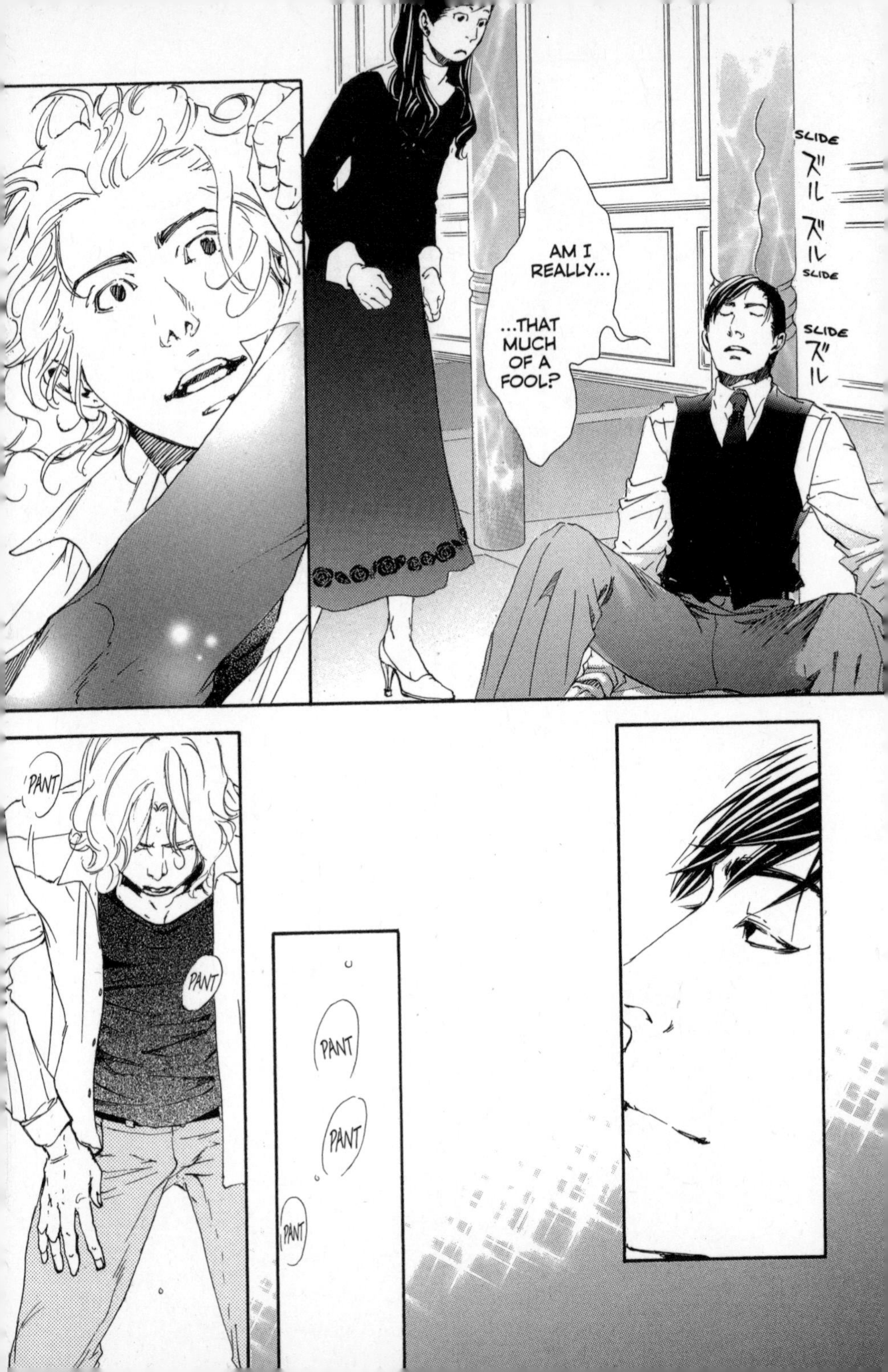

SLIDE
ズル
ズル
SLIDE
SLIDE
ズル
AM I REALLY...
...THAT MUCH OF A FOOL?
PANT
PANT
PANT
PANT
PANT
PANT

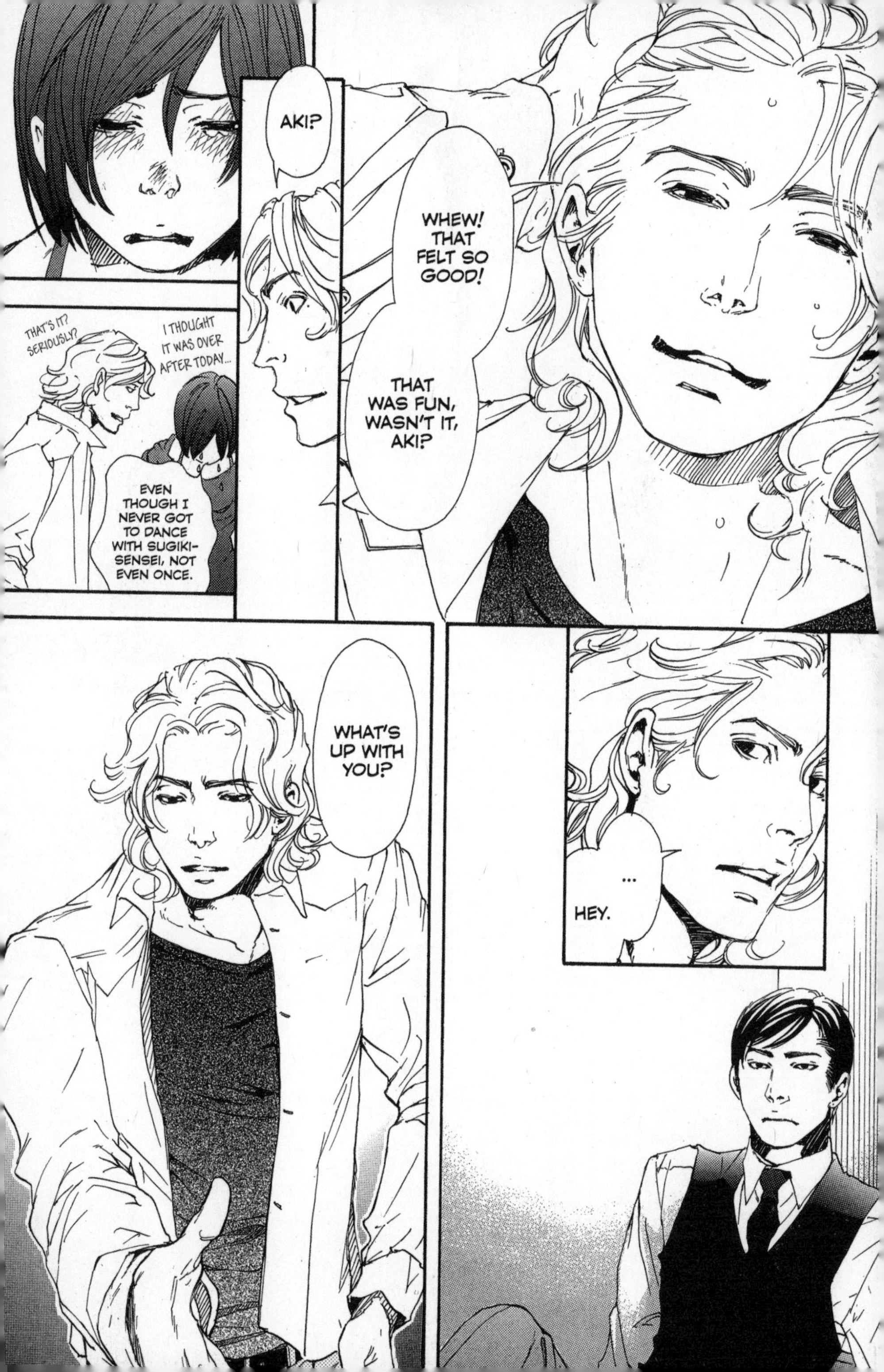
WHEW! THAT FELT SO GOOD!
THAT WAS FUN, WASN'T IT, AKI?
AKI?
I THOUGHT IT WAS OVER AFTER TODAY...
THAT'S IT? SERIOUSLY?
EVEN THOUGH I NEVER GOT TO DANCE WITH SUGIKI-SENSEI, NOT EVEN ONCE.
...
HEY.
WHAT'S UP WITH YOU?

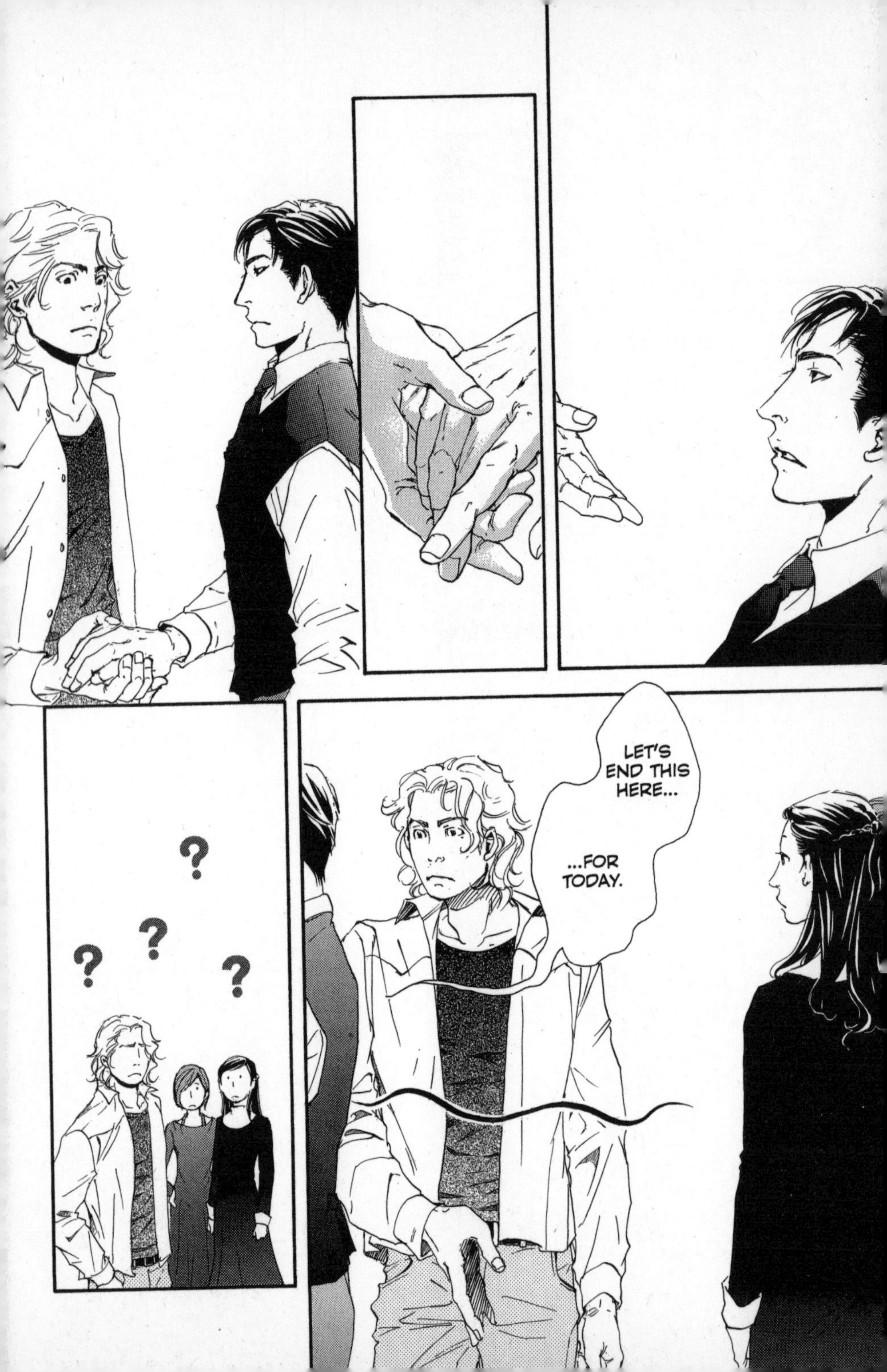
LET'S END THIS HERE...
...FOR TODAY.

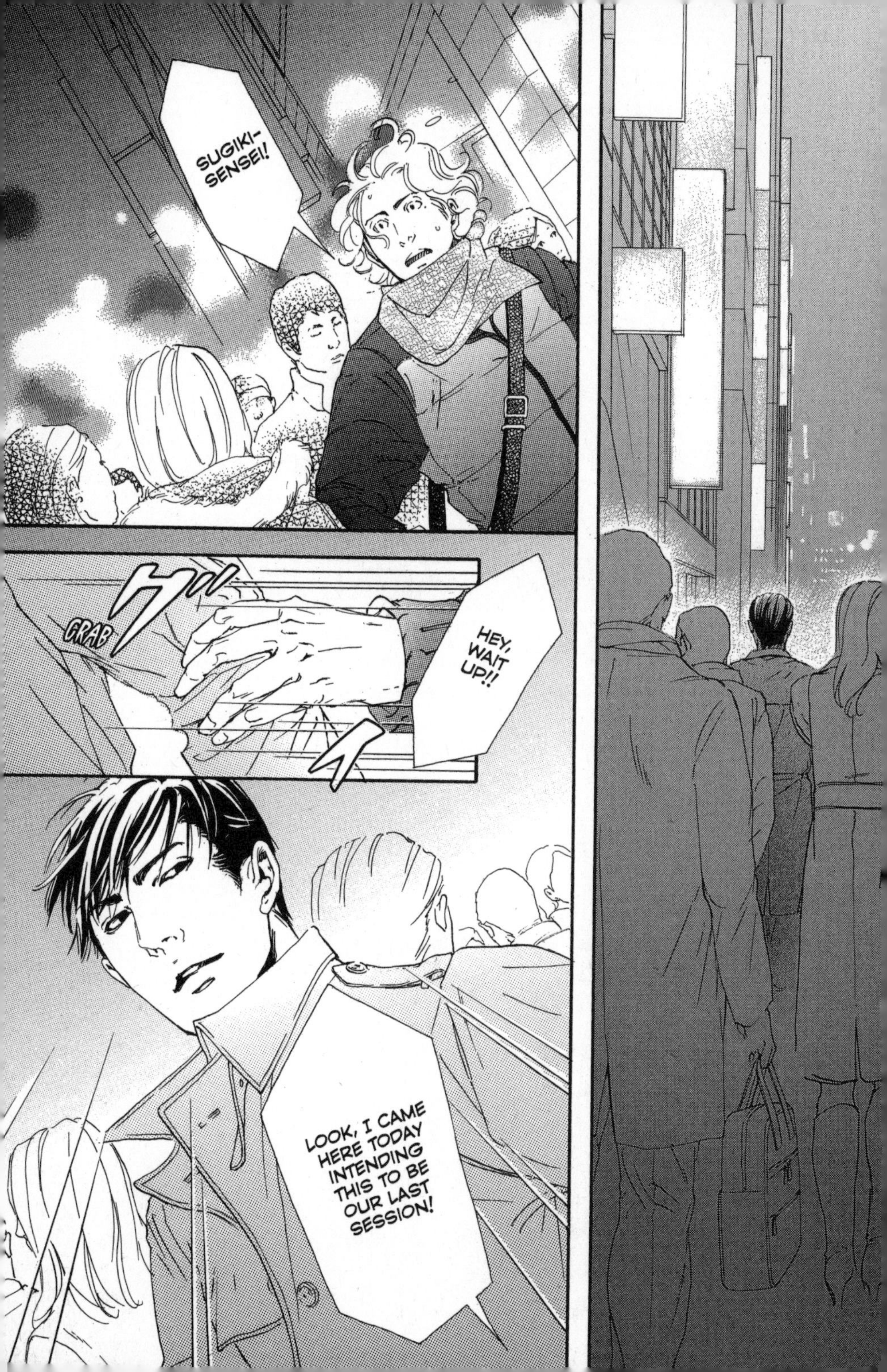
SUGIKI-SENSEI!
HEY, WAIT UP!!
グッ
GRAB
LOOK, I CAME HERE TODAY INTENDING THIS TO BE OUR LAST SESSION!

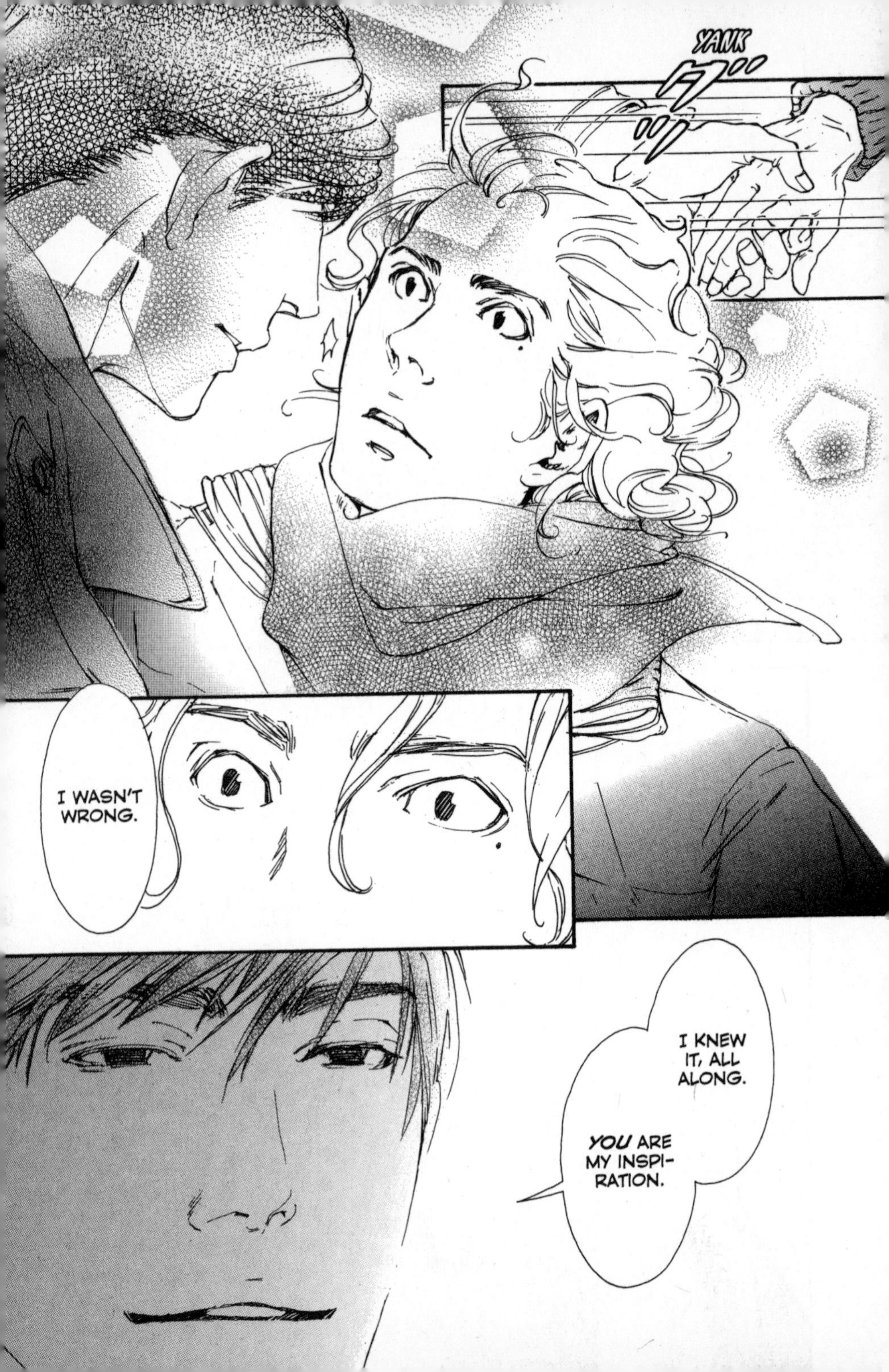
YANK
I WASN'T WRONG.
I KNEW IT, ALL ALONG.
YOU ARE MY INSPIRATION.

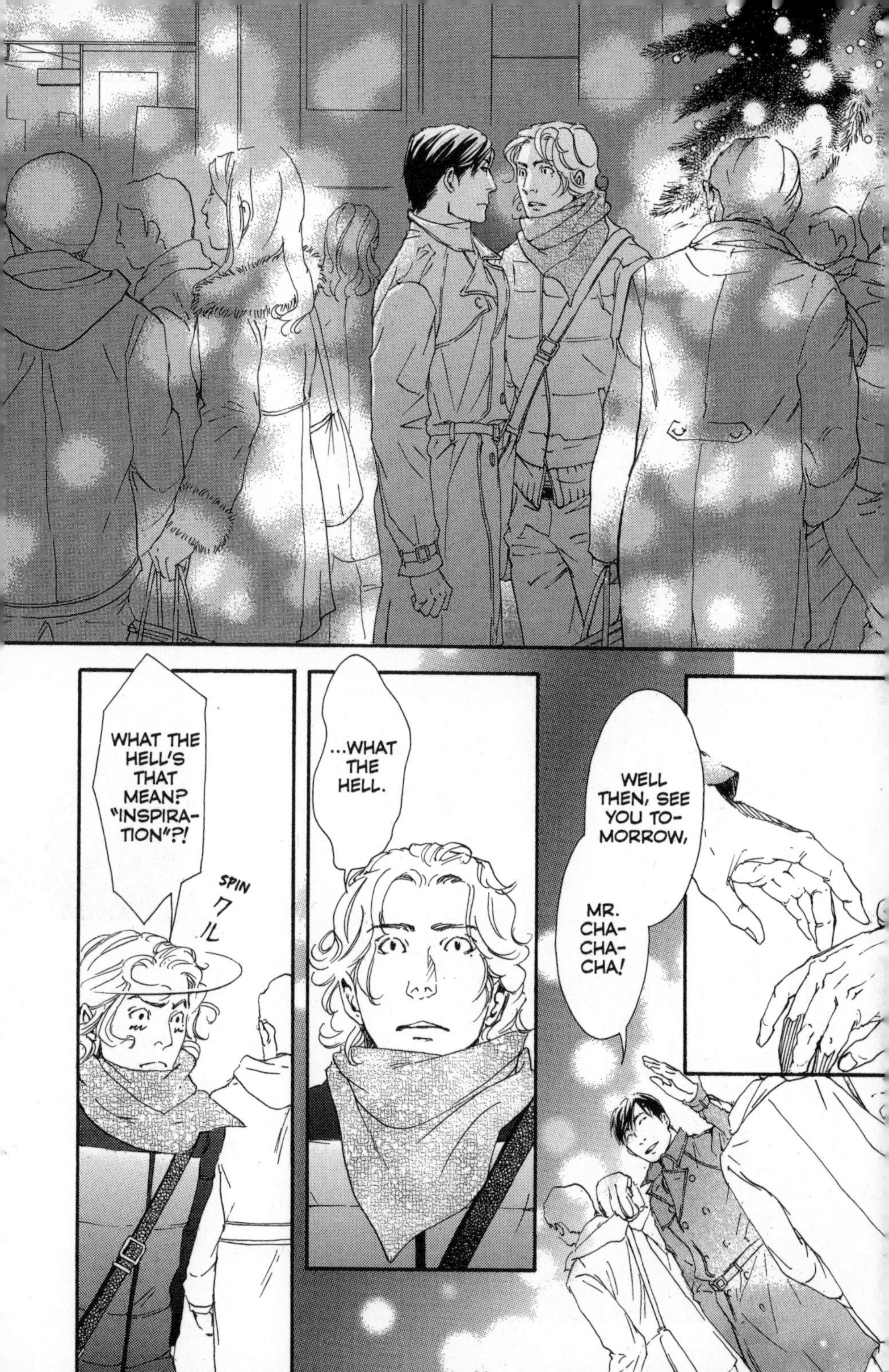
WELL THEN, SEE YOU TO-MORROW,
MR. CHA-CHA-CHA!
...WHAT THE HELL.
WHAT THE HELL'S THAT MEAN? "INSPIRATION"?!
SPIN
クル

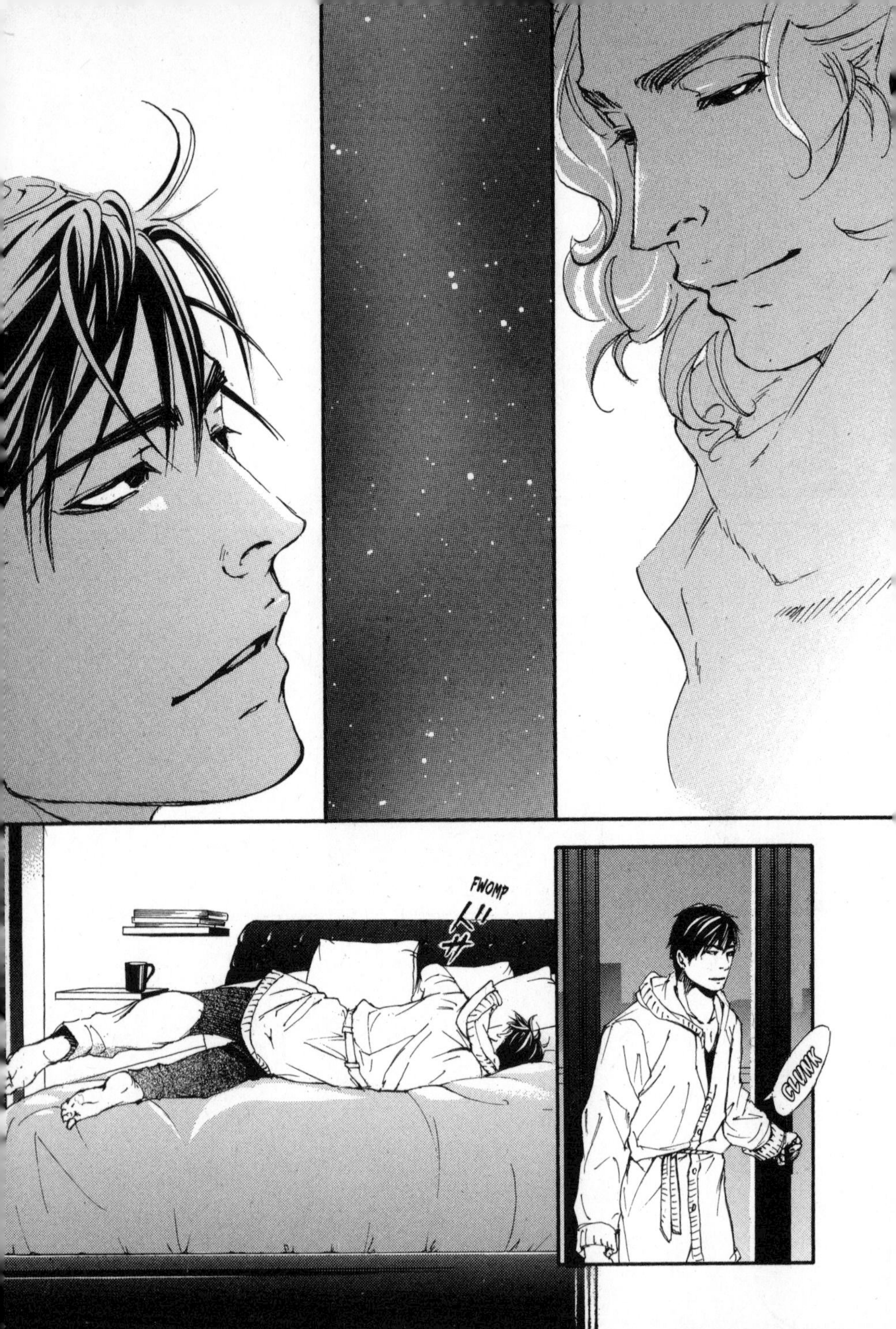
CLUNK
FWOMP

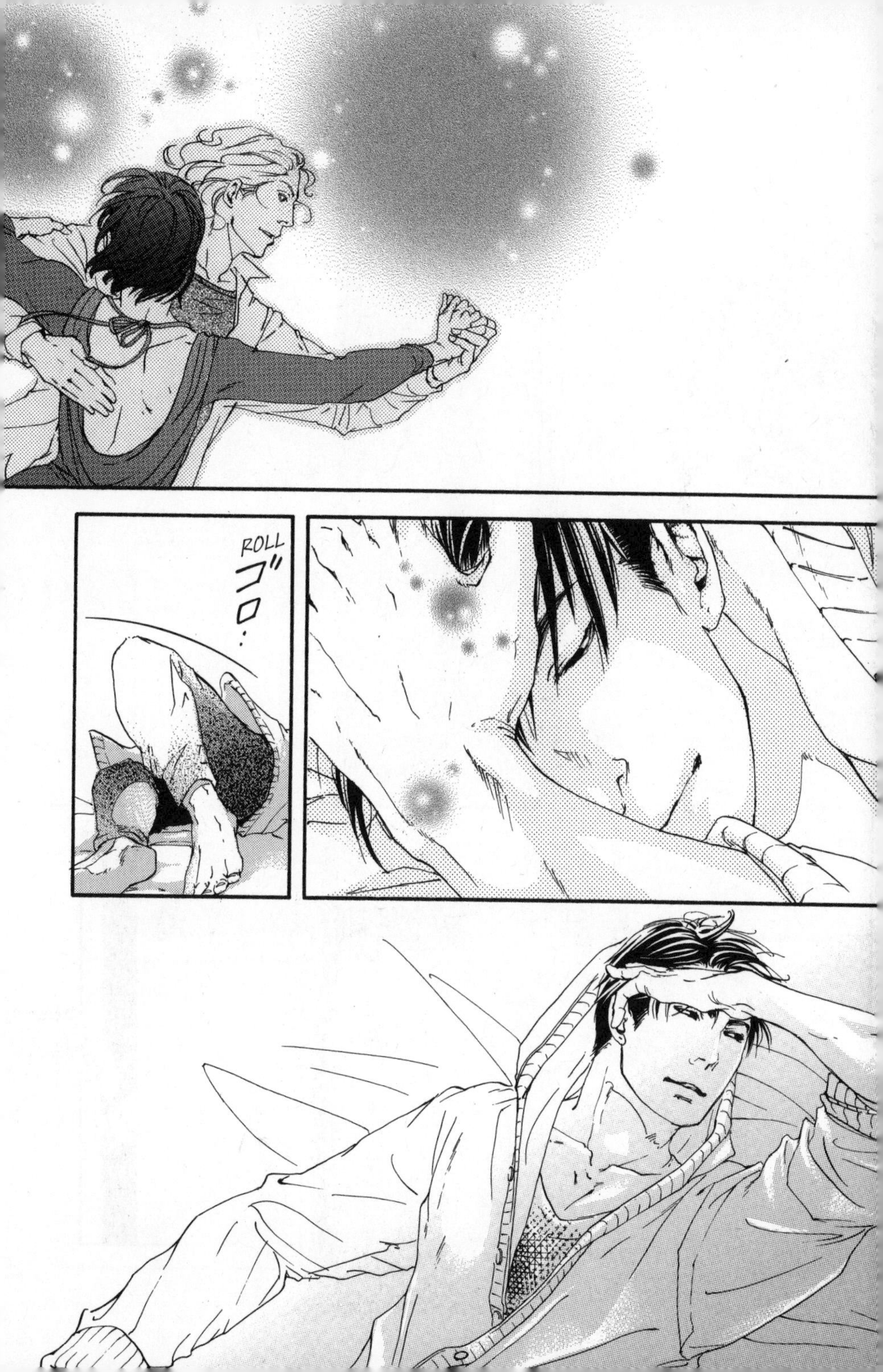
ROLL
ゴロ…

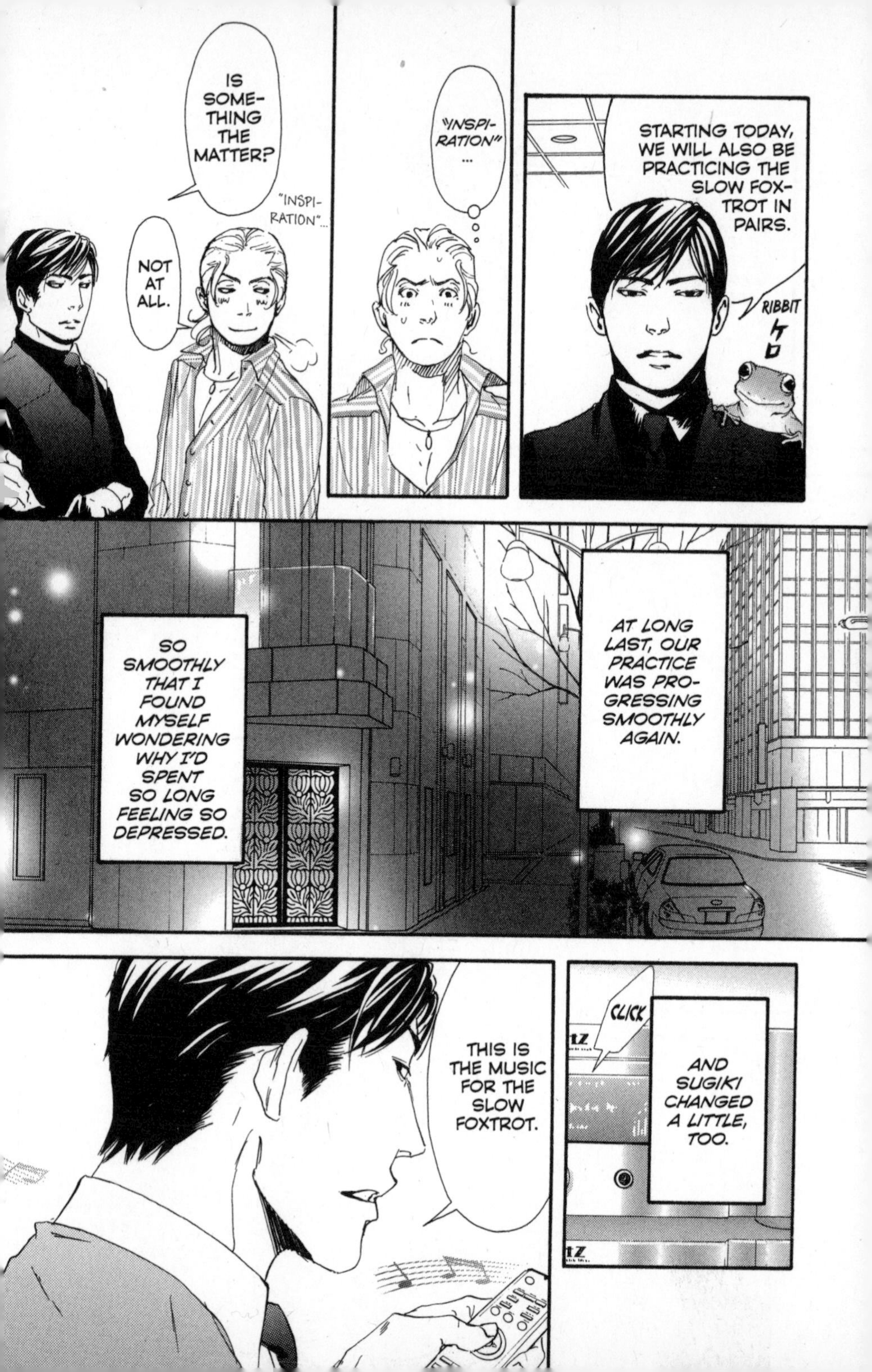
STARTING TODAY, WE WILL ALSO BE PRACTICING THE SLOW FOX-TROT IN PAIRS.
RIBBIT
ケロ
"INSPI-RATION" ...
IS SOME-THING THE MATTER?
"INSPI-RATION"...
NOT AT ALL.
AT LONG LAST, OUR PRACTICE WAS PRO-GRESSING SMOOTHLY AGAIN.
SO SMOOTHLY THAT I FOUND MYSELF WONDERING WHY I'D SPENT SO LONG FEELING SO DEPRESSED.
CLICK
AND SUGIKI CHANGED A LITTLE, TOO.
THIS IS THE MUSIC FOR THE SLOW FOXTROT.

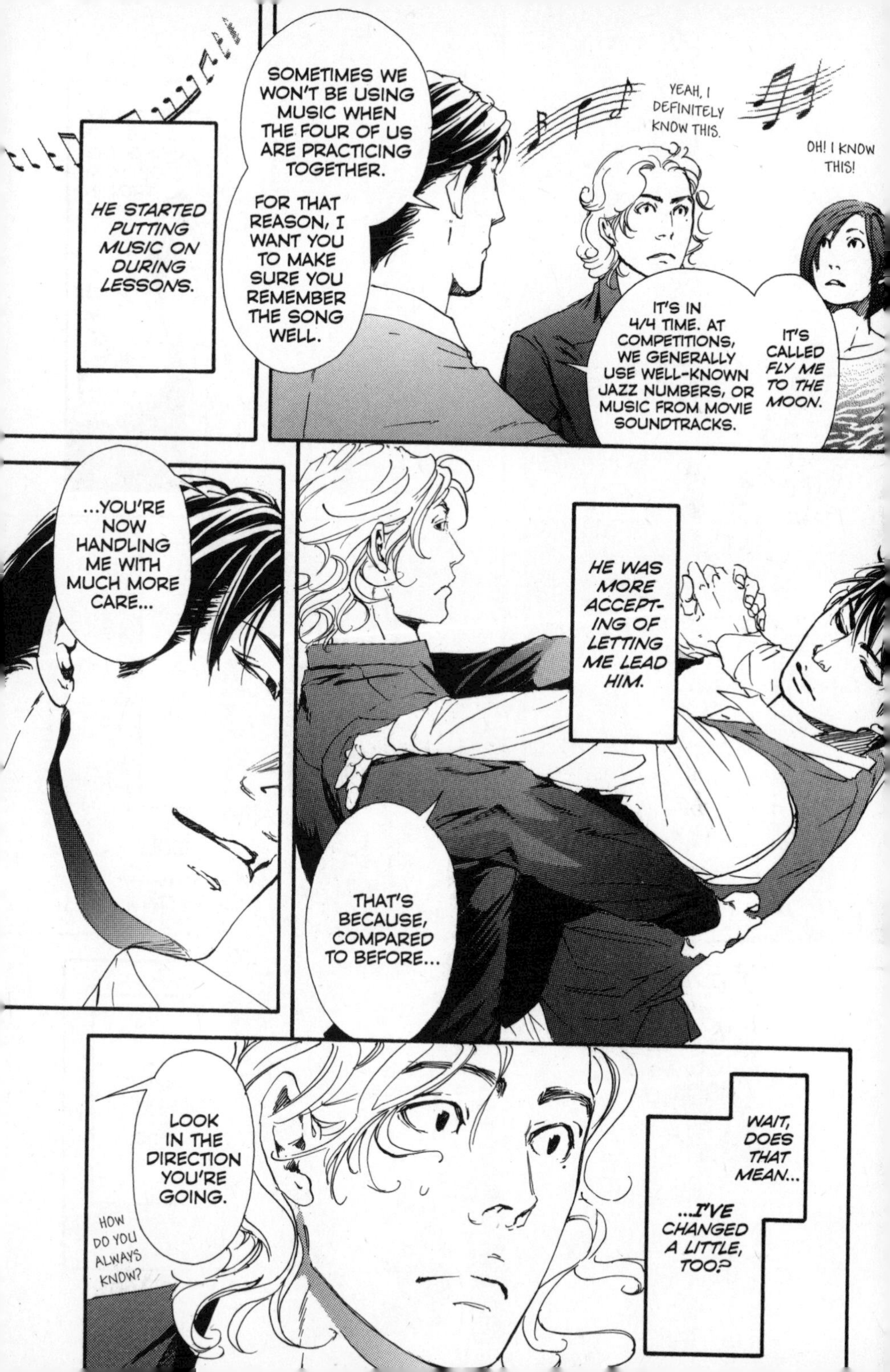
SOMETIMES WE WON'T BE USING MUSIC WHEN THE FOUR OF US ARE PRACTICING TOGETHER.
FOR THAT REASON, I WANT YOU TO MAKE SURE YOU REMEMBER THE SONG WELL.
YEAH, I DEFINITELY KNOW THIS.
OH! I KNOW THIS!
IT'S CALLED *FLY ME TO THE MOON*.
IT'S IN 4/4 TIME. AT COMPETITIONS, WE GENERALLY USE WELL-KNOWN JAZZ NUMBERS, OR MUSIC FROM MOVIE SOUNDTRACKS.
HE STARTED PUTTING MUSIC ON DURING LESSONS.
HE WAS MORE ACCEPTING OF LETTING ME LEAD HIM.
THAT'S BECAUSE, COMPARED TO BEFORE...
...YOU'RE NOW HANDLING ME WITH MUCH MORE CARE...
WAIT, DOES THAT MEAN...
...I'VE CHANGED A LITTLE, TOO?
LOOK IN THE DIRECTION YOU'RE GOING.
HOW DO YOU ALWAYS KNOW?

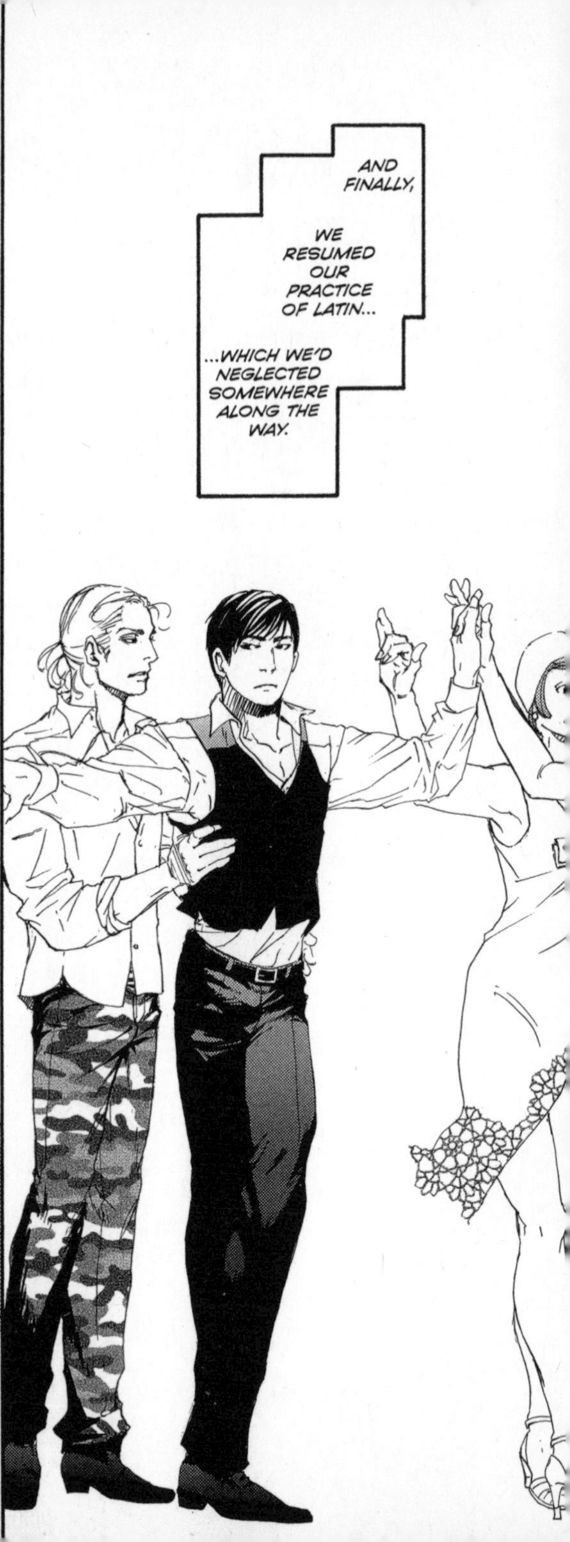
AND FINALLY,
WE RESUMED OUR PRACTICE OF LATIN...
...WHICH WE'D NEGLECTED SOMEWHERE ALONG THE WAY.
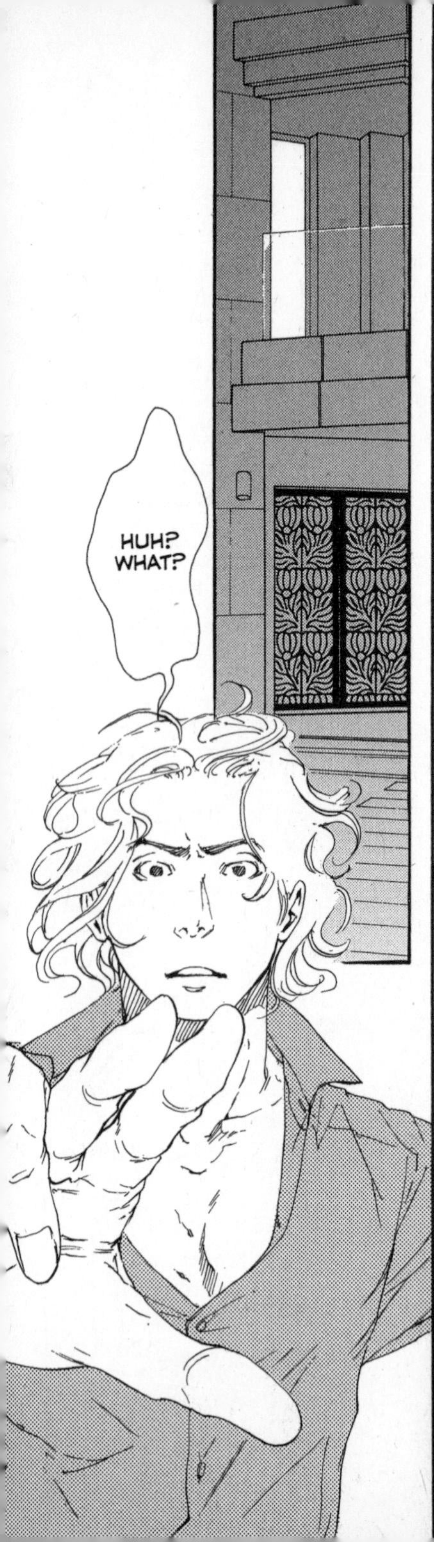
HUH? WHAT?

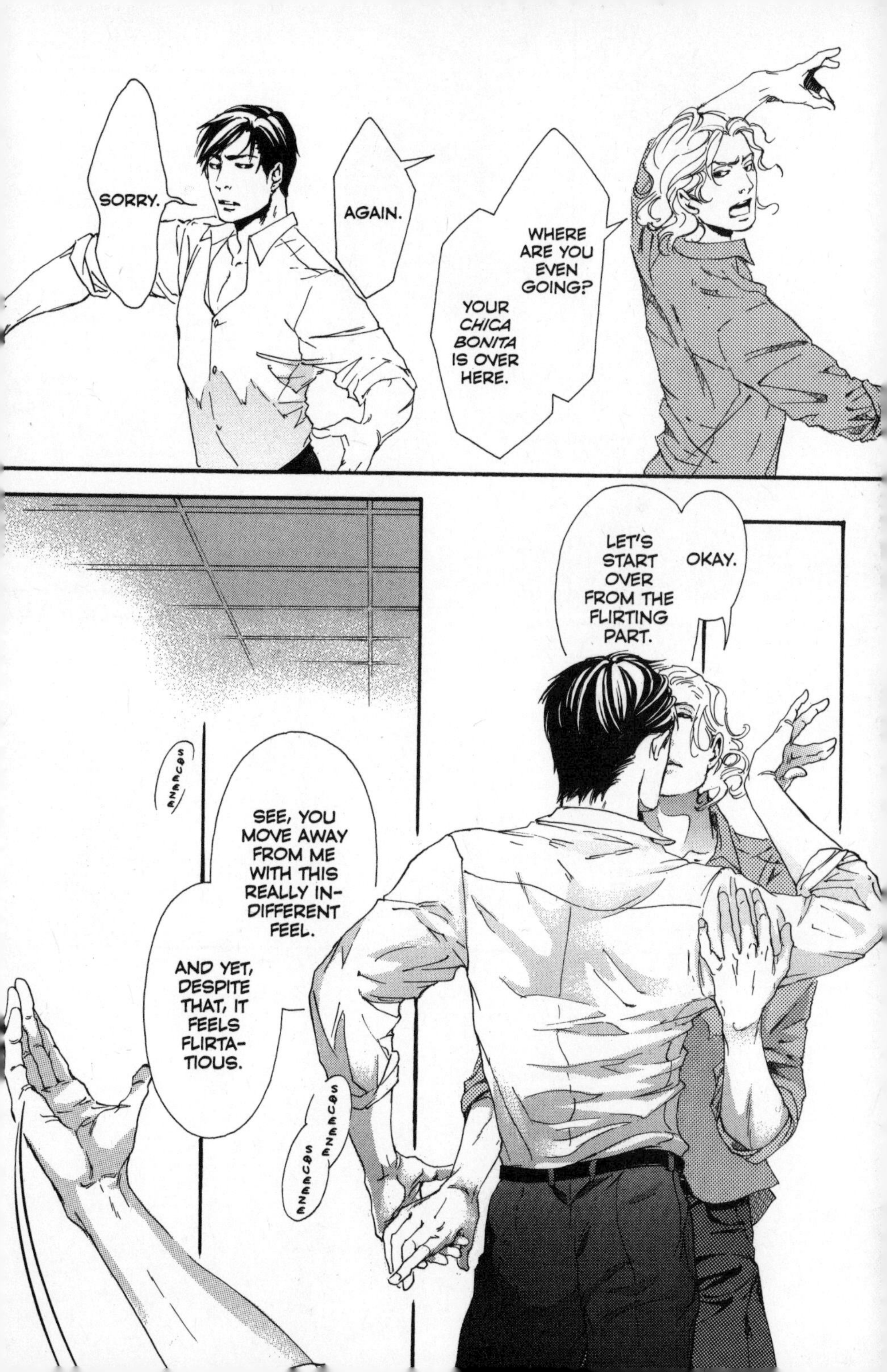
WHERE ARE YOU EVEN GOING?
YOUR *CHICA BONITA* IS OVER HERE.
AGAIN.
SORRY.
OKAY.
LET'S START OVER FROM THE FLIRTING PART.
SEE, YOU MOVE AWAY FROM ME WITH THIS REALLY IN-DIFFERENT FEEL.
AND YET, DESPITE THAT, IT FEELS FLIRTA-TIOUS.

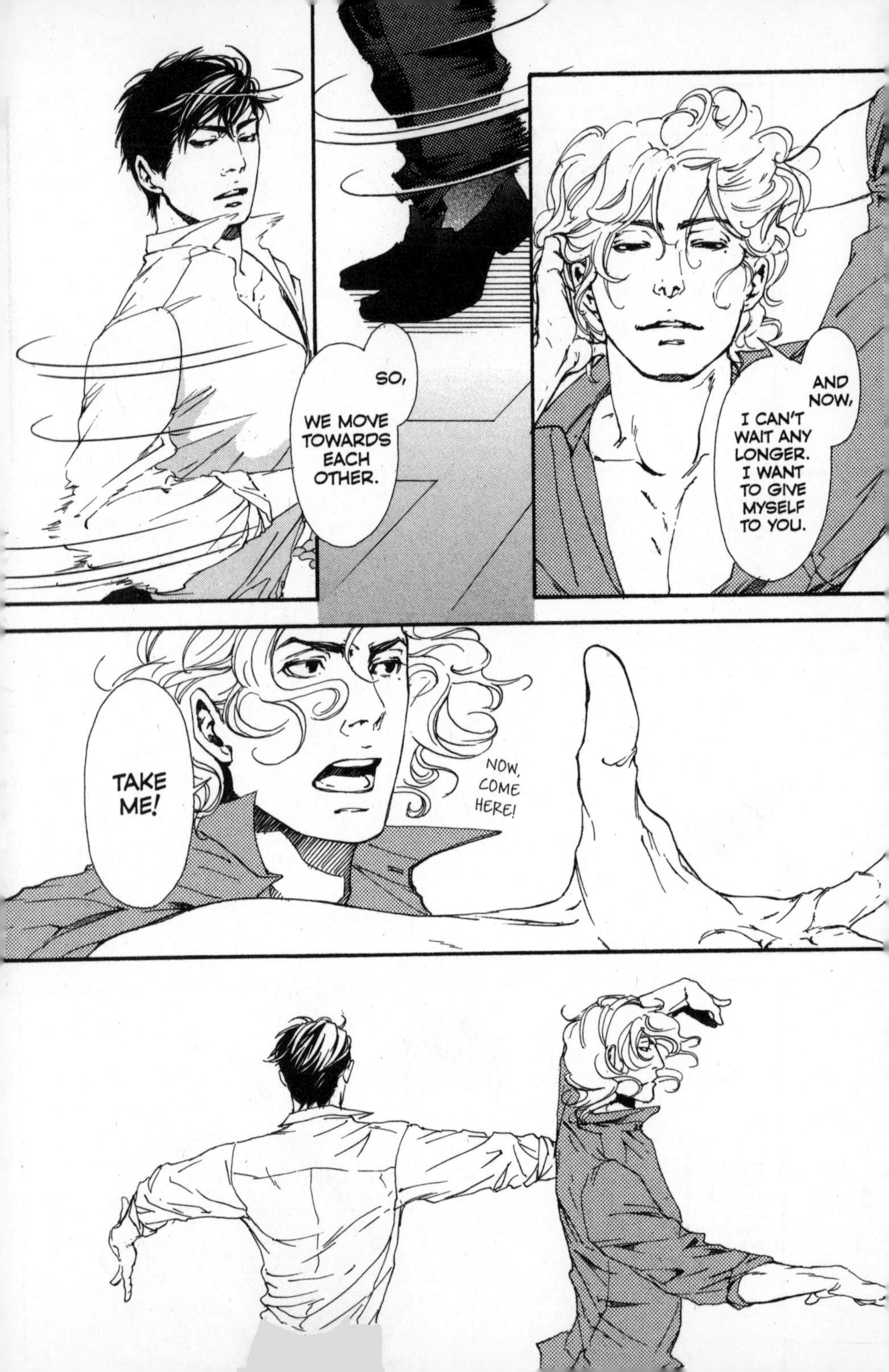
AND NOW, I CAN'T WAIT ANY LONGER. I WANT TO GIVE MYSELF TO YOU.
SO, WE MOVE TOWARDS EACH OTHER.
NOW, COME HERE!
TAKE ME!

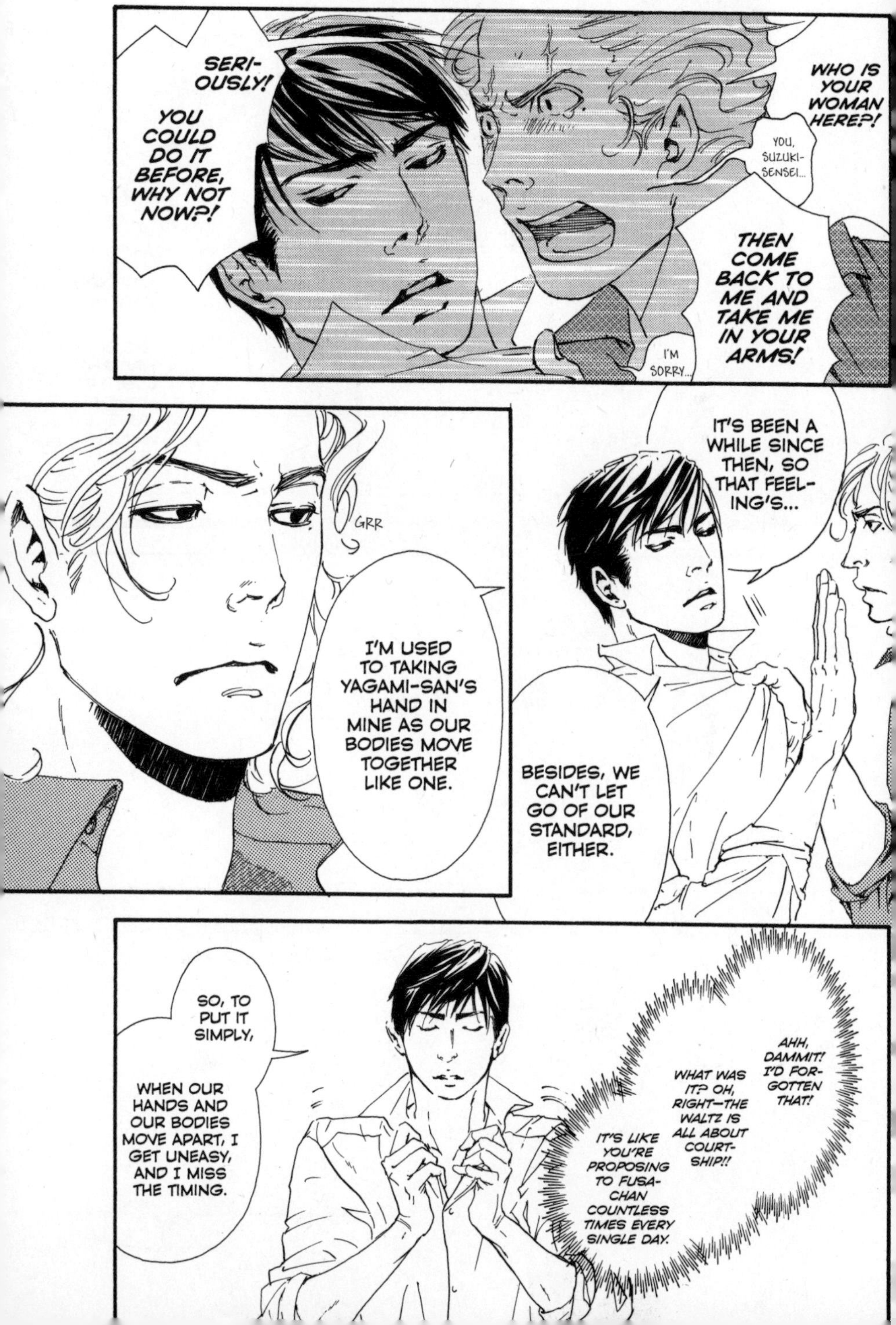
WHO IS YOUR WOMAN HERE?!
YOU, SUZUKI-SENSEI...
SERI-OUSLY!
YOU COULD DO IT BEFORE, WHY NOT NOW?!
THEN COME BACK TO ME AND TAKE ME IN YOUR ARMS!
I'M SORRY...
IT'S BEEN A WHILE SINCE THEN, SO THAT FEEL-ING'S...
BESIDES, WE CAN'T LET GO OF OUR STANDARD, EITHER.
GRR
I'M USED TO TAKING YAGAMI-SAN'S HAND IN MINE AS OUR BODIES MOVE TOGETHER LIKE ONE.
AHH, DAMMIT! I'D FOR-GOTTEN THAT!
WHAT WAS IT? OH, RIGHT—THE WALTZ IS ALL ABOUT COURT-SHIP!!
IT'S LIKE YOU'RE PROPOSING TO FUSA-CHAN COUNTLESS TIMES EVERY SINGLE DAY.
SO, TO PUT IT SIMPLY,
WHEN OUR HANDS AND OUR BODIES MOVE APART, I GET UNEASY, AND I MISS THE TIMING.

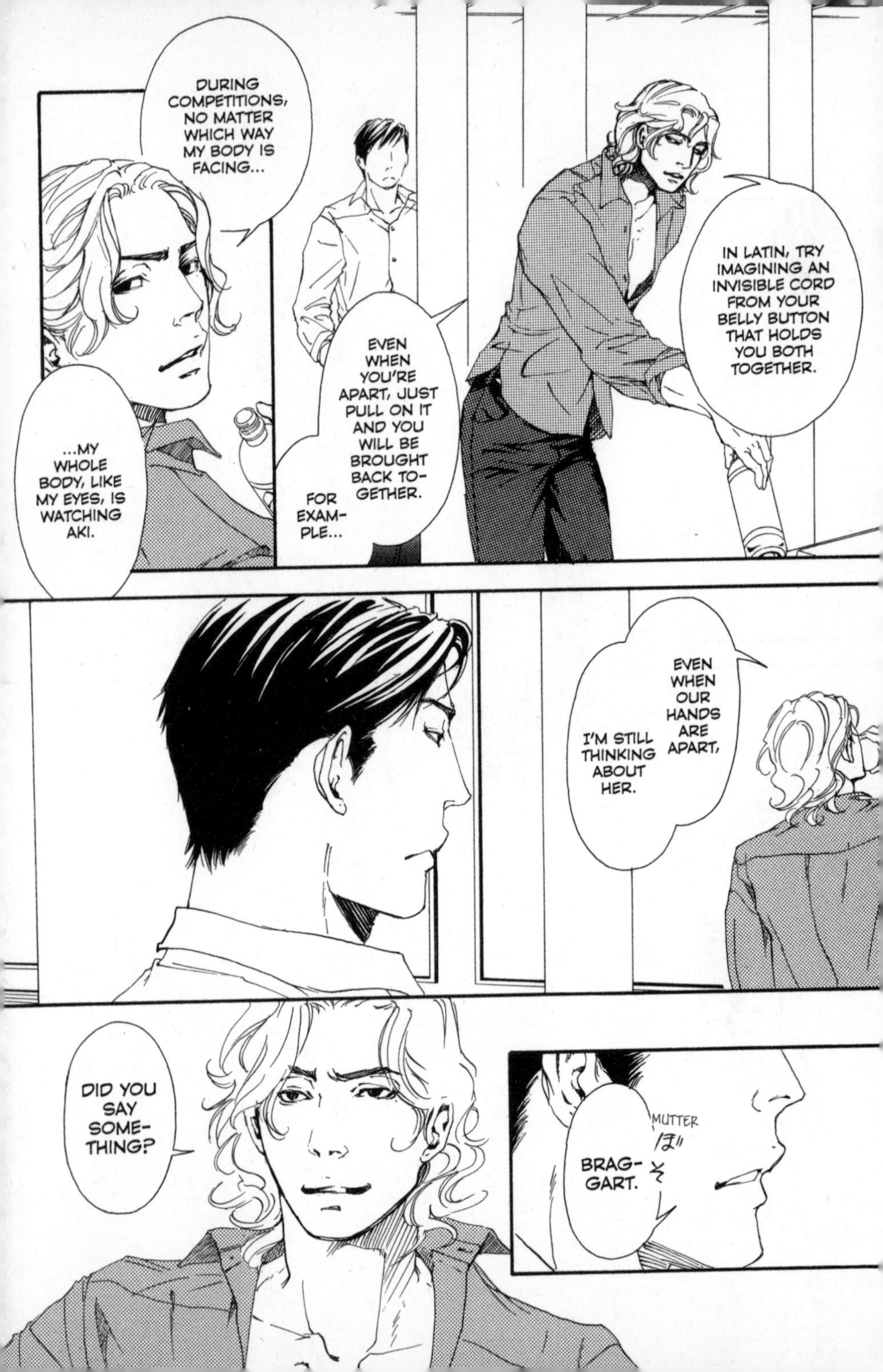
IN LATIN, TRY IMAGINING AN INVISIBLE CORD FROM YOUR BELLY BUTTON THAT HOLDS YOU BOTH TOGETHER.
EVEN WHEN YOU'RE APART, JUST PULL ON IT AND YOU WILL BE BROUGHT BACK TO-GETHER.
FOR EXAM-PLE...
DURING COMPETITIONS, NO MATTER WHICH WAY MY BODY IS FACING...
...MY WHOLE BODY, LIKE MY EYES, IS WATCHING AKI.
EVEN WHEN OUR HANDS ARE APART,
I'M STILL THINKING ABOUT HER.
MUTTER
ぼそ
BRAG-GART.
DID YOU SAY SOME-THING?

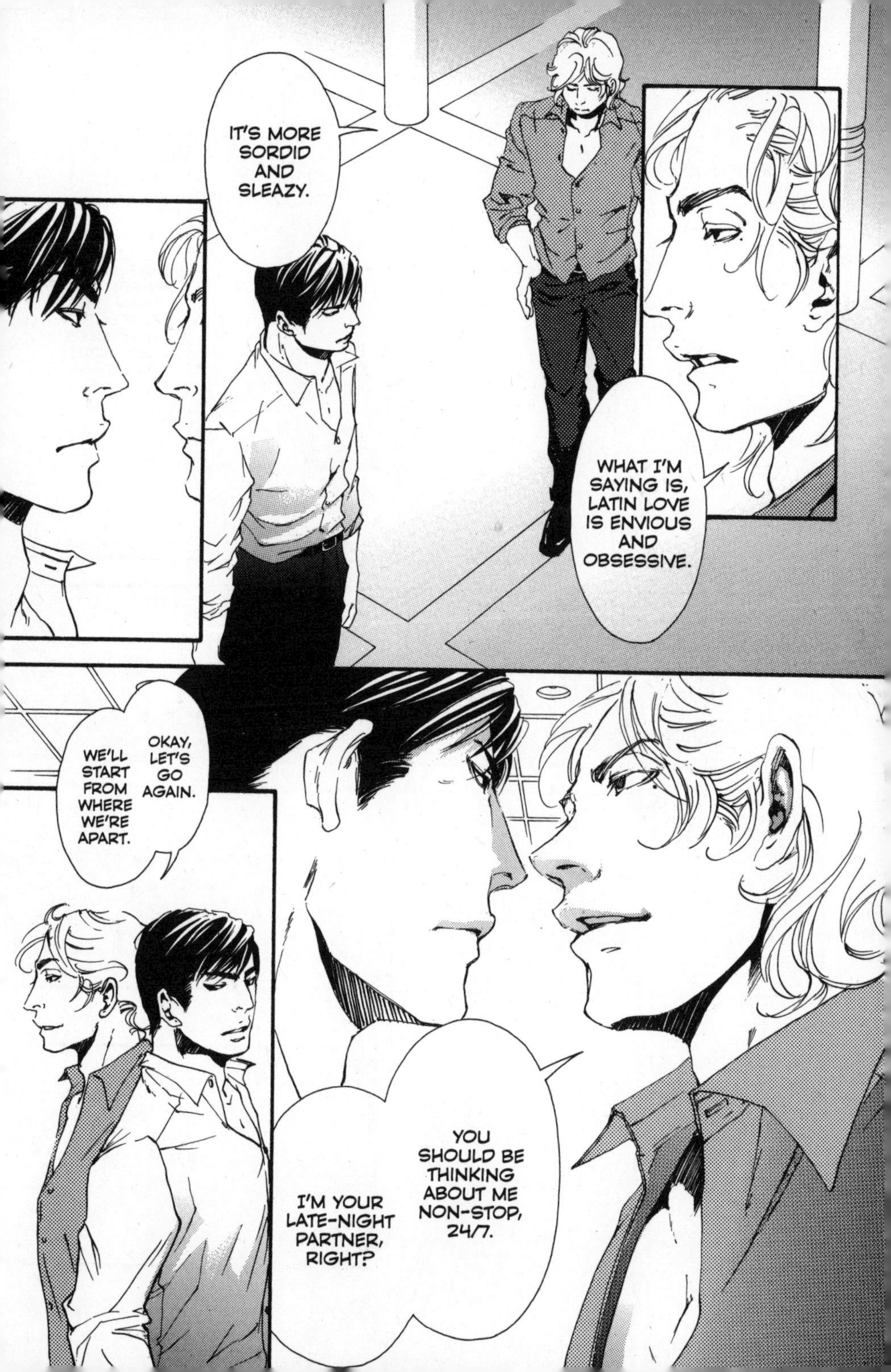
IT'S MORE SORDID AND SLEAZY.
WHAT I'M SAYING IS, LATIN LOVE IS ENVIOUS AND OBSESSIVE.
YOU SHOULD BE THINKING ABOUT ME NON-STOP, 24/7.
I'M YOUR LATE-NIGHT PARTNER, RIGHT?
OKAY, LET'S GO AGAIN.
WE'LL START FROM WHERE WE'RE APART.

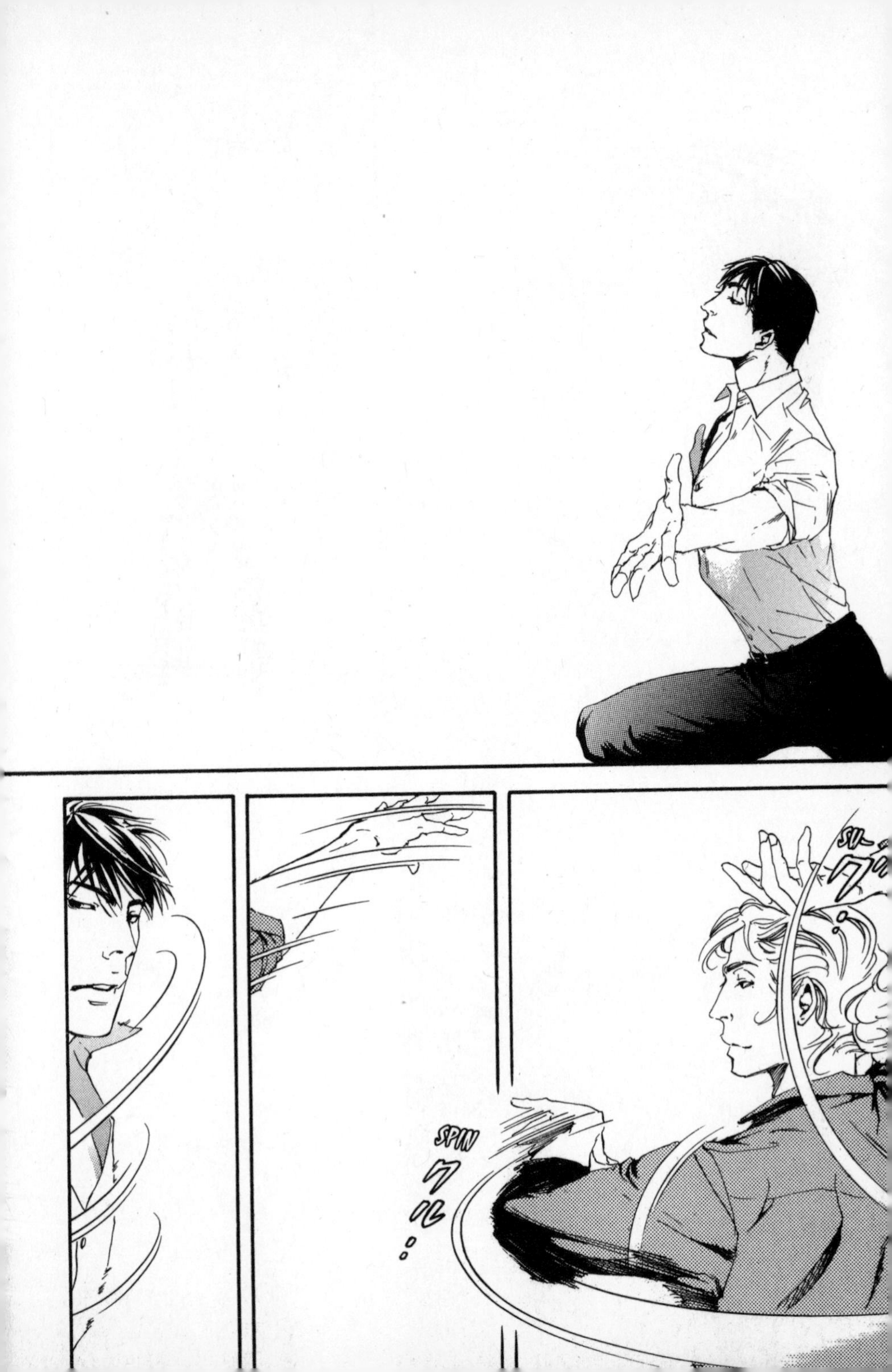
SU-
SPIN
クル

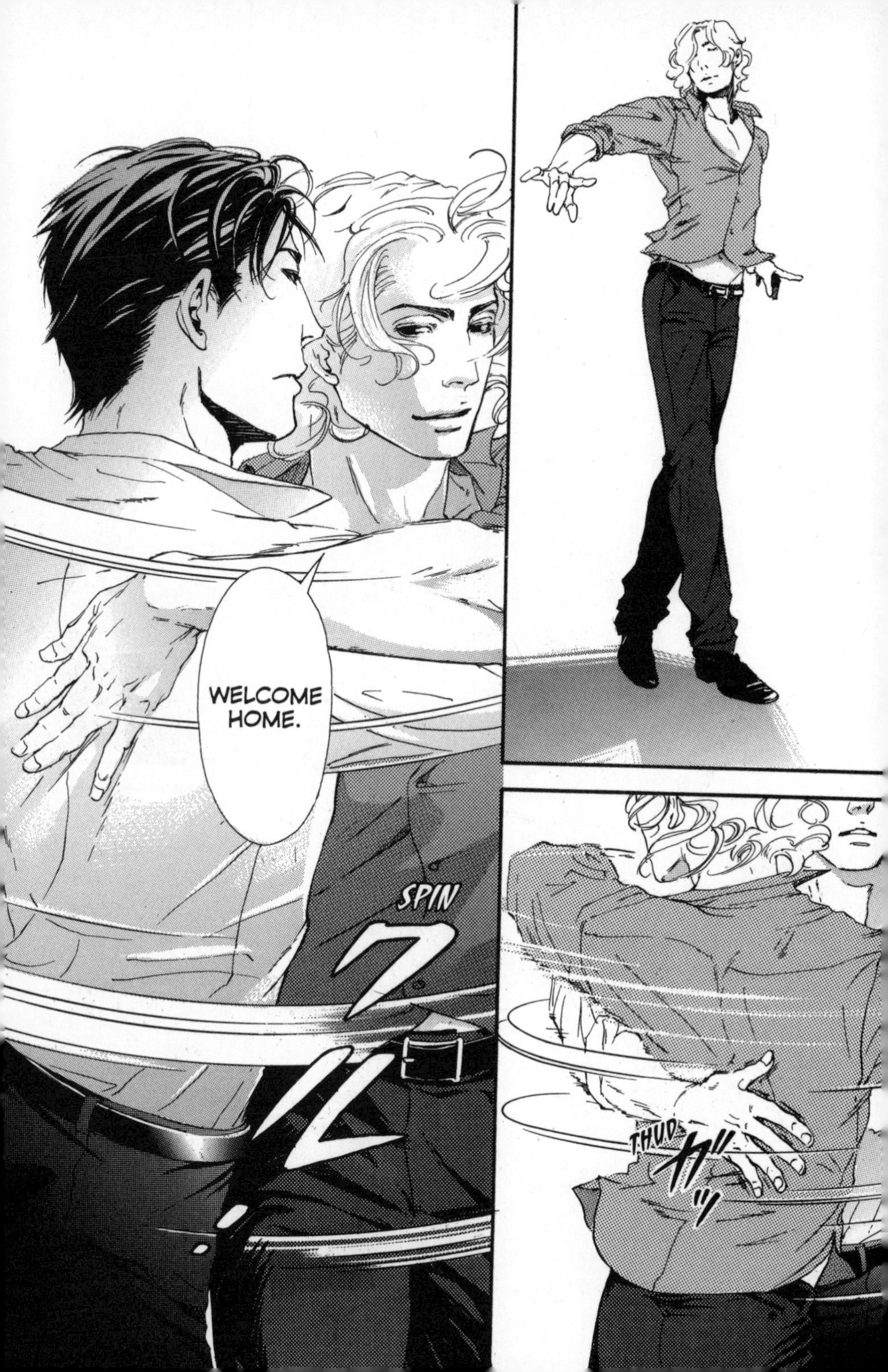
THUD
WELCOME HOME.
SPIN

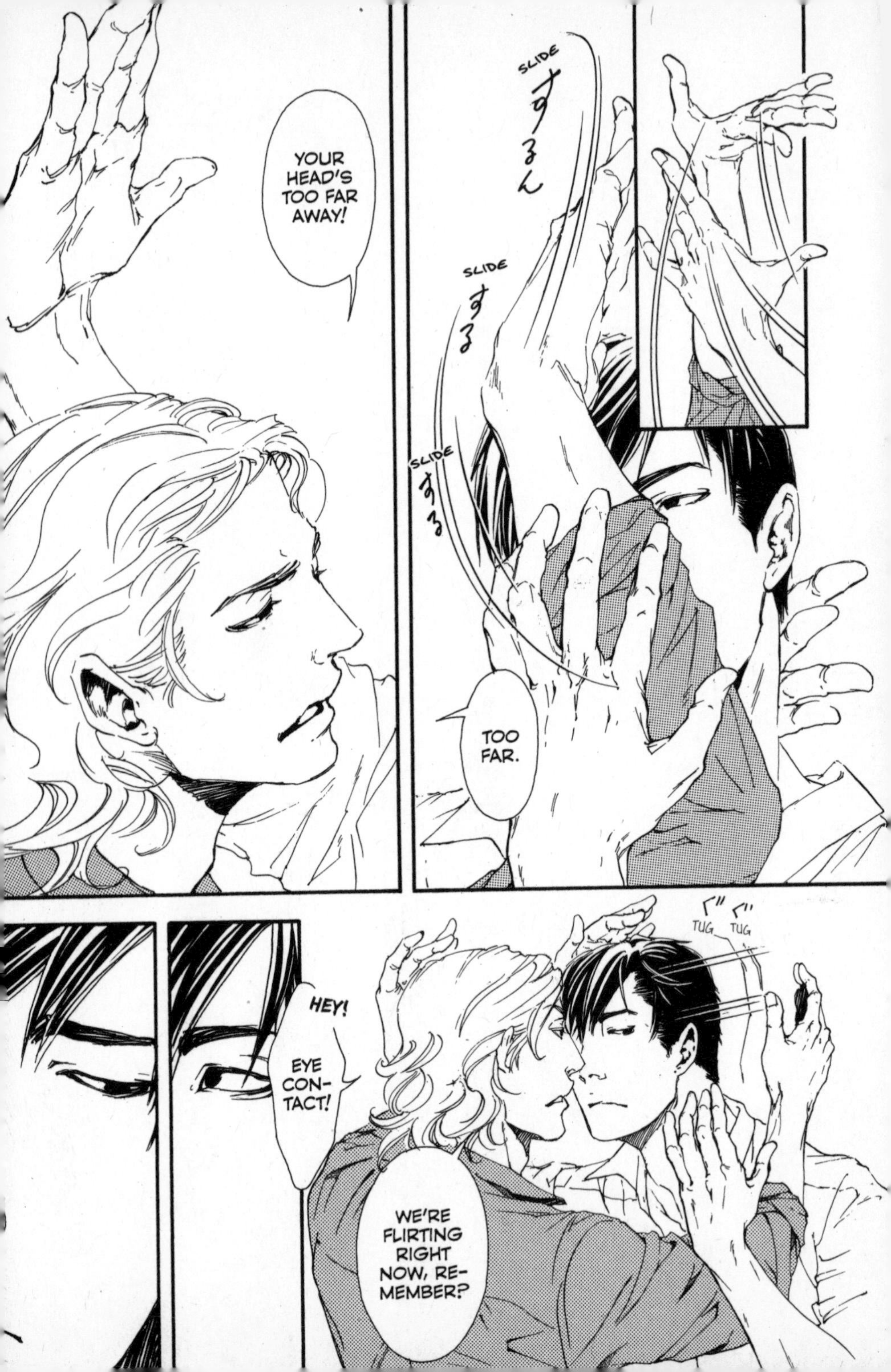
SLIDE すするん
SLIDE する
SLIDE する
TOO FAR.
YOUR HEAD'S TOO FAR AWAY!
ぐ" TUG
ぐ" TUG
HEY!
EYE CONTACT!
WE'RE FLIRTING RIGHT NOW, REMEMBER?

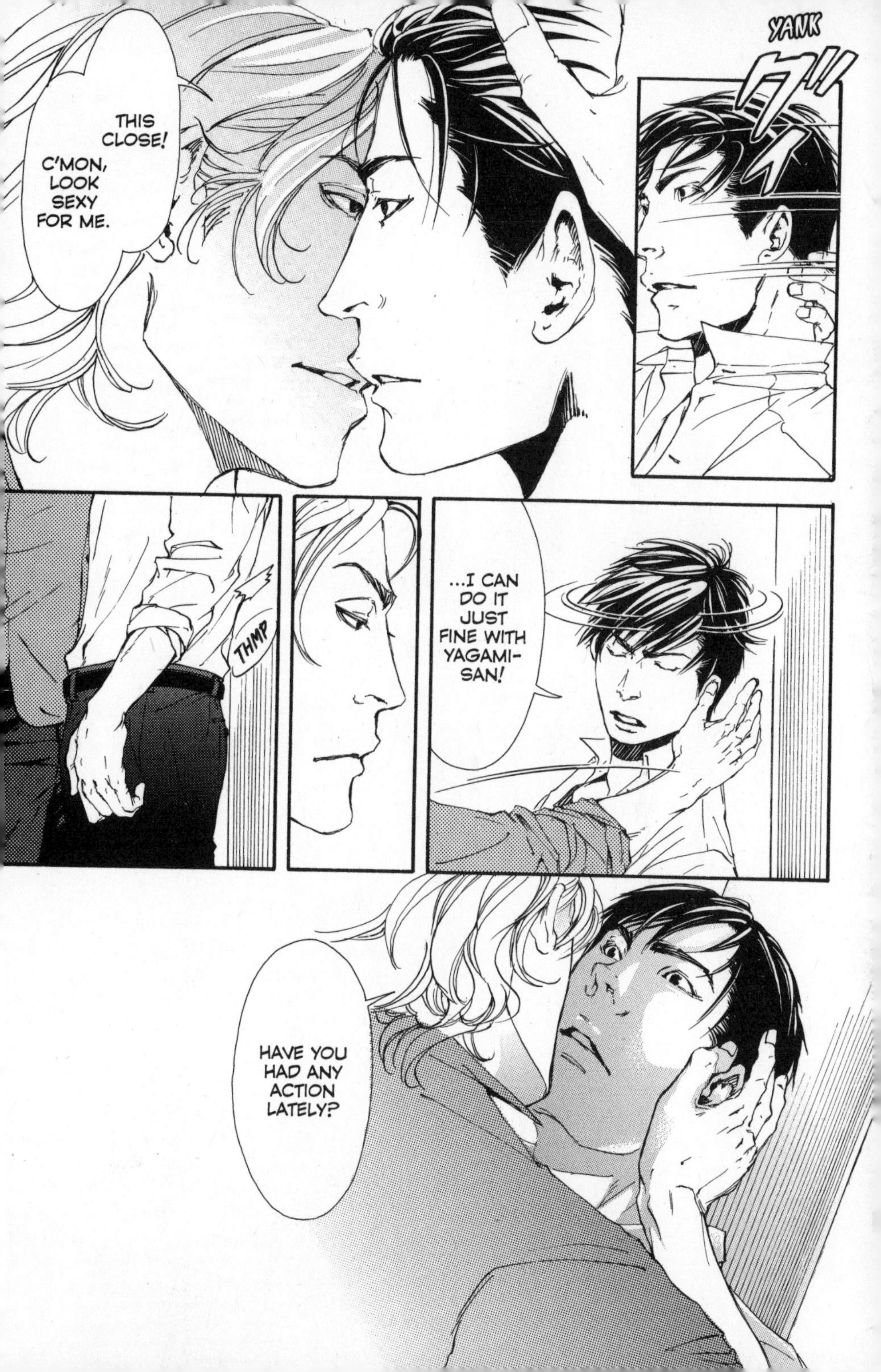
YANK
THIS CLOSE!
C'MON, LOOK SEXY FOR ME.
...I CAN DO IT JUST FINE WITH YAGAMI-SAN!
THMP
HAVE YOU HAD ANY ACTION LATELY?

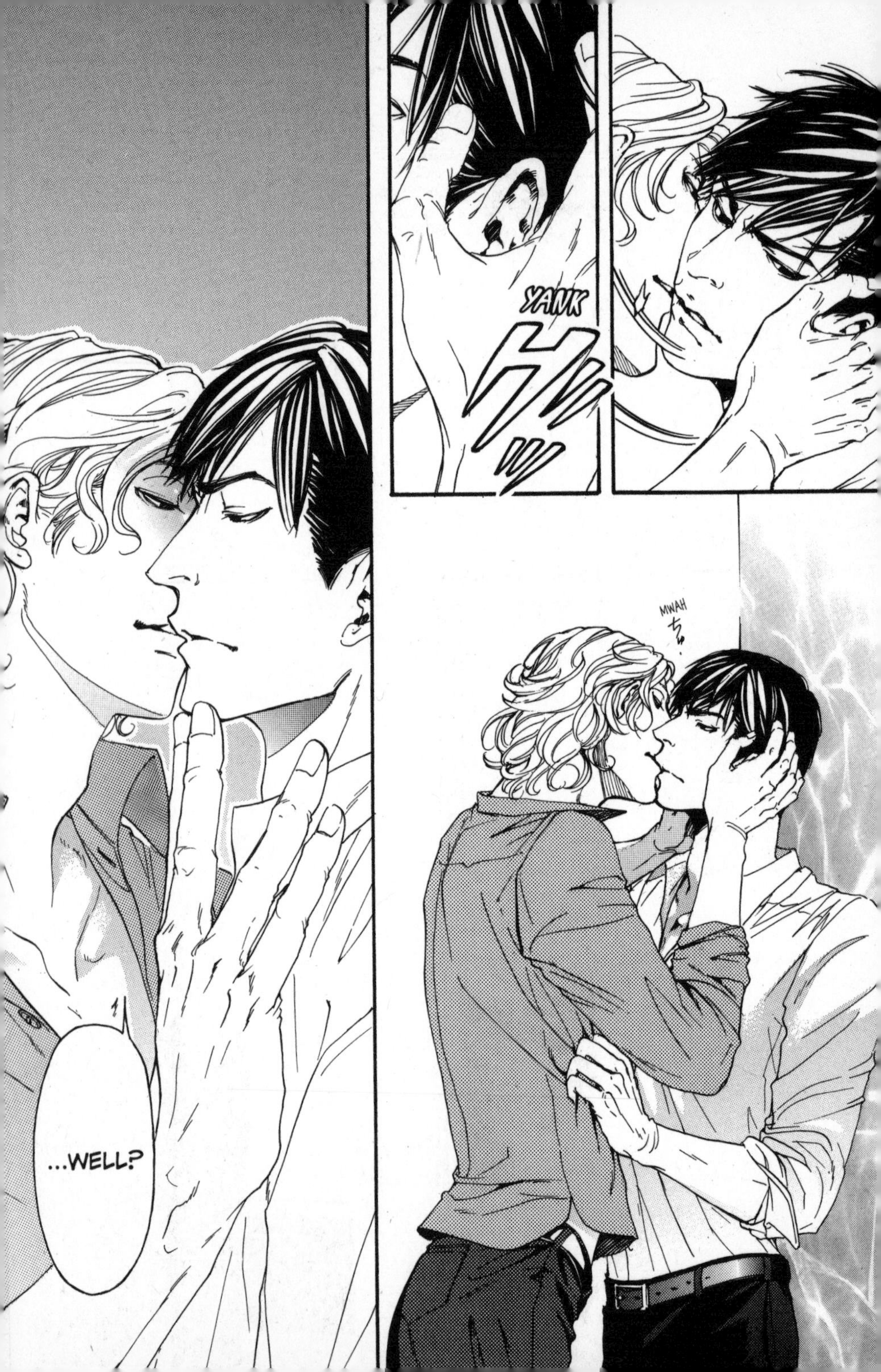
YANK
MWAH
...WELL?

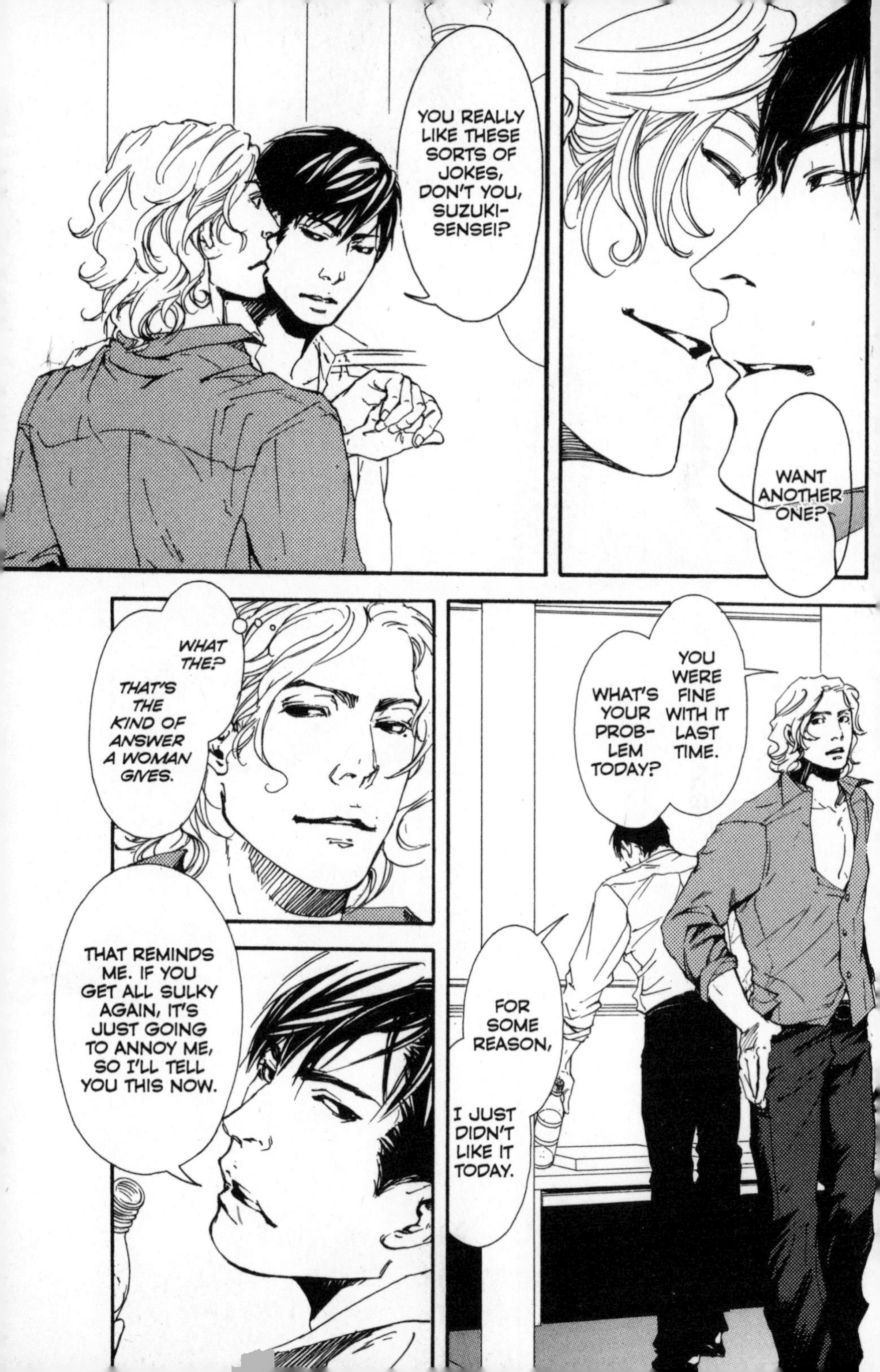
WANT ANOTHER ONE?
YOU REALLY LIKE THESE SORTS OF JOKES, DON'T YOU, SUZUKI-SENSEI?
YOU WERE FINE WITH IT LAST TIME.
WHAT'S YOUR PROBLEM TODAY?
FOR SOME REASON,
I JUST DIDN'T LIKE IT TODAY.
WHAT THE?
THAT'S THE KIND OF ANSWER A WOMAN GIVES.
THAT REMINDS ME. IF YOU GET ALL SULKY AGAIN, IT'S JUST GOING TO ANNOY ME, SO I'LL TELL YOU THIS NOW.

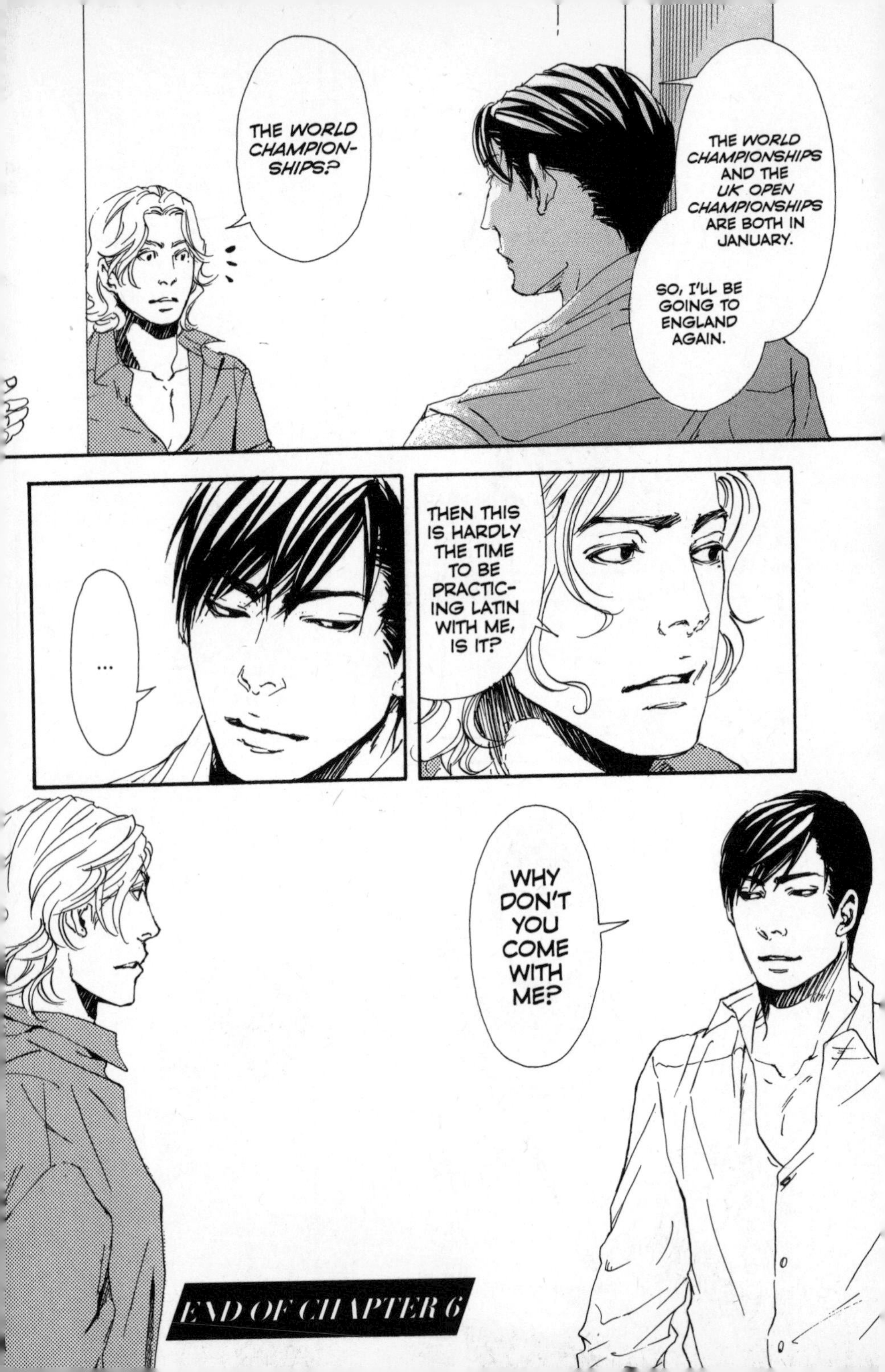
THE WORLD CHAMPIONSHIPS AND THE UK OPEN CHAMPIONSHIPS ARE BOTH IN JANUARY.
SO, I'LL BE GOING TO ENGLAND AGAIN.
THE WORLD CHAMPION-SHIPS?
THEN THIS IS HARDLY THE TIME TO BE PRACTIC-ING LATIN WITH ME, IS IT?
...
WHY DON'T YOU COME WITH ME?
END OF CHAPTER 6

BONUS CHAPTER
ONE MISSION

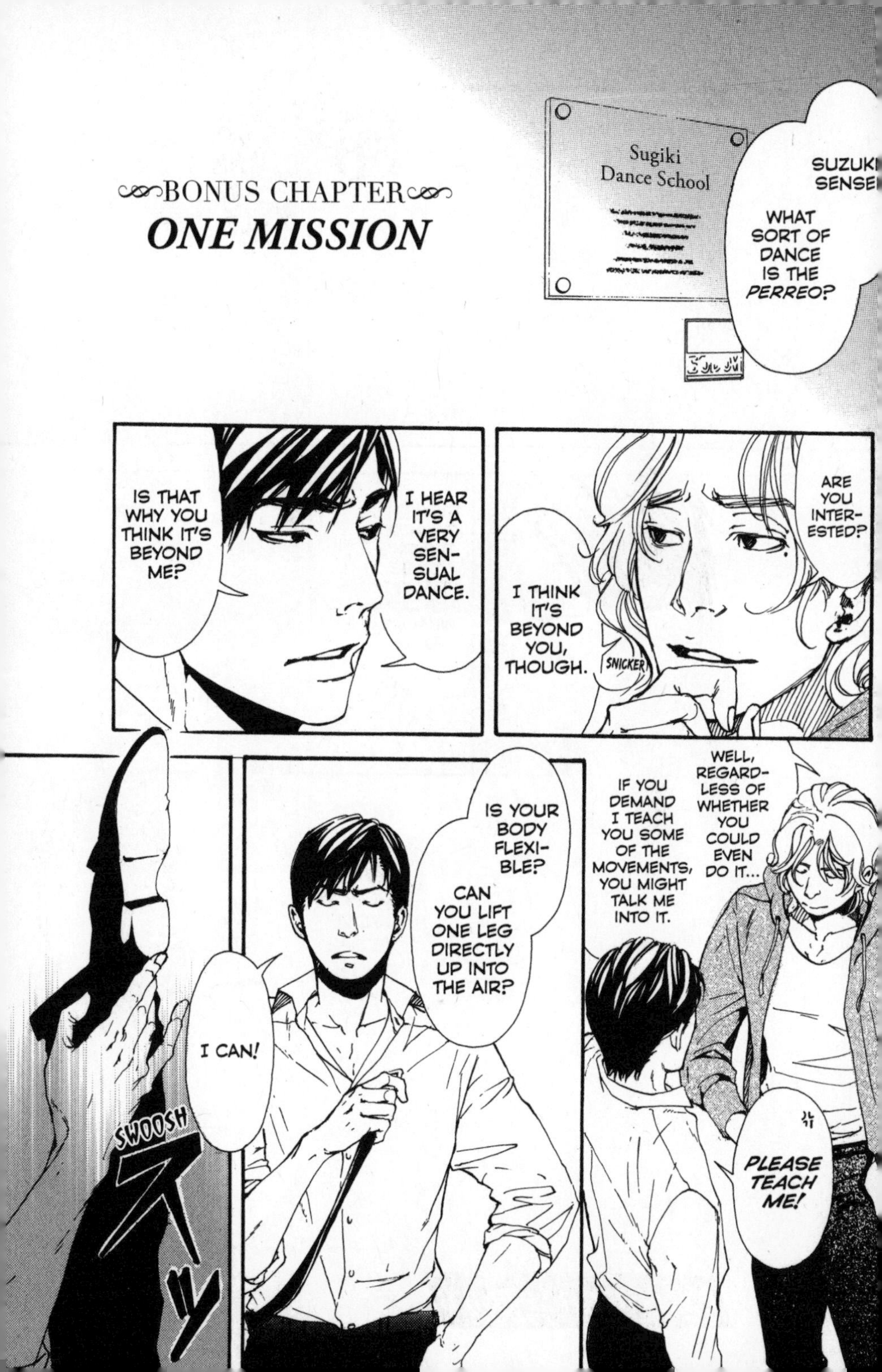
Sugiki Dance School
SUZUKI SENSE
WHAT SORT OF DANCE IS THE *PERREO*?
ARE YOU INTERESTED?
I THINK IT'S BEYOND YOU, THOUGH.
SNICKER
I HEAR IT'S A VERY SENSUAL DANCE.
IS THAT WHY YOU THINK IT'S BEYOND ME?
WELL, REGARDLESS OF WHETHER YOU COULD EVEN DO IT...
IF YOU DEMAND I TEACH YOU SOME OF THE MOVEMENTS, YOU MIGHT TALK ME INTO IT.
PLEASE TEACH ME!
IS YOUR BODY FLEXIBLE?
CAN YOU LIFT ONE LEG DIRECTLY UP INTO THE AIR?
I CAN!
SWOOSH

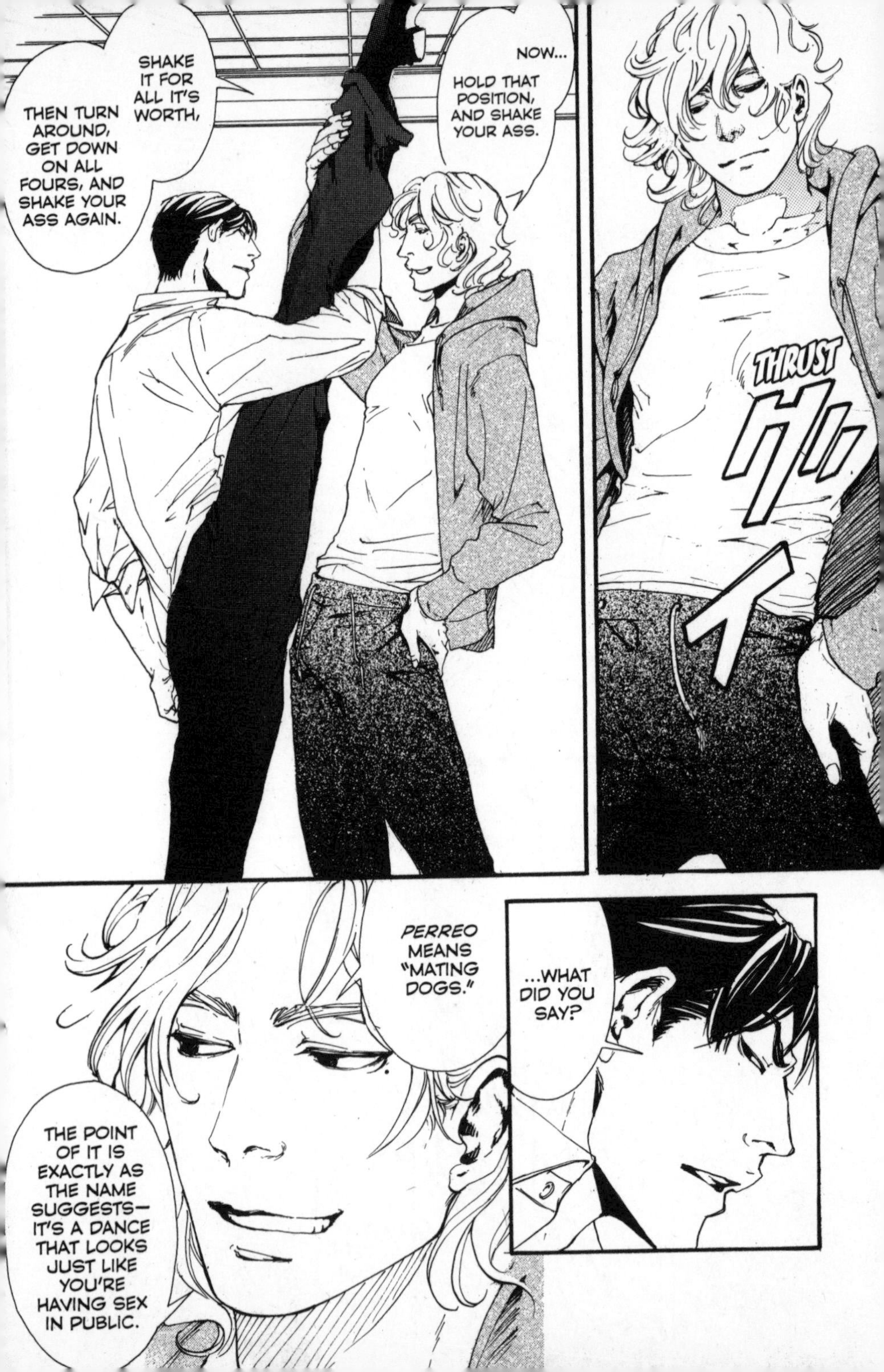
THRUST
NOW... HOLD THAT POSITION, AND SHAKE YOUR ASS.
SHAKE IT FOR ALL IT'S WORTH,
THEN TURN AROUND, GET DOWN ON ALL FOURS, AND SHAKE YOUR ASS AGAIN.
PERREO MEANS "MATING DOGS."
...WHAT DID YOU SAY?
THE POINT OF IT IS EXACTLY AS THE NAME SUGGESTS—IT'S A DANCE THAT LOOKS JUST LIKE YOU'RE HAVING SEX IN PUBLIC.

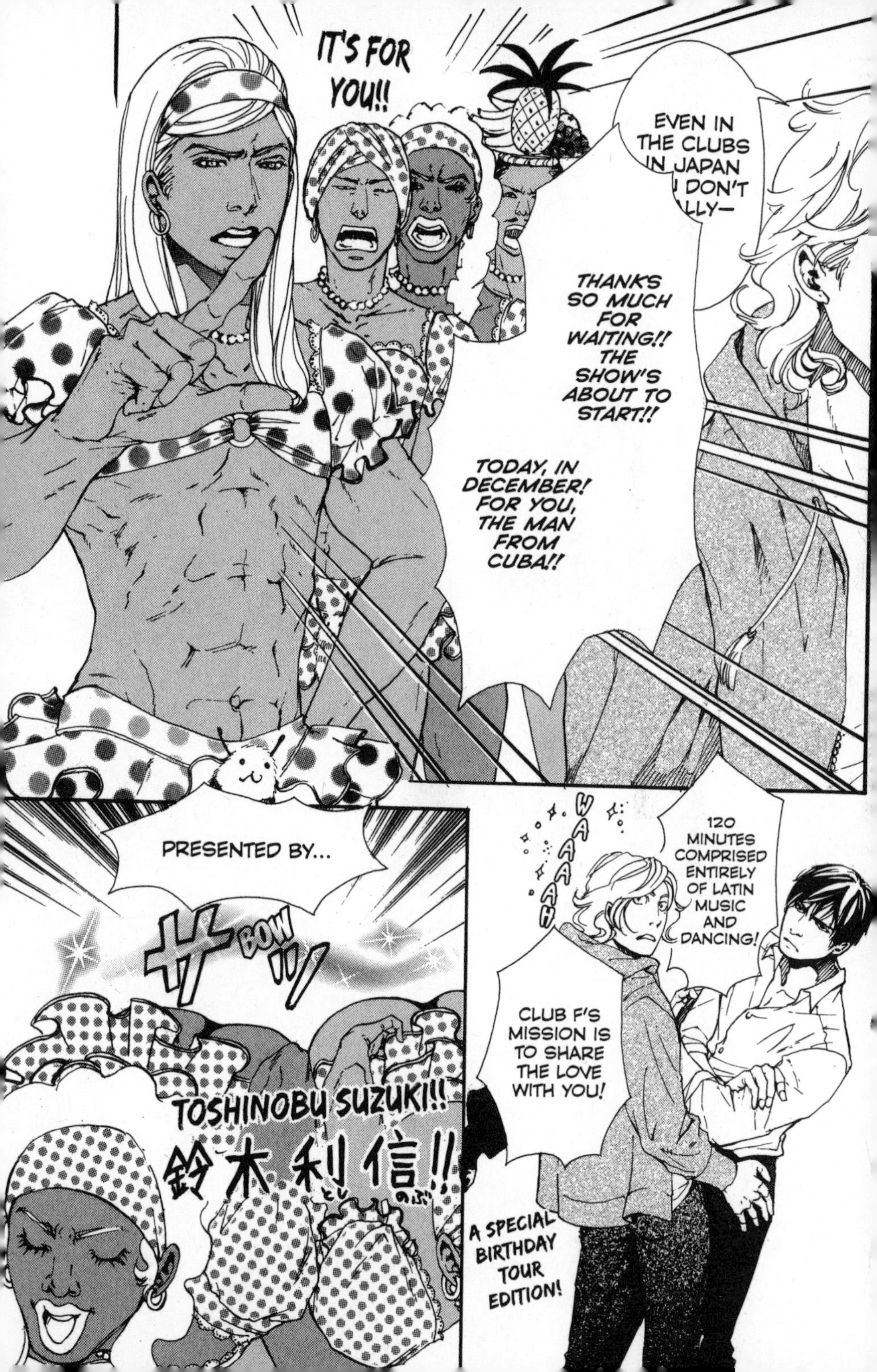
EVEN IN THE CLUBS IN JAPAN U DON'T ALLY—
THANKS SO MUCH FOR WAITING!! THE SHOW'S ABOUT TO START!!
TODAY, IN DECEMBER! FOR YOU, THE MAN FROM CUBA!!
IT'S FOR YOU!!
120 MINUTES COMPRISED ENTIRELY OF LATIN MUSIC AND DANCING!
WAAAAAH
CLUB F'S MISSION IS TO SHARE THE LOVE WITH YOU!
A SPECIAL BIRTHDAY TOUR EDITION!
PRESENTED BY...
BOW
TOSHINOBU SUZUKI!!
鈴木利信!!
とし のぶ

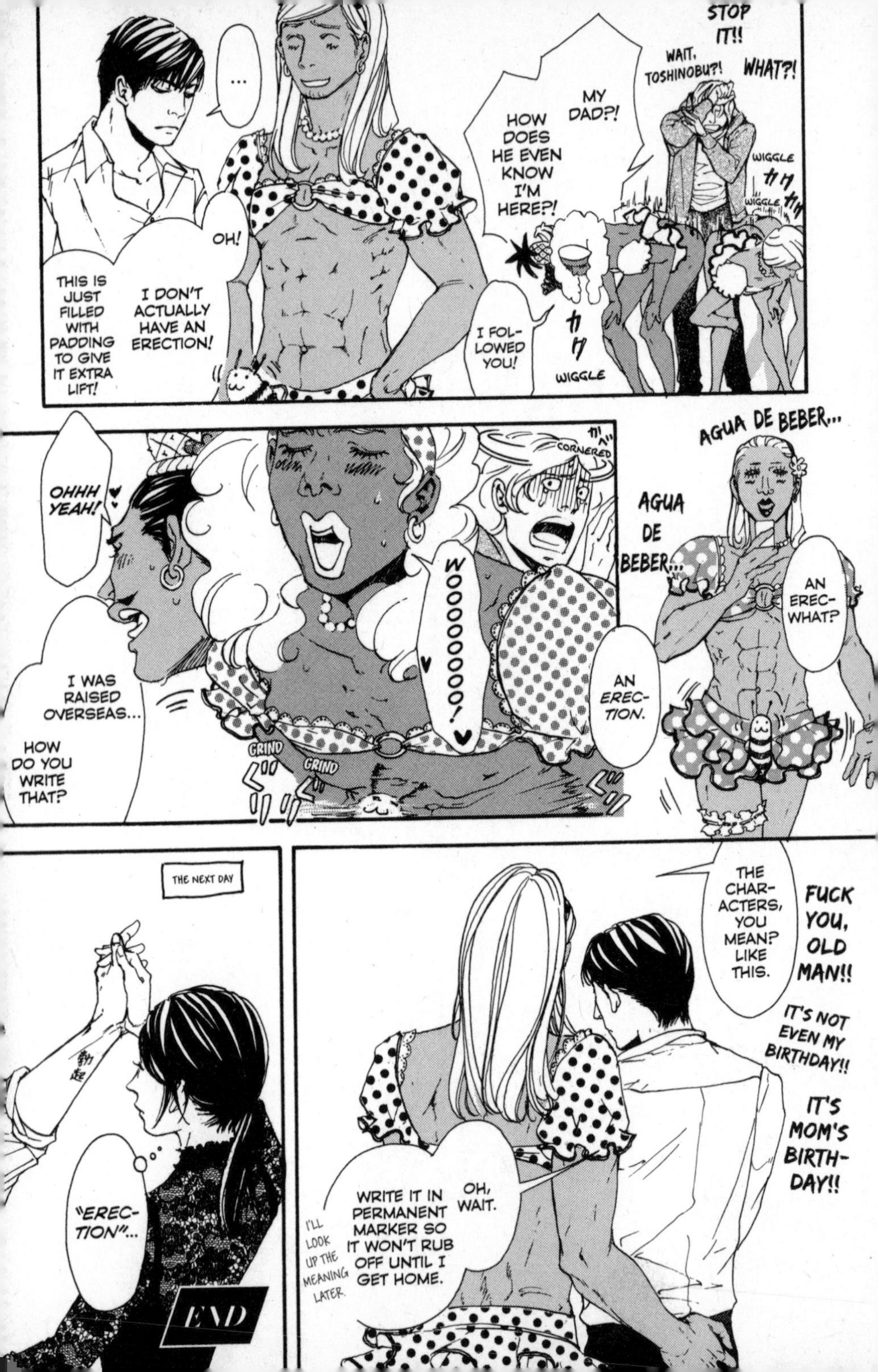
STOP IT!!
WAIT, TOSHINOBU?!
WHAT?!
MY DAD?!
HOW DOES HE EVEN KNOW I'M HERE?!
WIGGLE
WIGGLE
...
OH!
I FOL-LOWED YOU!
WIGGLE
I DON'T ACTUALLY HAVE AN ERECTION!
THIS IS JUST FILLED WITH PADDING TO GIVE IT EXTRA LIFT!
AGUA DE BEBER...
AGUA DE BEBER...
AN EREC-WHAT?
CORNERED
AN EREC-TION.
WOOOOOOOO!
OHHH YEAH!
I WAS RAISED OVERSEAS...
HOW DO YOU WRITE THAT?
GRIND
GRIND
THE CHAR-ACTERS, YOU MEAN? LIKE THIS.
FUCK YOU, OLD MAN!!
IT'S NOT EVEN MY BIRTHDAY!!
IT'S MOM'S BIRTH-DAY!!
OH, WAIT.
WRITE IT IN PERMANENT MARKER SO IT WON'T RUB OFF UNTIL I GET HOME.
I'LL LOOK UP THE MEANING LATER.
THE NEXT DAY
"ERECTION"...
END

#07
FROM GIULIO WITH LOVE

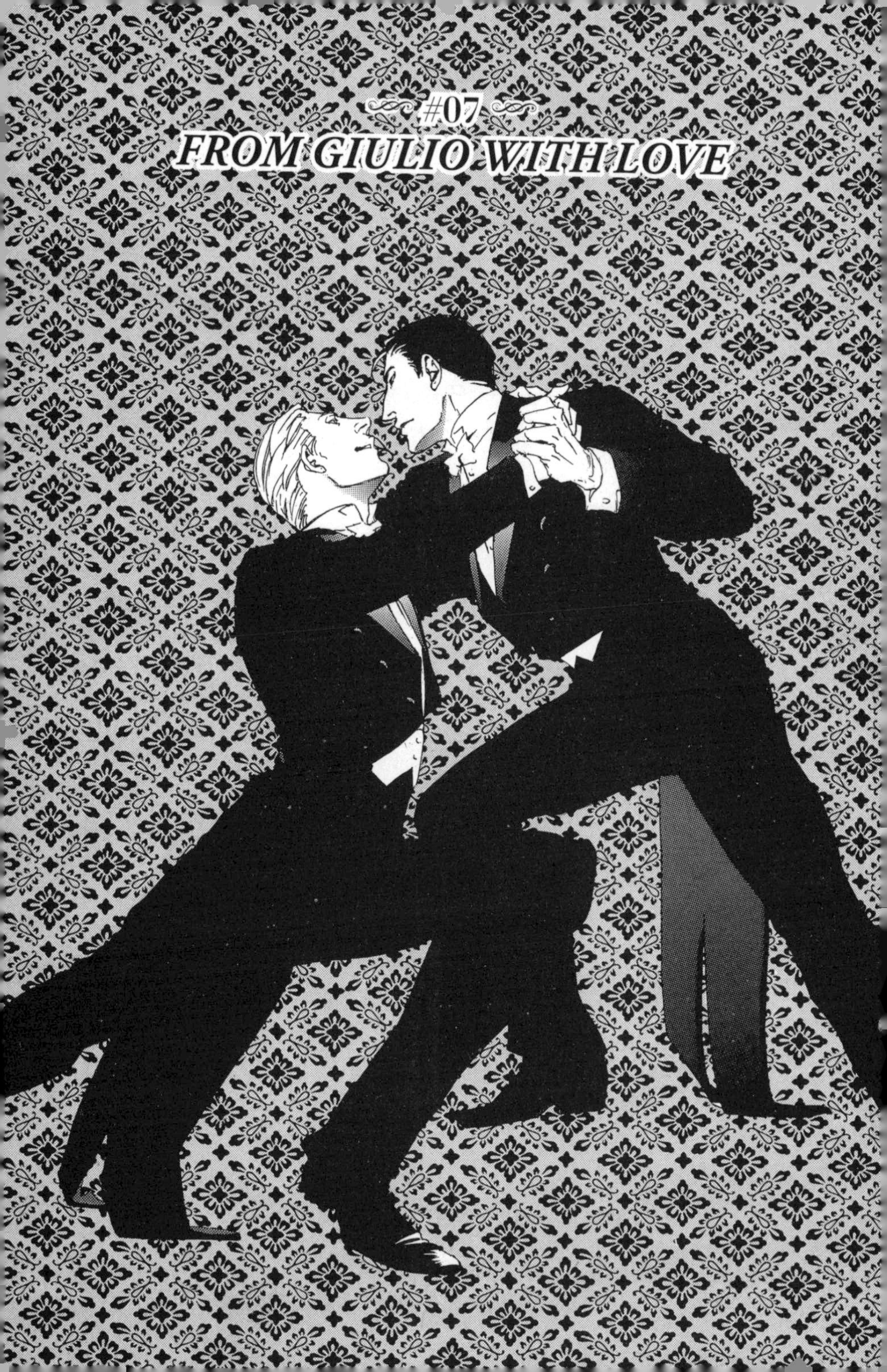

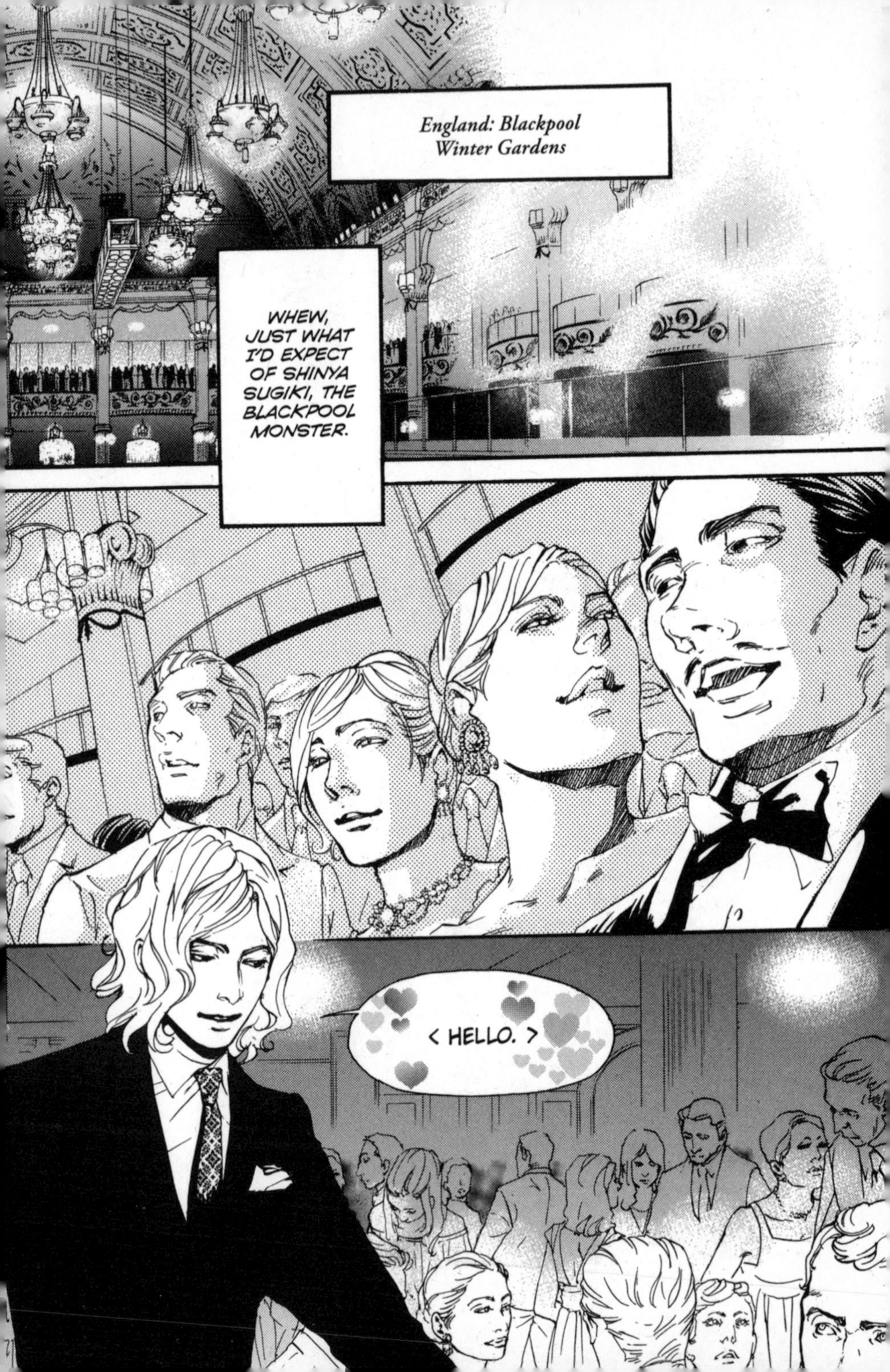
England: Blackpool Winter Gardens
WHEW, JUST WHAT I'D EXPECT OF SHINYA SUGIKI, THE BLACKPOOL MONSTER.
< HELLO. >

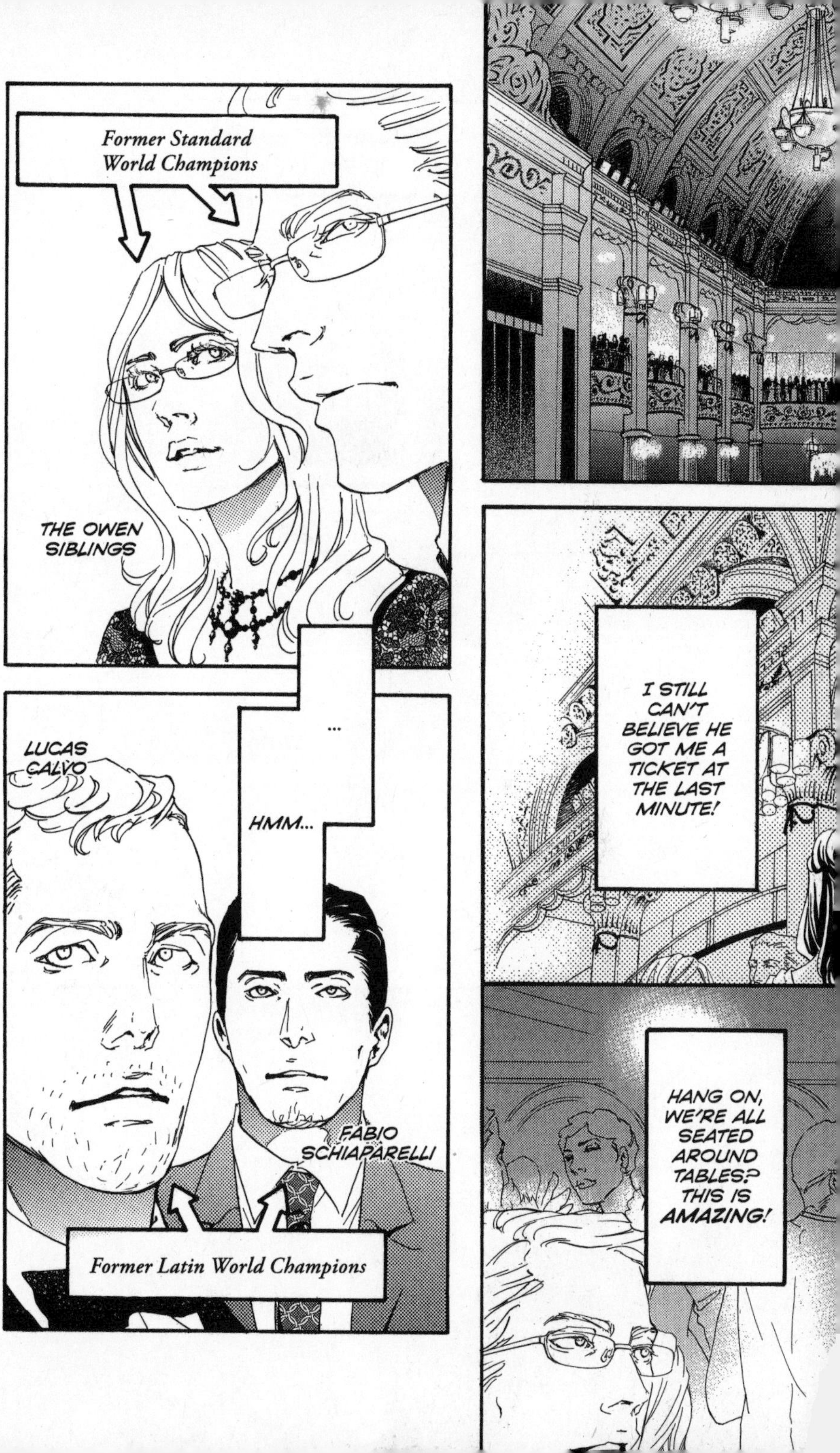
I STILL CAN'T BELIEVE HE GOT ME A TICKET AT THE LAST MINUTE!
HANG ON, WE'RE ALL SEATED AROUND TABLES? THIS IS AMAZING!
Former Standard World Champions
THE OWEN SIBLINGS
...
HMM...
LUCAS CALVO
FABIO SCHIAPARELLI
Former Latin World Champions

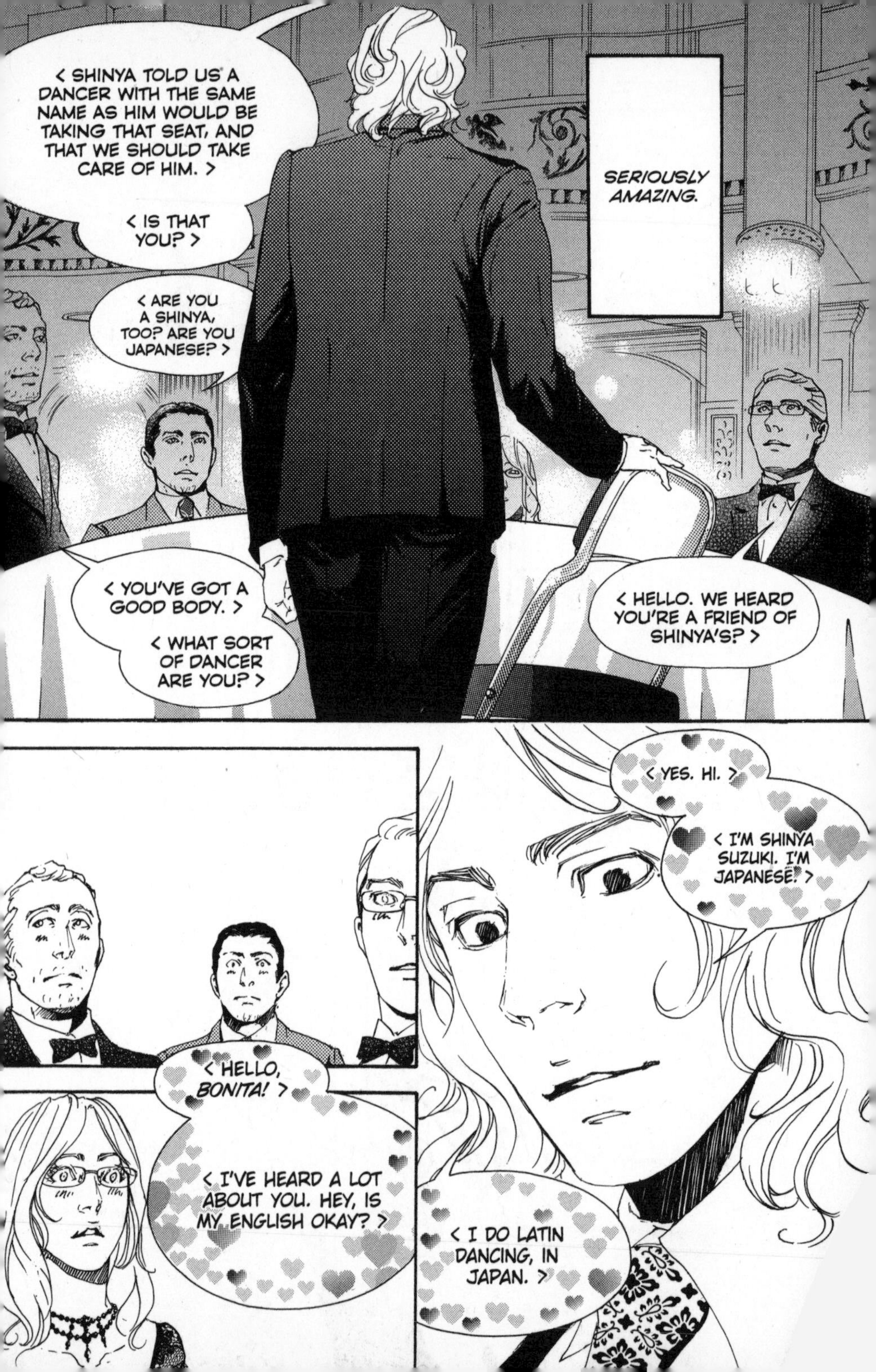
SERIOUSLY AMAZING.
< SHINYA TOLD US A DANCER WITH THE SAME NAME AS HIM WOULD BE TAKING THAT SEAT, AND THAT WE SHOULD TAKE CARE OF HIM. >
< IS THAT YOU? >
< ARE YOU A SHINYA, TOO? ARE YOU JAPANESE? >
< HELLO. WE HEARD YOU'RE A FRIEND OF SHINYA'S? >
< YOU'VE GOT A GOOD BODY. >
< WHAT SORT OF DANCER ARE YOU? >
< YES. HI. >
< I'M SHINYA SUZUKI. I'M JAPANESE. >
< I DO LATIN DANCING, IN JAPAN. >
< HELLO, *BONITA!* >
< I'VE HEARD A LOT ABOUT YOU. HEY, IS MY ENGLISH OKAY? >

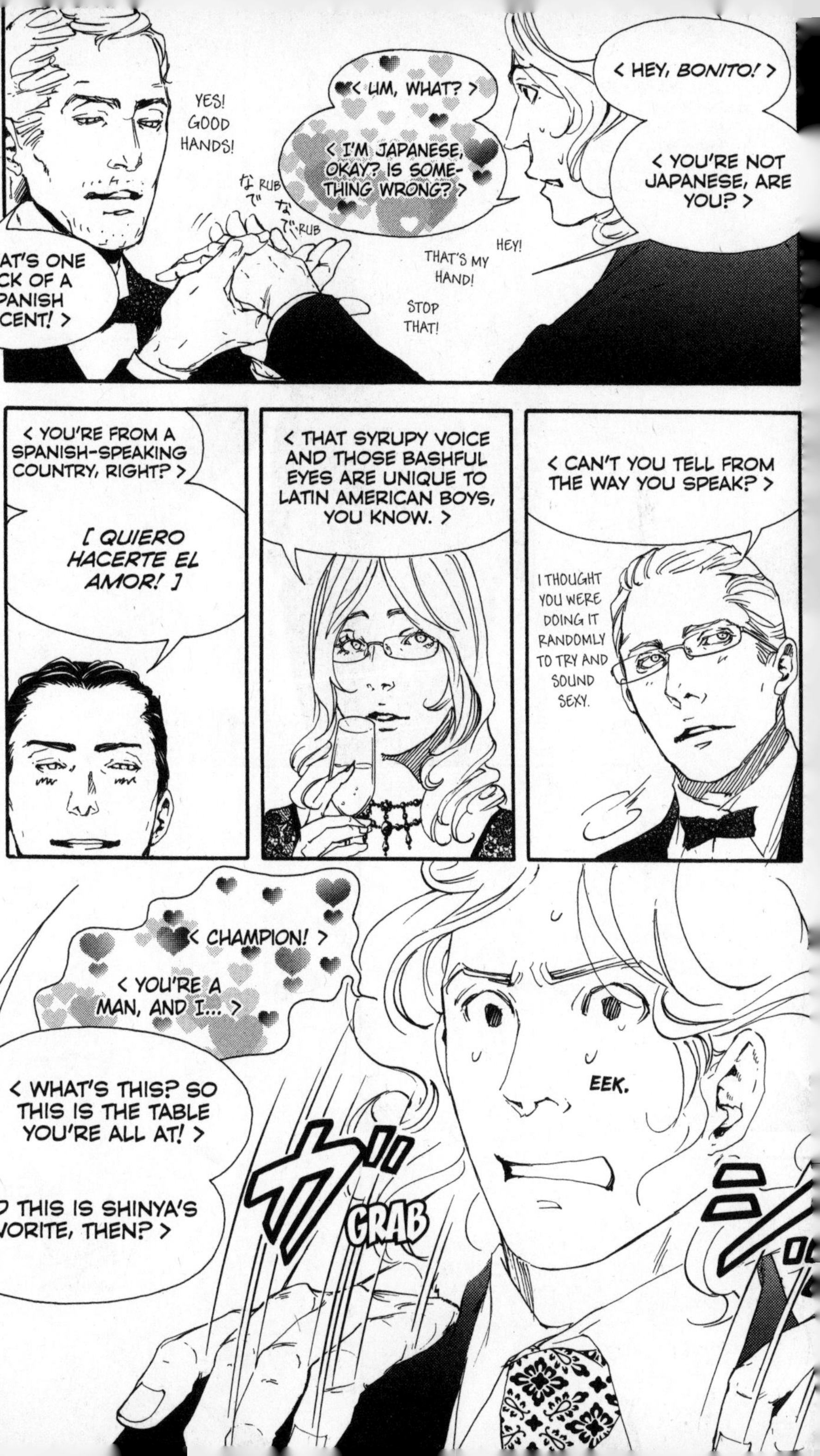
< HEY, BONITO! >
< YOU'RE NOT JAPANESE, ARE YOU? >
< UM, WHAT? >
< I'M JAPANESE, OKAY? IS SOMETHING WRONG? >
HEY!
THAT'S MY HAND!
STOP THAT!
YES! GOOD HANDS!
なで RUB
なで RUB
< THAT'S ONE HECK OF A SPANISH ACCENT! >
< CAN'T YOU TELL FROM THE WAY YOU SPEAK? >
I THOUGHT YOU WERE DOING IT RANDOMLY TO TRY AND SOUND SEXY.
< THAT SYRUPY VOICE AND THOSE BASHFUL EYES ARE UNIQUE TO LATIN AMERICAN BOYS, YOU KNOW. >
< YOU'RE FROM A SPANISH-SPEAKING COUNTRY, RIGHT? >
[QUIERO HACERTE EL AMOR!]
EEK.
< CHAMPION! >
< YOU'RE A MAN, AND I... >
< WHAT'S THIS? SO THIS IS THE TABLE YOU'RE ALL AT! >
< AND THIS IS SHINYA'S FAVORITE, THEN? >
GRAB

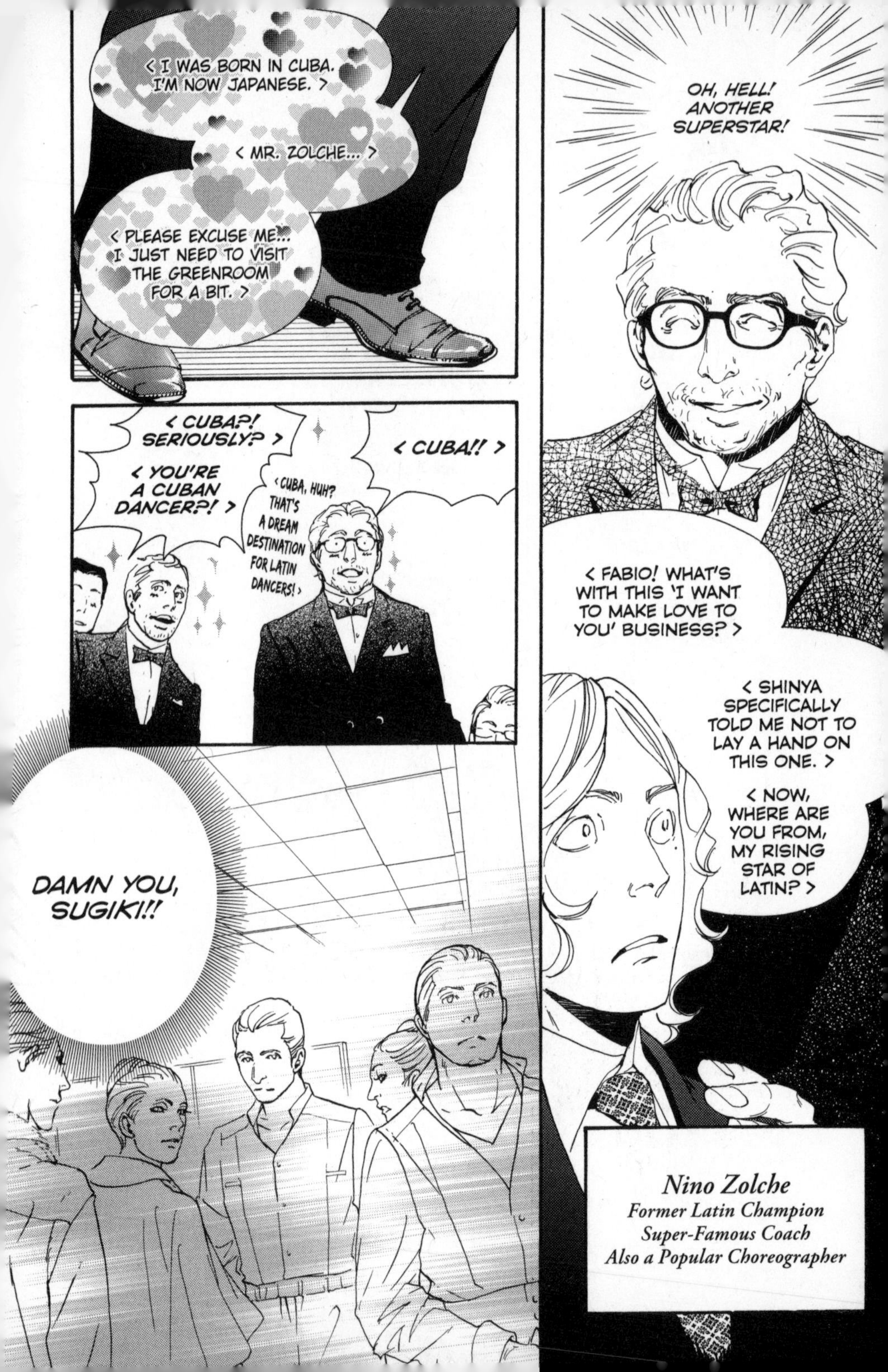
OH, HELL! ANOTHER SUPERSTAR!
< FABIO! WHAT'S WITH THIS 'I WANT TO MAKE LOVE TO YOU' BUSINESS? >
< SHINYA SPECIFICALLY TOLD ME NOT TO LAY A HAND ON THIS ONE. >
< NOW, WHERE ARE YOU FROM, MY RISING STAR OF LATIN? >
Nino Zolche
Former Latin Champion
Super-Famous Coach
Also a Popular Choreographer
< I WAS BORN IN CUBA. I'M NOW JAPANESE. >
< MR. ZOLCHE... >
< PLEASE EXCUSE ME... I JUST NEED TO VISIT THE GREENROOM FOR A BIT. >
< CUBA!! >
< CUBA, HUH? THAT'S A DREAM DESTINATION FOR LATIN DANCERS! >
< CUBA?! SERIOUSLY? >
< YOU'RE A CUBAN DANCER?! >
DAMN YOU, SUGIKI!!

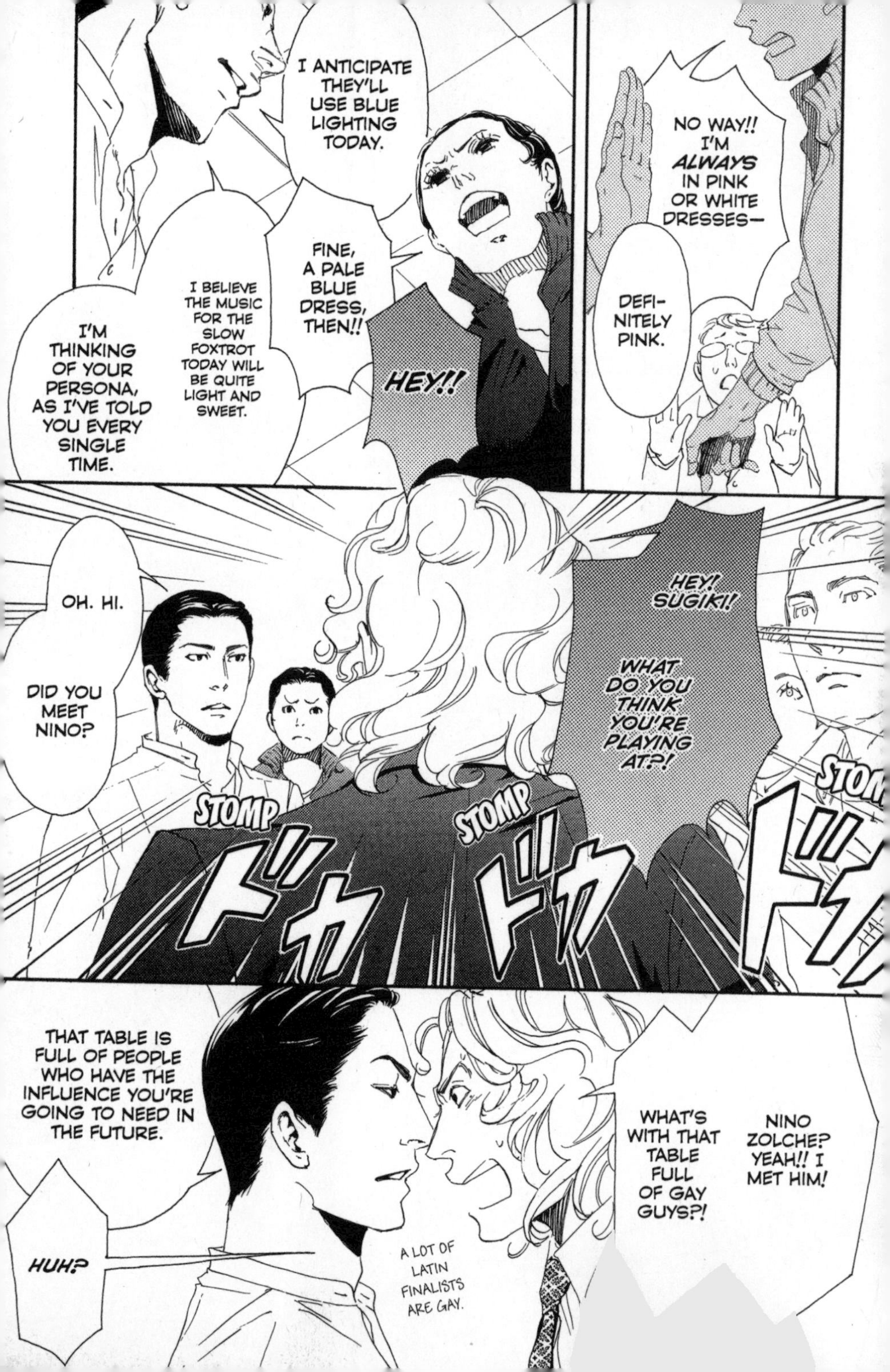
NO WAY!! I'M *ALWAYS* IN PINK OR WHITE DRESSES—
DEFI- NITELY PINK.
I ANTICIPATE THEY'LL USE BLUE LIGHTING TODAY.
HEY!!
FINE, A PALE BLUE DRESS, THEN!!
I BELIEVE THE MUSIC FOR THE SLOW FOXTROT TODAY WILL BE QUITE LIGHT AND SWEET.
I'M THINKING OF YOUR PERSONA, AS I'VE TOLD YOU EVERY SINGLE TIME.
HEY! SUGIKI!
WHAT DO YOU THINK YOU'RE PLAYING AT?!
STOM
ドカ
STOMP
ドカ
STOMP
ドカ
OH. HI.
DID YOU MEET NINO?
NINO ZOLCHE? YEAH!! I MET HIM!
WHAT'S WITH THAT TABLE FULL OF GAY GUYS?!
A LOT OF LATIN FINALISTS ARE GAY.
THAT TABLE IS FULL OF PEOPLE WHO HAVE THE INFLUENCE YOU'RE GOING TO NEED IN THE FUTURE.
HUH?

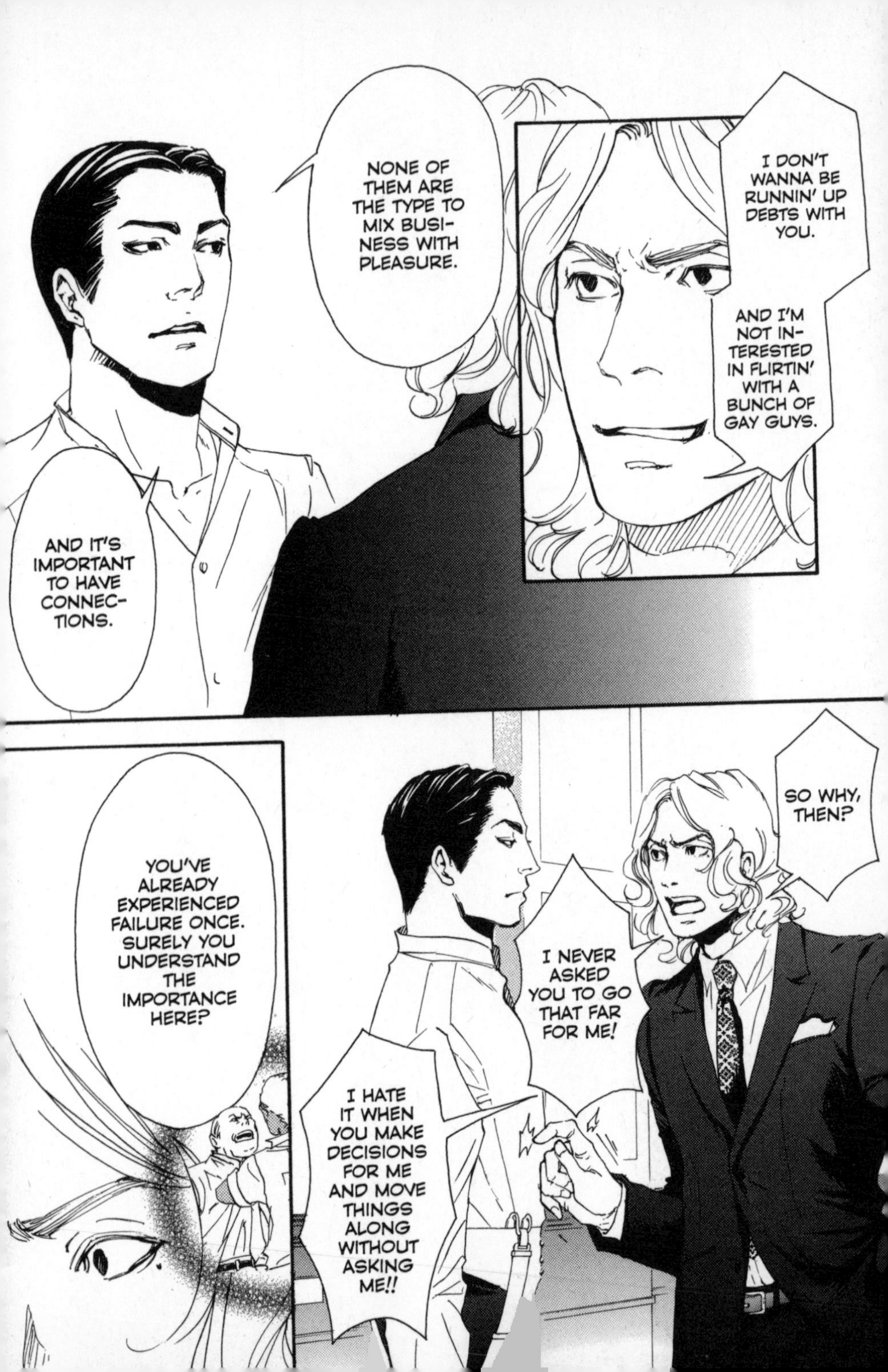
I DON'T WANNA BE RUNNIN' UP DEBTS WITH YOU.
AND I'M NOT INTERESTED IN FLIRTIN' WITH A BUNCH OF GAY GUYS.
NONE OF THEM ARE THE TYPE TO MIX BUSINESS WITH PLEASURE.
AND IT'S IMPORTANT TO HAVE CONNECTIONS.
SO WHY, THEN?
I NEVER ASKED YOU TO GO THAT FAR FOR ME!
I HATE IT WHEN YOU MAKE DECISIONS FOR ME AND MOVE THINGS ALONG WITHOUT ASKING ME!!
YOU'VE ALREADY EXPERIENCED FAILURE ONCE. SURELY YOU UNDERSTAND THE IMPORTANCE HERE?

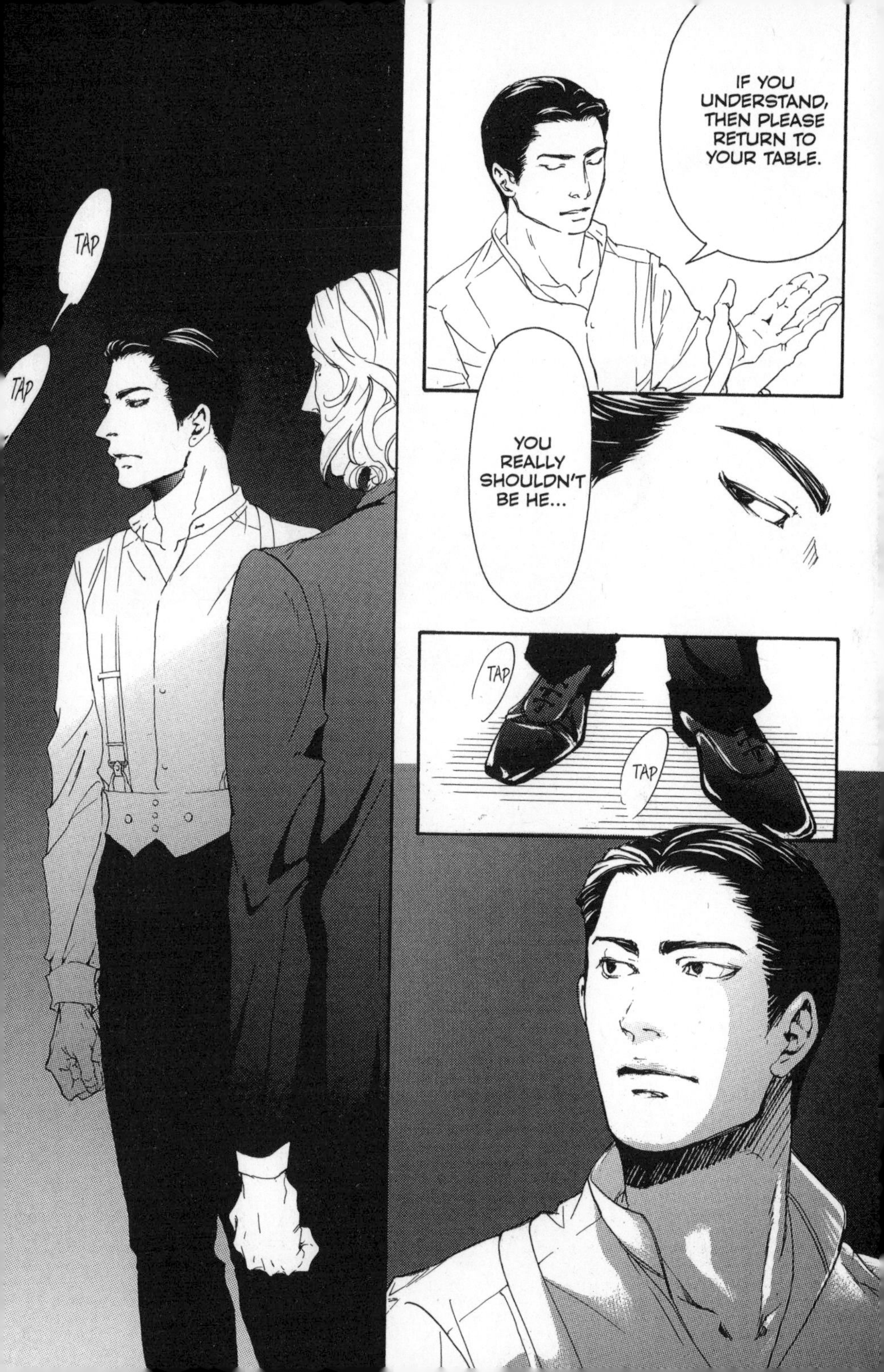
IF YOU UNDERSTAND, THEN PLEASE RETURN TO YOUR TABLE.
YOU REALLY SHOULDN'T BE HE...
TAP
TAP
TAP
TAP

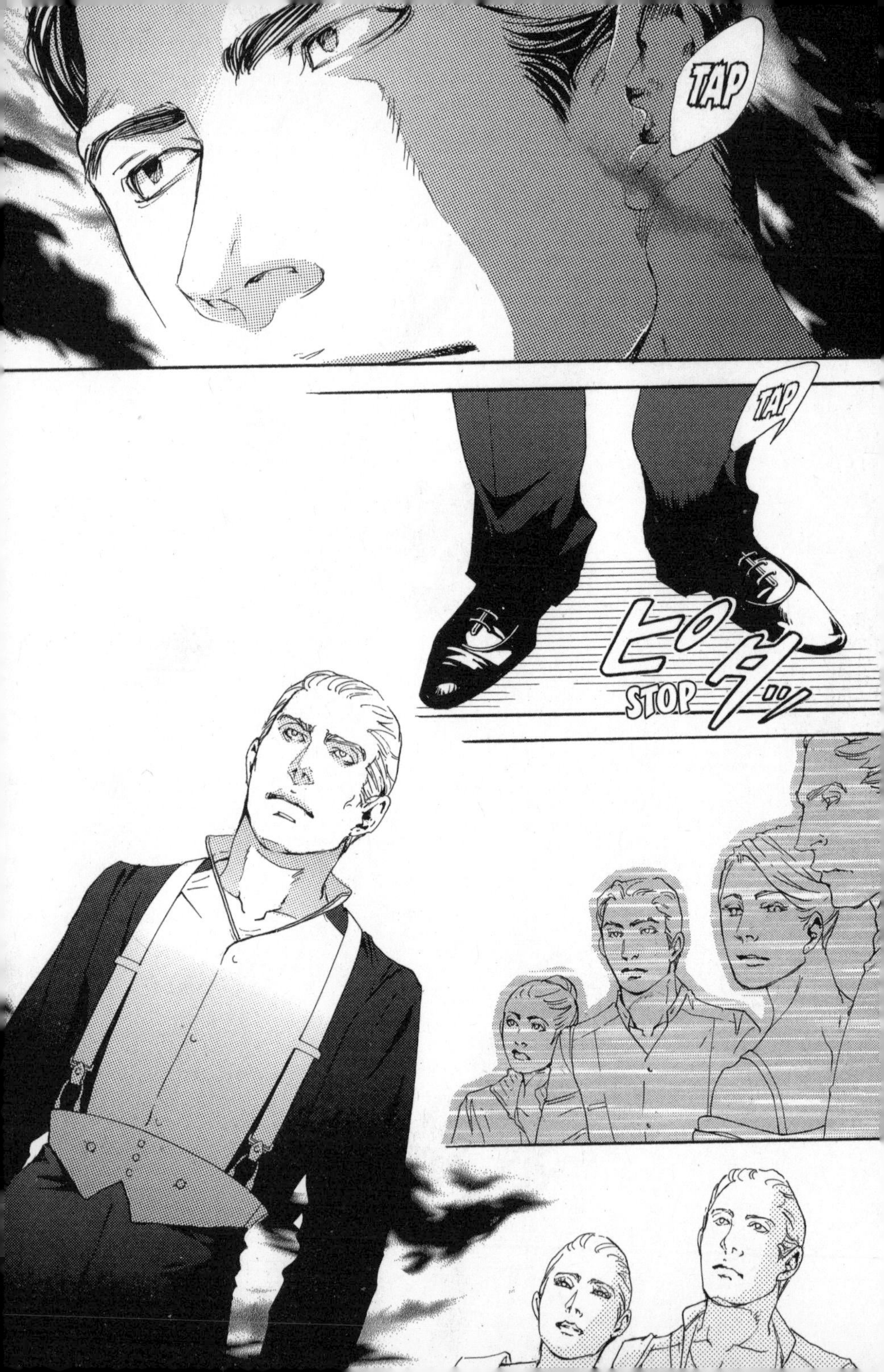
TAP
TAP
ピタッ
STOP

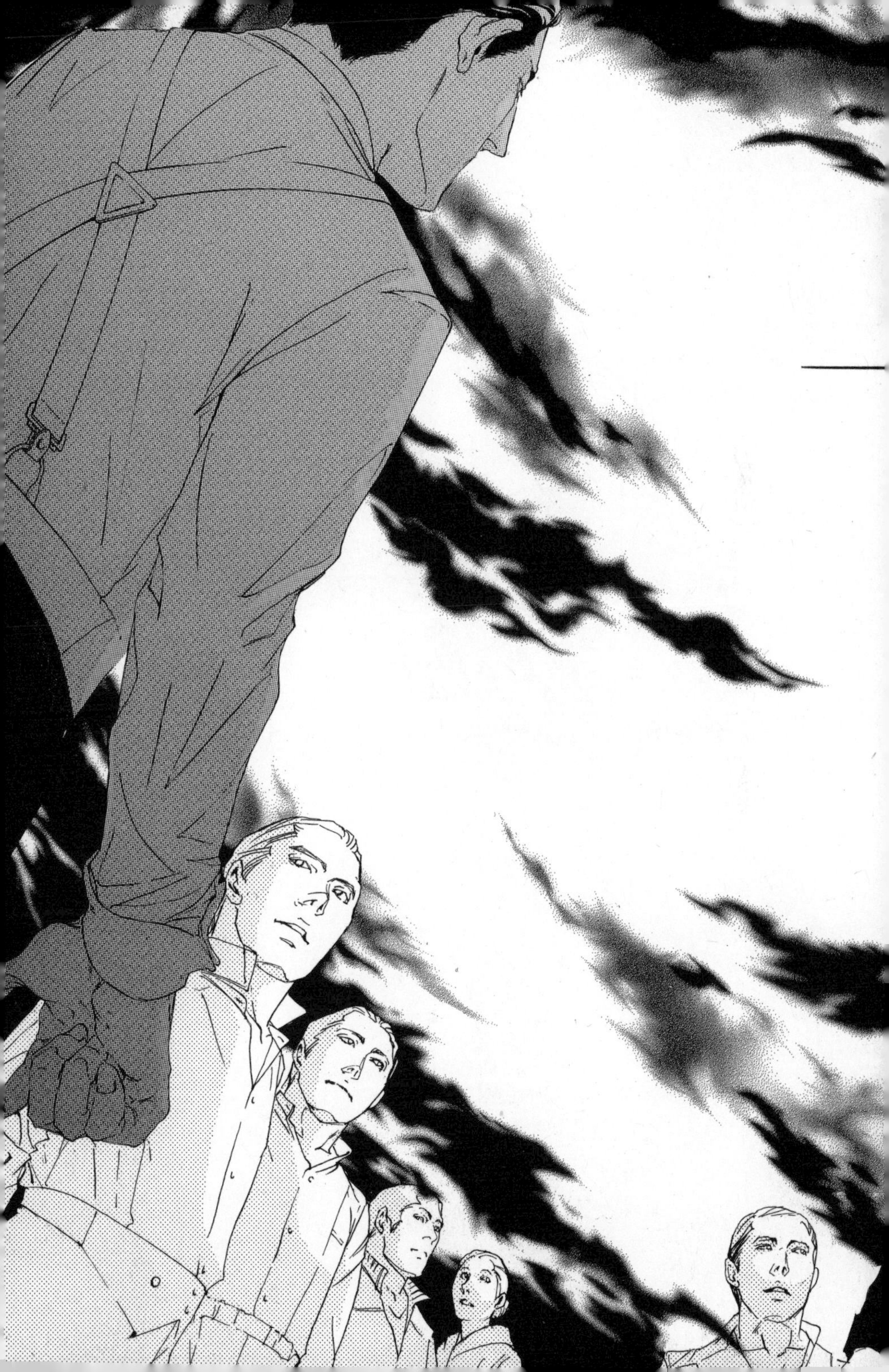

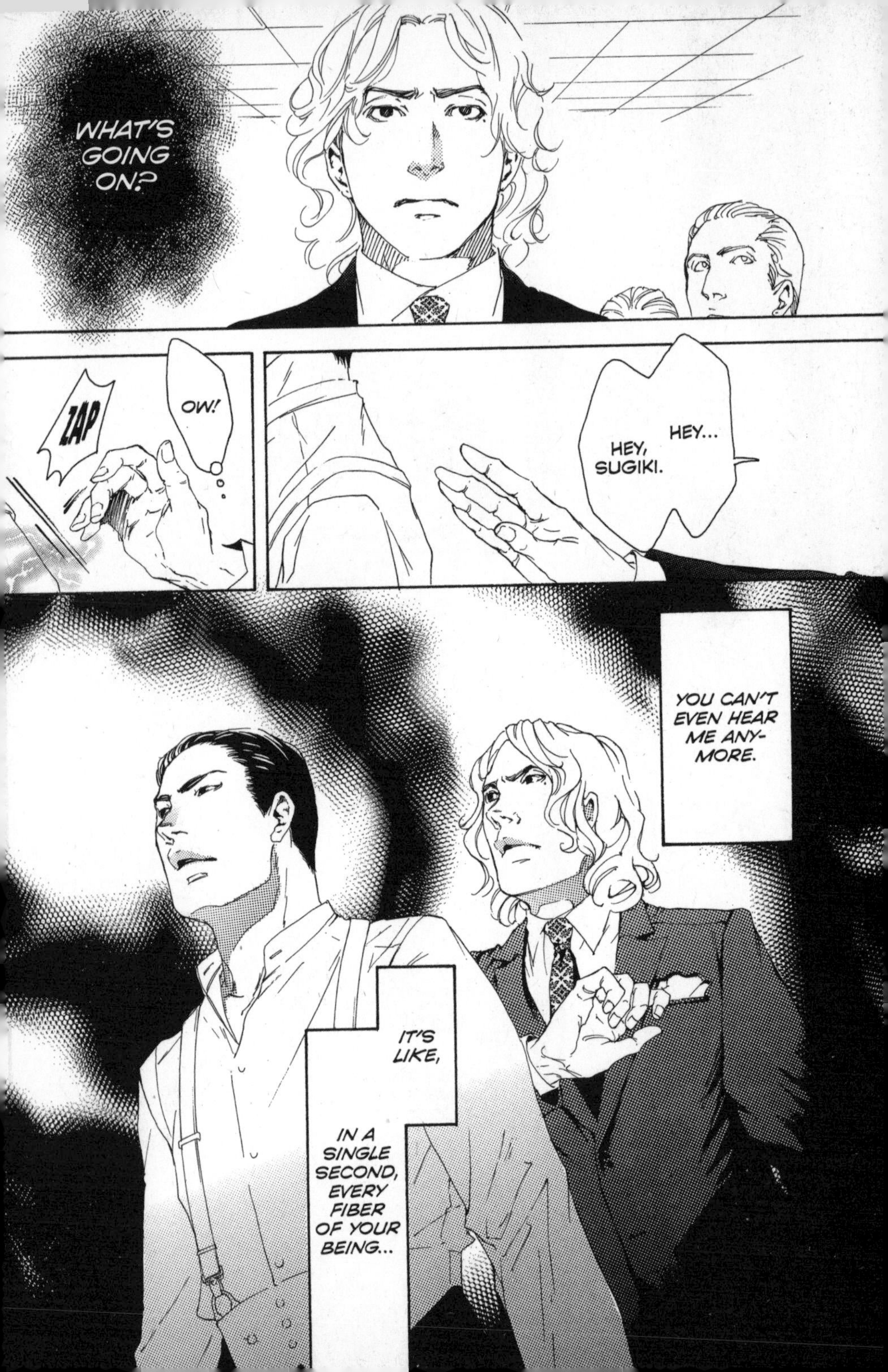
WHAT'S GOING ON?
HEY... HEY, SUGIKI.
ZAP
OW!
YOU CAN'T EVEN HEAR ME ANY-MORE.
IT'S LIKE,
IN A SINGLE SECOND, EVERY FIBER OF YOUR BEING...

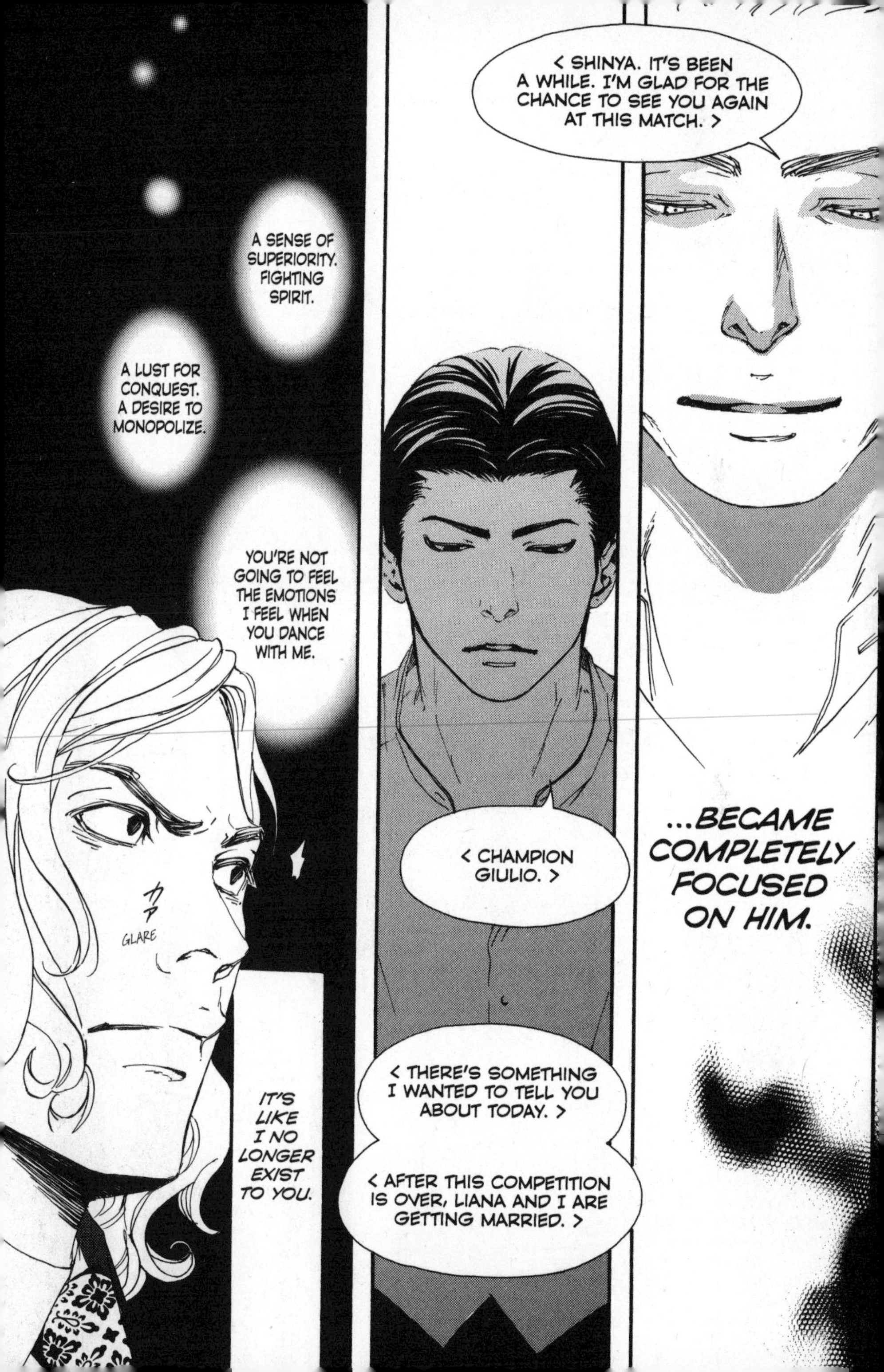
< SHINYA. IT'S BEEN A WHILE. I'M GLAD FOR THE CHANCE TO SEE YOU AGAIN AT THIS MATCH. >
...BECAME COMPLETELY FOCUSED ON HIM.
< CHAMPION GIULIO. >
< THERE'S SOMETHING I WANTED TO TELL YOU ABOUT TODAY. >
< AFTER THIS COMPETITION IS OVER, LIANA AND I ARE GETTING MARRIED. >
A SENSE OF SUPERIORITY. FIGHTING SPIRIT.
A LUST FOR CONQUEST. A DESIRE TO MONOPOLIZE.
YOU'RE NOT GOING TO FEEL THE EMOTIONS I FEEL WHEN YOU DANCE WITH ME.
GLARE
IT'S LIKE I NO LONGER EXIST TO YOU.

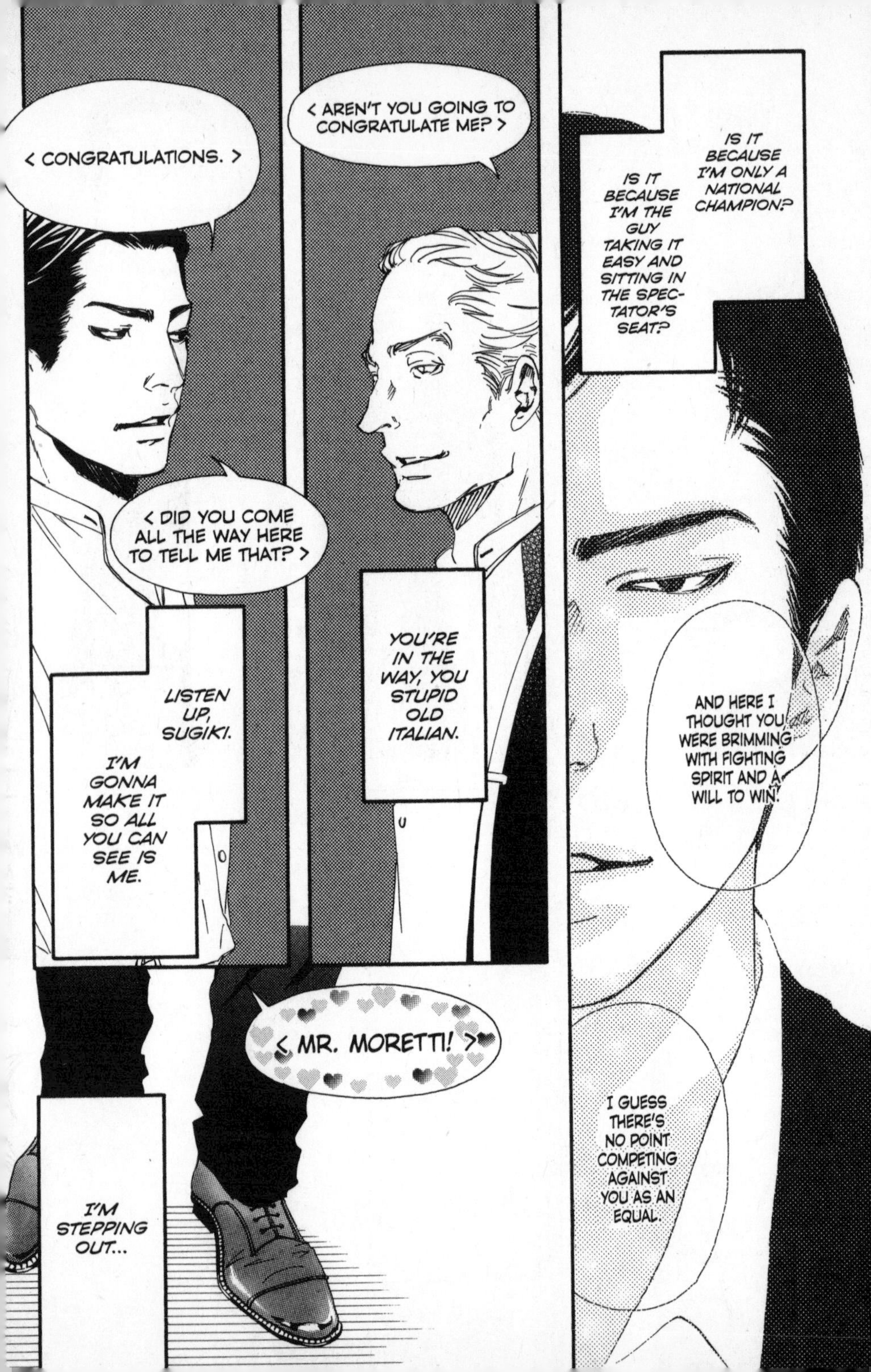
IS IT BECAUSE I'M ONLY A NATIONAL CHAMPION?
IS IT BECAUSE I'M THE GUY TAKING IT EASY AND SITTING IN THE SPEC-TATOR'S SEAT?
AND HERE I THOUGHT YOU WERE BRIMMING WITH FIGHTING SPIRIT AND A WILL TO WIN.
I GUESS THERE'S NO POINT COMPETING AGAINST YOU AS AN EQUAL.
< AREN'T YOU GOING TO CONGRATULATE ME? >
YOU'RE IN THE WAY, YOU STUPID OLD ITALIAN.
< CONGRATULATIONS. >
< DID YOU COME ALL THE WAY HERE TO TELL ME THAT? >
LISTEN UP, SUGIKI.
I'M GONNA MAKE IT SO ALL YOU CAN SEE IS ME.
< MR. MORETTI! >
I'M STEPPING OUT...

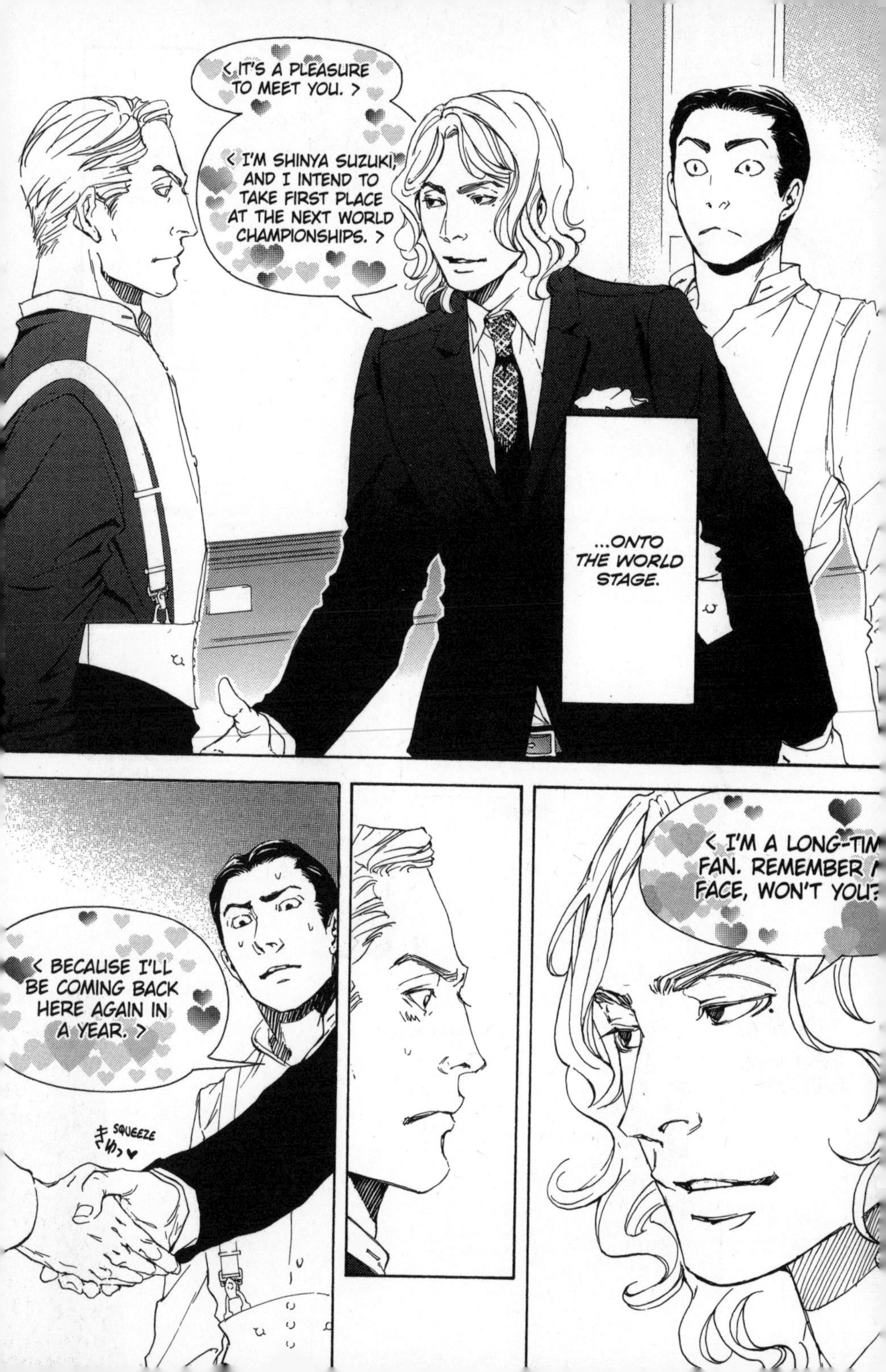
< IT'S A PLEASURE TO MEET YOU. > < I'M SHINYA SUZUKI, AND I INTEND TO TAKE FIRST PLACE AT THE NEXT WORLD CHAMPIONSHIPS. >
...ONTO THE WORLD STAGE.
< I'M A LONG-TIM FAN. REMEMBER FACE, WON'T YOU?
< BECAUSE I'LL BE COMING BACK HERE AGAIN IN A YEAR. >
きゅっ SQUEEZE

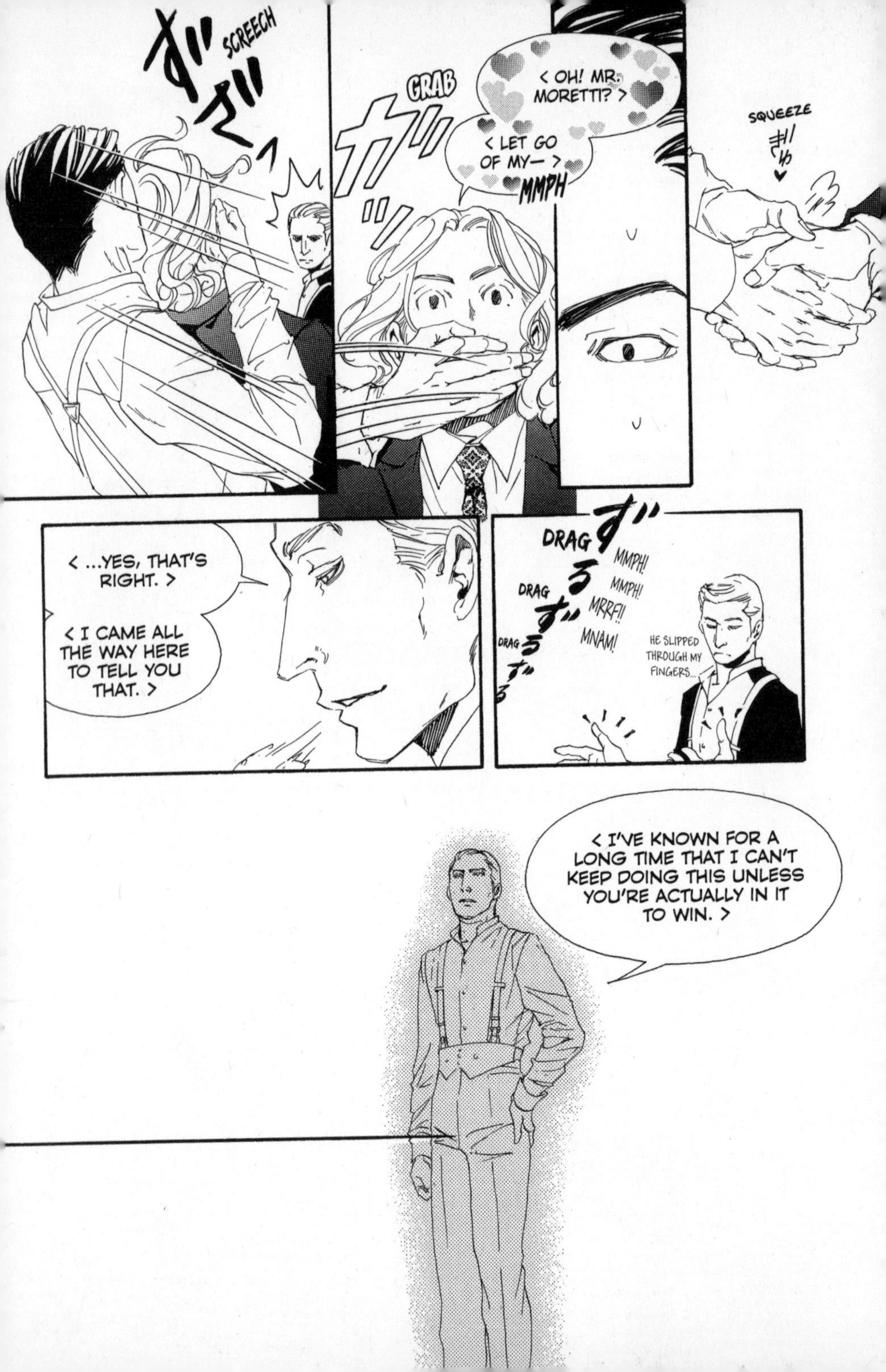
SQUEEZE
GRAB
< OH! MR. MORETTI? >
< LET GO OF MY— >
MMPH
SCREECH
DRAG
MMPH!
MMPH!
DRAG
MRRF!!
MNAM!
DRAG
HE SLIPPED THROUGH MY FINGERS...
< ...YES, THAT'S RIGHT. >
< I CAME ALL THE WAY HERE TO TELL YOU THAT. >
< I'VE KNOWN FOR A LONG TIME THAT I CAN'T KEEP DOING THIS UNLESS YOU'RE ACTUALLY IN IT TO WIN. >

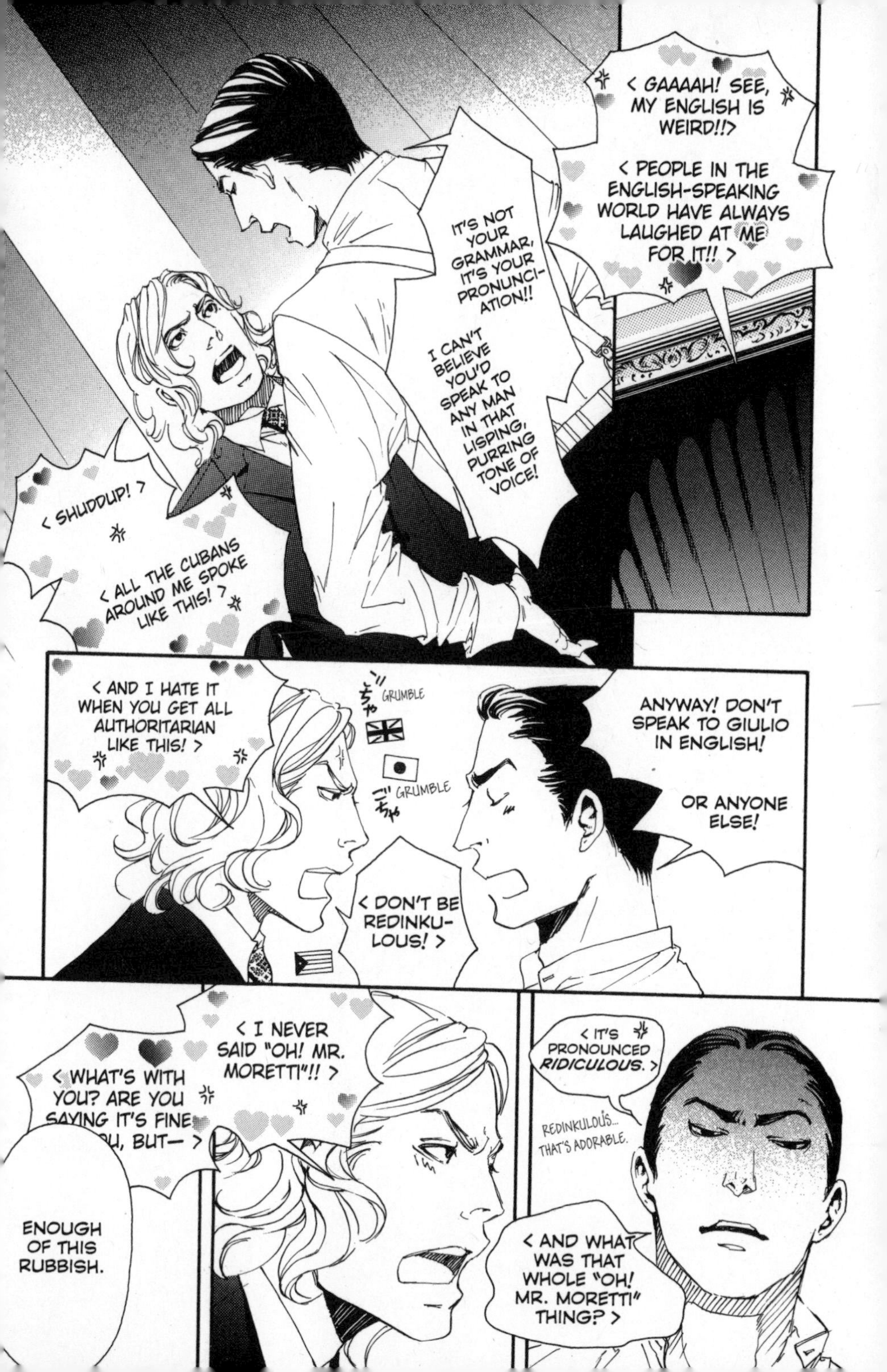
< GAAAAH! SEE, MY ENGLISH IS WEIRD!! >
< PEOPLE IN THE ENGLISH-SPEAKING WORLD HAVE ALWAYS LAUGHED AT ME FOR IT!! >
IT'S NOT YOUR GRAMMAR, IT'S YOUR PRONUNCIATION!!
I CAN'T BELIEVE YOU'D SPEAK TO ANY MAN IN THAT LISPING, PURRING TONE OF VOICE!
< SHUDDUP! >
< ALL THE CUBANS AROUND ME SPOKE LIKE THIS! >
ANYWAY! DON'T SPEAK TO GIULIO IN ENGLISH!
OR ANYONE ELSE!
GRUMBLE
GRUMBLE
< AND I HATE IT WHEN YOU GET ALL AUTHORITARIAN LIKE THIS! >
< DON'T BE REDINKULOUS! >
< IT'S PRONOUNCED *RIDICULOUS*. >
REDINKULOUS... THAT'S ADORABLE.
< AND WHAT WAS THAT WHOLE "OH! MR. MORETTI" THING? >
< I NEVER SAID "OH! MR. MORETTI"!! >
< WHAT'S WITH YOU? ARE YOU SAYING IT'S FINE
U, BUT— >
ENOUGH OF THIS RUBBISH.

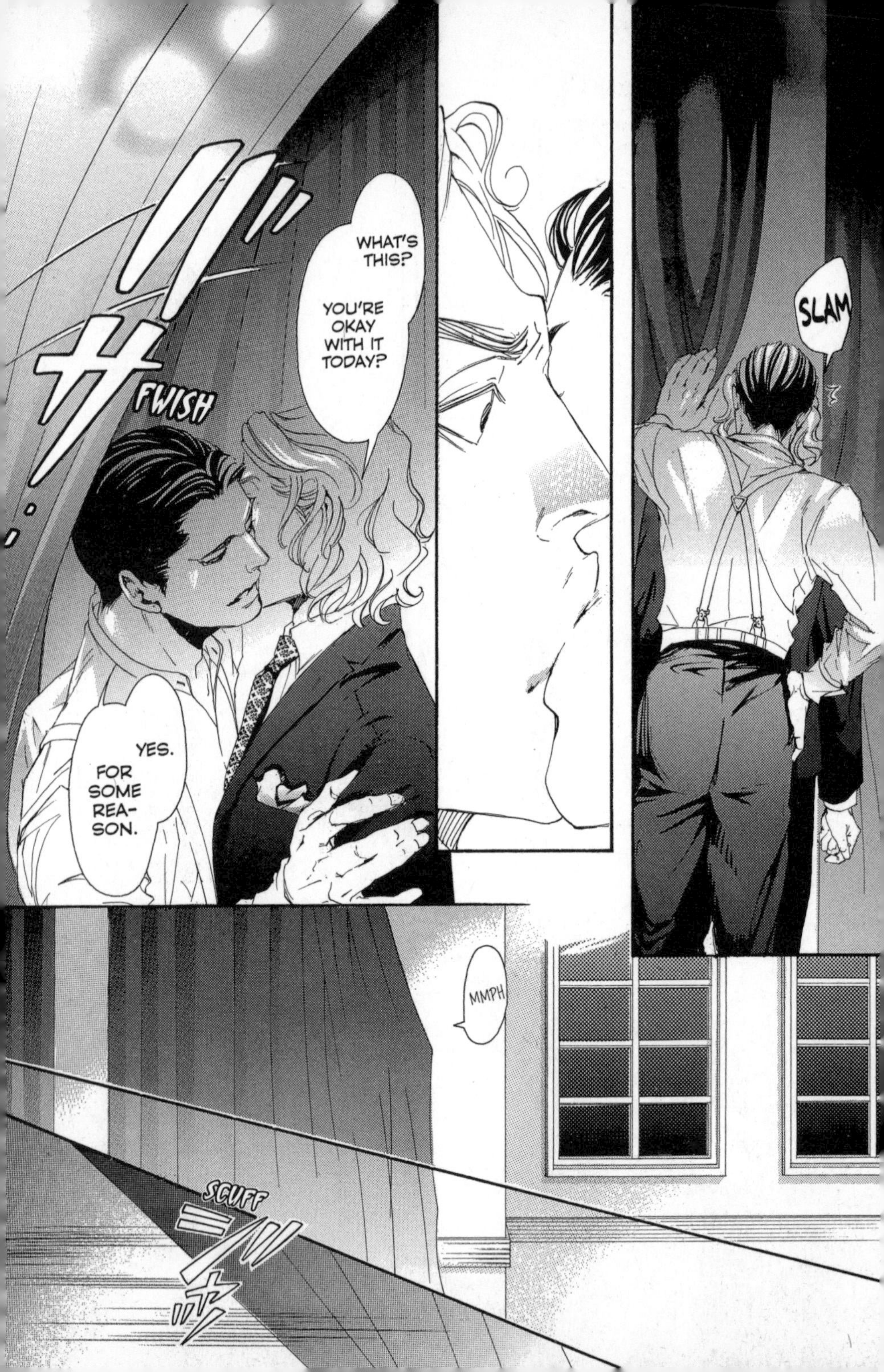
SLAM
WHAT'S THIS? YOU'RE OKAY WITH IT TODAY?
FWISH
YES. FOR SOME REA-SON.
MMPH
SCUFF

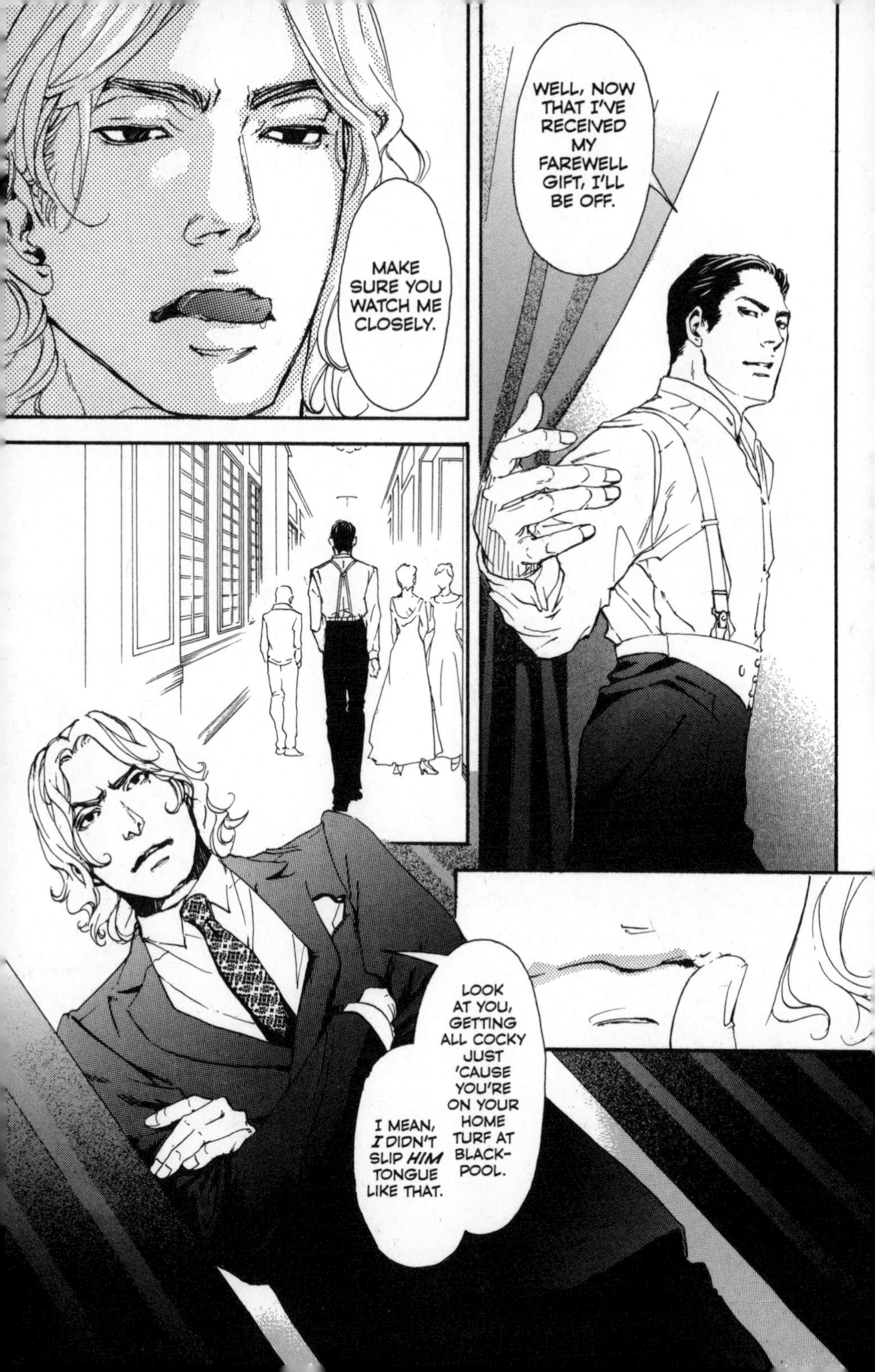
WELL, NOW THAT I'VE RECEIVED MY FAREWELL GIFT, I'LL BE OFF.
MAKE SURE YOU WATCH ME CLOSELY.
LOOK AT YOU, GETTING ALL COCKY JUST 'CAUSE YOU'RE ON YOUR HOME TURF AT BLACK-POOL.
I MEAN, *I* DIDN'T SLIP *HIM* TONGUE LIKE THAT.

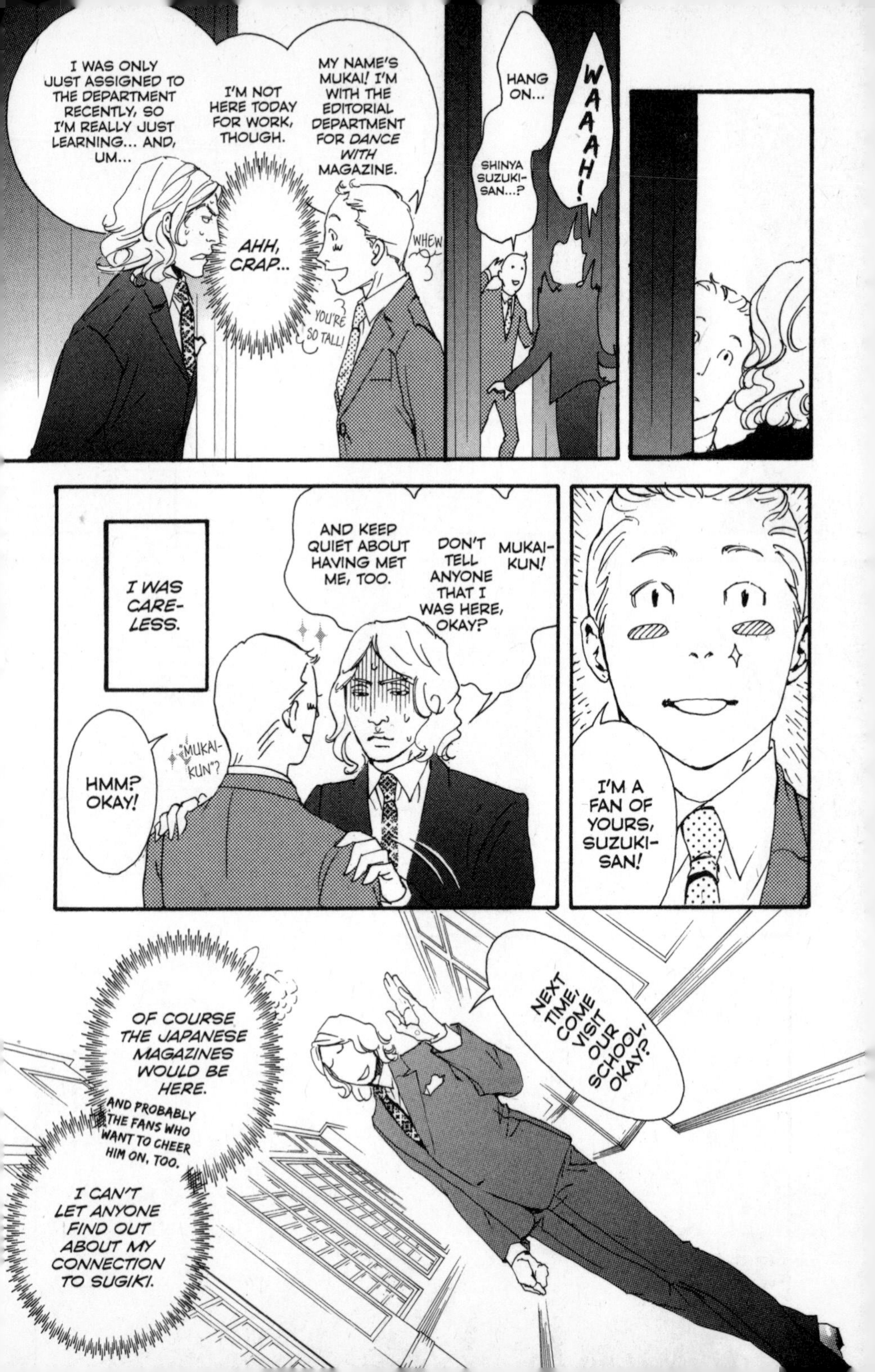
WAAAAH!
HANG ON...
SHINYA SUZUKI-SAN...?
MY NAME'S MUKAI! I'M WITH THE EDITORIAL DEPARTMENT FOR DANCE WITH MAGAZINE.
I'M NOT HERE TODAY FOR WORK, THOUGH.
I WAS ONLY JUST ASSIGNED TO THE DEPARTMENT RECENTLY, SO I'M REALLY JUST LEARNING... AND, UM...
WHEW
AHH, CRAP...
YOU'RE SO TALL!
I'M A FAN OF YOURS, SUZUKI-SAN!
MUKAI-KUN!
DON'T TELL ANYONE THAT I WAS HERE, OKAY?
AND KEEP QUIET ABOUT HAVING MET ME, TOO.
I WAS CARELESS.
"MUKAI-KUN"?
HMM? OKAY!
NEXT TIME, COME VISIT OUR SCHOOL, OKAY?
OF COURSE THE JAPANESE MAGAZINES WOULD BE HERE.
AND PROBABLY THE FANS WHO WANT TO CHEER HIM ON, TOO.
I CAN'T LET ANYONE FIND OUT ABOUT MY CONNECTION TO SUGIKI.

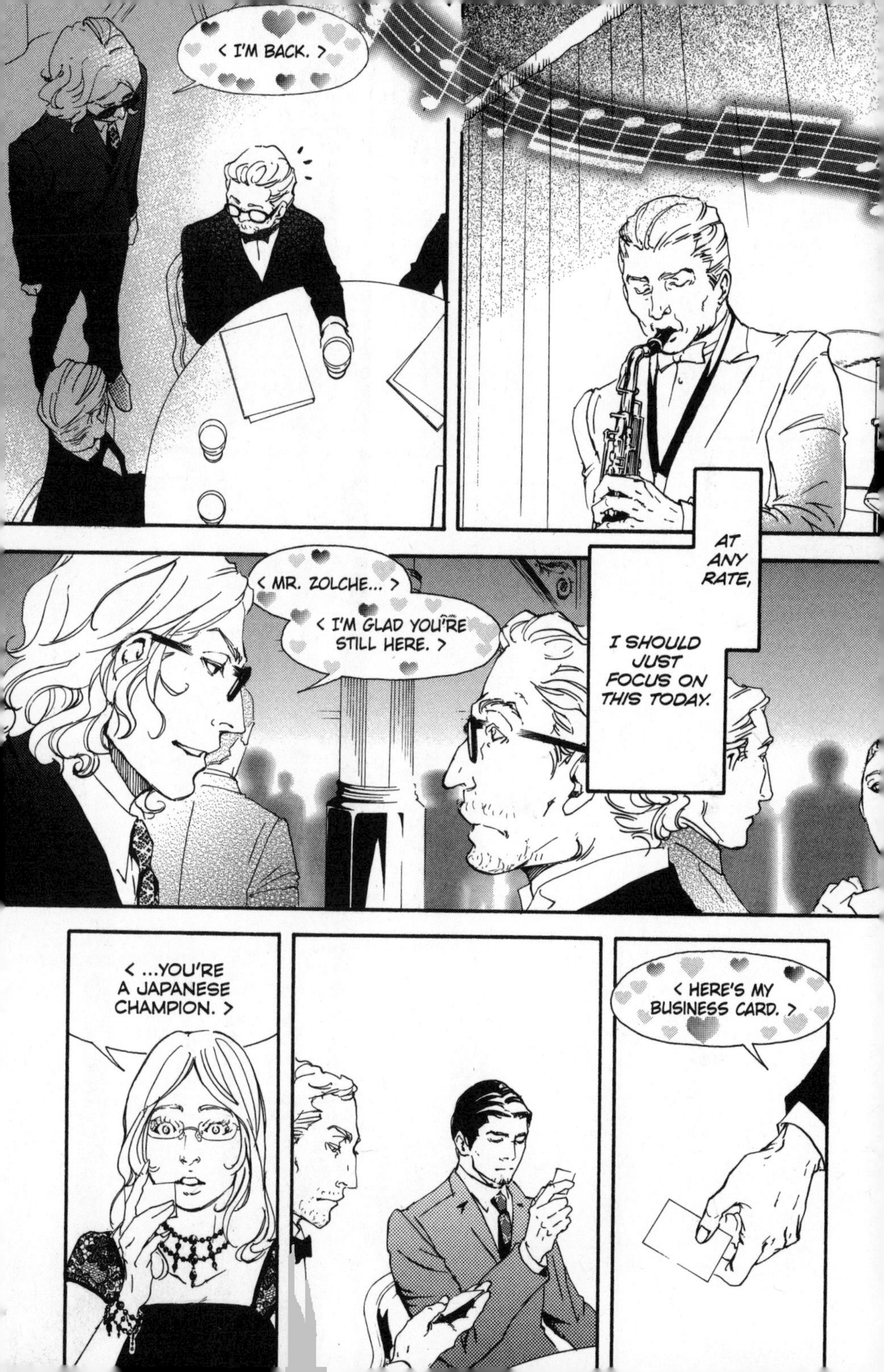
< I'M BACK. >
AT ANY RATE,
I SHOULD JUST FOCUS ON THIS TODAY.
< MR. ZOLCHE... >
< I'M GLAD YOU'RE STILL HERE. >
< HERE'S MY BUSINESS CARD. >
< ...YOU'RE A JAPANESE CHAMPION. >

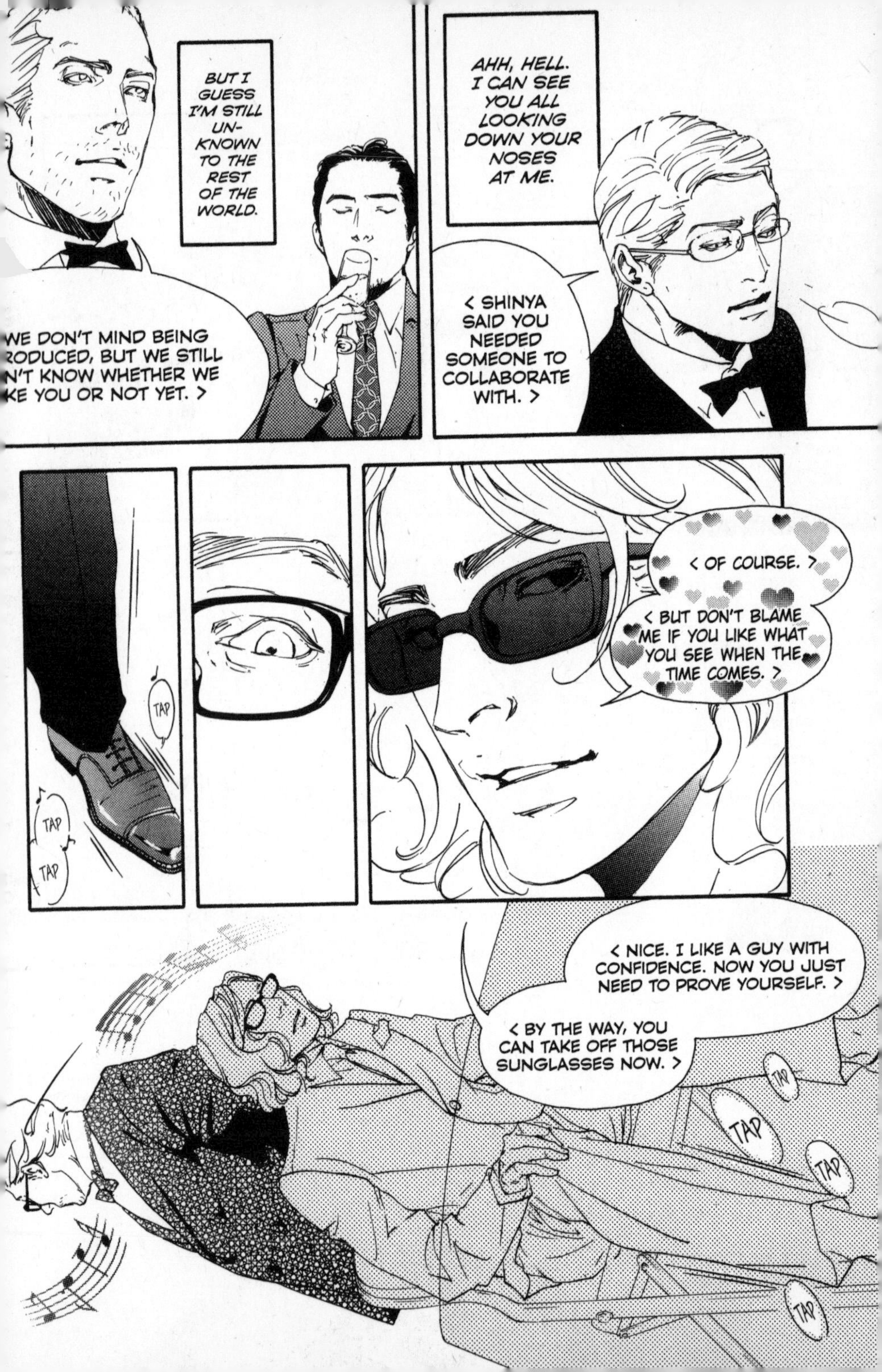
AHH, HELL. I CAN SEE YOU ALL LOOKING DOWN YOUR NOSES AT ME.
< SHINYA SAID YOU NEEDED SOMEONE TO COLLABORATE WITH. >
BUT I GUESS I'M STILL UN-KNOWN TO THE REST OF THE WORLD.
WE DON'T MIND BEING RODUCED, BUT WE STILL N'T KNOW WHETHER WE KE YOU OR NOT YET. >
< OF COURSE. >
< BUT DON'T BLAME ME IF YOU LIKE WHAT YOU SEE WHEN THE TIME COMES. >
TAP
TAP
TAP
< NICE. I LIKE A GUY WITH CONFIDENCE. NOW YOU JUST NEED TO PROVE YOURSELF. >
< BY THE WAY, YOU CAN TAKE OFF THOSE SUNGLASSES NOW. >
TAP
TAP
TAP
TAP

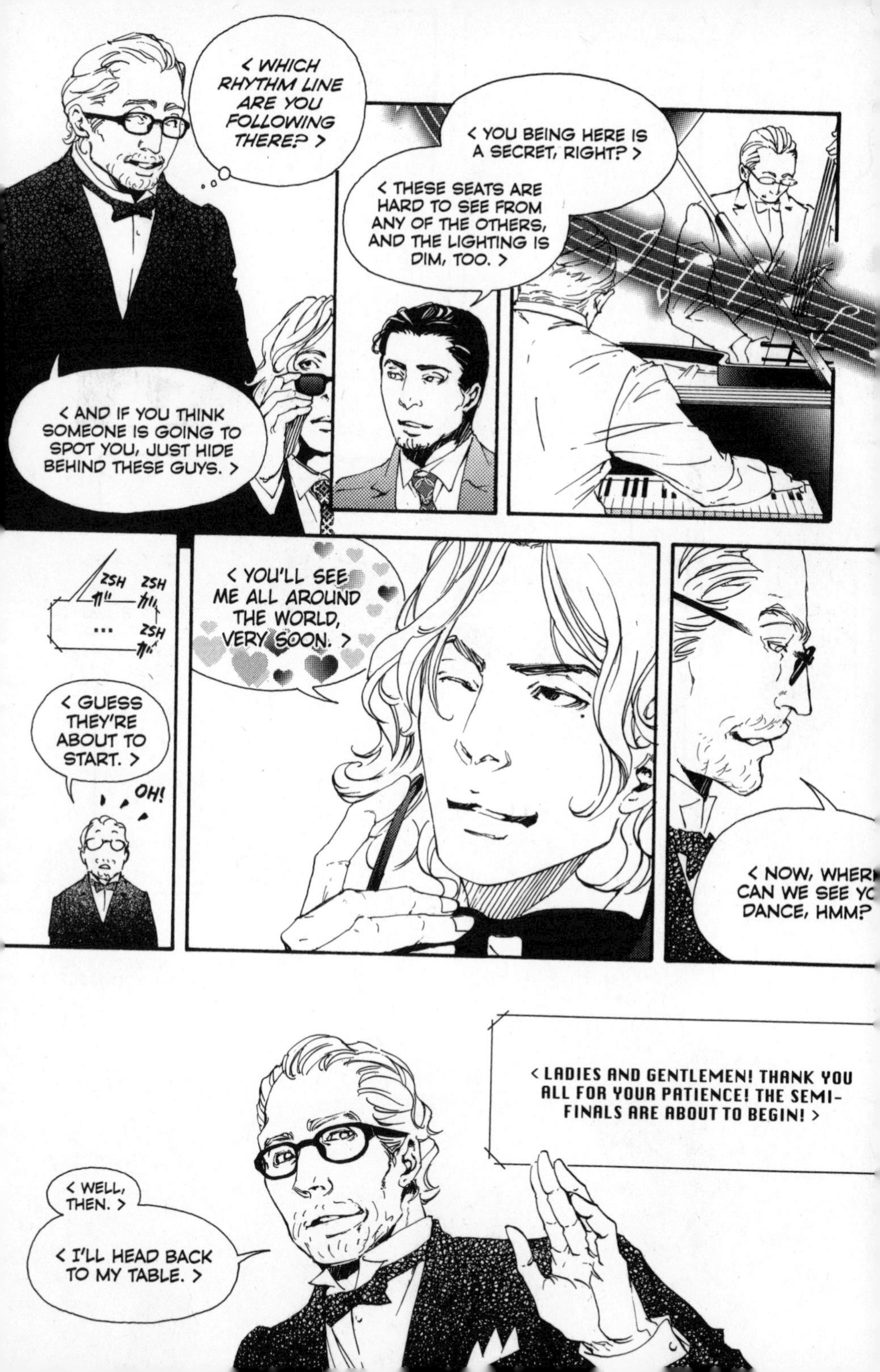
< YOU BEING HERE IS A SECRET, RIGHT? >
< THESE SEATS ARE HARD TO SEE FROM ANY OF THE OTHERS, AND THE LIGHTING IS DIM, TOO. >
< WHICH RHYTHM LINE ARE YOU FOLLOWING THERE? >
< AND IF YOU THINK SOMEONE IS GOING TO SPOT YOU, JUST HIDE BEHIND THESE GUYS. >
< NOW, WHER CAN WE SEE YC DANCE, HMM?
< YOU'LL SEE ME ALL AROUND THE WORLD, VERY SOON. >
ZSH ZSH
...
ZSH
< GUESS THEY'RE ABOUT TO START. >
OH!
< LADIES AND GENTLEMEN! THANK YOU ALL FOR YOUR PATIENCE! THE SEMI-FINALS ARE ABOUT TO BEGIN! >
< WELL, THEN. >
< I'LL HEAD BACK TO MY TABLE. >

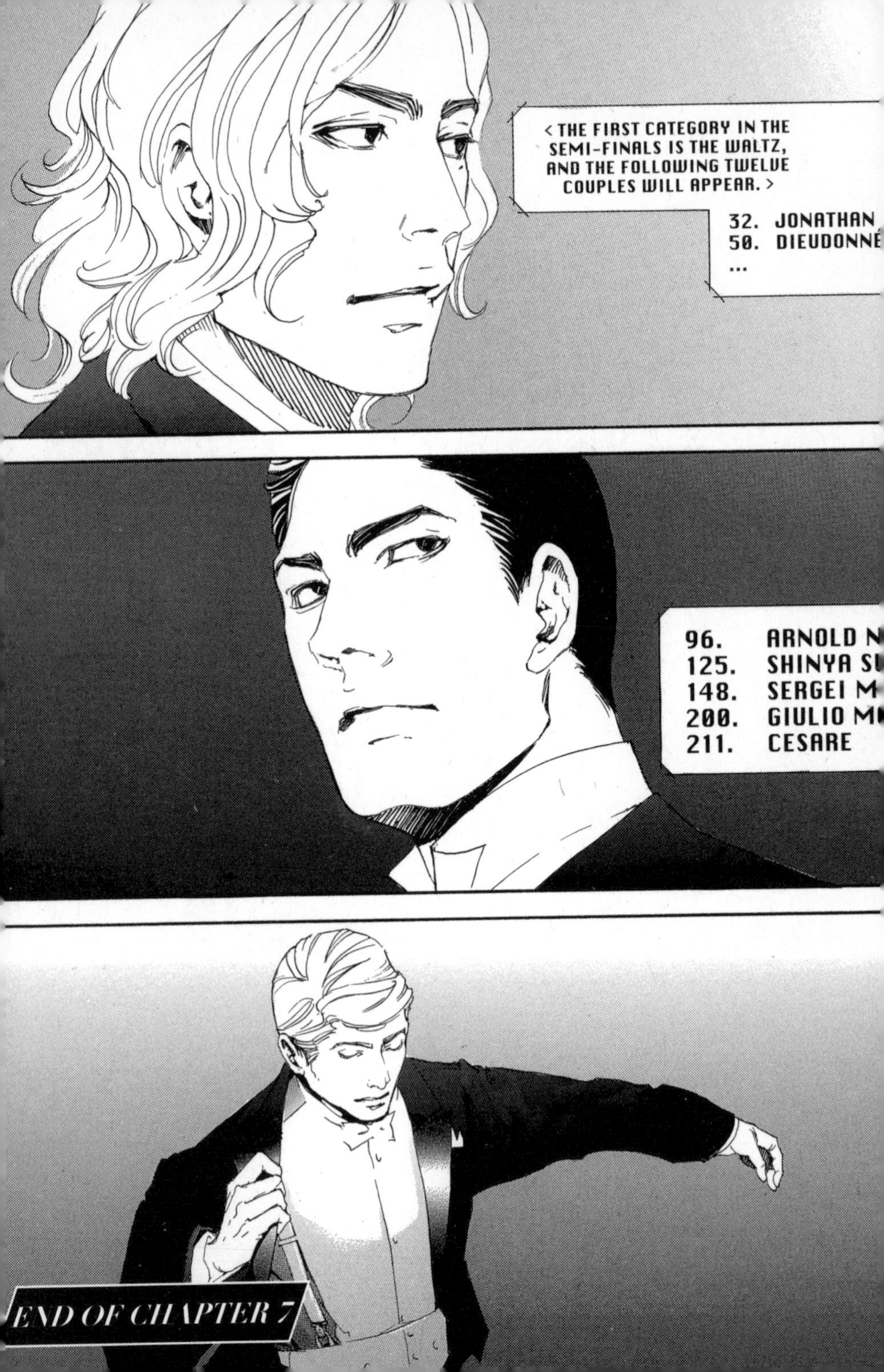
< THE FIRST CATEGORY IN THE SEMI-FINALS IS THE WALTZ, AND THE FOLLOWING TWELVE COUPLES WILL APPEAR. >
32. JONATHAN
50. DIEUDONNÉ
...
96. ARNOLD N
125. SHINYA S
148. SERGEI M
200. GIULIO M
211. CESARE
END OF CHAPTER 7

#08

CAN'T TAKE MY EYES OFF YOU

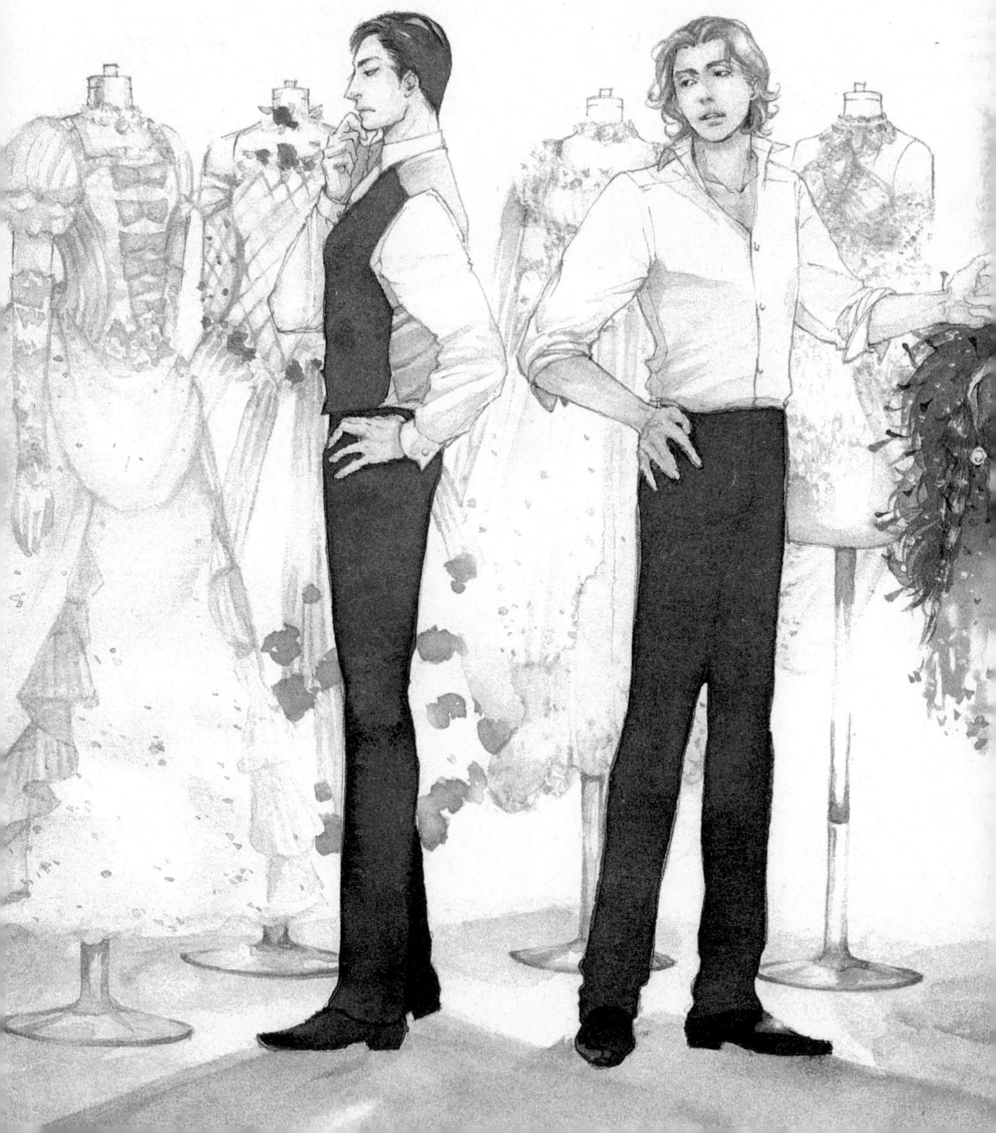

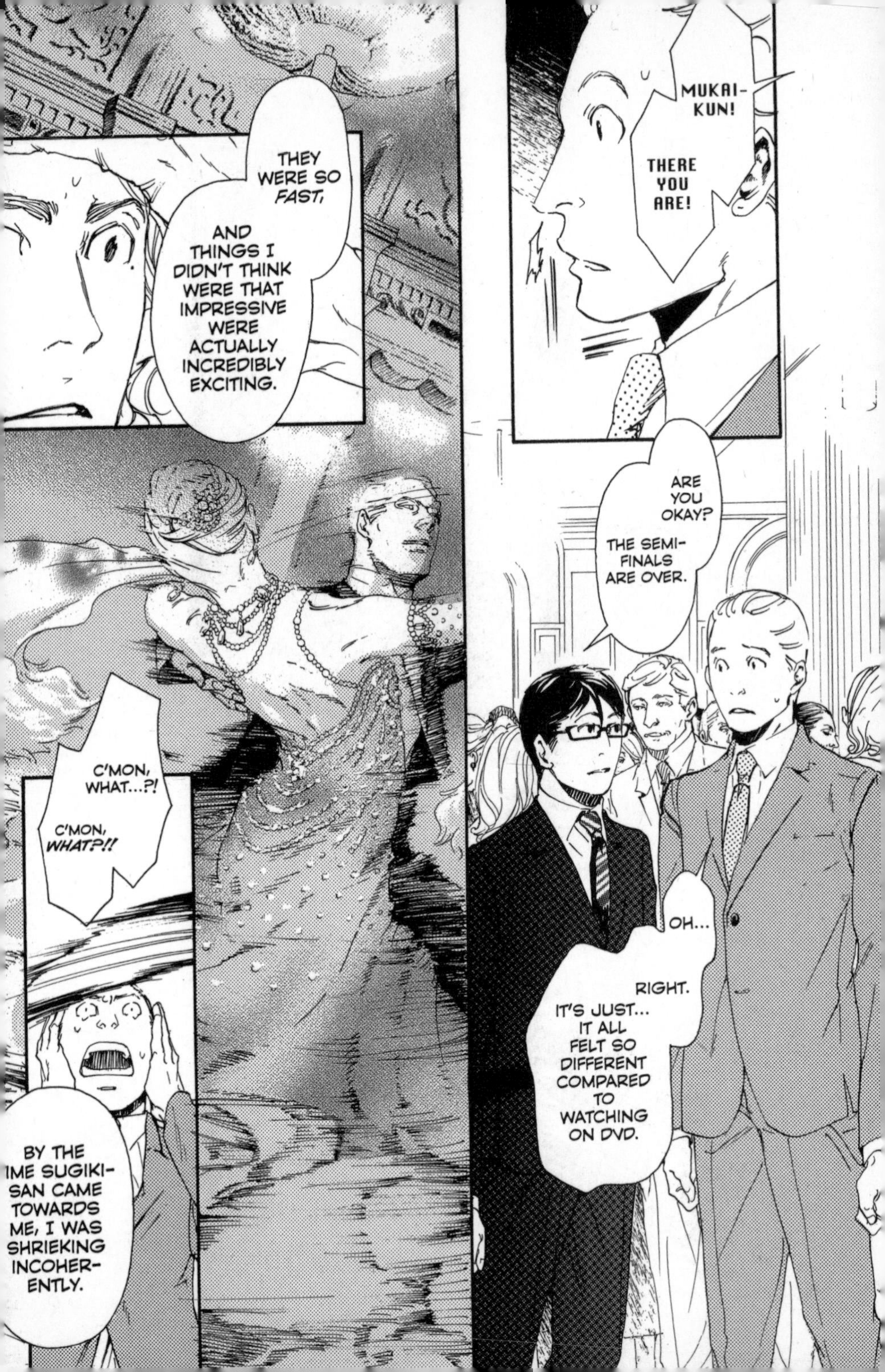
MUKAI-KUN!
THERE YOU ARE!
ARE YOU OKAY?
THE SEMI-FINALS ARE OVER.
OH...
RIGHT.
IT'S JUST... IT ALL FELT SO DIFFERENT COMPARED TO WATCHING ON DVD.
THEY WERE SO *FAST*,
AND THINGS I DIDN'T THINK WERE THAT IMPRESSIVE WERE ACTUALLY INCREDIBLY EXCITING.
C'MON, WHAT...?!
C'MON, ***WHAT?!!***
BY THE IME SUGIKI-SAN CAME TOWARDS ME, I WAS SHRIEKING INCOHER-ENTLY.

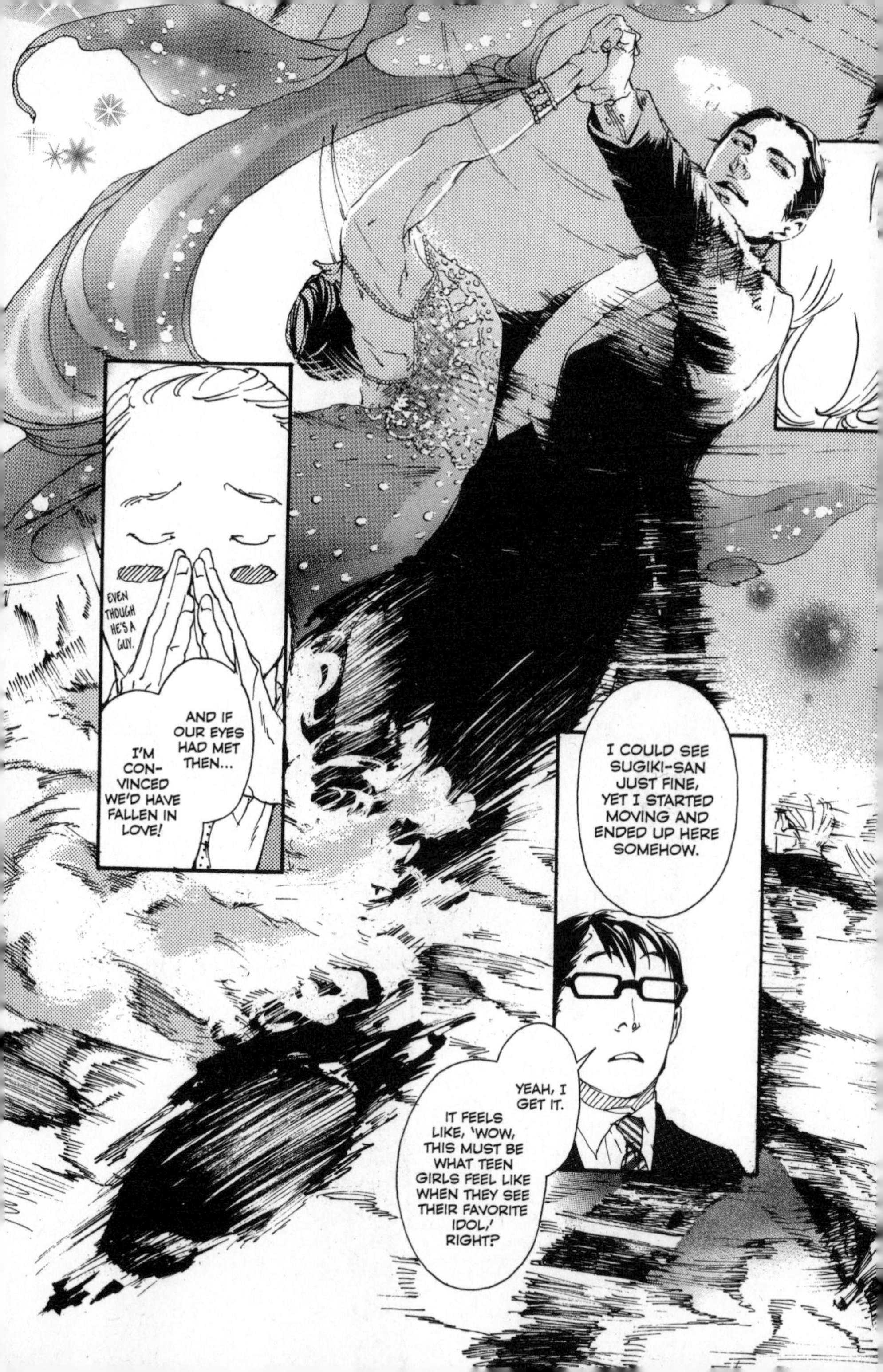
I COULD SEE SUGIKI-SAN JUST FINE, YET I STARTED MOVING AND ENDED UP HERE SOMEHOW.
AND IF OUR EYES HAD MET THEN...
I'M CON-VINCED WE'D HAVE FALLEN IN LOVE!
EVEN THOUGH HE'S A GUY.
YEAH, I GET IT.
IT FEELS LIKE, 'WOW, THIS MUST BE WHAT TEEN GIRLS FEEL LIKE WHEN THEY SEE THEIR FAVORITE IDOL,' RIGHT?

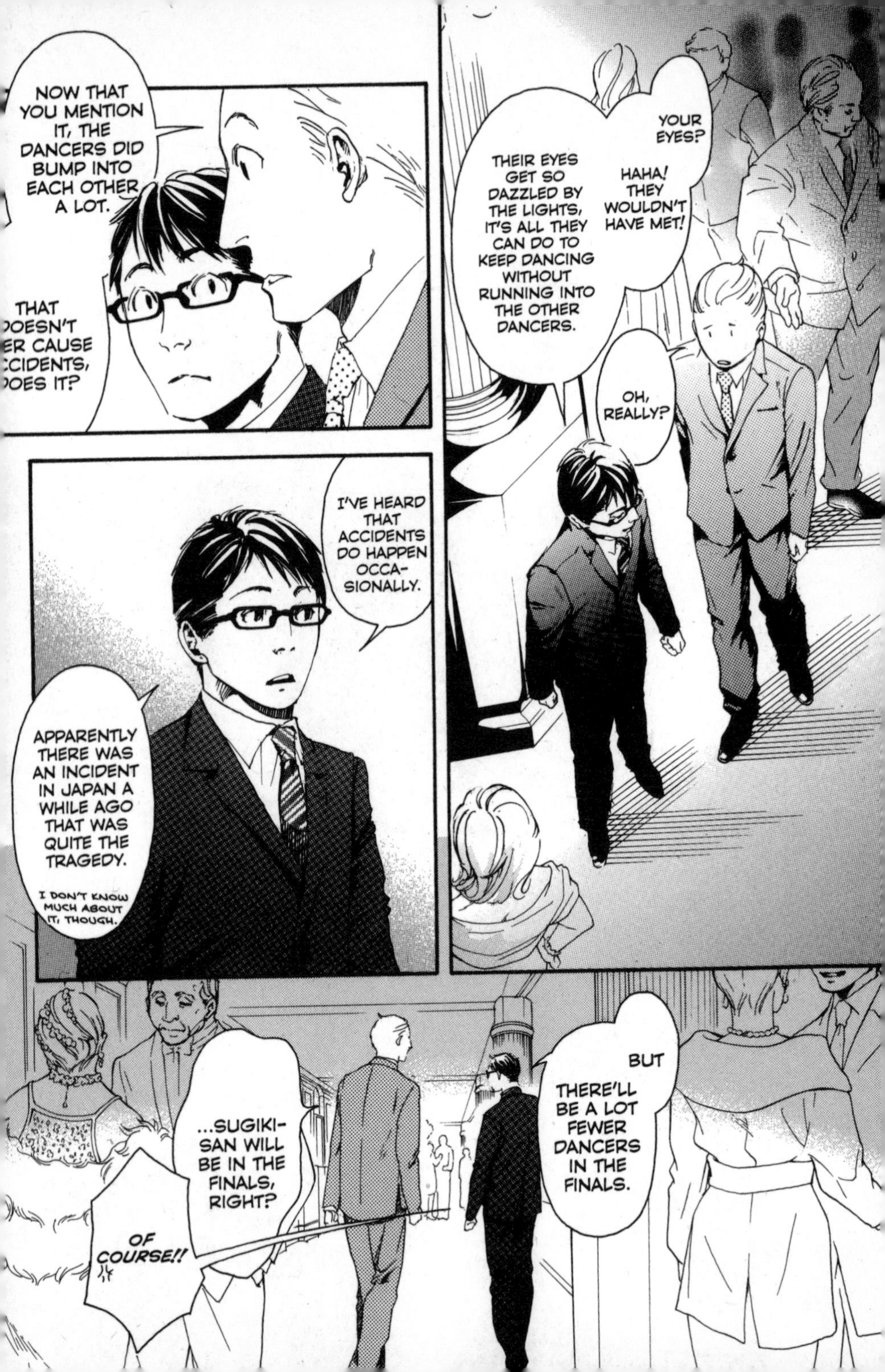
YOUR EYES?
HAHA! THEY WOULDN'T HAVE MET!
THEIR EYES GET SO DAZZLED BY THE LIGHTS, IT'S ALL THEY CAN DO TO KEEP DANCING WITHOUT RUNNING INTO THE OTHER DANCERS.
OH, REALLY?
NOW THAT YOU MENTION IT, THE DANCERS DID BUMP INTO EACH OTHER A LOT.
THAT OESN'T ER CAUSE CIDENTS, OES IT?
I'VE HEARD THAT ACCIDENTS DO HAPPEN OCCA-SIONALLY.
APPARENTLY THERE WAS AN INCIDENT IN JAPAN A WHILE AGO THAT WAS QUITE THE TRAGEDY.
I DON'T KNOW MUCH ABOUT IT, THOUGH.
BUT THERE'LL BE A LOT FEWER DANCERS IN THE FINALS.
...SUGIKI-SAN WILL BE IN THE FINALS, RIGHT?
OF COURSE!!

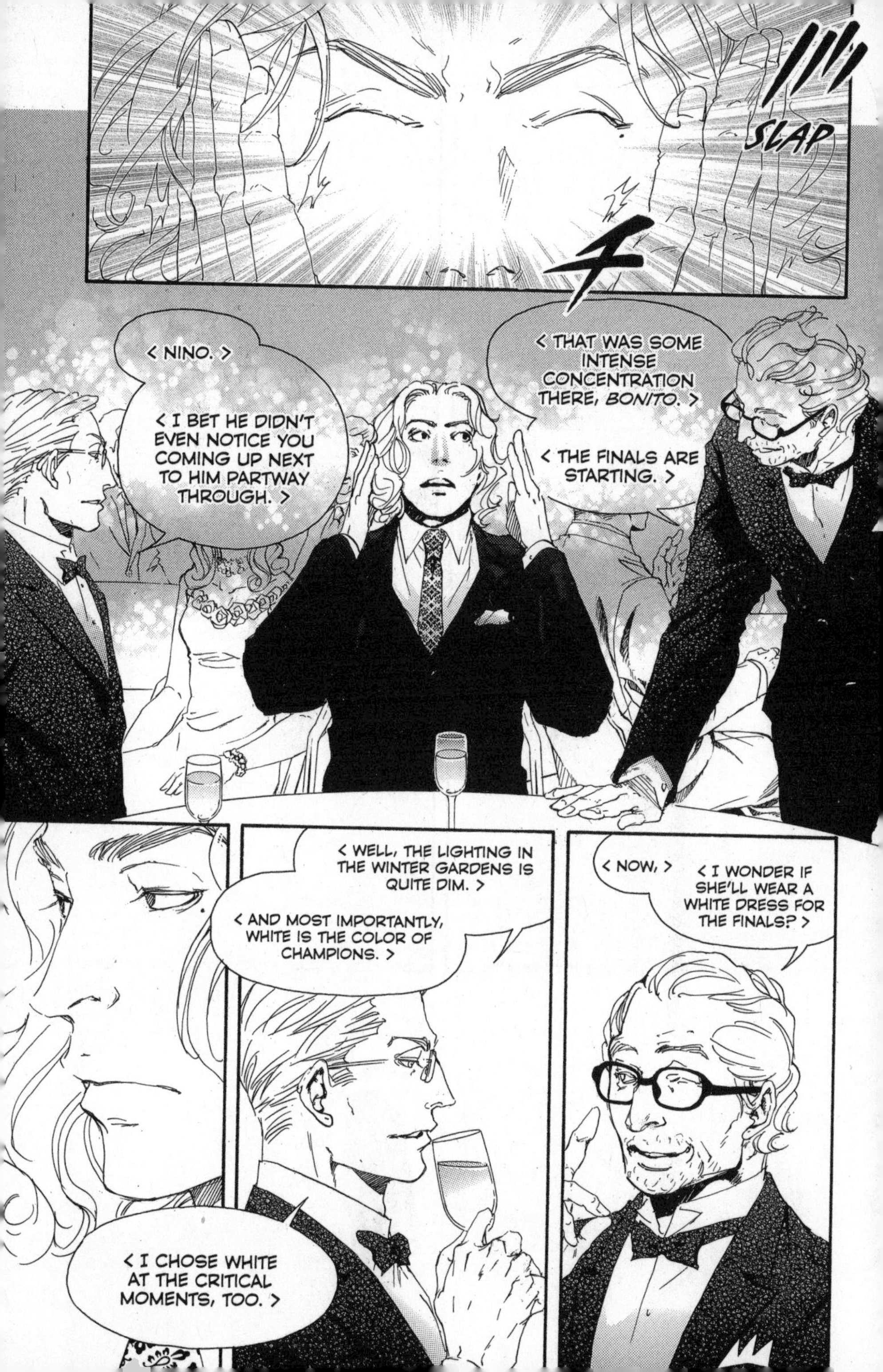
SLAP
< THAT WAS SOME INTENSE CONCENTRATION THERE, *BONITO*. >
< THE FINALS ARE STARTING. >
< NINO. >
< I BET HE DIDN'T EVEN NOTICE YOU COMING UP NEXT TO HIM PARTWAY THROUGH. >
< NOW, >
< I WONDER IF SHE'LL WEAR A WHITE DRESS FOR THE FINALS? >
< WELL, THE LIGHTING IN THE WINTER GARDENS IS QUITE DIM. >
< AND MOST IMPORTANTLY, WHITE IS THE COLOR OF CHAMPIONS. >
< I CHOSE WHITE AT THE CRITICAL MOMENTS, TOO. >

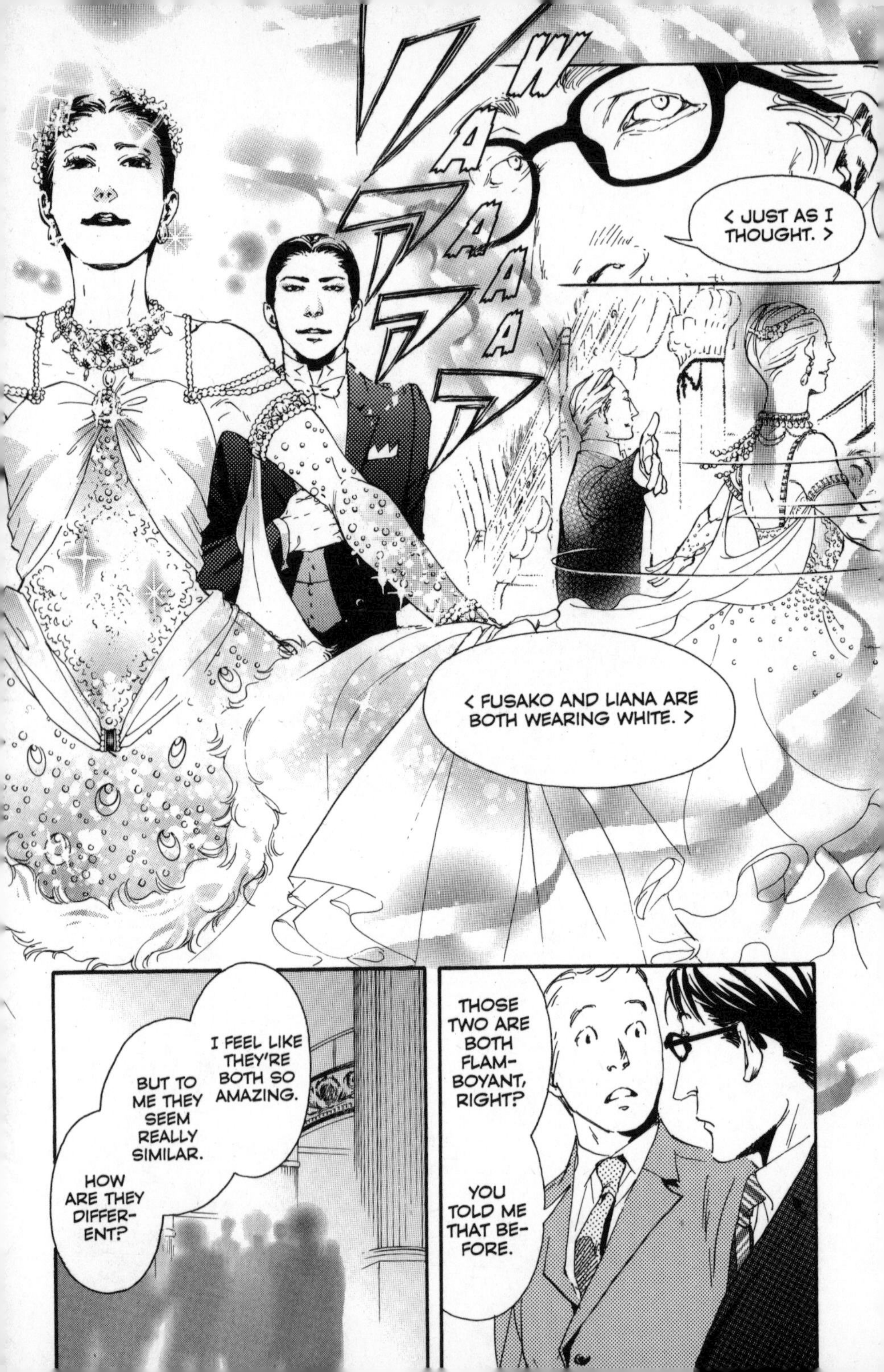
< JUST AS I THOUGHT. >
WAAAA
< FUSAKO AND LIANA ARE BOTH WEARING WHITE. >
THOSE TWO ARE BOTH FLAM- BOYANT, RIGHT?
YOU TOLD ME THAT BE- FORE.
I FEEL LIKE THEY'RE BOTH SO AMAZING.
BUT TO ME THEY SEEM REALLY SIMILAR.
HOW ARE THEY DIFFER- ENT?

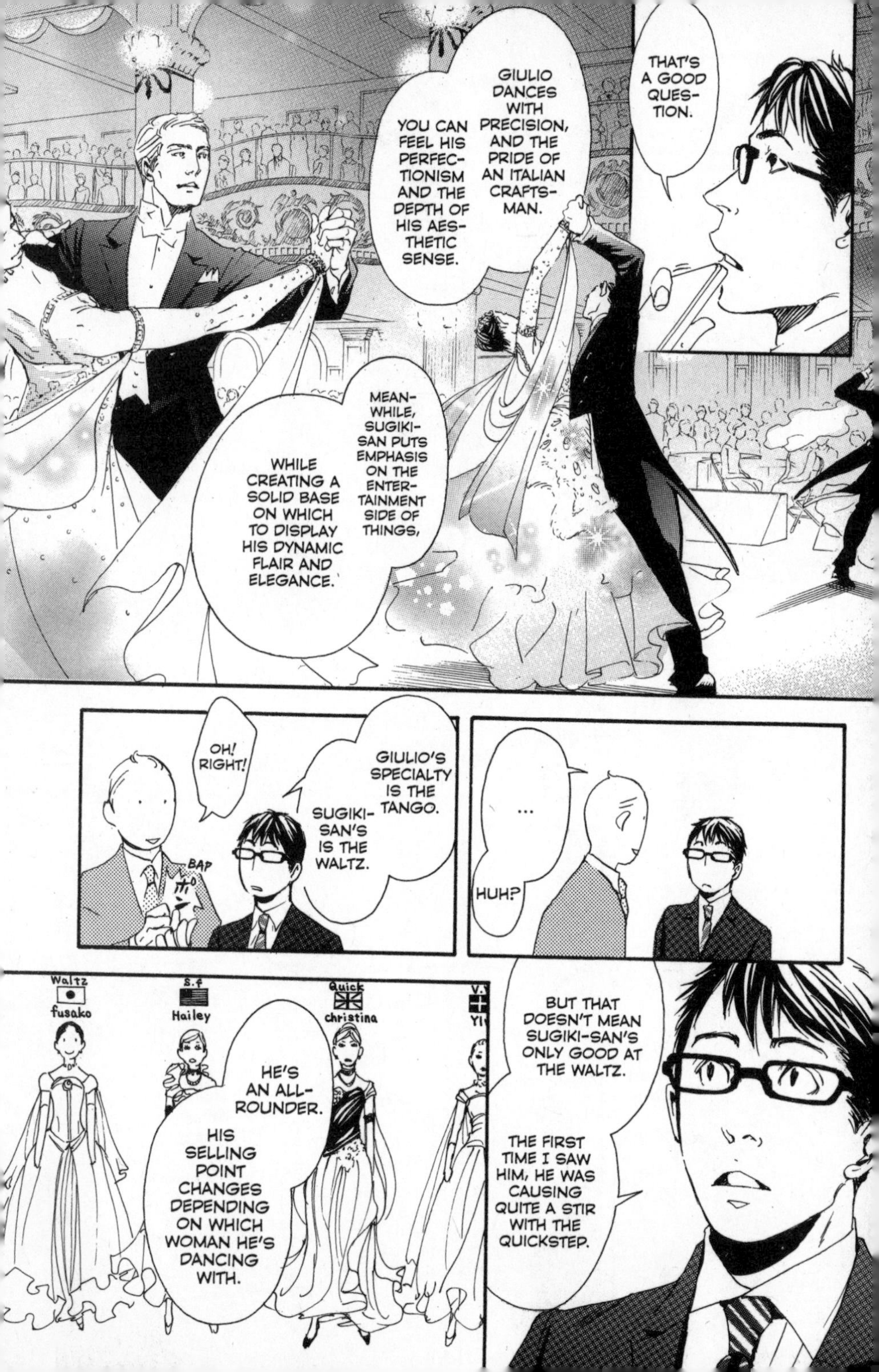
THAT'S A GOOD QUESTION.
GIULIO DANCES WITH PRECISION, AND THE PRIDE OF AN ITALIAN CRAFTSMAN.
YOU CAN FEEL HIS PERFECTIONISM AND THE DEPTH OF HIS AESTHETIC SENSE.
MEANWHILE, SUGIKI-SAN PUTS EMPHASIS ON THE ENTERTAINMENT SIDE OF THINGS,
WHILE CREATING A SOLID BASE ON WHICH TO DISPLAY HIS DYNAMIC FLAIR AND ELEGANCE.
...
HUH?
GIULIO'S SPECIALTY IS THE TANGO.
SUGIKI-SAN'S IS THE WALTZ.
OH! RIGHT!
BAP
BUT THAT DOESN'T MEAN SUGIKI-SAN'S ONLY GOOD AT THE WALTZ.
THE FIRST TIME I SAW HIM, HE WAS CAUSING QUITE A STIR WITH THE QUICKSTEP.
Quick christina
S.f Hailey
Waltz fusako
HE'S AN ALL-ROUNDER.
HIS SELLING POINT CHANGES DEPENDING ON WHICH WOMAN HE'S DANCING WITH.

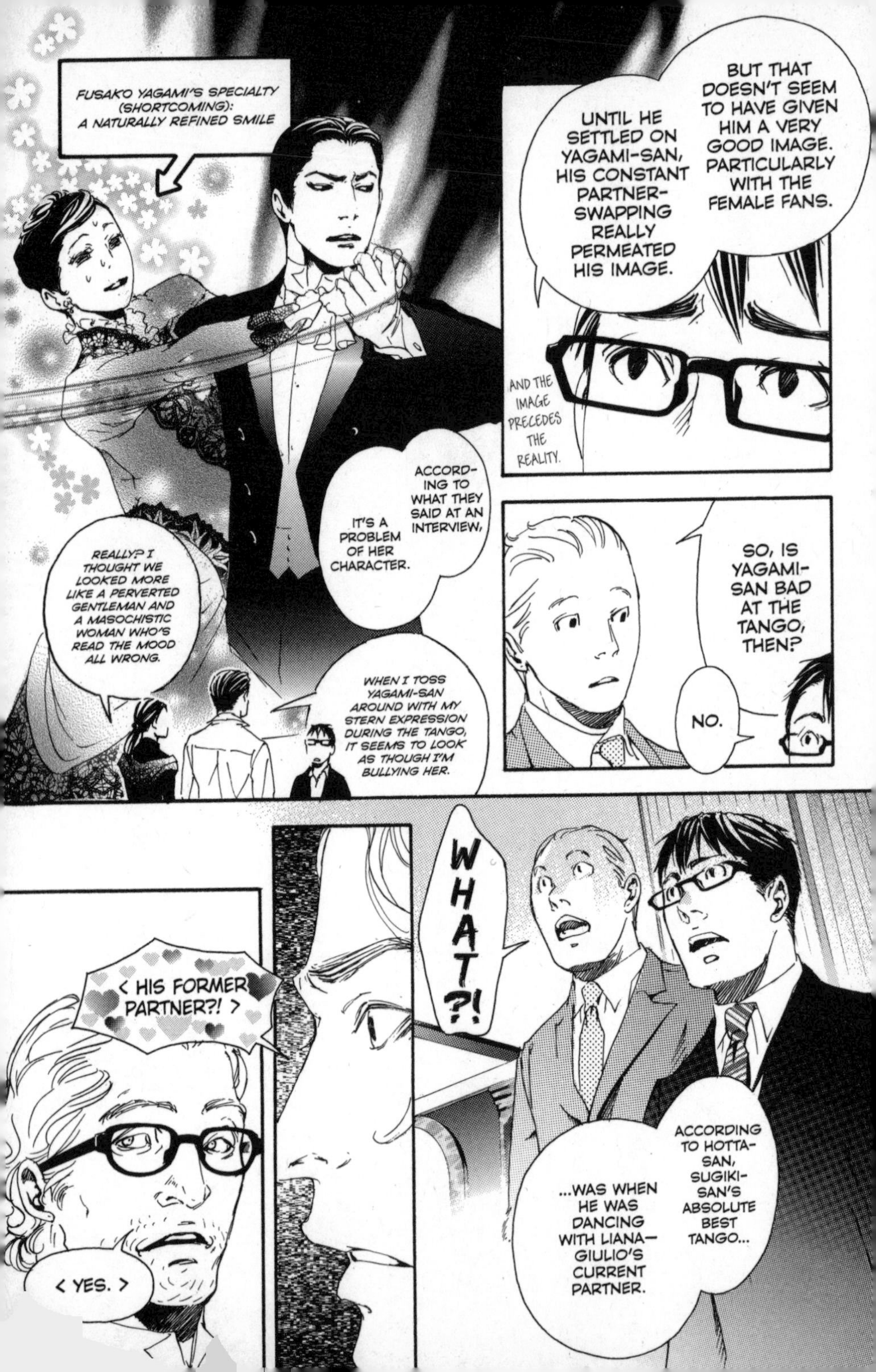
UNTIL HE SETTLED ON YAGAMI-SAN, HIS CONSTANT PARTNER-SWAPPING REALLY PERMEATED HIS IMAGE.
BUT THAT DOESN'T SEEM TO HAVE GIVEN HIM A VERY GOOD IMAGE. PARTICULARLY WITH THE FEMALE FANS.
AND THE IMAGE PRECEDES THE REALITY.
SO, IS YAGAMI-SAN BAD AT THE TANGO, THEN?
NO.
ACCORDING TO WHAT THEY SAID AT AN INTERVIEW,
IT'S A PROBLEM OF HER CHARACTER.
FUSAKO YAGAMI'S SPECIALTY (SHORTCOMING): A NATURALLY REFINED SMILE
WHEN I TOSS YAGAMI-SAN AROUND WITH MY STERN EXPRESSION DURING THE TANGO, IT SEEMS TO LOOK AS THOUGH I'M BULLYING HER.
REALLY? I THOUGHT WE LOOKED MORE LIKE A PERVERTED GENTLEMAN AND A MASOCHISTIC WOMAN WHO'S READ THE MOOD ALL WRONG.
ACCORDING TO HOTTA-SAN, SUGIKI-SAN'S ABSOLUTE BEST TANGO...
...WAS WHEN HE WAS DANCING WITH LIANA-GIULIO'S CURRENT PARTNER.
WHAT?!
< HIS FORMER PARTNER?! >
< YES. >

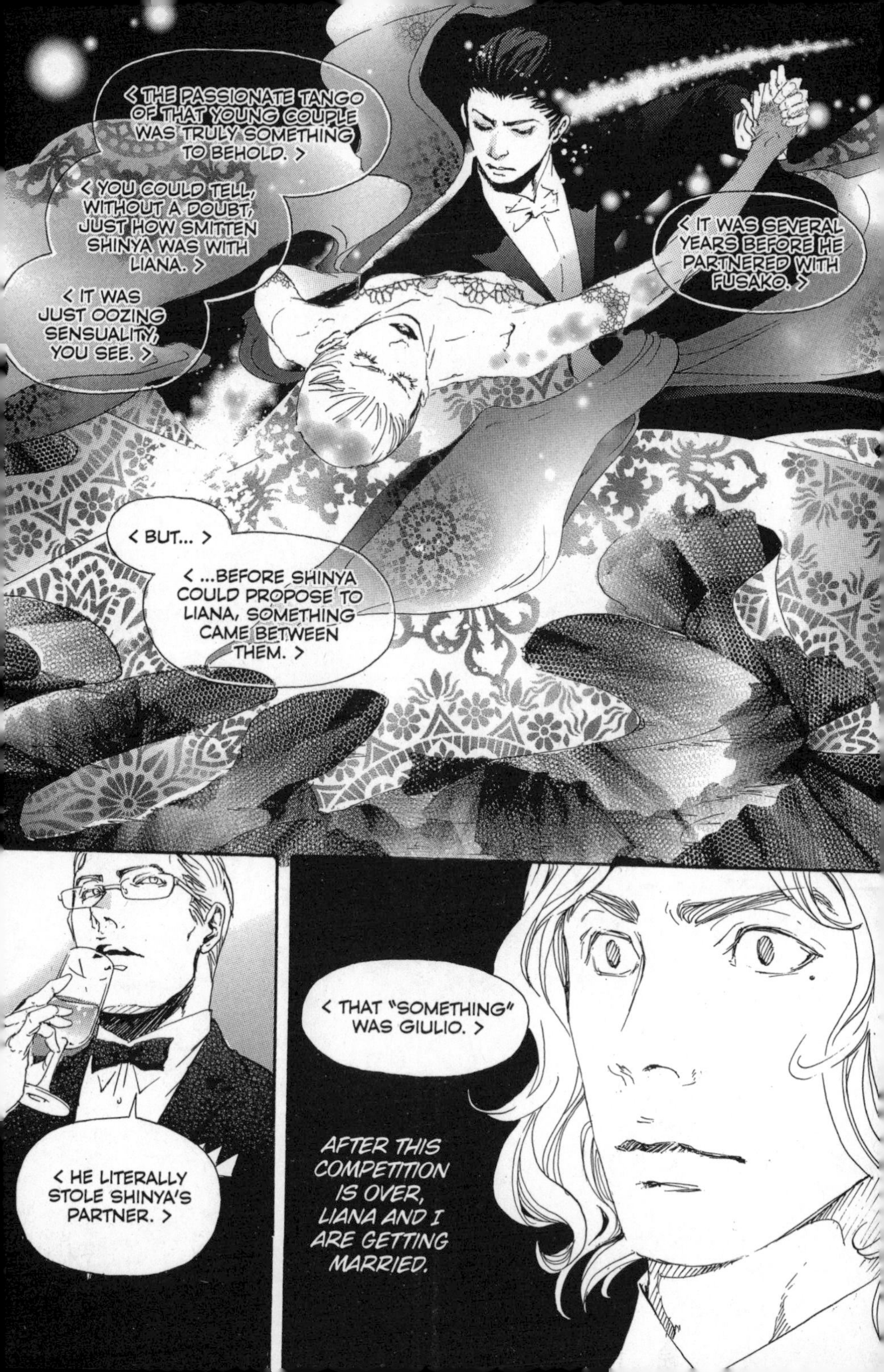
< THE PASSIONATE TANGO OF THAT YOUNG COUPLE WAS TRULY SOMETHING TO BEHOLD. >
< YOU COULD TELL, WITHOUT A DOUBT, JUST HOW SMITTEN SHINYA WAS WITH LIANA. >
< IT WAS JUST OOZING SENSUALITY, YOU SEE. >
< IT WAS SEVERAL YEARS BEFORE HE PARTNERED WITH FUSAKO. >
< BUT... >
< ...BEFORE SHINYA COULD PROPOSE TO LIANA, SOMETHING CAME BETWEEN THEM. >
< THAT "SOMETHING" WAS GIULIO. >
AFTER THIS COMPETITION IS OVER, LIANA AND I ARE GETTING MARRIED.
< HE LITERALLY STOLE SHINYA'S PARTNER. >

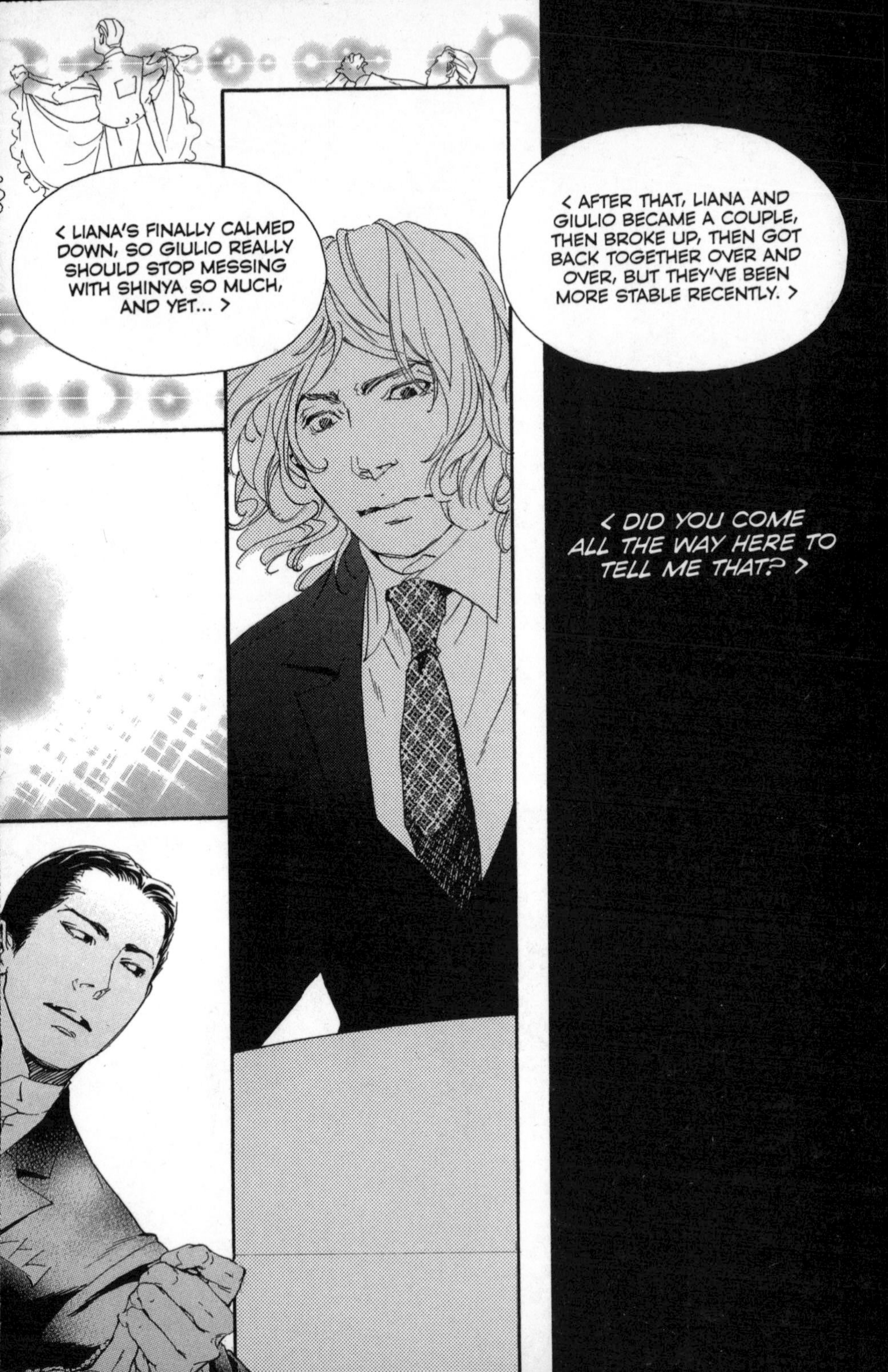
< AFTER THAT, LIANA AND GIULIO BECAME A COUPLE, THEN BROKE UP, THEN GOT BACK TOGETHER OVER AND OVER, BUT THEY'VE BEEN MORE STABLE RECENTLY. >
< LIANA'S FINALLY CALMED DOWN, SO GIULIO REALLY SHOULD STOP MESSING WITH SHINYA SO MUCH, AND YET... >
< DID YOU COME ALL THE WAY HERE TO TELL ME THAT? >

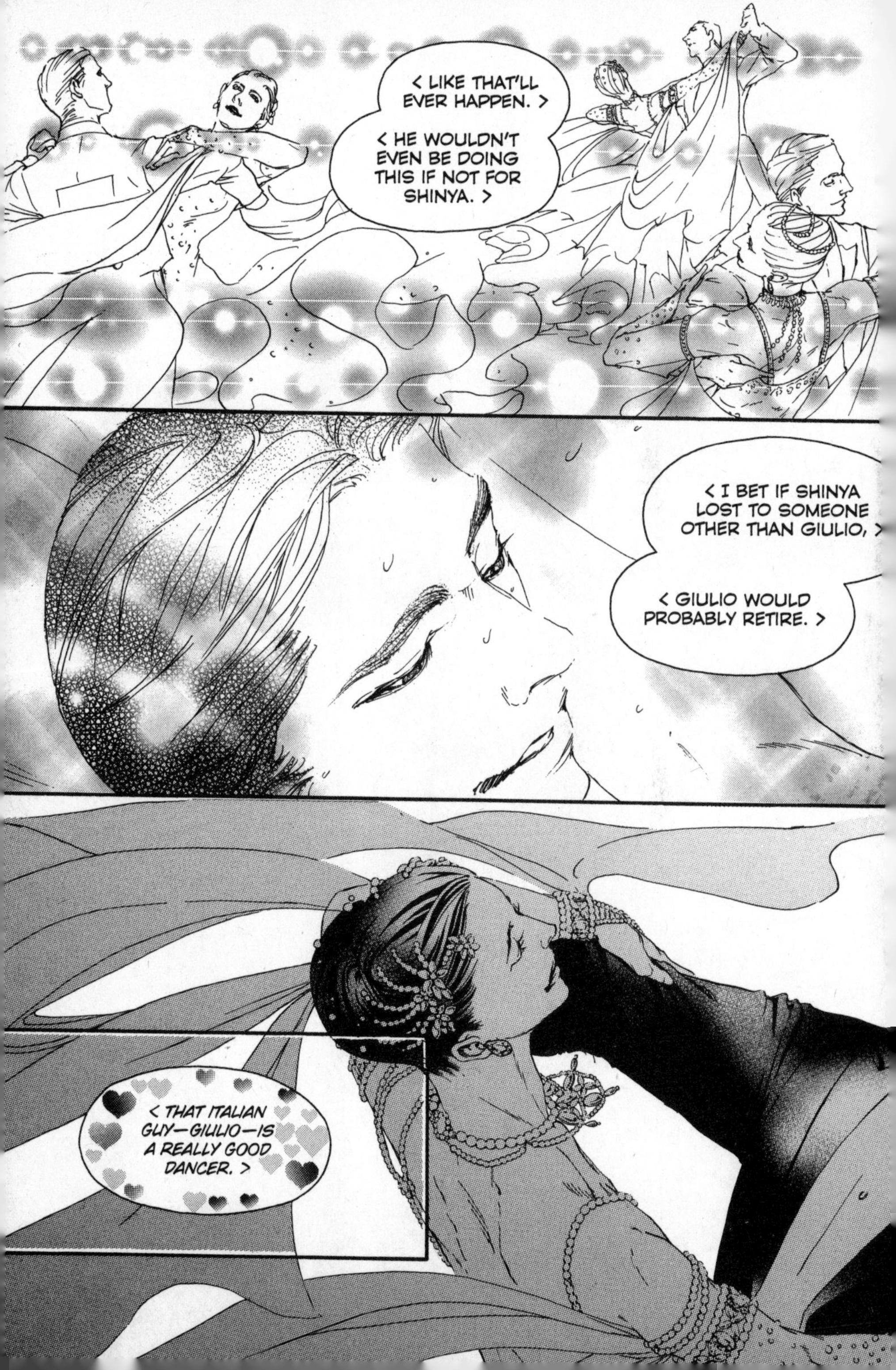
< LIKE THAT'LL EVER HAPPEN. >
< HE WOULDN'T EVEN BE DOING THIS IF NOT FOR SHINYA. >
< I BET IF SHINYA LOST TO SOMEONE OTHER THAN GIULIO, >
< GIULIO WOULD PROBABLY RETIRE. >
< THAT ITALIAN GUY—GIULIO—IS A REALLY GOOD DANCER. >

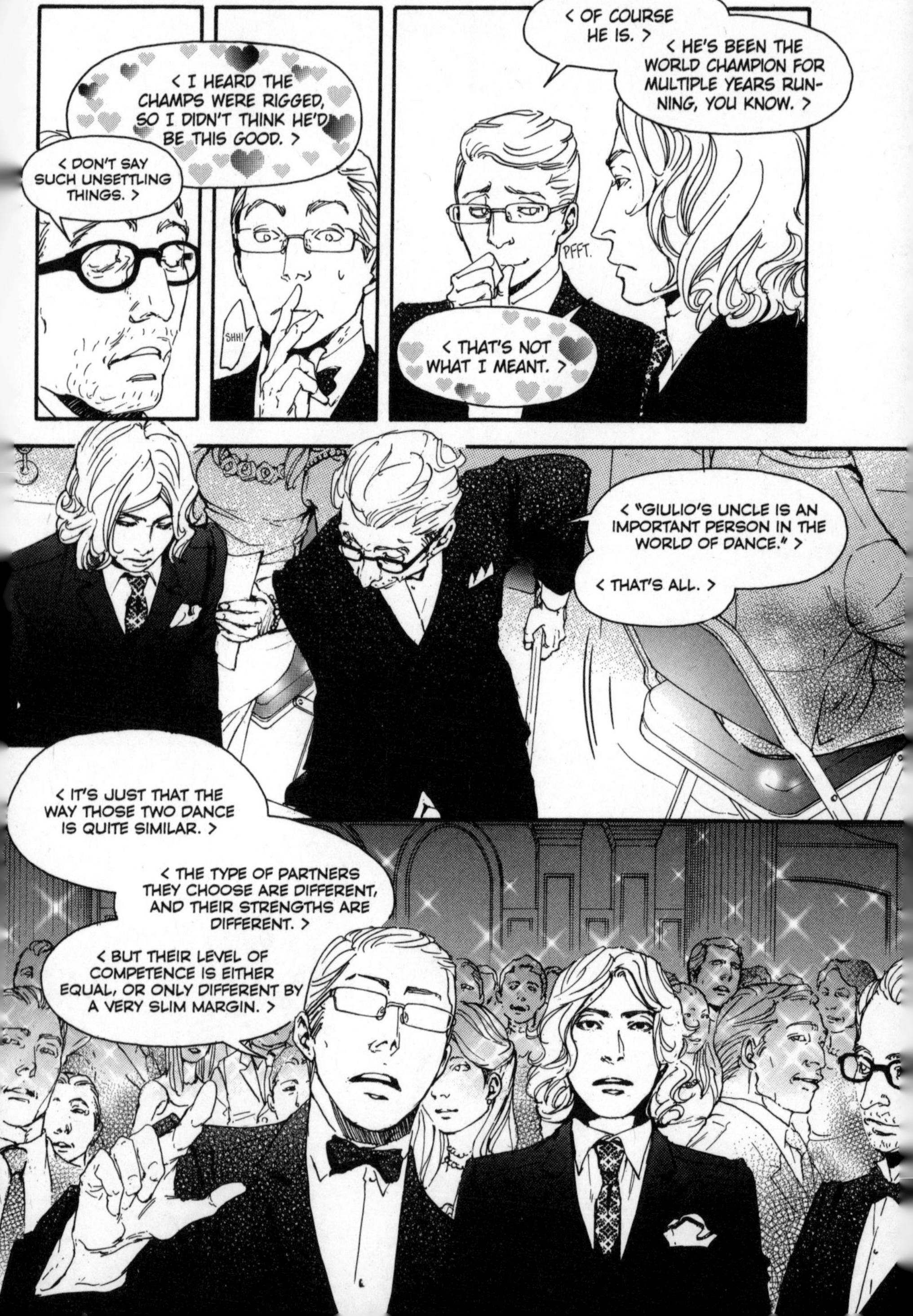

< OF COURSE HE IS. >
< HE'S BEEN THE WORLD CHAMPION FOR MULTIPLE YEARS RUN- NING, YOU KNOW. >
PFFT.
< THAT'S NOT WHAT I MEANT. >
SHH!
< I HEARD THE CHAMPS WERE RIGGED, SO I DIDN'T THINK HE'D BE THIS GOOD. >
< DON'T SAY SUCH UNSETTLING THINGS. >
< "GIULIO'S UNCLE IS AN IMPORTANT PERSON IN THE WORLD OF DANCE." >
< THAT'S ALL. >
< IT'S JUST THAT THE WAY THOSE TWO DANCE IS QUITE SIMILAR. >
< THE TYPE OF PARTNERS THEY CHOOSE ARE DIFFERENT, AND THEIR STRENGTHS ARE DIFFERENT. >
< BUT THEIR LEVEL OF COMPETENCE IS EITHER EQUAL, OR ONLY DIFFERENT BY A VERY SLIM MARGIN. >

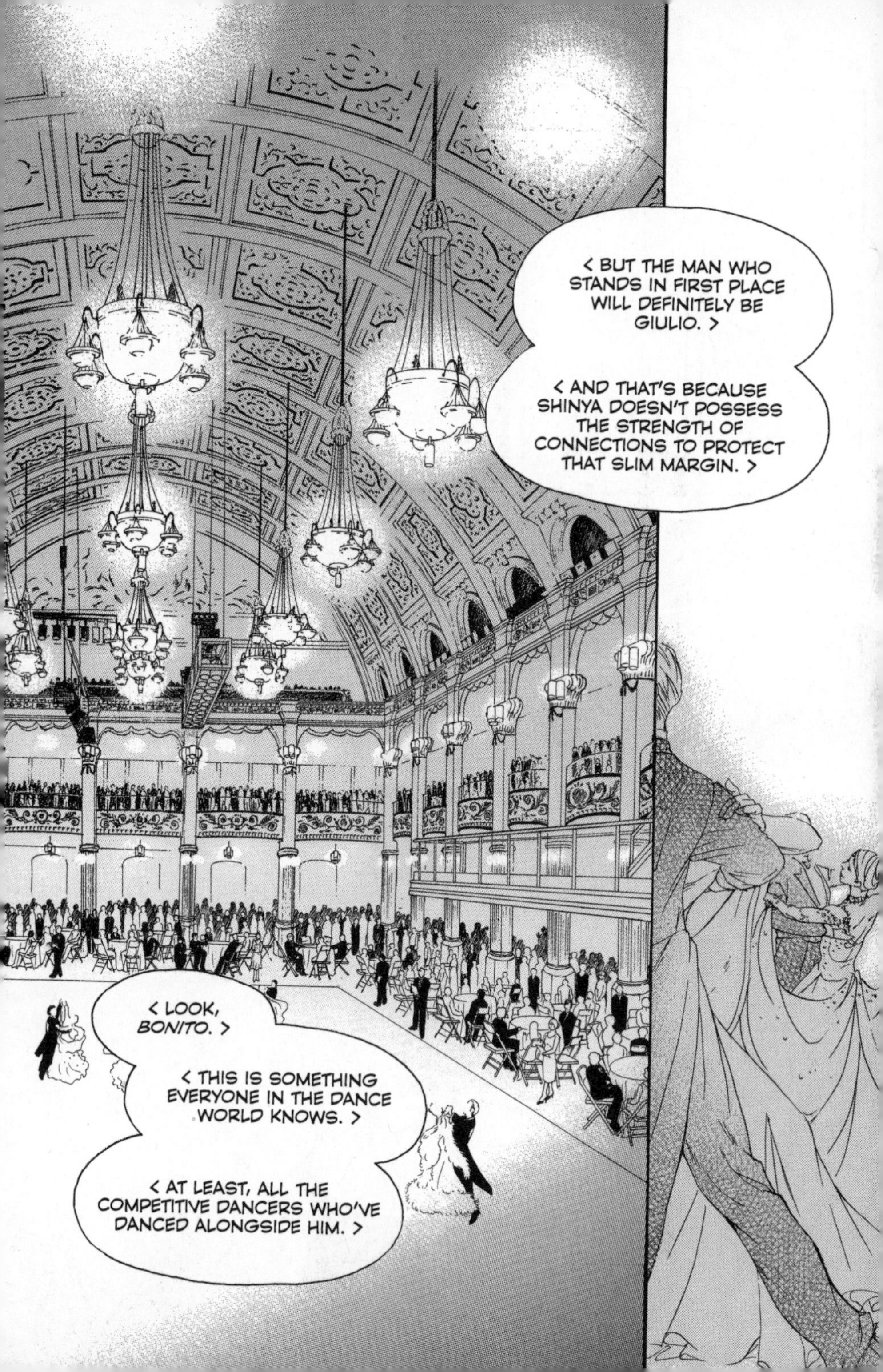
< BUT THE MAN WHO STANDS IN FIRST PLACE WILL DEFINITELY BE GIULIO. >
< AND THAT'S BECAUSE SHINYA DOESN'T POSSESS THE STRENGTH OF CONNECTIONS TO PROTECT THAT SLIM MARGIN. >
< LOOK, BONITO. >
< THIS IS SOMETHING EVERYONE IN THE DANCE WORLD KNOWS. >
< AT LEAST, ALL THE COMPETITIVE DANCERS WHO'VE DANCED ALONGSIDE HIM. >

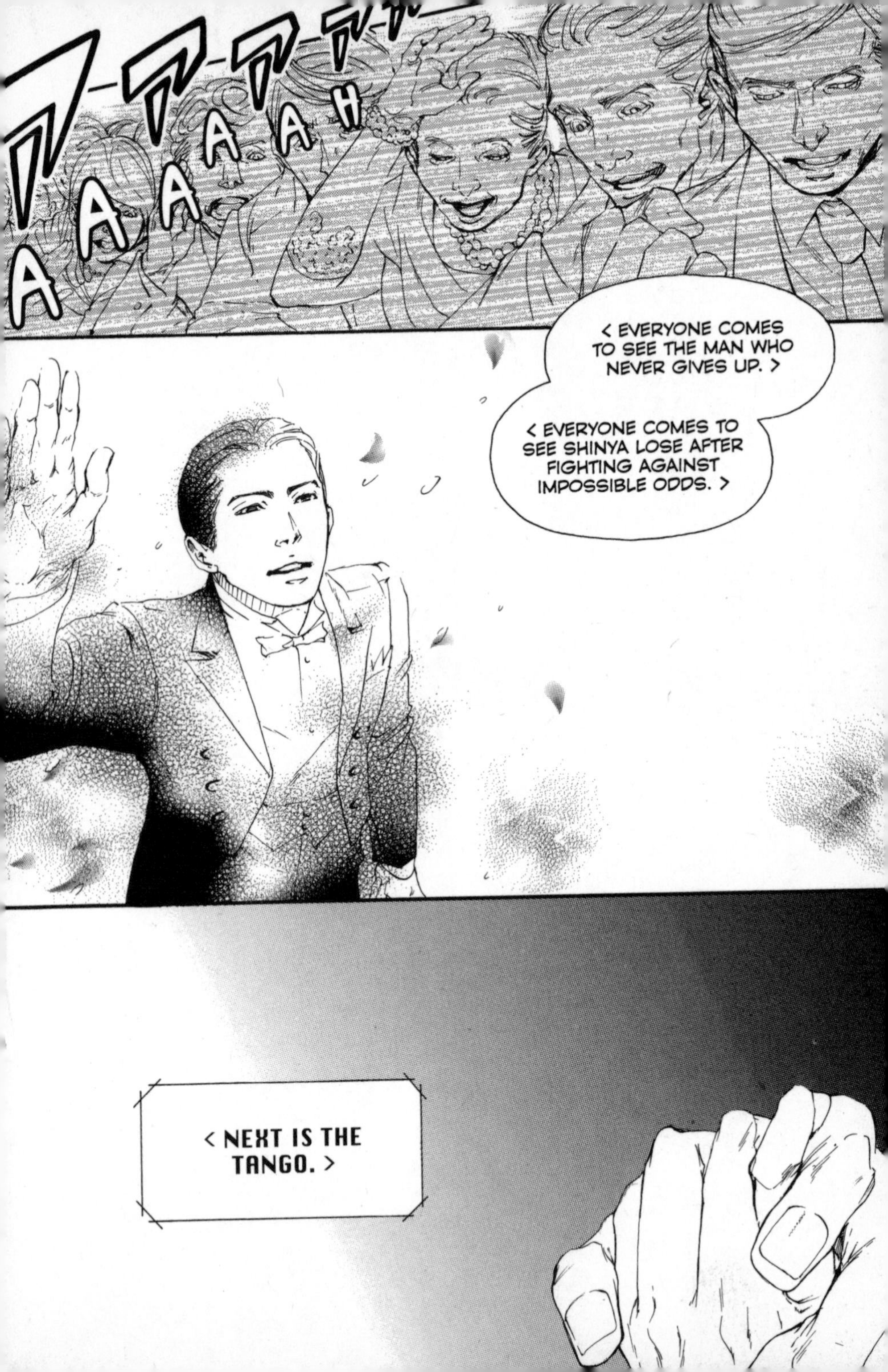
AAAAAAH
< EVERYONE COMES TO SEE THE MAN WHO NEVER GIVES UP. >
< EVERYONE COMES TO SEE SHINYA LOSE AFTER FIGHTING AGAINST IMPOSSIBLE ODDS. >
< NEXT IS THE TANGO. >

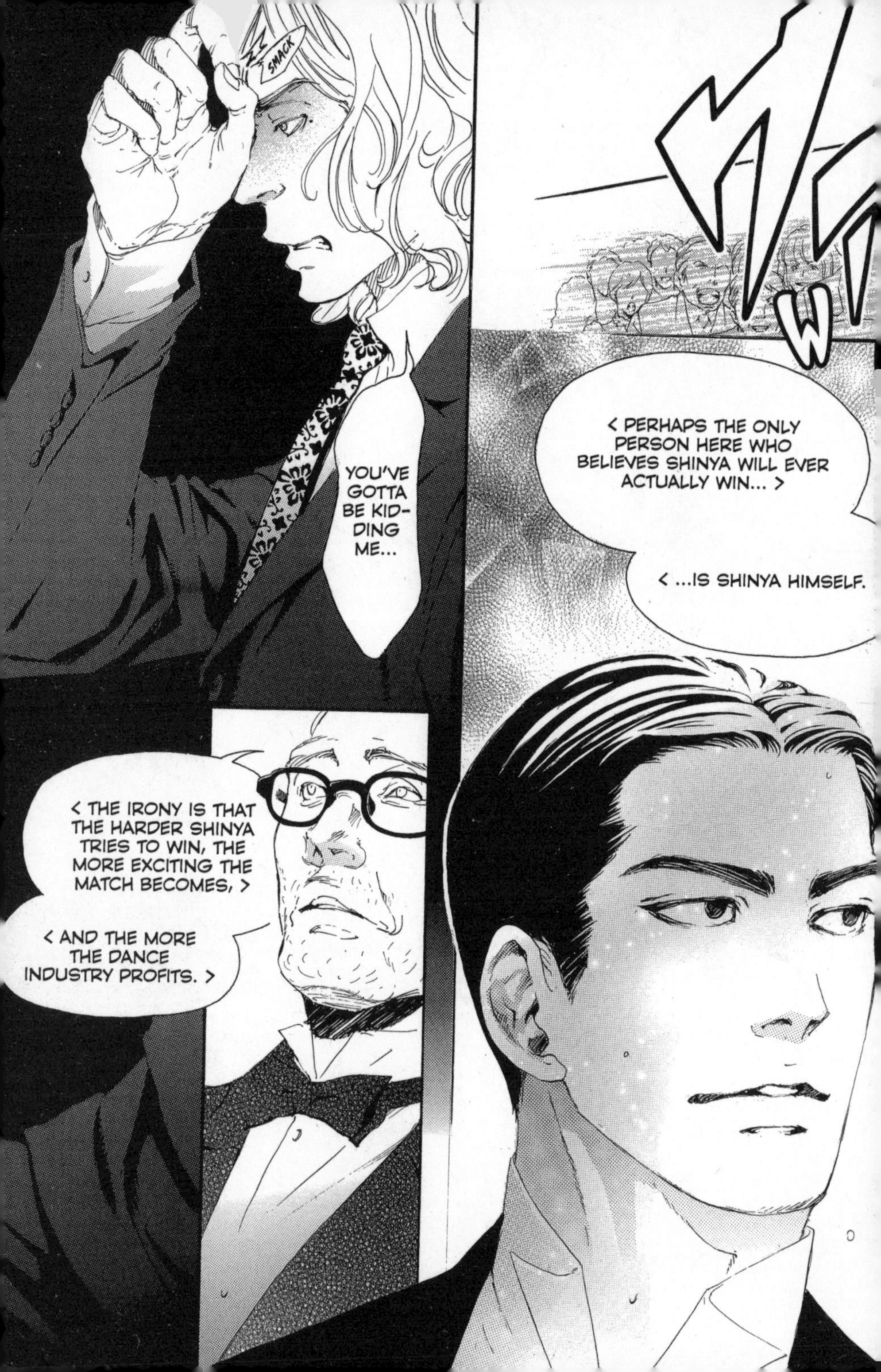
WOW
SMACK
YOU'VE GOTTA BE KID-DING ME...
< PERHAPS THE ONLY PERSON HERE WHO BELIEVES SHINYA WILL EVER ACTUALLY WIN... >
< ...IS SHINYA HIMSELF.
< THE IRONY IS THAT THE HARDER SHINYA TRIES TO WIN, THE MORE EXCITING THE MATCH BECOMES, >
< AND THE MORE THE DANCE INDUSTRY PROFITS. >

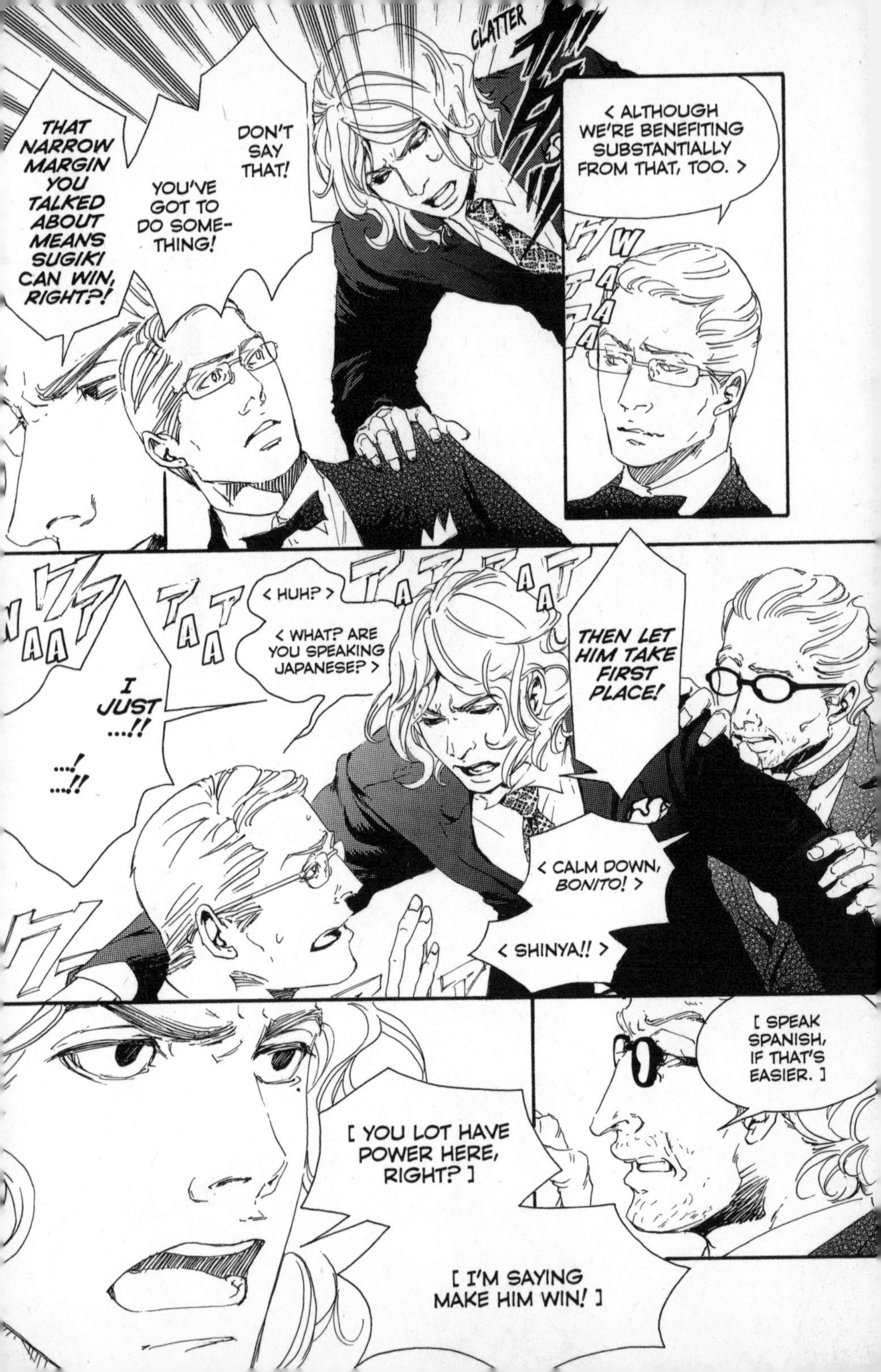
< ALTHOUGH WE'RE BENEFITING SUBSTANTIALLY FROM THAT, TOO. >
CLATTER
DON'T SAY THAT!
YOU'VE GOT TO DO SOME-THING!
THAT NARROW MARGIN YOU TALKED ABOUT MEANS SUGIKI CAN WIN, RIGHT?!
THEN LET HIM TAKE FIRST PLACE!
< HUH? >
< WHAT? ARE YOU SPEAKING JAPANESE? >
I JUST ...!!
...! ...!!
< CALM DOWN, BONITO! >
< SHINYA!! >
[SPEAK SPANISH, IF THAT'S EASIER.]
[YOU LOT HAVE POWER HERE, RIGHT?]
[I'M SAYING MAKE HIM WIN!]

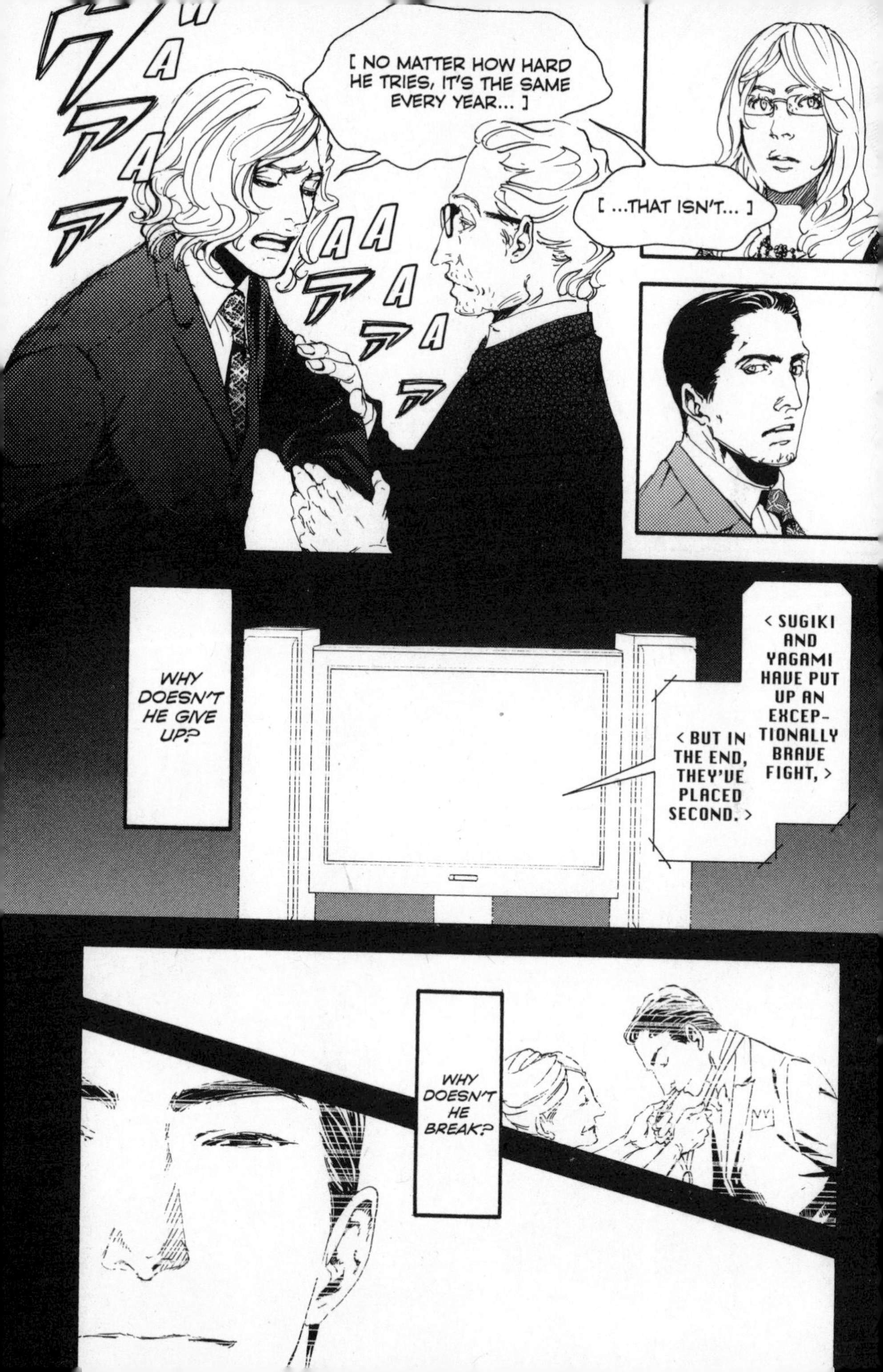
[...THAT ISN'T...]
WAAA
[NO MATTER HOW HARD HE TRIES, IT'S THE SAME EVERY YEAR...]
AAAA
< SUGIKI AND YAGAMI HAVE PUT UP AN EXCEPTIONALLY BRAVE FIGHT, >
< BUT IN THE END, THEY'VE PLACED SECOND. >
WHY DOESN'T HE GIVE UP?
WHY DOESN'T HE BREAK?

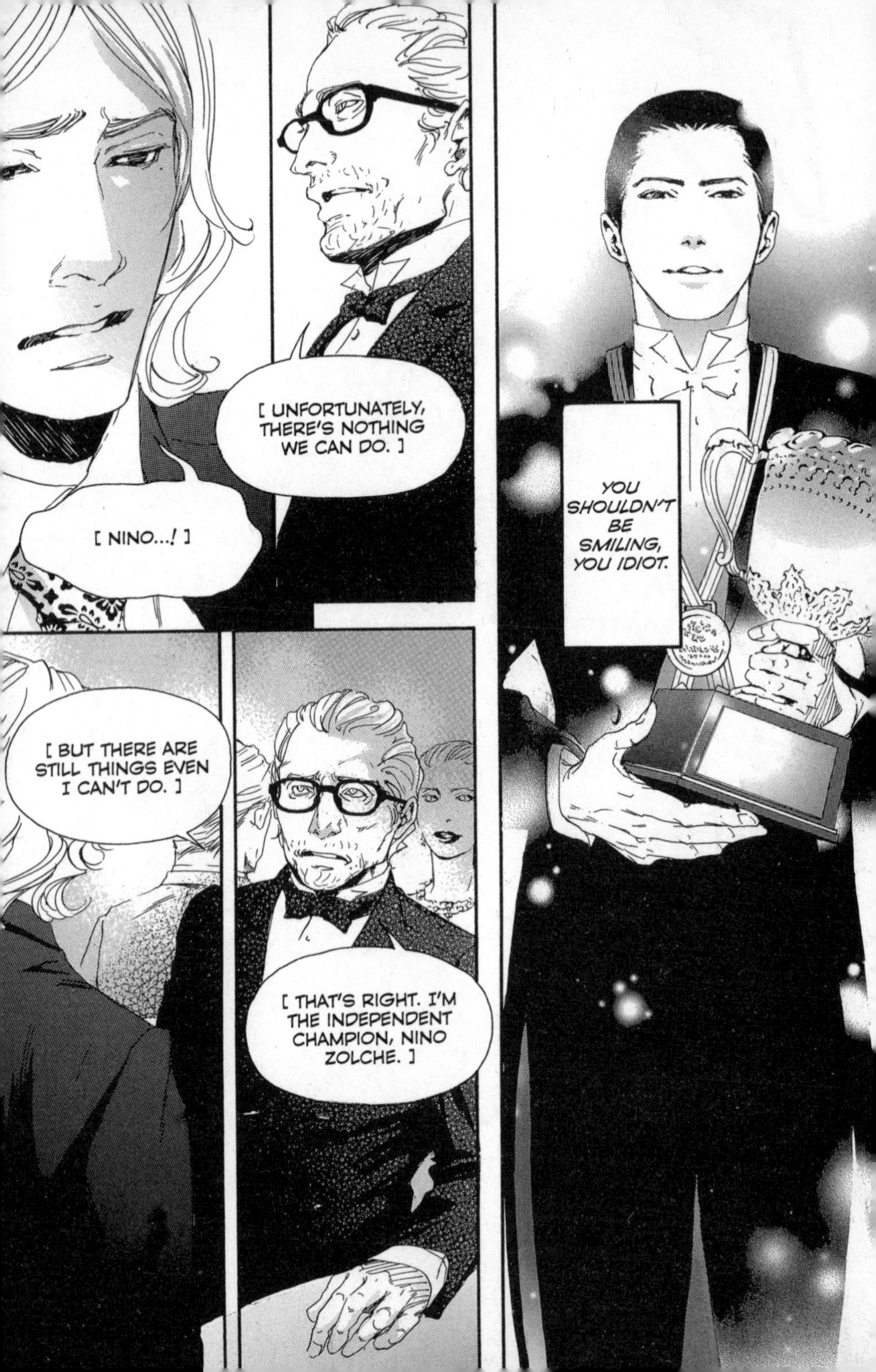
YOU SHOULDN'T BE SMILING, YOU IDIOT.
[UNFORTUNATELY, THERE'S NOTHING WE CAN DO.]
[NINO...!]
[THAT'S RIGHT. I'M THE INDEPENDENT CHAMPION, NINO ZOLCHE.]
[BUT THERE ARE STILL THINGS EVEN I CAN'T DO.]

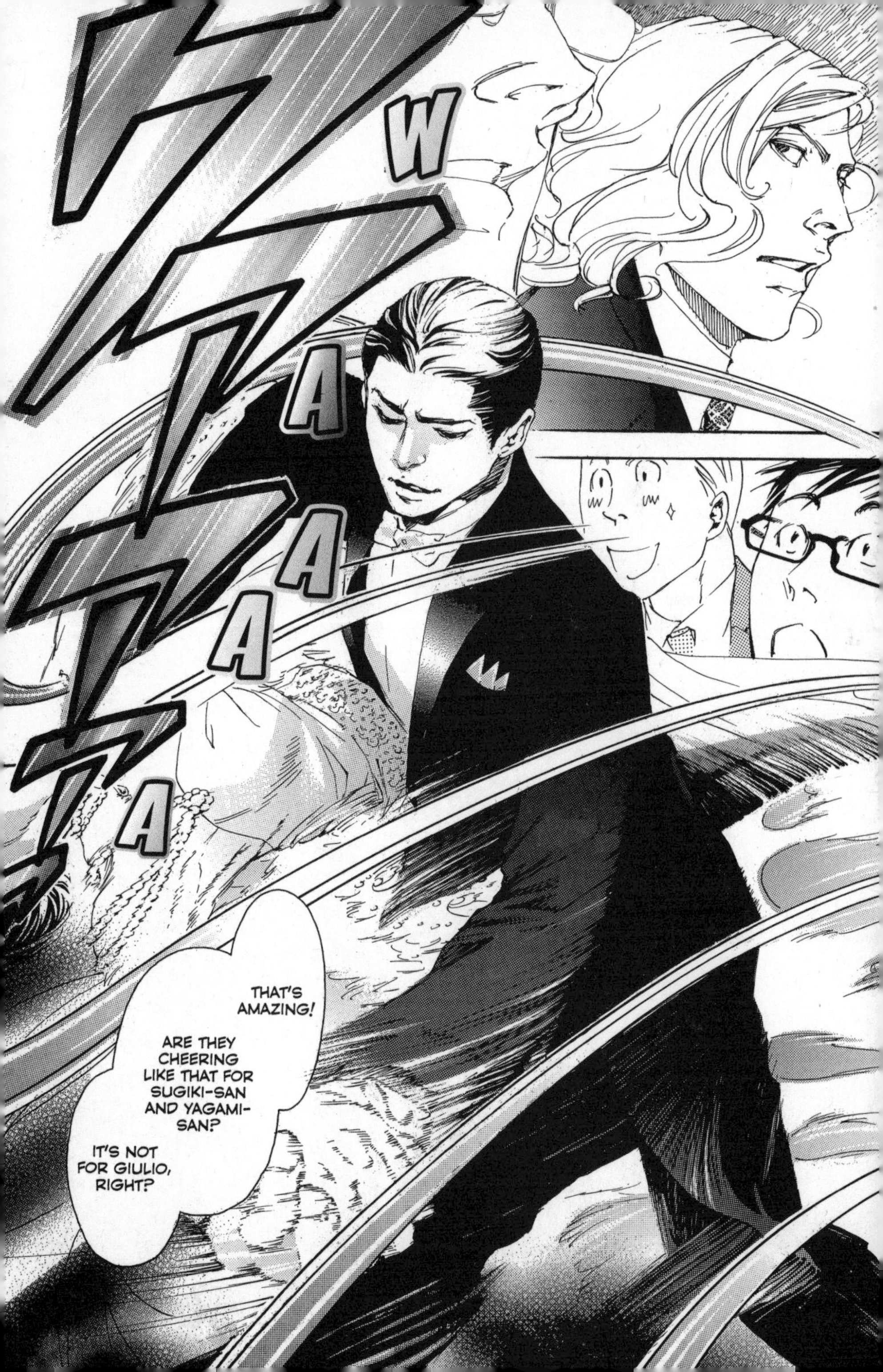
WAAAAA
THAT'S AMAZING!
ARE THEY CHEERING LIKE THAT FOR SUGIKI-SAN AND YAGAMI-SAN?
IT'S NOT FOR GIULIO, RIGHT?

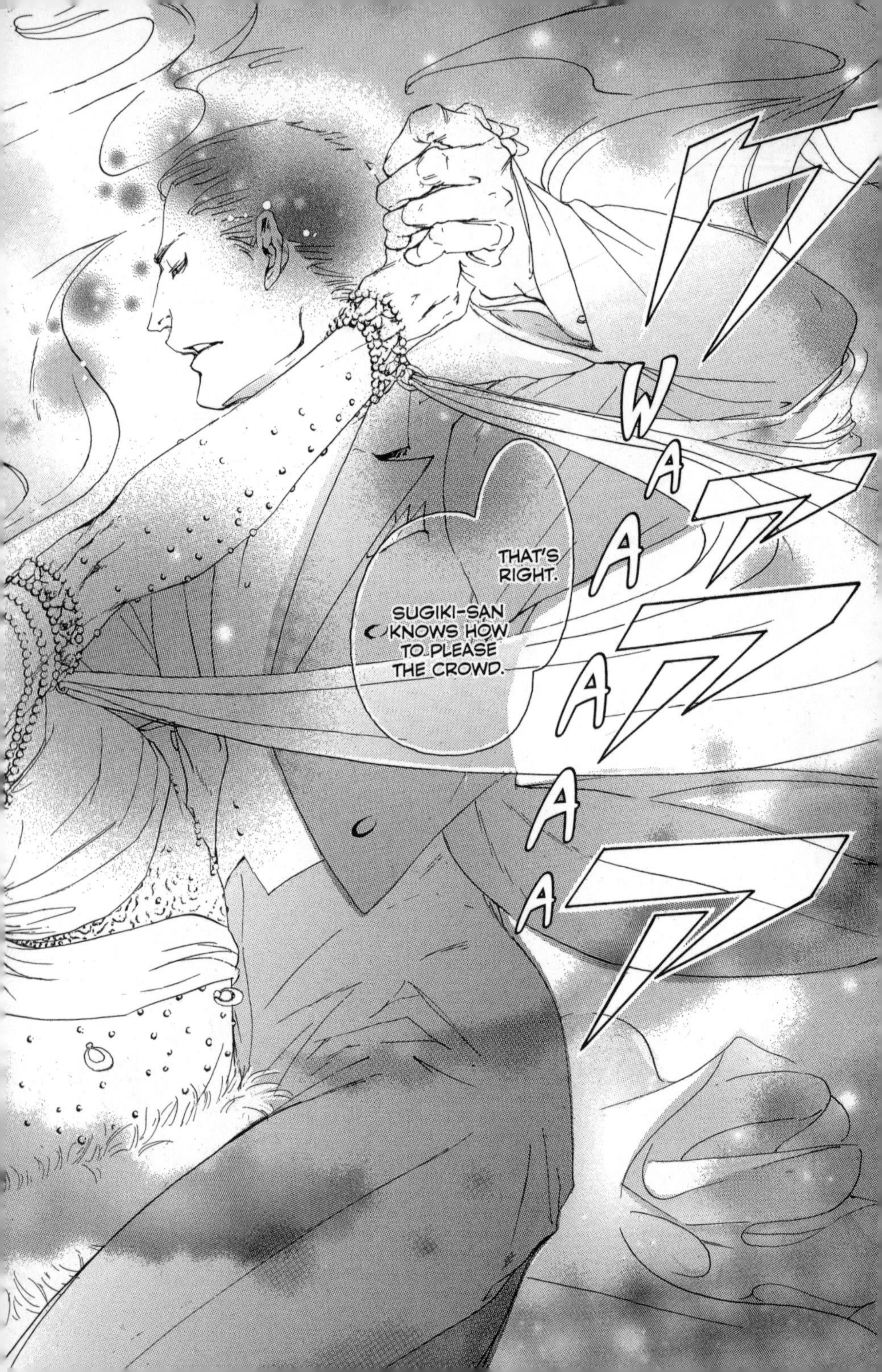

WAAAAAA
THAT'S RIGHT.
SUGIKI-SAN KNOWS HOW TO PLEASE THE CROWD.

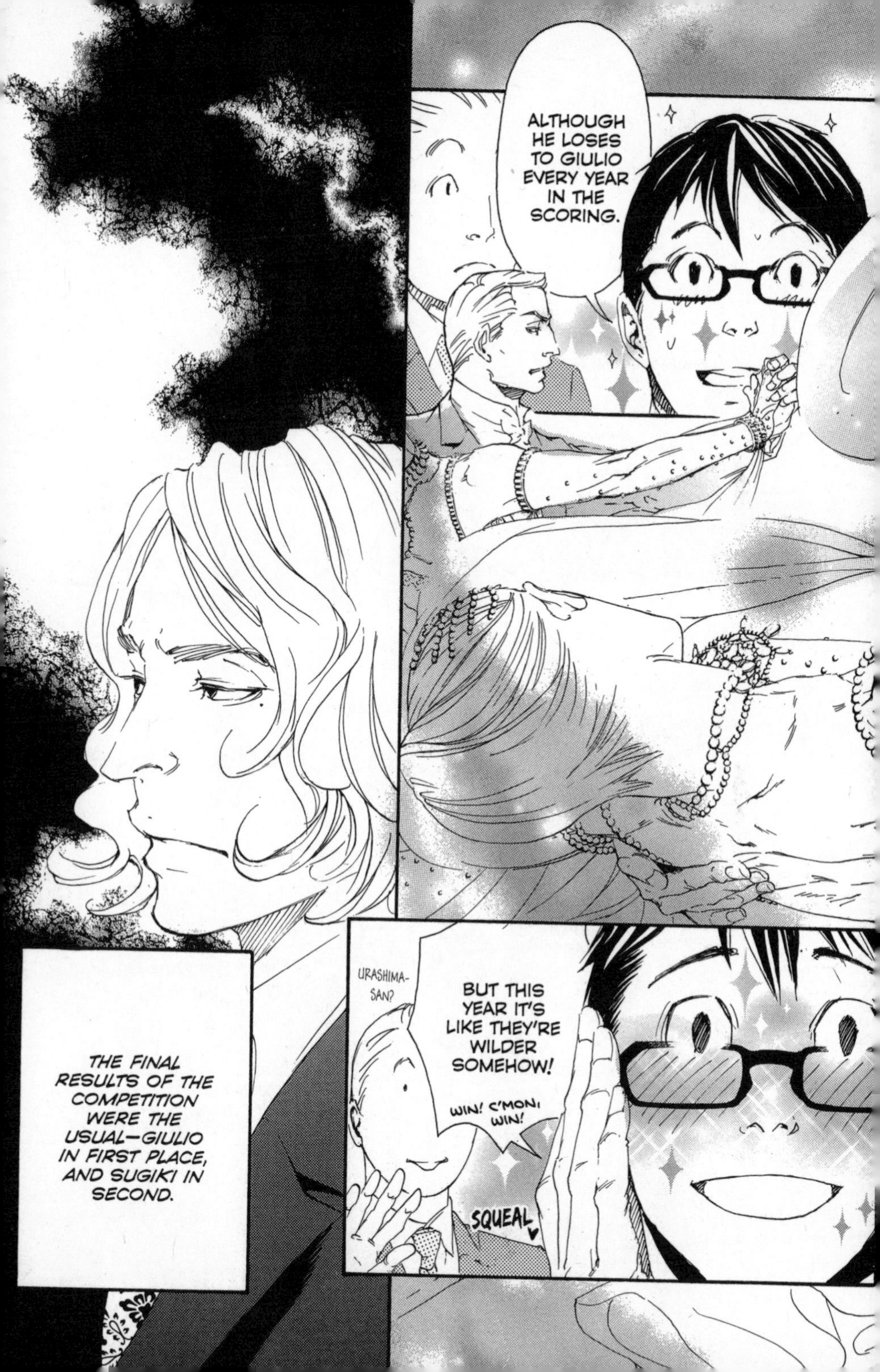
ALTHOUGH HE LOSES TO GIULIO EVERY YEAR IN THE SCORING.
BUT THIS YEAR IT'S LIKE THEY'RE WILDER SOMEHOW!
URASHIMA-SAN?
WIN! C'MON! WIN!
SQUEAL
THE FINAL RESULTS OF THE COMPETITION WERE THE USUAL—GIULIO IN FIRST PLACE, AND SUGIKI IN SECOND.

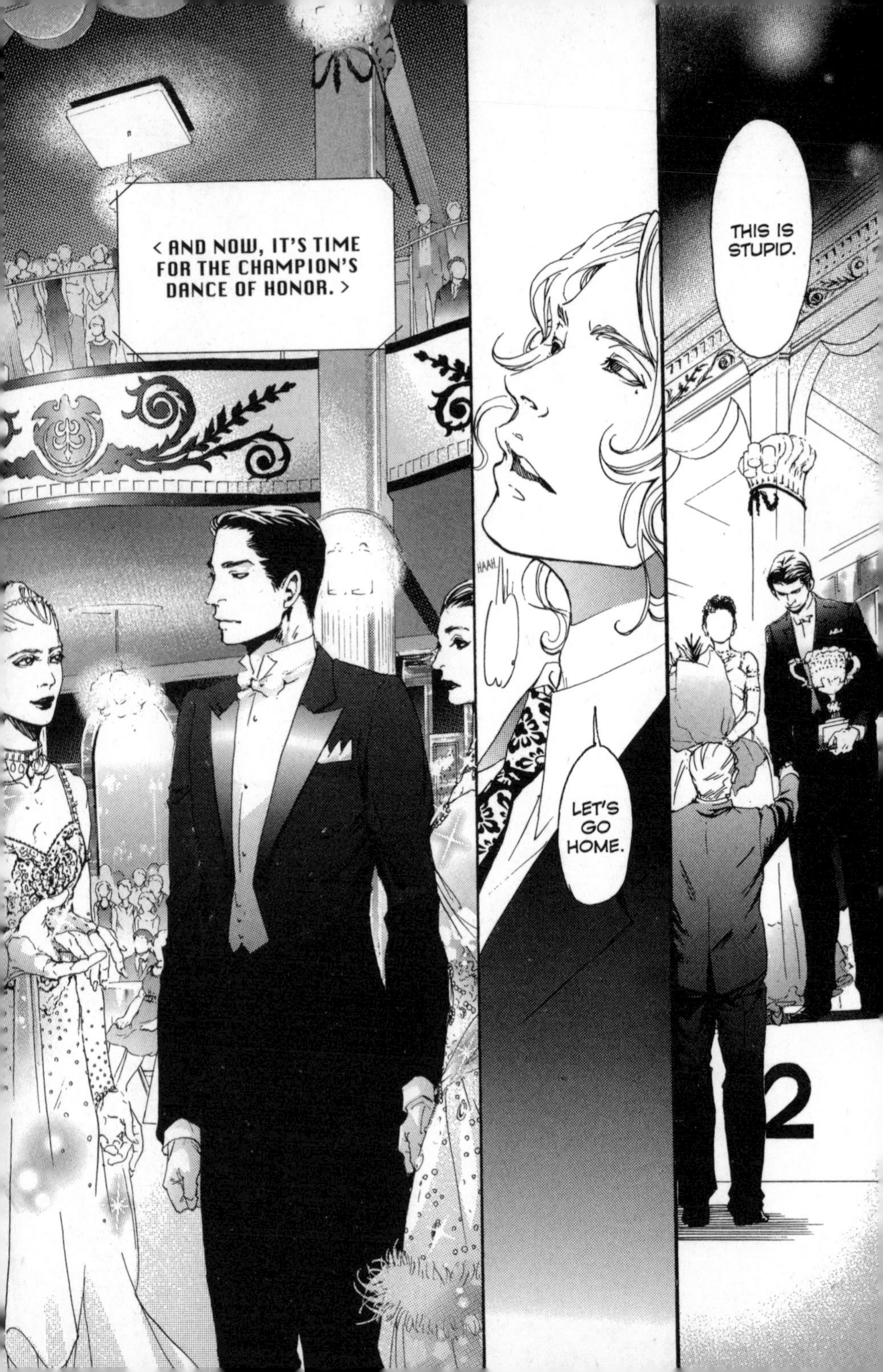
THIS IS STUPID.
HAAH.
LET'S GO HOME.
< AND NOW, IT'S TIME FOR THE CHAMPION'S DANCE OF HONOR. >

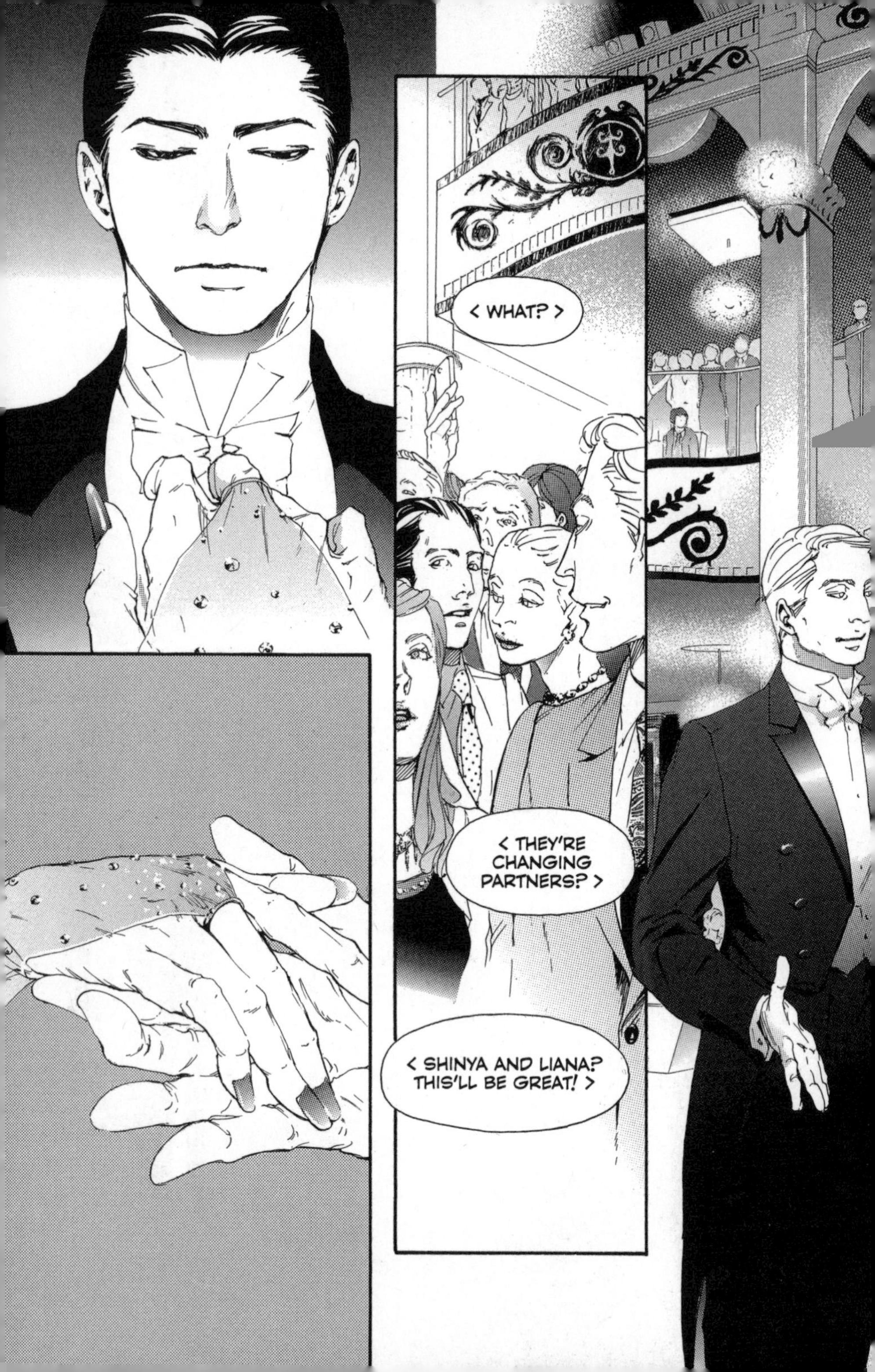
< WHAT? >
< THEY'RE CHANGING PARTNERS? >
< SHINYA AND LIANA? THIS'LL BE GREAT! >

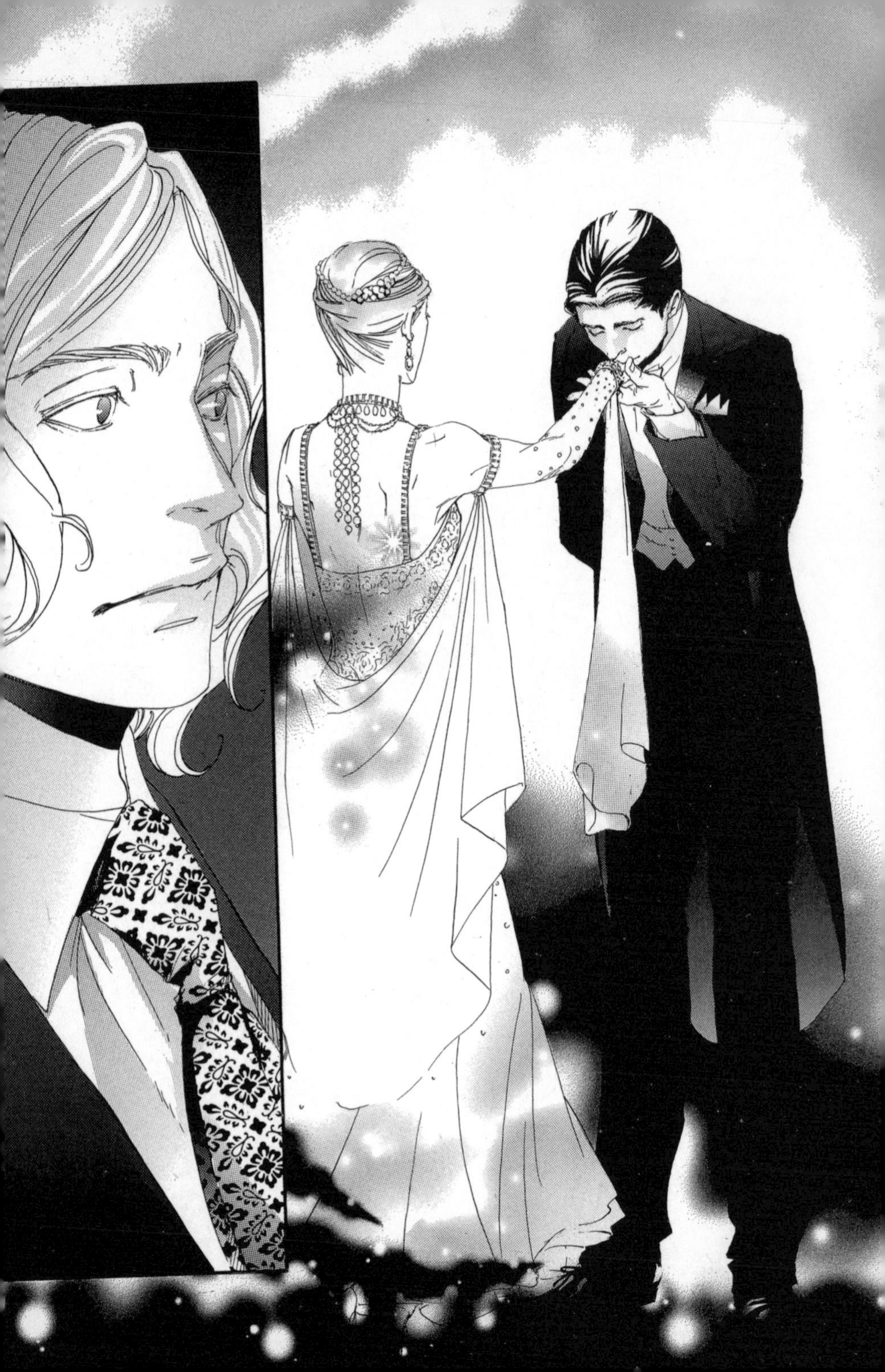

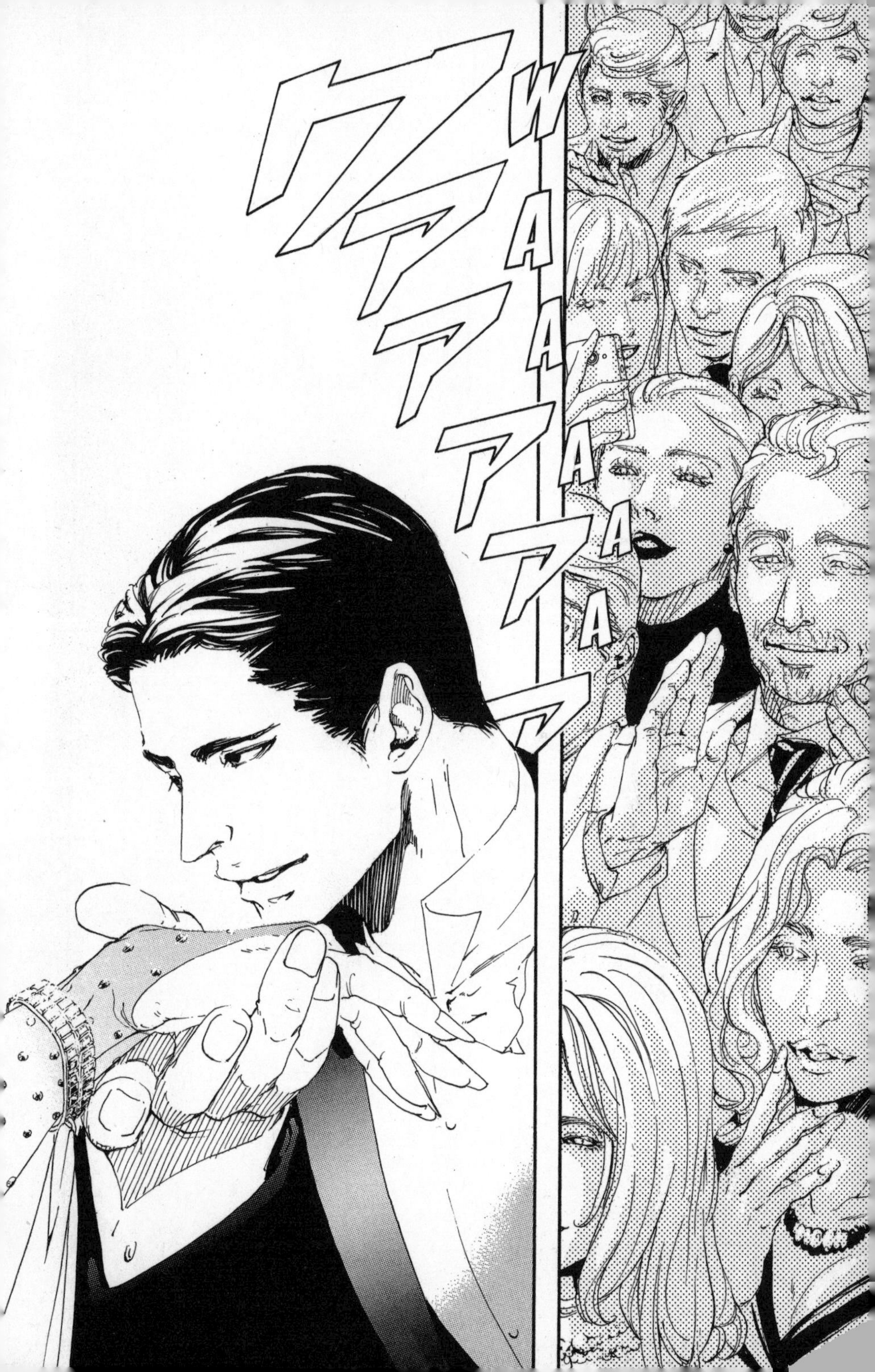
ワアアアアア
WAAAAA

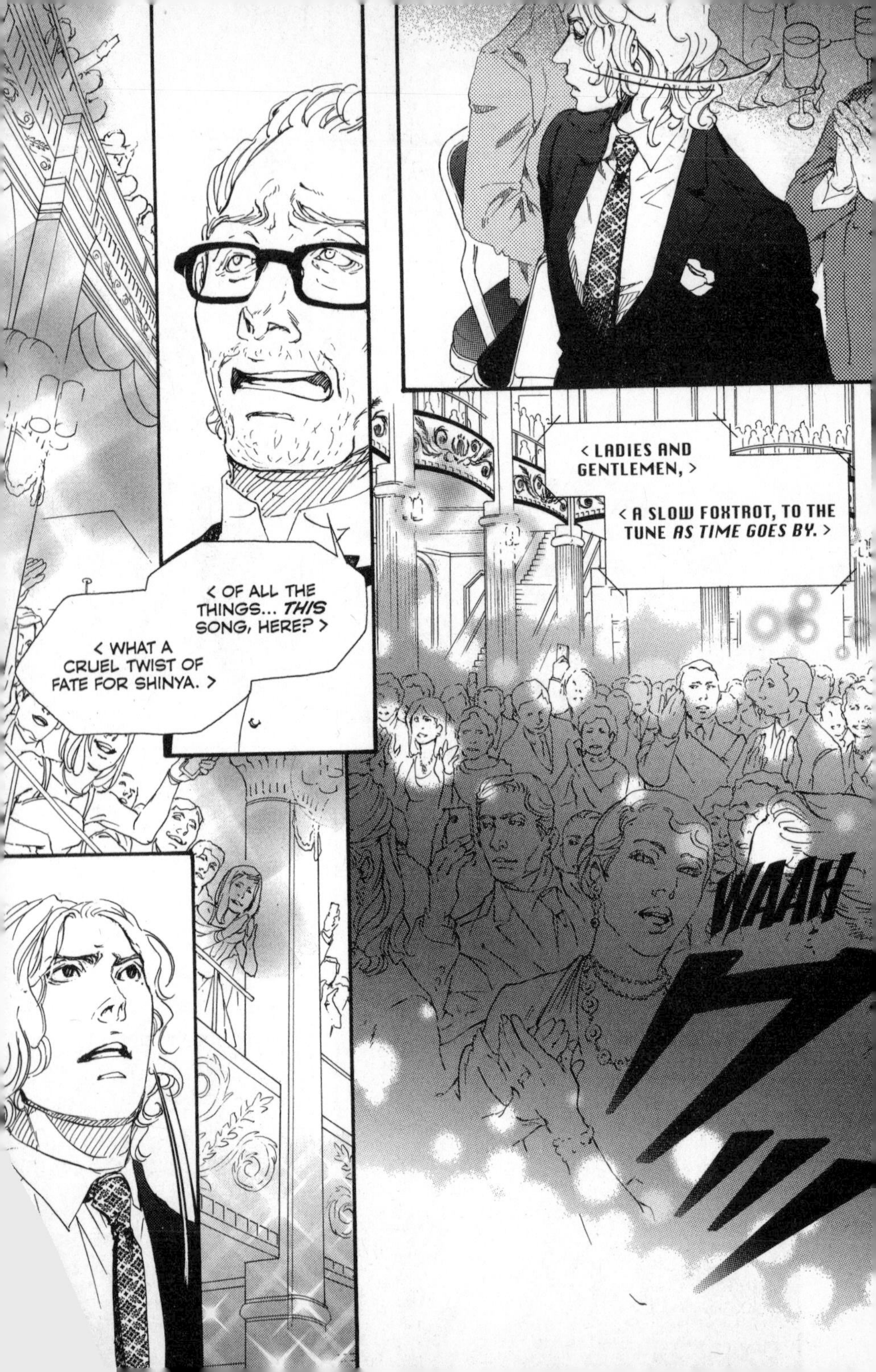

< LADIES AND GENTLEMEN, >
< A SLOW FOXTROT, TO THE TUNE *AS TIME GOES BY.* >
WAAH
< OF ALL THE THINGS... *THIS* SONG, HERE? >
< WHAT A CRUEL TWIST OF FATE FOR SHINYA. >

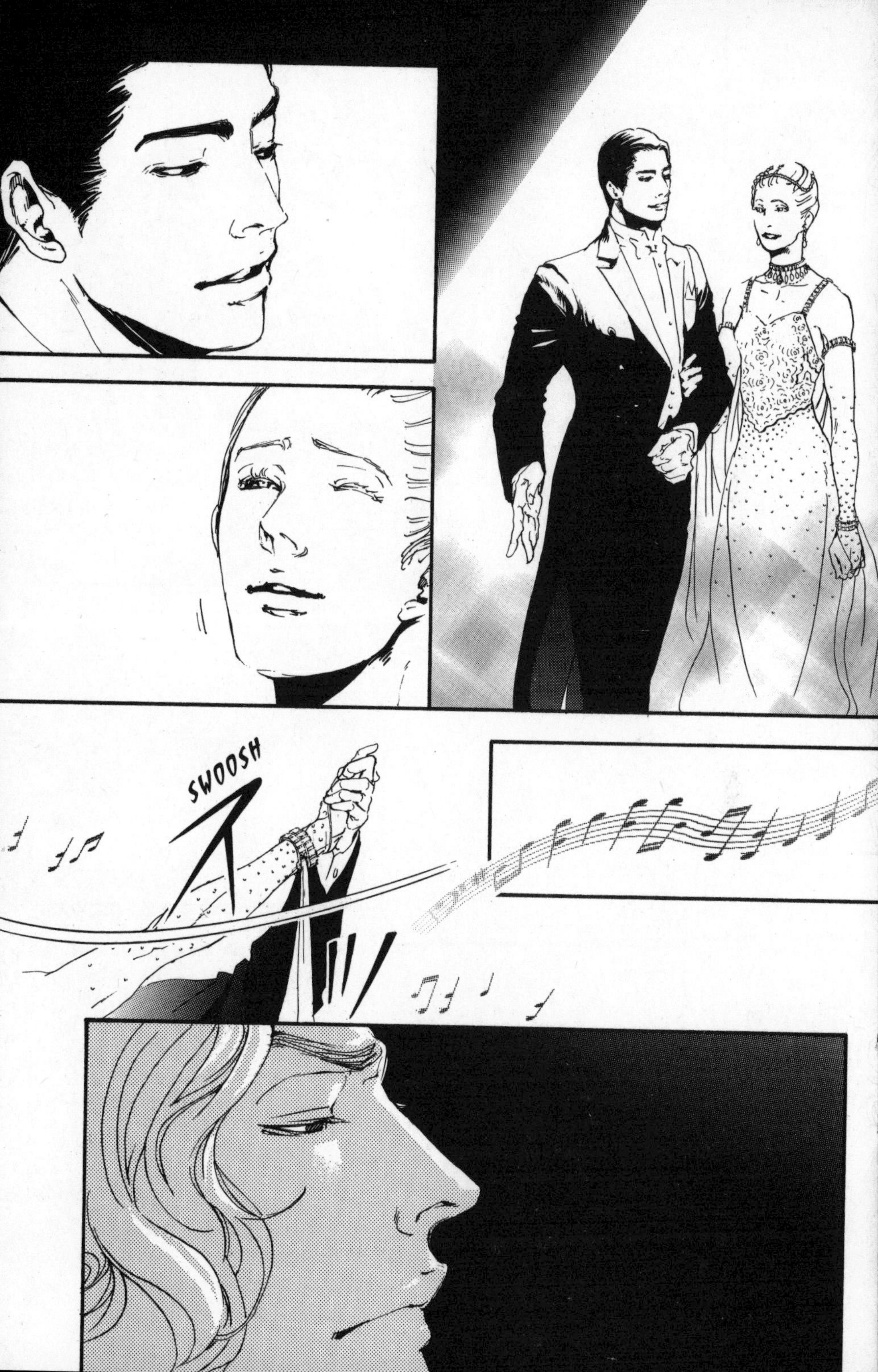
SWOOSH

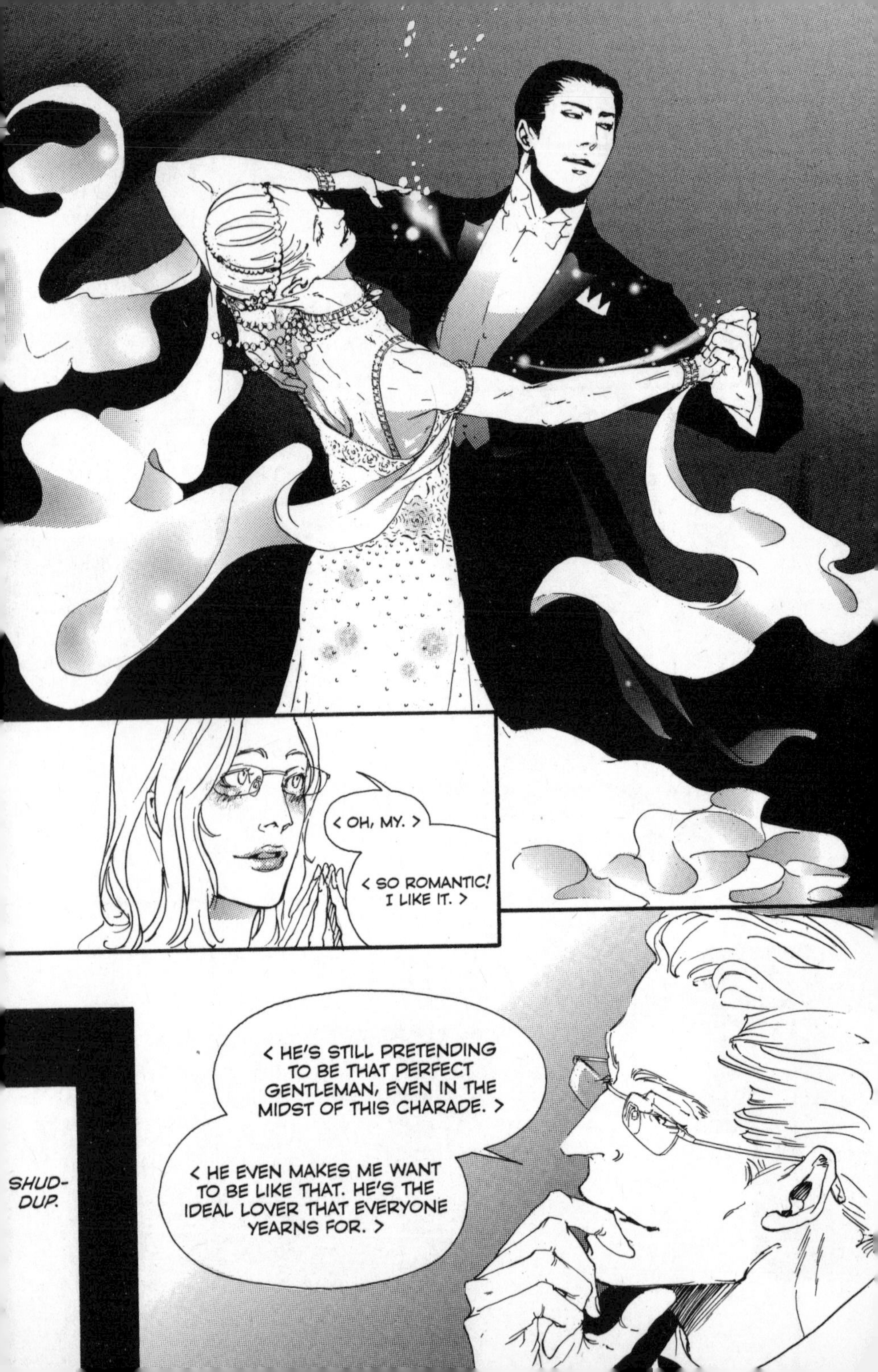
< OH, MY. >
< SO ROMANTIC! I LIKE IT. >
< HE'S STILL PRETENDING TO BE THAT PERFECT GENTLEMAN, EVEN IN THE MIDST OF THIS CHARADE. >
< HE EVEN MAKES ME WANT TO BE LIKE THAT. HE'S THE IDEAL LOVER THAT EVERYONE YEARNS FOR. >
SHUD-DUP.

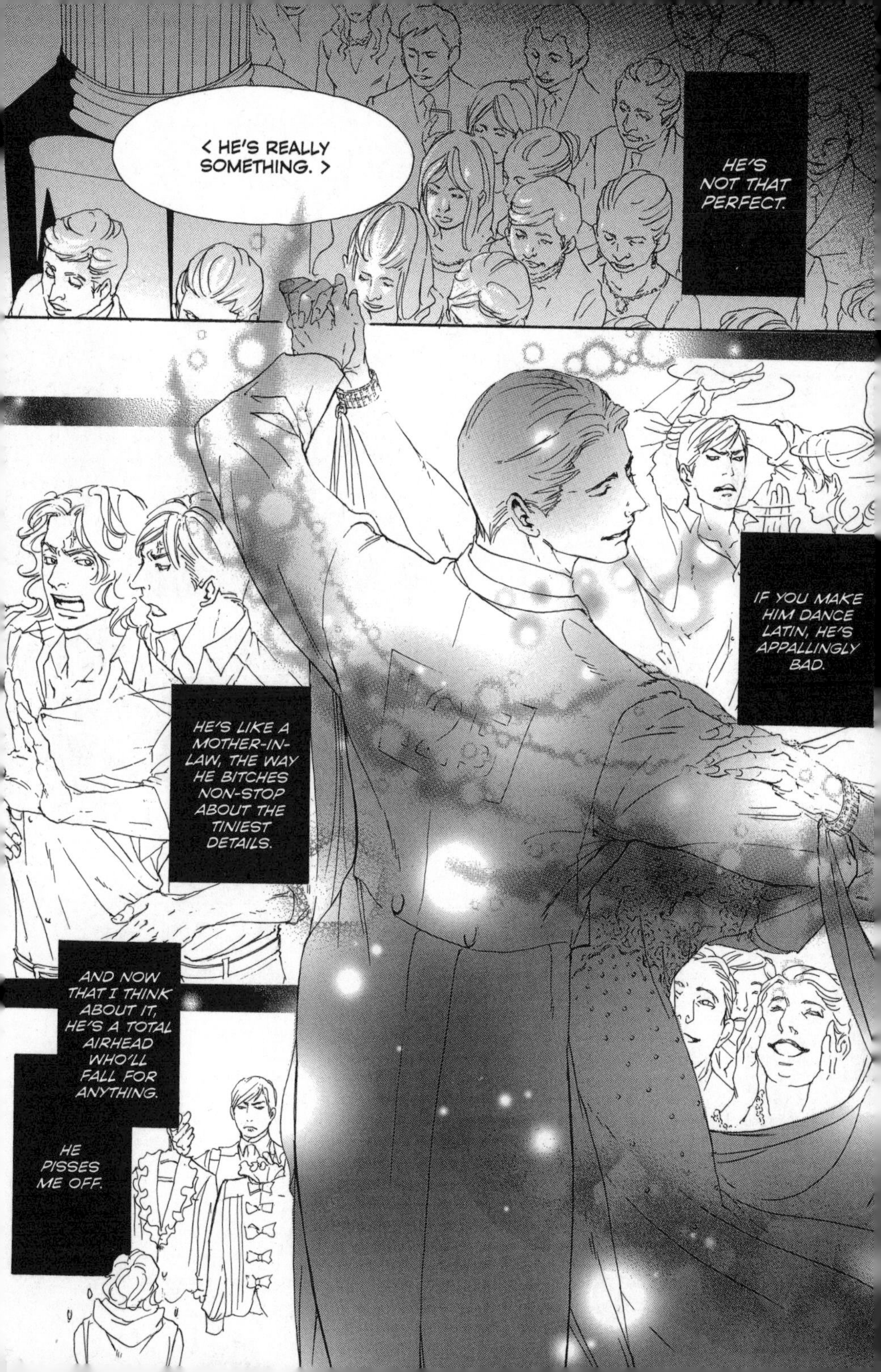
HE'S NOT THAT PERFECT.
< HE'S REALLY SOMETHING. >
IF YOU MAKE HIM DANCE LATIN, HE'S APPALLINGLY BAD.
HE'S LIKE A MOTHER-IN-LAW, THE WAY HE BITCHES NON-STOP ABOUT THE TINIEST DETAILS.
AND NOW THAT I THINK ABOUT IT, HE'S A TOTAL AIRHEAD WHO'LL FALL FOR ANYTHING.
HE PISSES ME OFF.

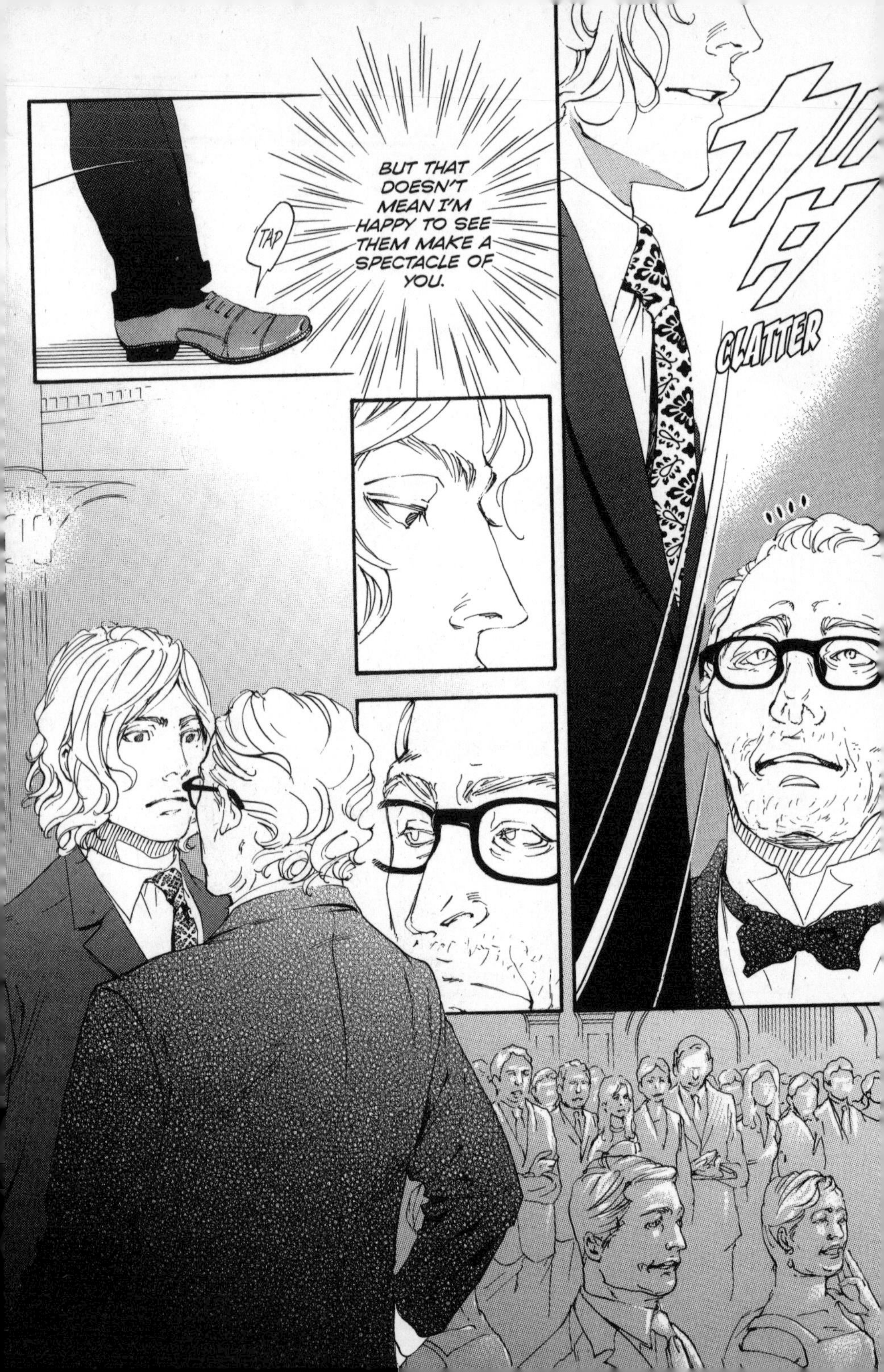
CLATTER
TAP
BUT THAT DOESN'T MEAN I'M HAPPY TO SEE THEM MAKE A SPECTACLE OF YOU.
....

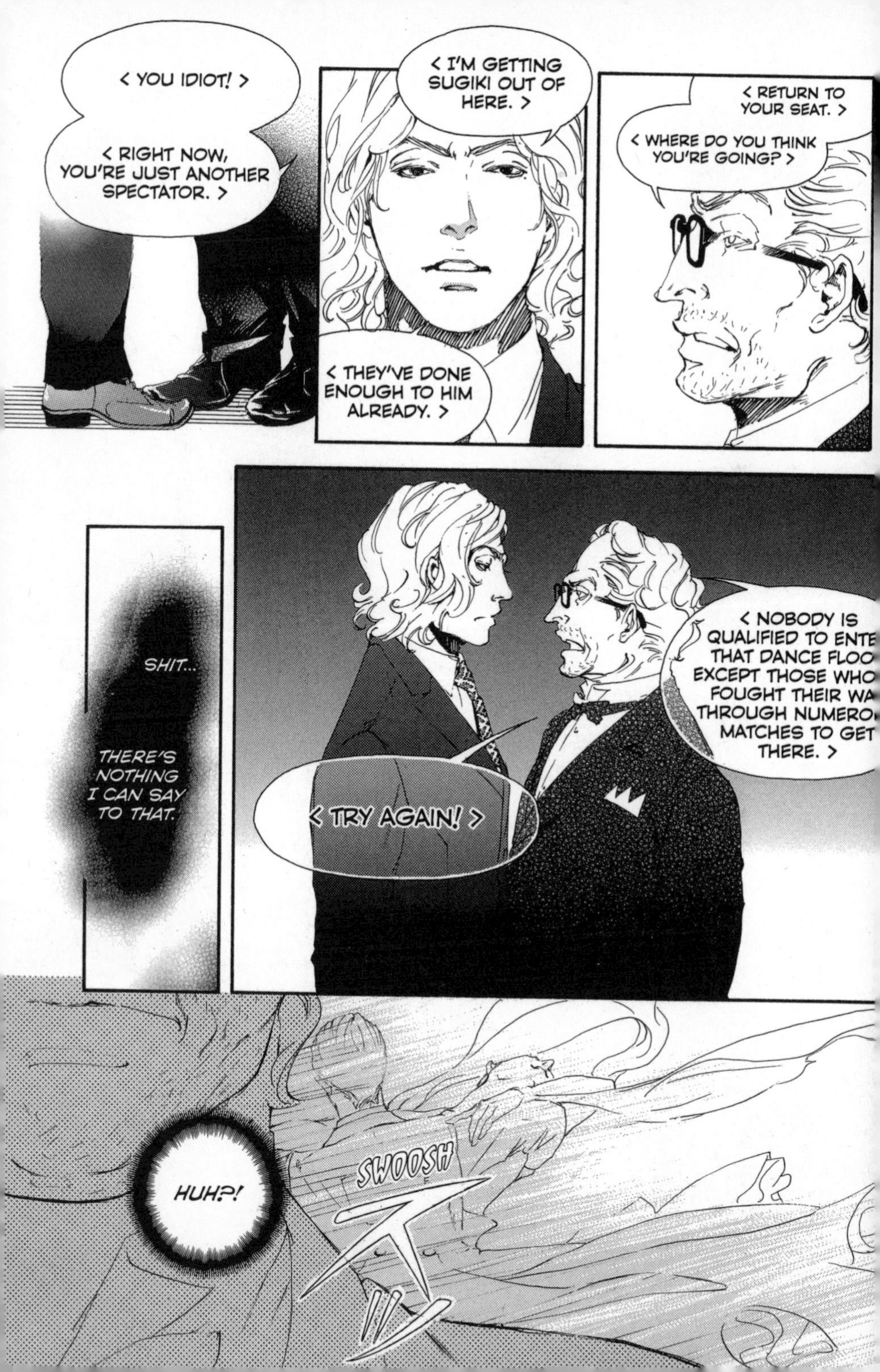
< RETURN TO YOUR SEAT. >
< WHERE DO YOU THINK YOU'RE GOING? >
< I'M GETTING SUGIKI OUT OF HERE. >
< THEY'VE DONE ENOUGH TO HIM ALREADY. >
< YOU IDIOT! >
< RIGHT NOW, YOU'RE JUST ANOTHER SPECTATOR. >
< NOBODY IS QUALIFIED TO ENTE THAT DANCE FLOO EXCEPT THOSE WHO FOUGHT THEIR WA THROUGH NUMERO MATCHES TO GET THERE. >
< TRY AGAIN! >
SHIT...
THERE'S NOTHING I CAN SAY TO THAT.
SWOOSH
HUH?!

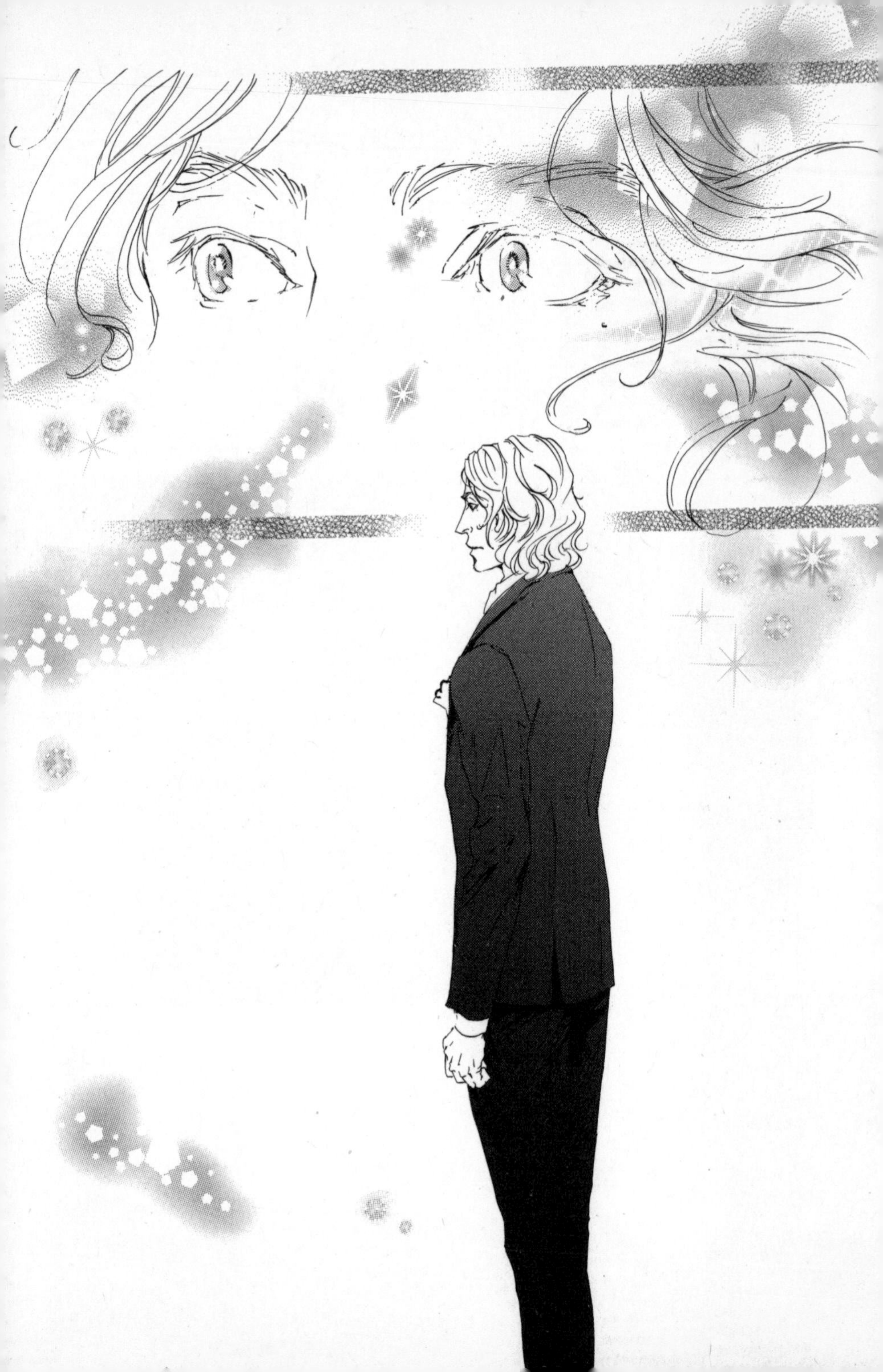

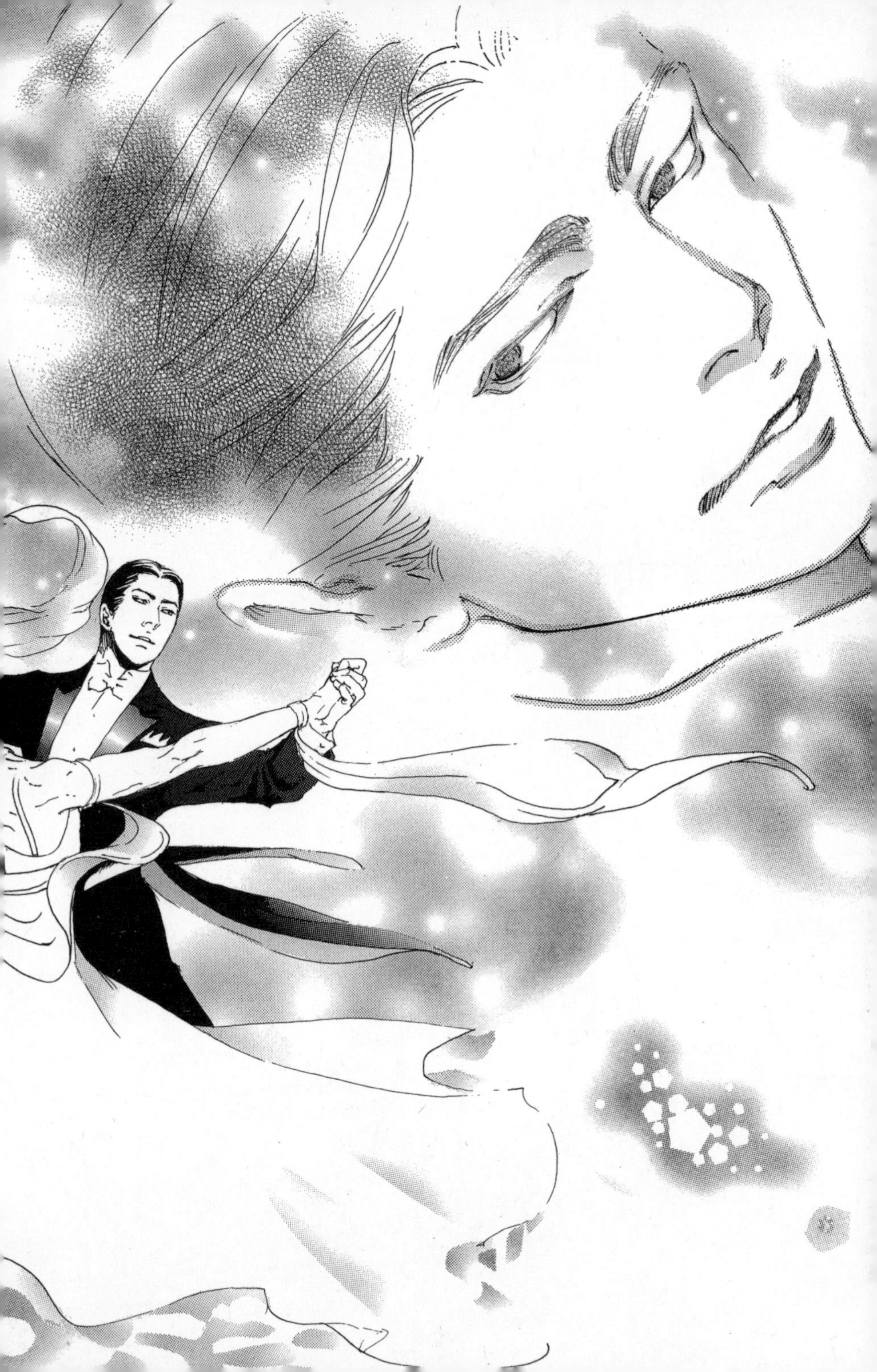

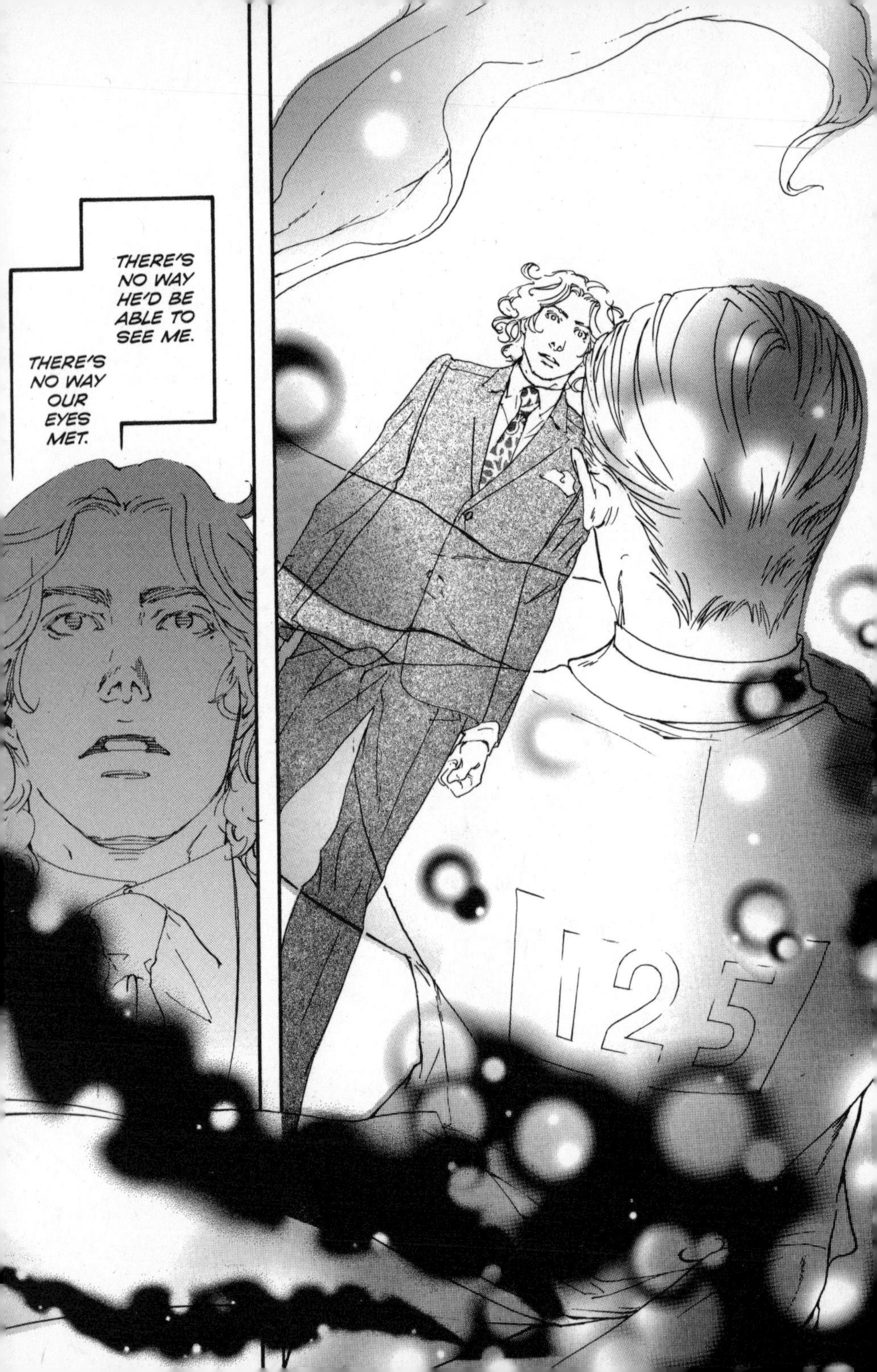
125
THERE'S NO WAY HE'D BE ABLE TO SEE ME.
THERE'S NO WAY OUR EYES MET.

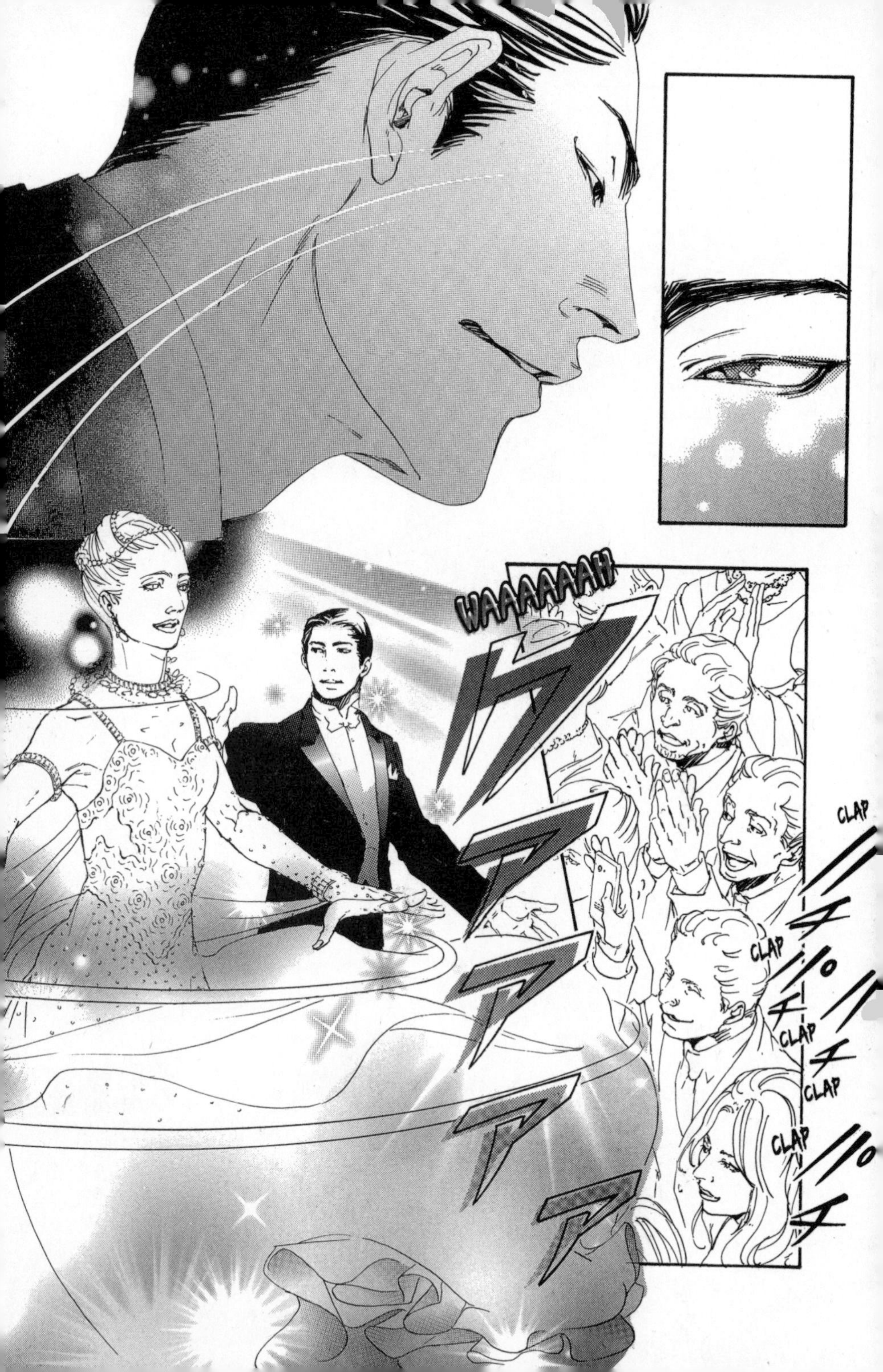
CLAP
CLAP
CLAP
CLAP
CLAP
WAAAAAAH

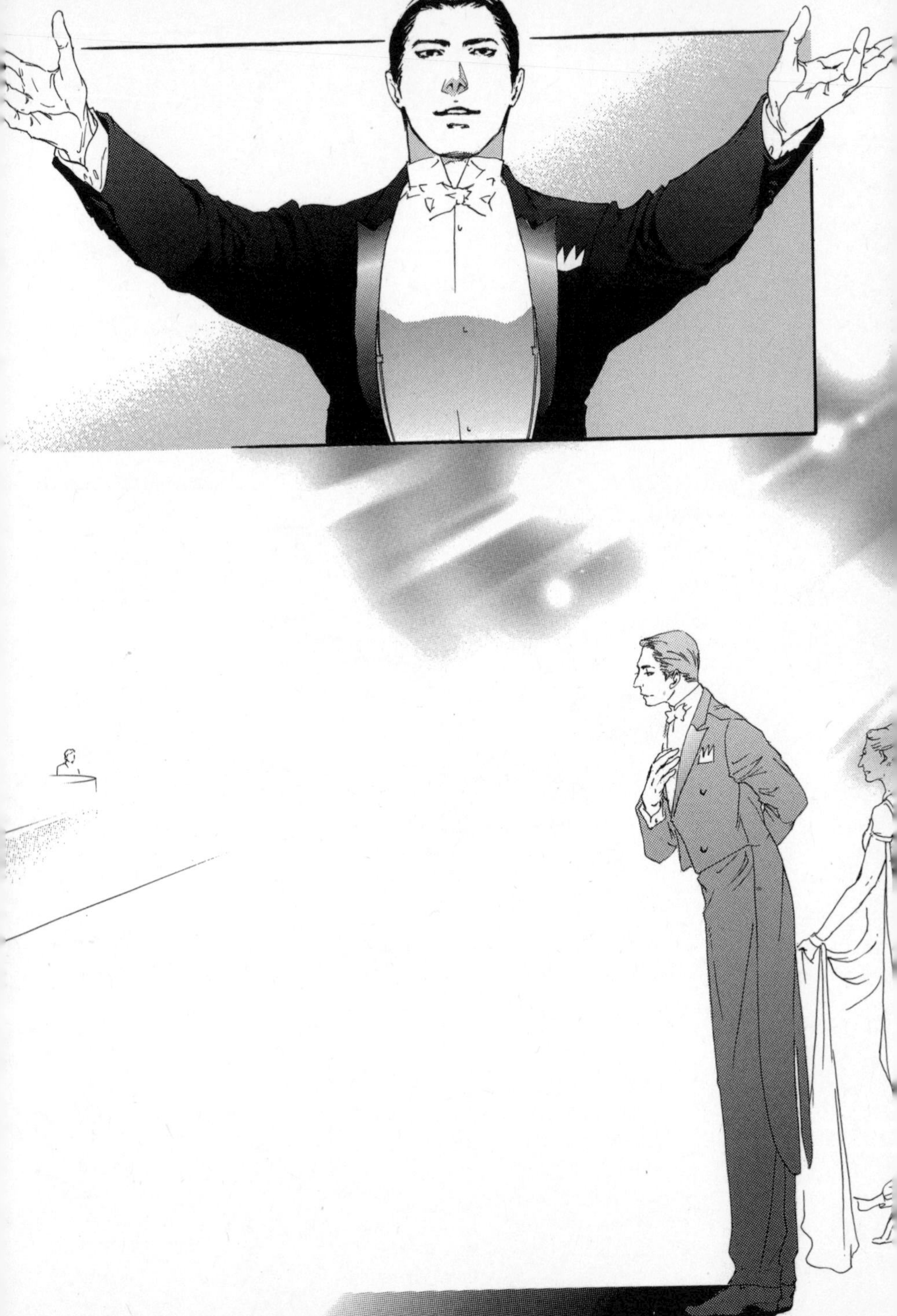

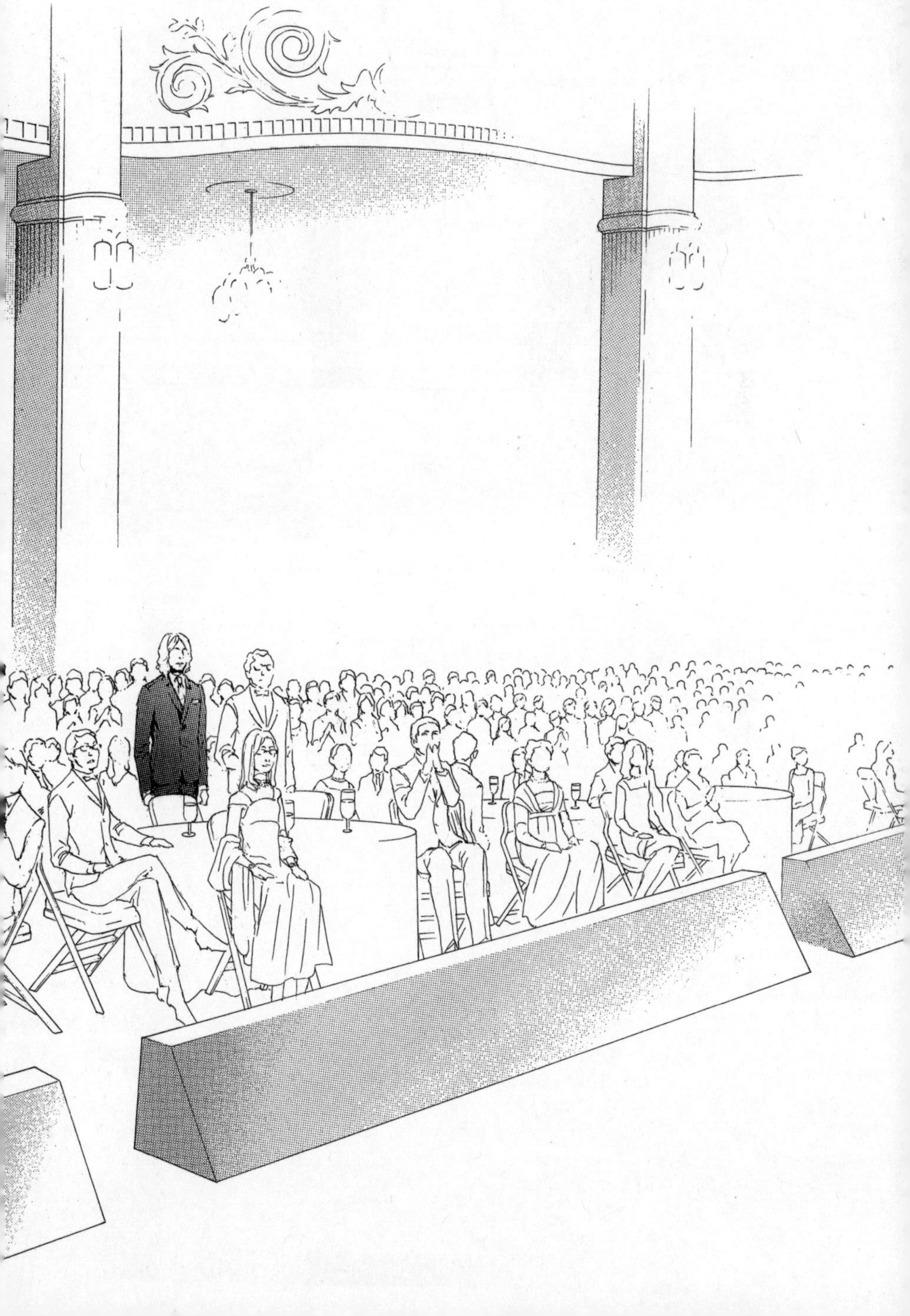

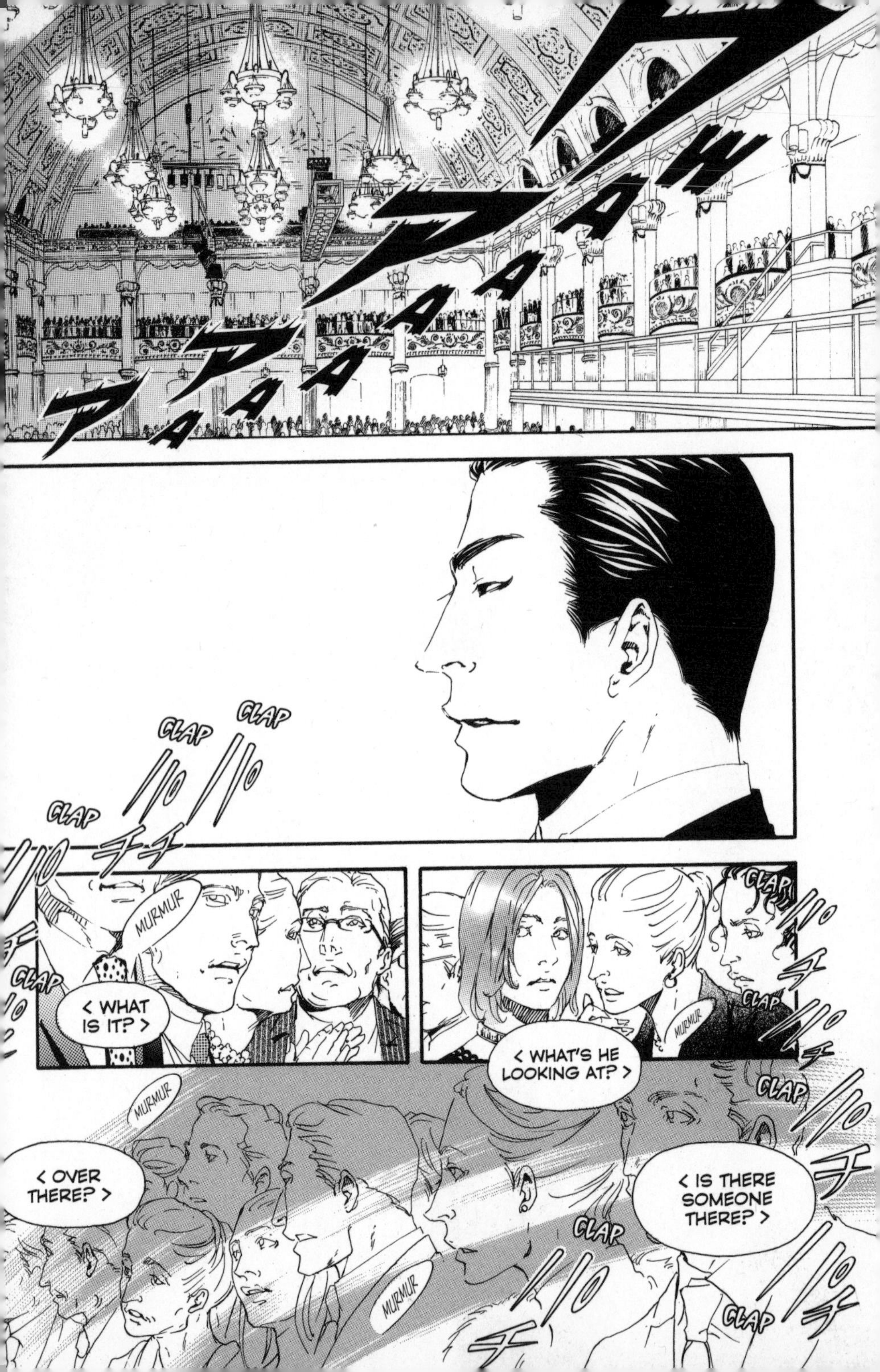
WAAAAAA
CLAP
CLAP
CLAP
CLAP
CLAP
MURMUR
< WHAT'S HE LOOKING AT? >
MURMUR
< WHAT IS IT? >
CLAP
CLAP
< IS THERE SOMEONE THERE? >
CLAP
CLAP
MURMUR
MURMUR
< OVER THERE? >

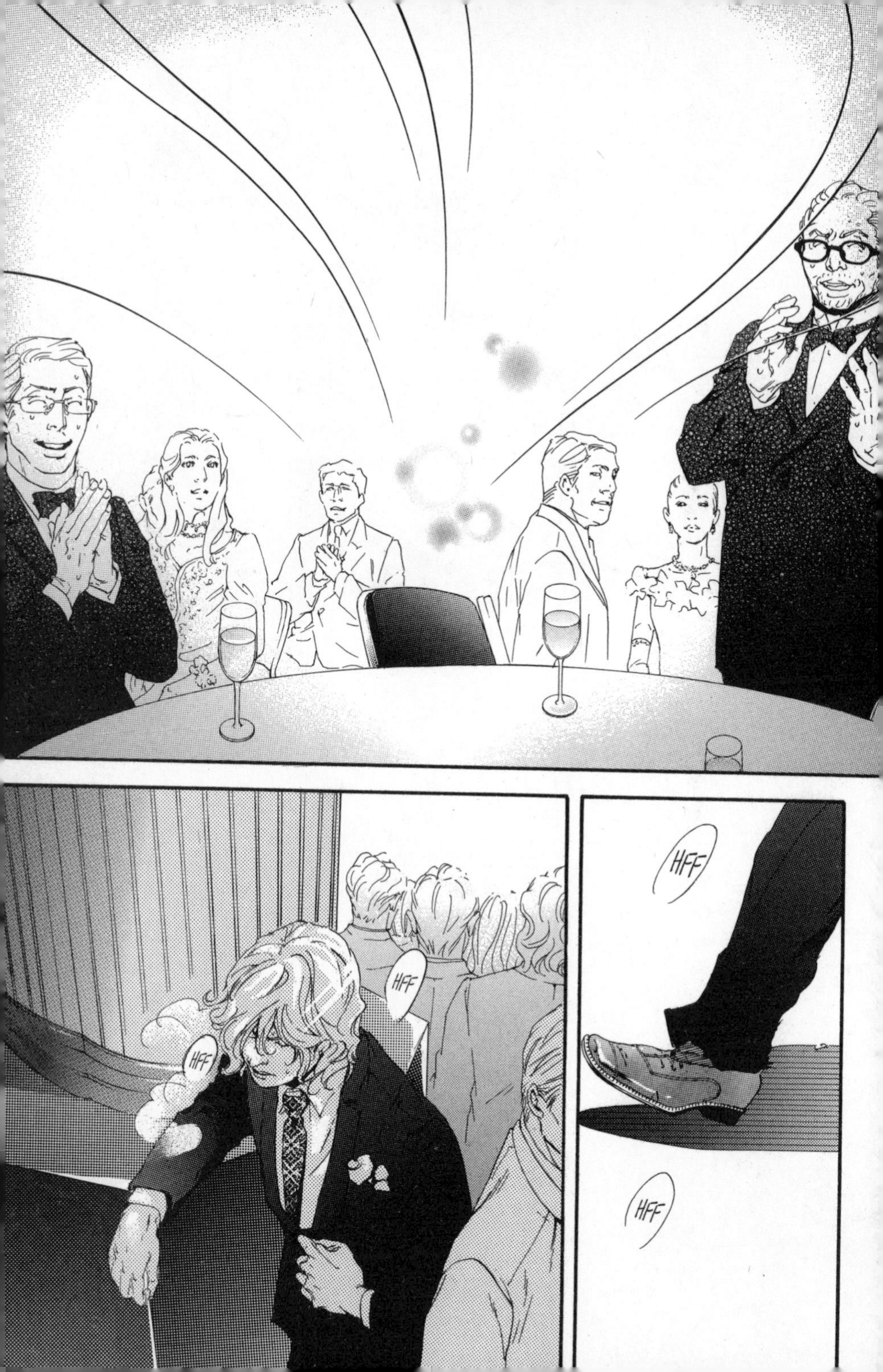
HFF
HFF
HFF
HFF

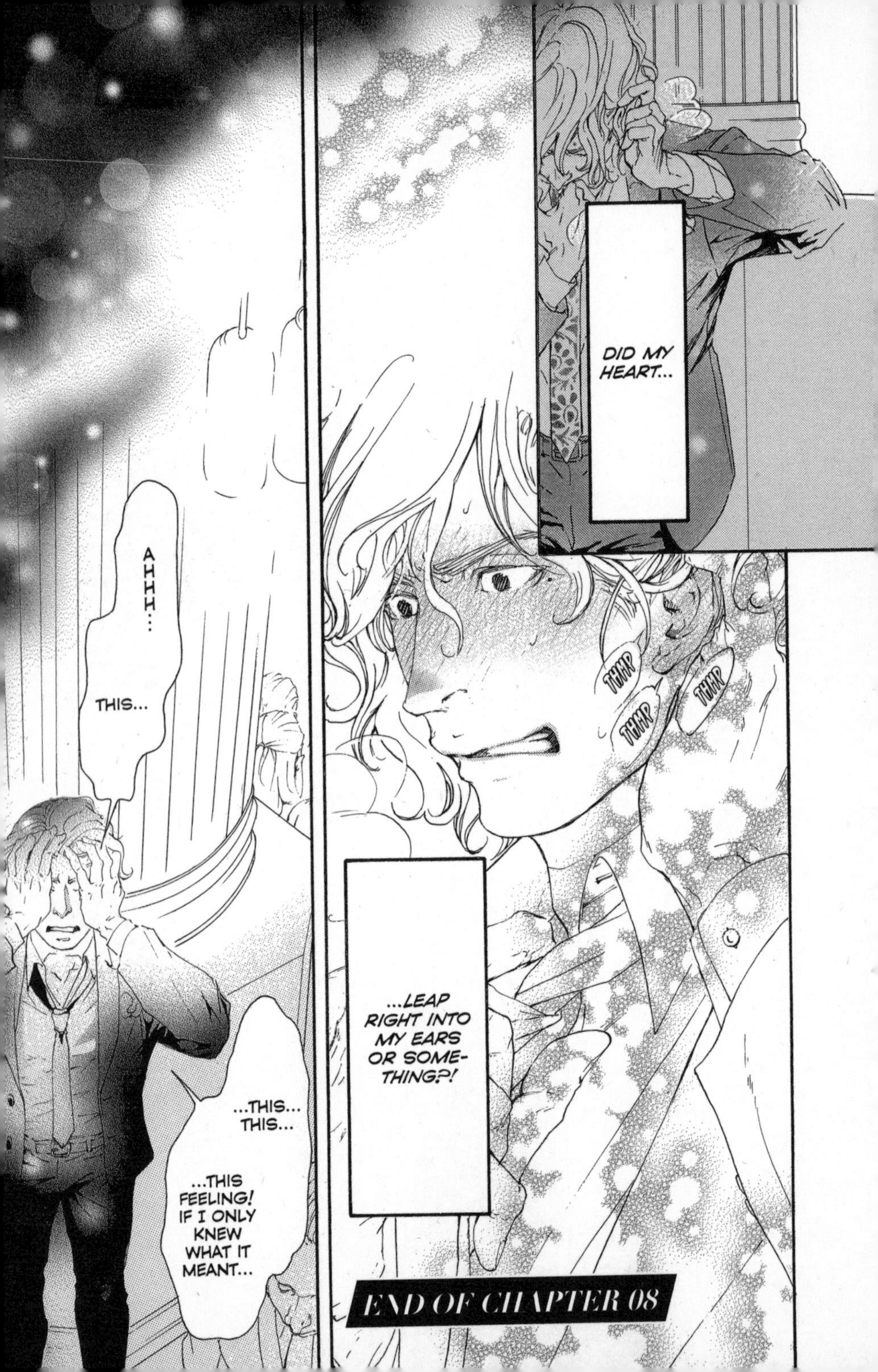
DID MY HEART...
THMP
THMP
THMP
...LEAP RIGHT INTO MY EARS OR SOME-THING?!
AHHH...
THIS...
...THIS... THIS...
...THIS FEELING! IF I ONLY KNEW WHAT IT MEANT...
END OF CHAPTER 08

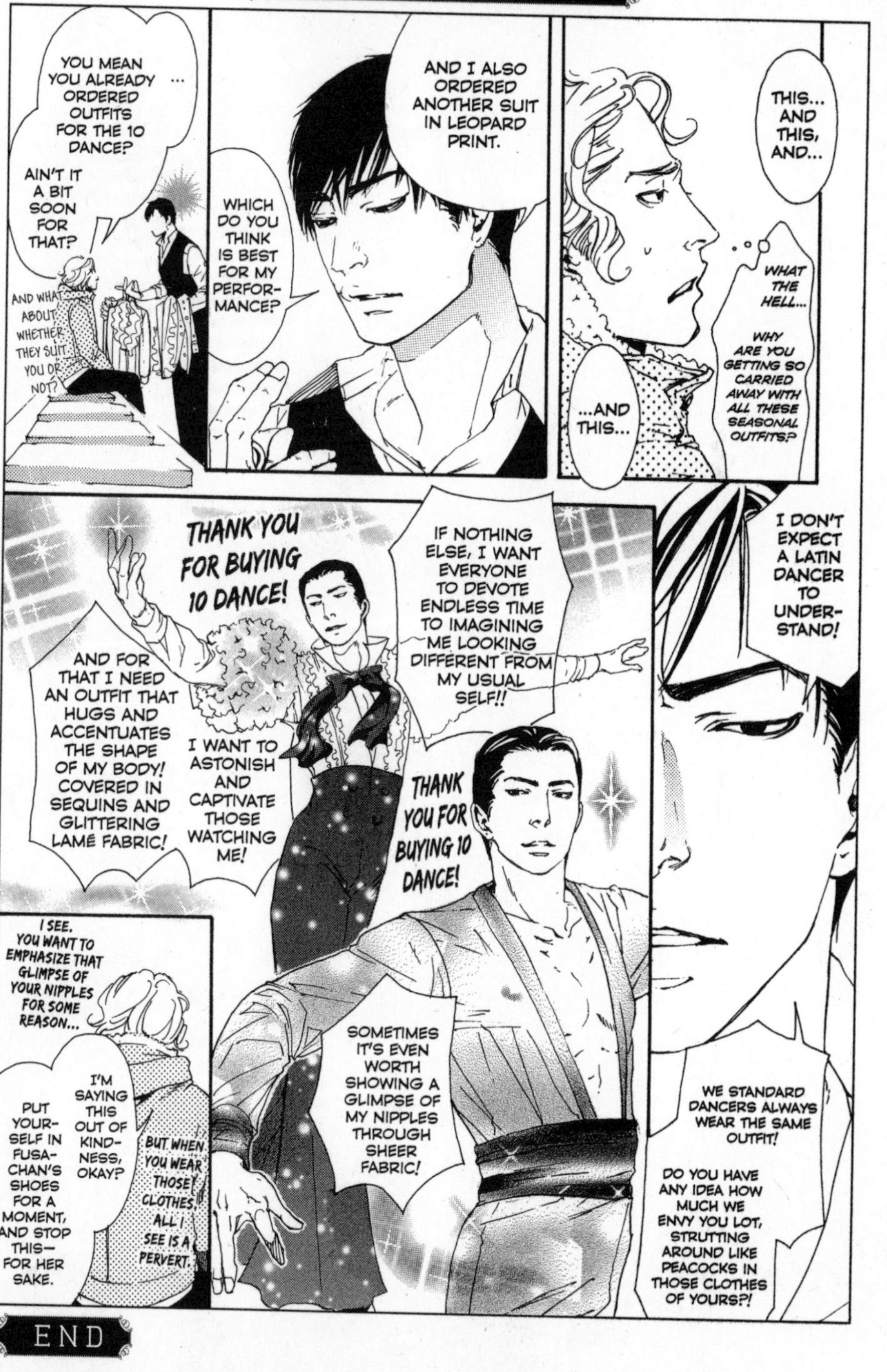
THIS... AND THIS, AND...
...AND THIS...
WHAT THE HELL... WHY ARE YOU GETTING SO CARRIED AWAY WITH ALL THESE SEASONAL OUTFITS?
AND I ALSO ORDERED ANOTHER SUIT IN LEOPARD PRINT.
WHICH DO YOU THINK IS BEST FOR MY PERFORMANCE?
YOU MEAN YOU ALREADY ORDERED OUTFITS FOR THE 10 DANCE?
...
AIN'T IT A BIT SOON FOR THAT?
AND WHAT ABOUT WHETHER THEY SUIT YOU OR NOT?
I DON'T EXPECT A LATIN DANCER TO UNDERSTAND!
WE STANDARD DANCERS ALWAYS WEAR THE SAME OUTFIT!
DO YOU HAVE ANY IDEA HOW MUCH WE ENVY YOU LOT, STRUTTING AROUND LIKE PEACOCKS IN THOSE CLOTHES OF YOURS?!
IF NOTHING ELSE, I WANT EVERYONE TO DEVOTE ENDLESS TIME TO IMAGINING ME LOOKING DIFFERENT FROM MY USUAL SELF!!
THANK YOU FOR BUYING 10 DANCE!
AND FOR THAT I NEED AN OUTFIT THAT HUGS AND ACCENTUATES THE SHAPE OF MY BODY! COVERED IN SEQUINS AND GLITTERING LAMÉ FABRIC!
I WANT TO ASTONISH AND CAPTIVATE THOSE WATCHING ME!
THANK YOU FOR BUYING 10 DANCE!
SOMETIMES IT'S EVEN WORTH SHOWING A GLIMPSE OF MY NIPPLES THROUGH SHEER FABRIC!
I SEE. YOU WANT TO EMPHASIZE THAT GLIMPSE OF YOUR NIPPLES FOR SOME REASON...
I'M SAYING THIS OUT OF KINDNESS, OKAY?
BUT WHEN YOU WEAR THOSE CLOTHES, ALL I SEE IS A PERVERT.
PUT YOURSELF IN FUSA-CHAN'S SHOES FOR A MOMENT, AND STOP THIS— FOR HER SAKE.

END

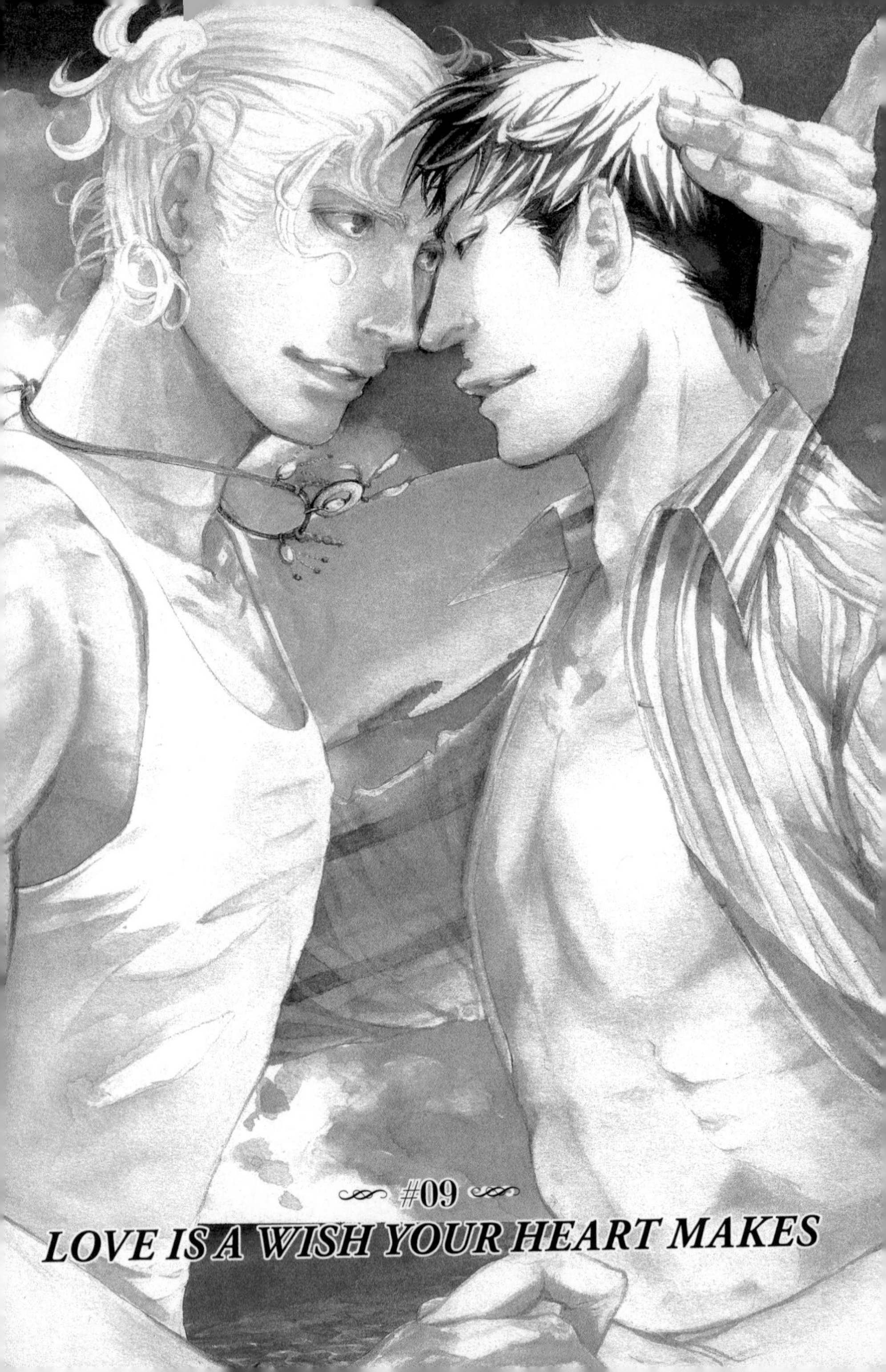
#09
LOVE IS A WISH YOUR HEART MAKES

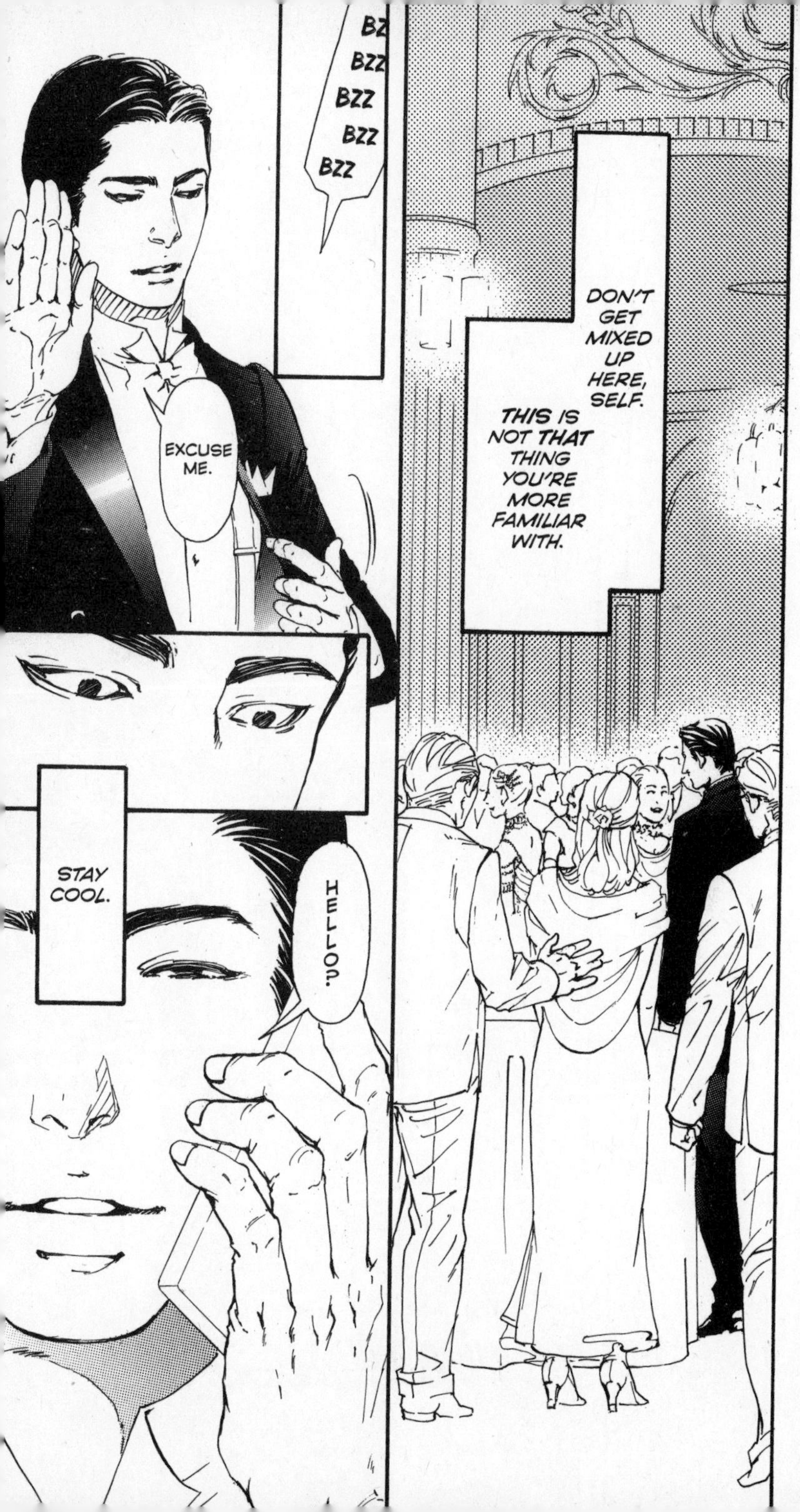
DON'T GET MIXED UP HERE, SELF.
THIS IS NOT THAT THING YOU'RE MORE FAMILIAR WITH.
BZZ BZZ BZZ BZZ BZZ
EXCUSE ME.
HELLO?
STAY COOL.

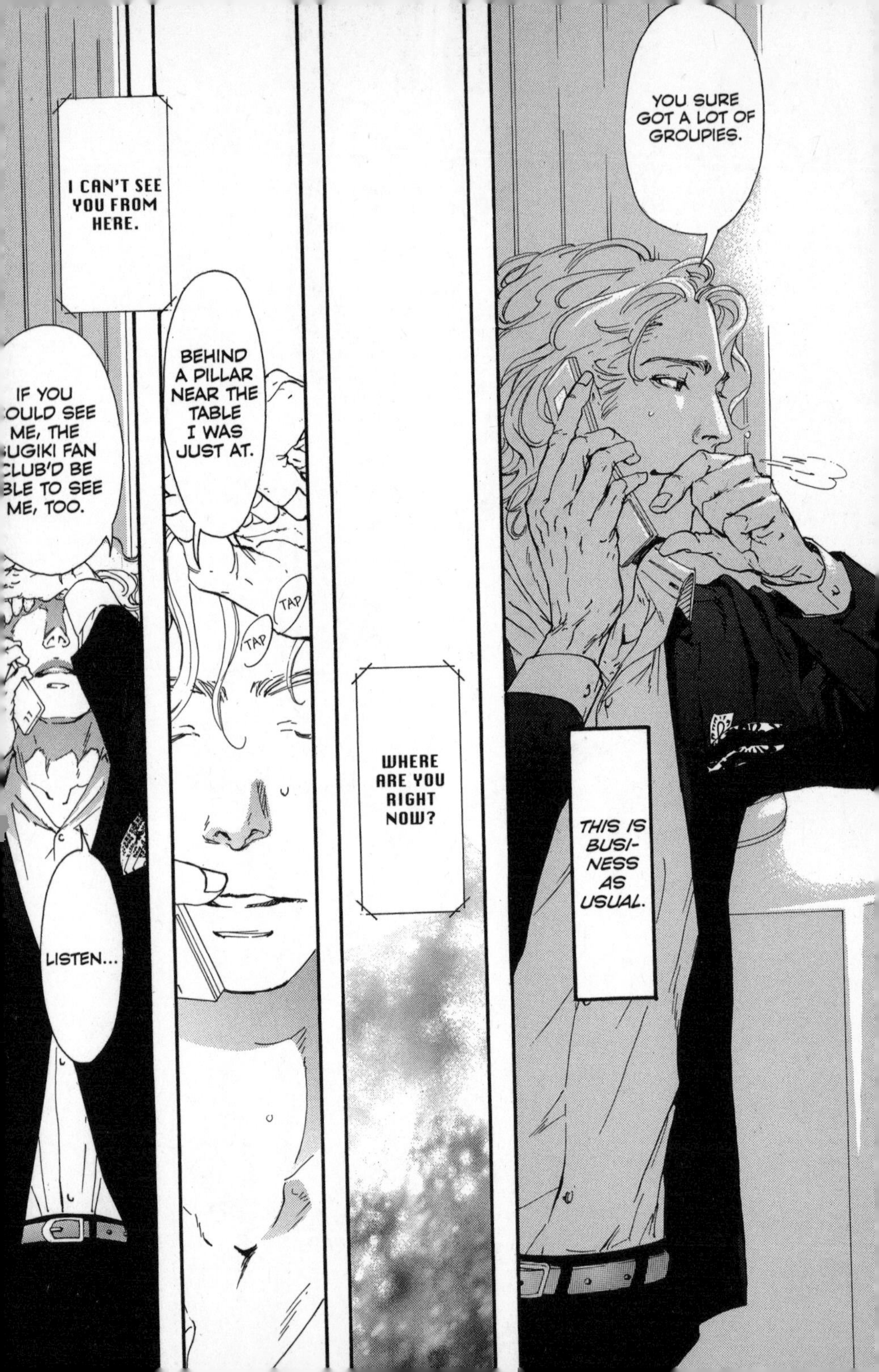

YOU SURE GOT A LOT OF GROUPIES.
THIS IS BUSINESS AS USUAL.
WHERE ARE YOU RIGHT NOW?
BEHIND A PILLAR NEAR THE TABLE I WAS JUST AT.
TAP
TAP
I CAN'T SEE YOU FROM HERE.
IF YOU OULD SEE ME, THE UGIKI FAN CLUB'D BE BLE TO SEE ME, TOO.
LISTEN...

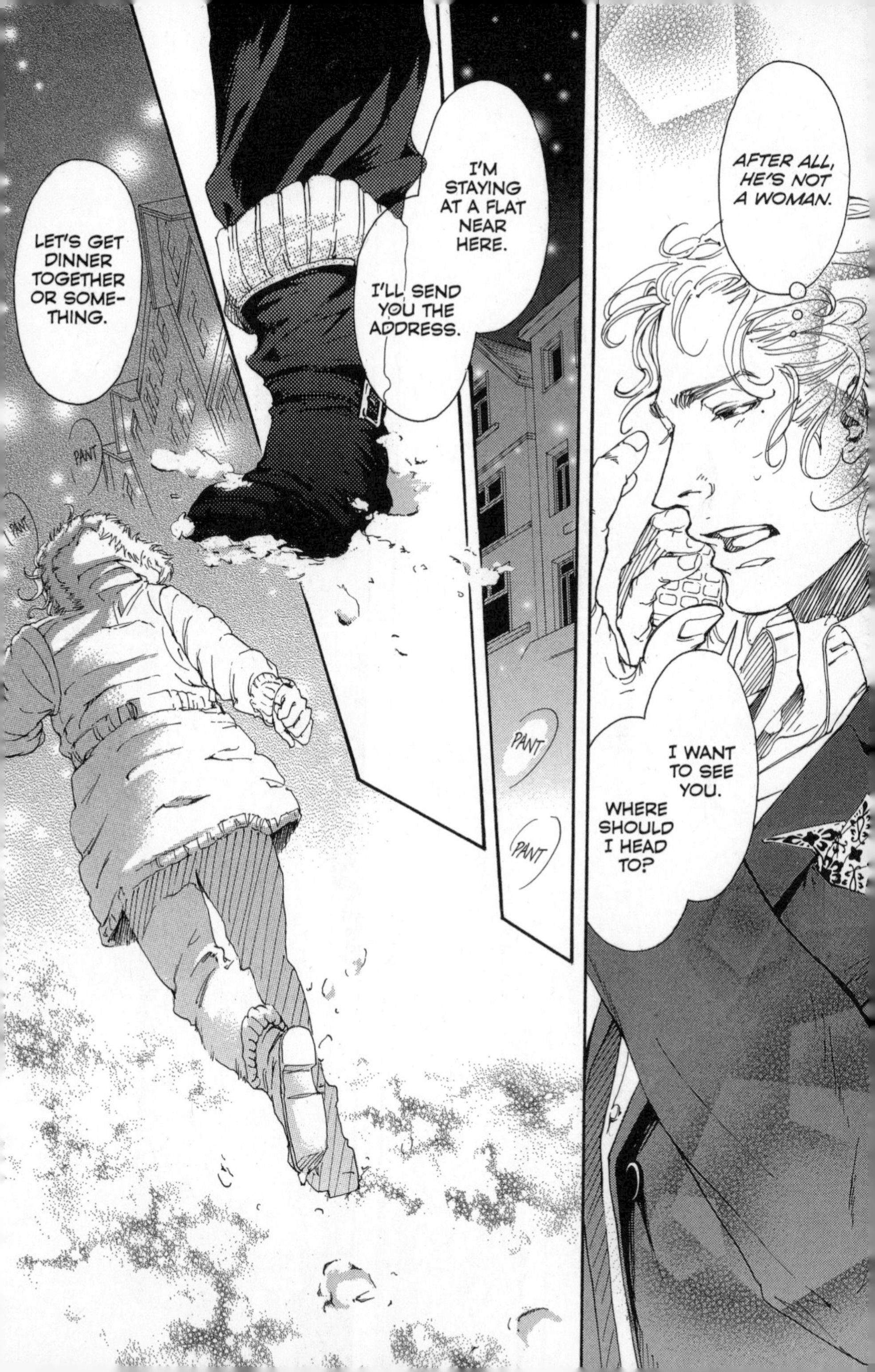
AFTER ALL, HE'S NOT A WOMAN.
I WANT TO SEE YOU.
WHERE SHOULD I HEAD TO?
I'M STAYING AT A FLAT NEAR HERE.
I'LL SEND YOU THE ADDRESS.
PANT
PANT
LET'S GET DINNER TOGETHER OR SOME-THING.
PANT
PANT

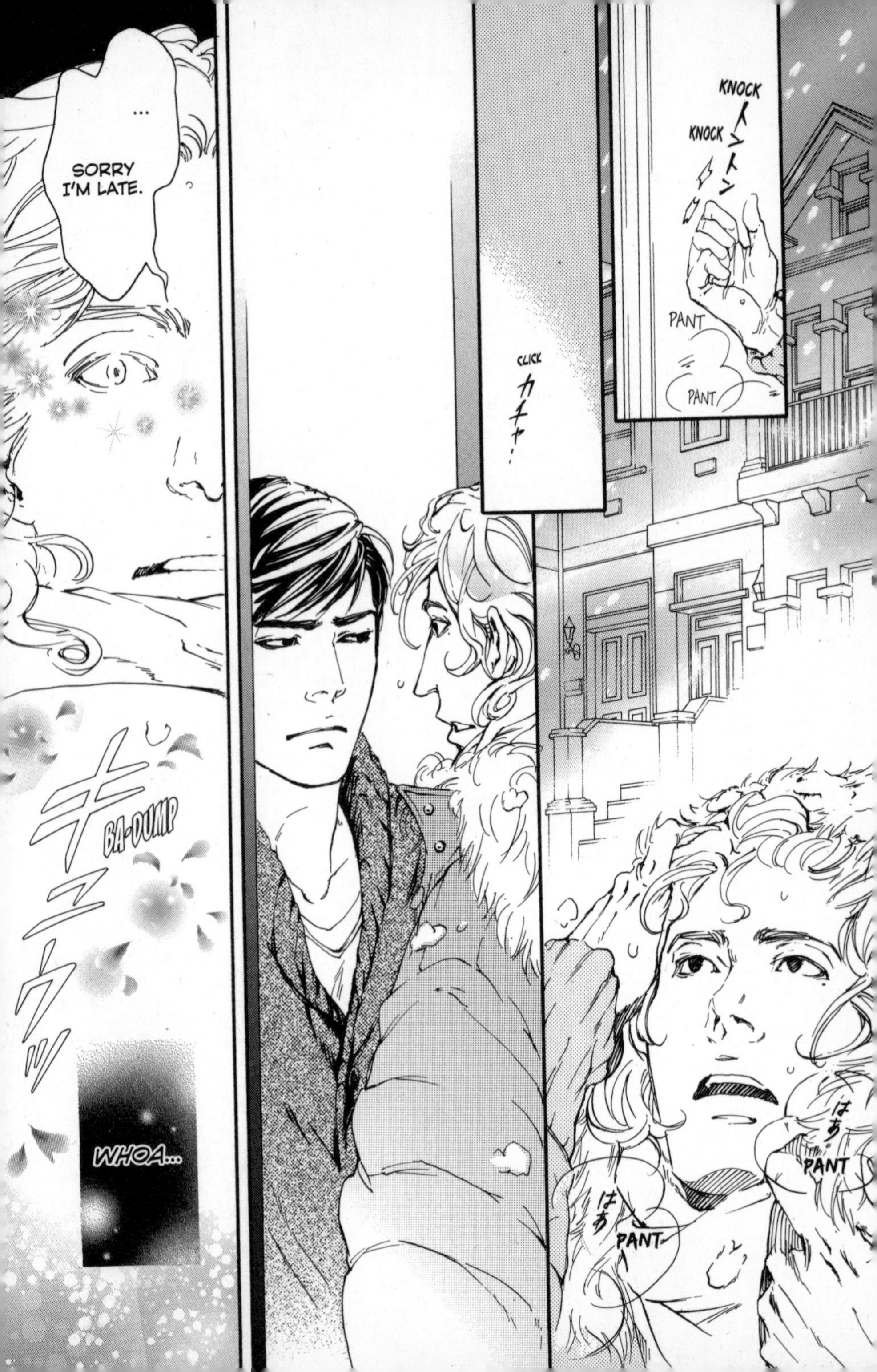
KNOCK
KNOCK
PANT
PANT
PANT
PANT
CLICK
カチャ!
...
SORRY I'M LATE.
BA-DUMP
WHOA...

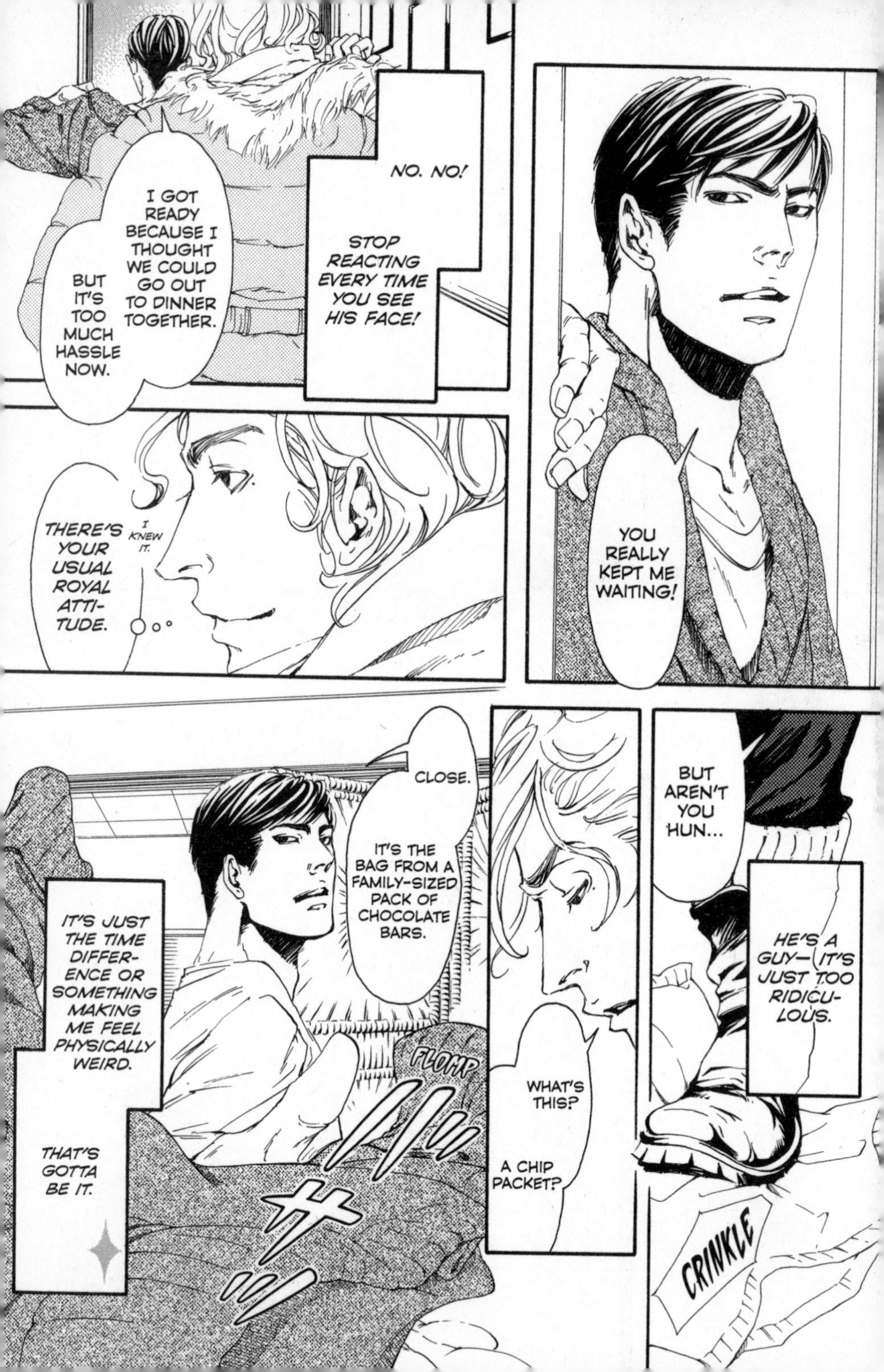
YOU REALLY KEPT ME WAITING!
NO. NO!
STOP REACTING EVERY TIME YOU SEE HIS FACE!
I GOT READY BECAUSE I THOUGHT WE COULD GO OUT TO DINNER TOGETHER.
BUT IT'S TOO MUCH HASSLE NOW.
I KNEW IT.
THERE'S YOUR USUAL ROYAL ATTI-TUDE.
BUT AREN'T YOU HUN...
HE'S A GUY—IT'S JUST TOO RIDICU-LOUS.
CRINKLE
WHAT'S THIS?
A CHIP PACKET?
CLOSE.
IT'S THE BAG FROM A FAMILY-SIZED PACK OF CHOCOLATE BARS.
IT'S JUST THE TIME DIFFER-ENCE OR SOMETHING MAKING ME FEEL PHYSICALLY WEIRD.
FLOMP
THAT'S GOTTA BE IT.

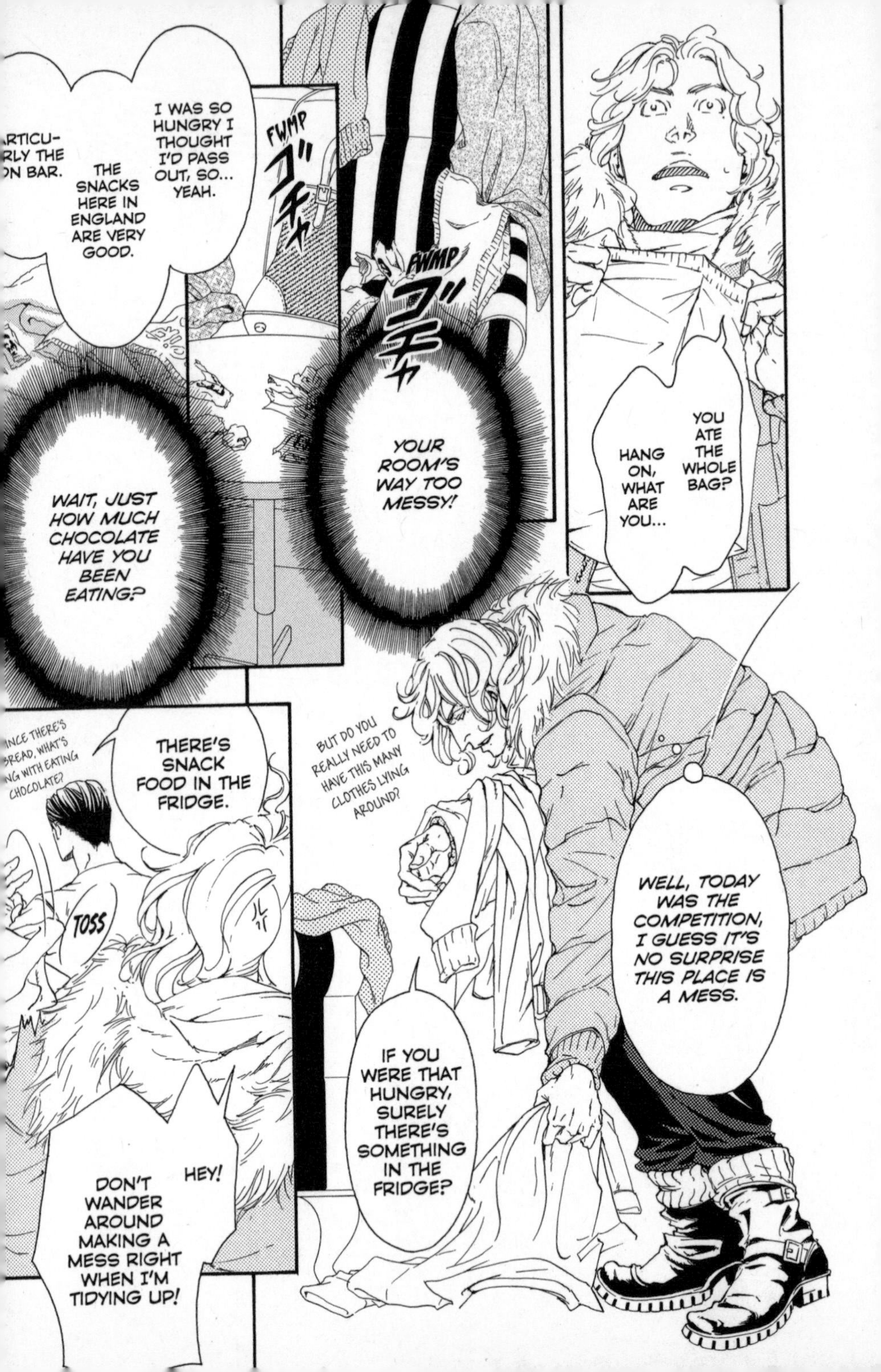
HANG ON, WHAT ARE YOU...
YOU ATE THE WHOLE BAG?
FWMP
FWMP
YOUR ROOM'S WAY TOO MESSY!
I WAS SO HUNGRY I THOUGHT I'D PASS OUT, SO... YEAH.
THE SNACKS HERE IN ENGLAND ARE VERY GOOD.
ARTICU-RLY THE ON BAR.
WAIT, JUST HOW MUCH CHOCOLATE HAVE YOU BEEN EATING?
WELL, TODAY WAS THE COMPETITION, I GUESS IT'S NO SURPRISE THIS PLACE IS A MESS.
BUT DO YOU REALLY NEED TO HAVE THIS MANY CLOTHES LYING AROUND?
IF YOU WERE THAT HUNGRY, SURELY THERE'S SOMETHING IN THE FRIDGE?
THERE'S SNACK FOOD IN THE FRIDGE.
NCE THERE'S BREAD, WHAT'S NG WITH EATING CHOCOLATE?
TOSS
HEY!
DON'T WANDER AROUND MAKING A MESS RIGHT WHEN I'M TIDYING UP!

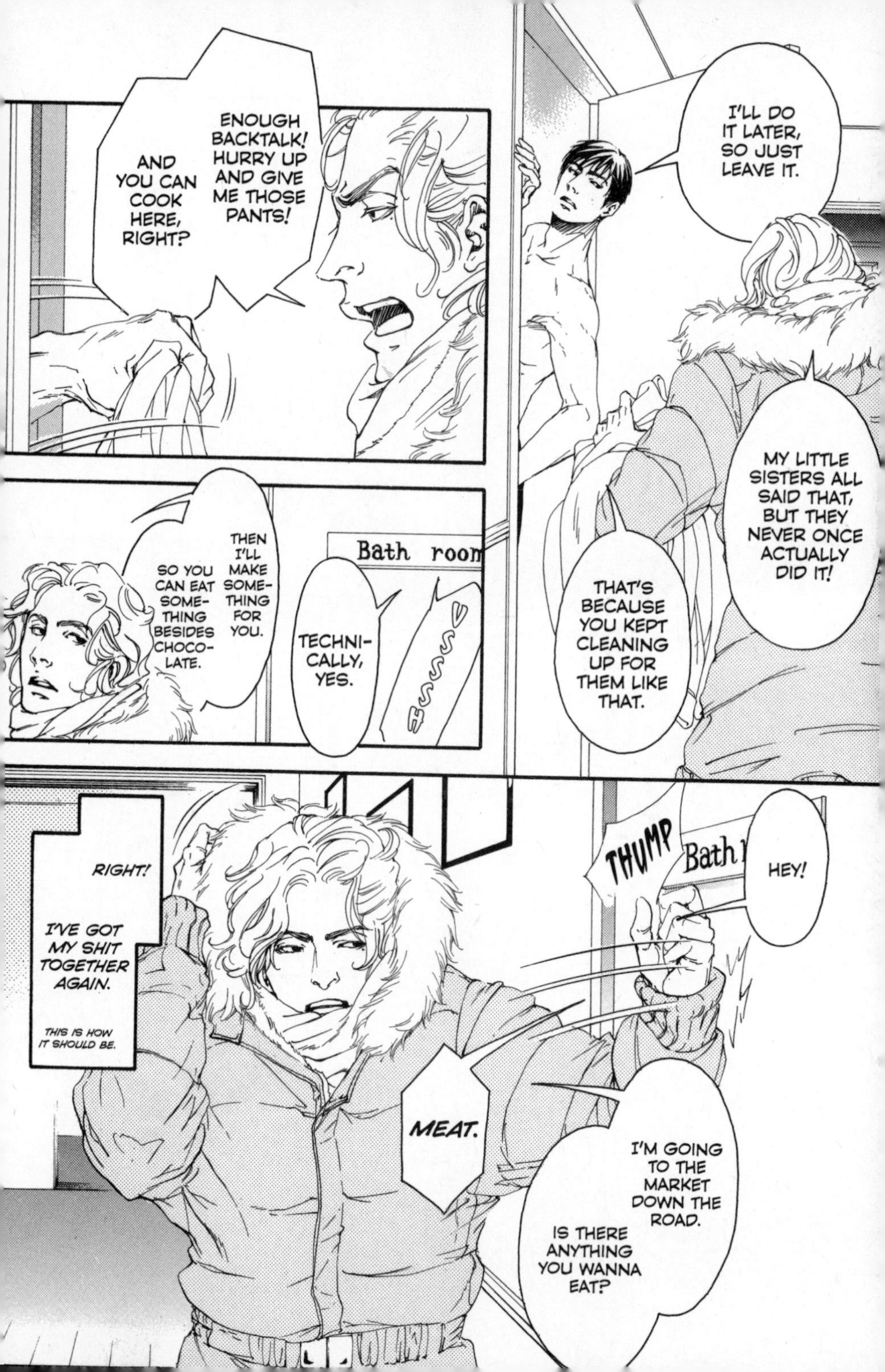
I'LL DO IT LATER, SO JUST LEAVE IT.
MY LITTLE SISTERS ALL SAID THAT, BUT THEY NEVER ONCE ACTUALLY DID IT!
THAT'S BECAUSE YOU KEPT CLEANING UP FOR THEM LIKE THAT.
ENOUGH BACKTALK! HURRY UP AND GIVE ME THOSE PANTS!
AND YOU CAN COOK HERE, RIGHT?
Bath room
TECHNICALLY, YES.
HSSSS
THEN I'LL MAKE SOMETHING FOR YOU.
SO YOU CAN EAT SOMETHING BESIDES CHOCOLATE.
HEY!
THUMP
Bath r
I'M GOING TO THE MARKET DOWN THE ROAD.
IS THERE ANYTHING YOU WANNA EAT?
MEAT.
RIGHT!
I'VE GOT MY SHIT TOGETHER AGAIN.
THIS IS HOW IT SHOULD BE.

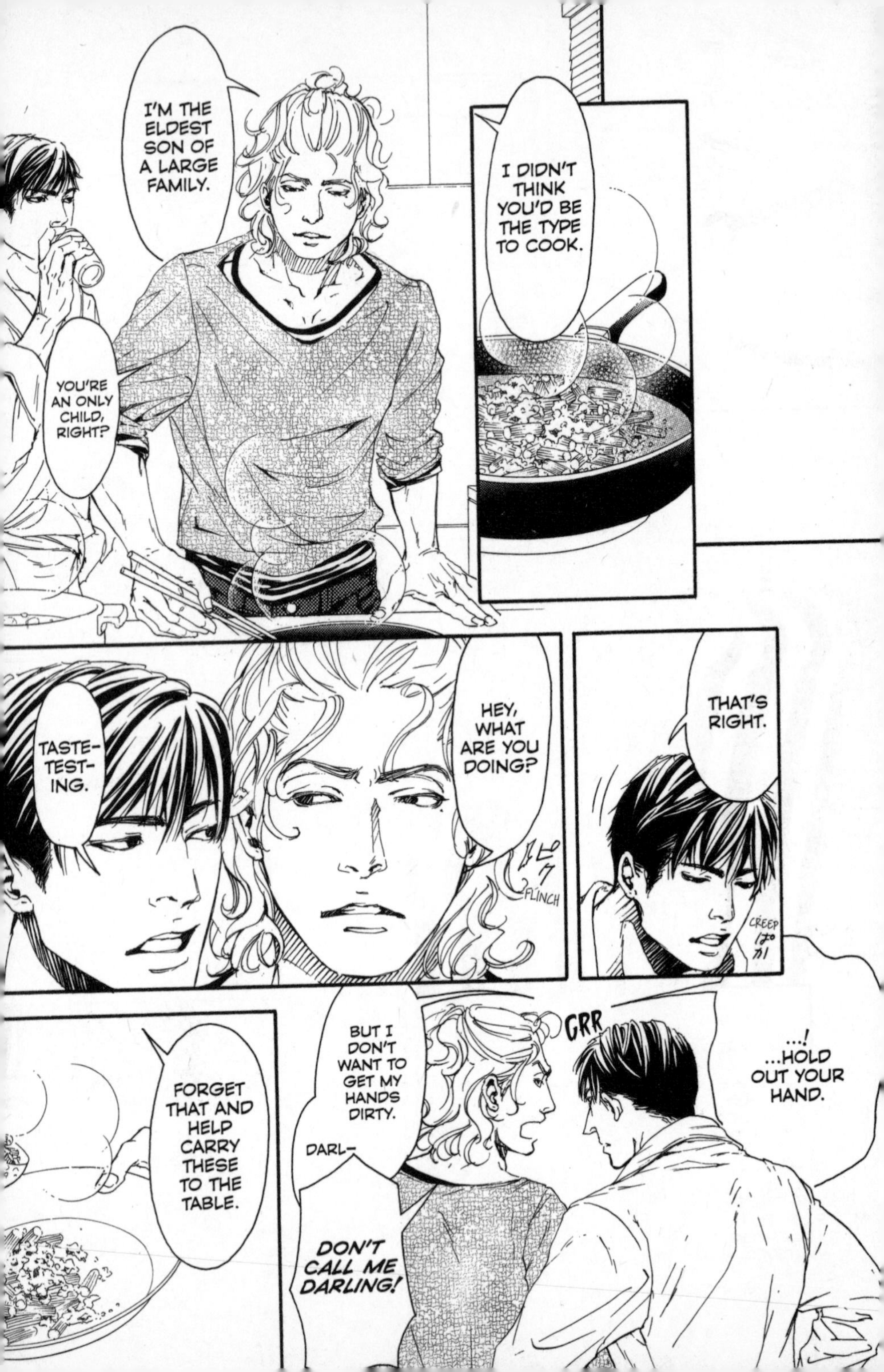
I DIDN'T THINK YOU'D BE THE TYPE TO COOK.
I'M THE ELDEST SON OF A LARGE FAMILY.
YOU'RE AN ONLY CHILD, RIGHT?
THAT'S RIGHT.
CREEP
HEY, WHAT ARE YOU DOING?
FLINCH
TASTE-TESTING.
...! ...HOLD OUT YOUR HAND.
GRR
BUT I DON'T WANT TO GET MY HANDS DIRTY.
DARL—
DON'T CALL ME DARLING!
FORGET THAT AND HELP CARRY THESE TO THE TABLE.

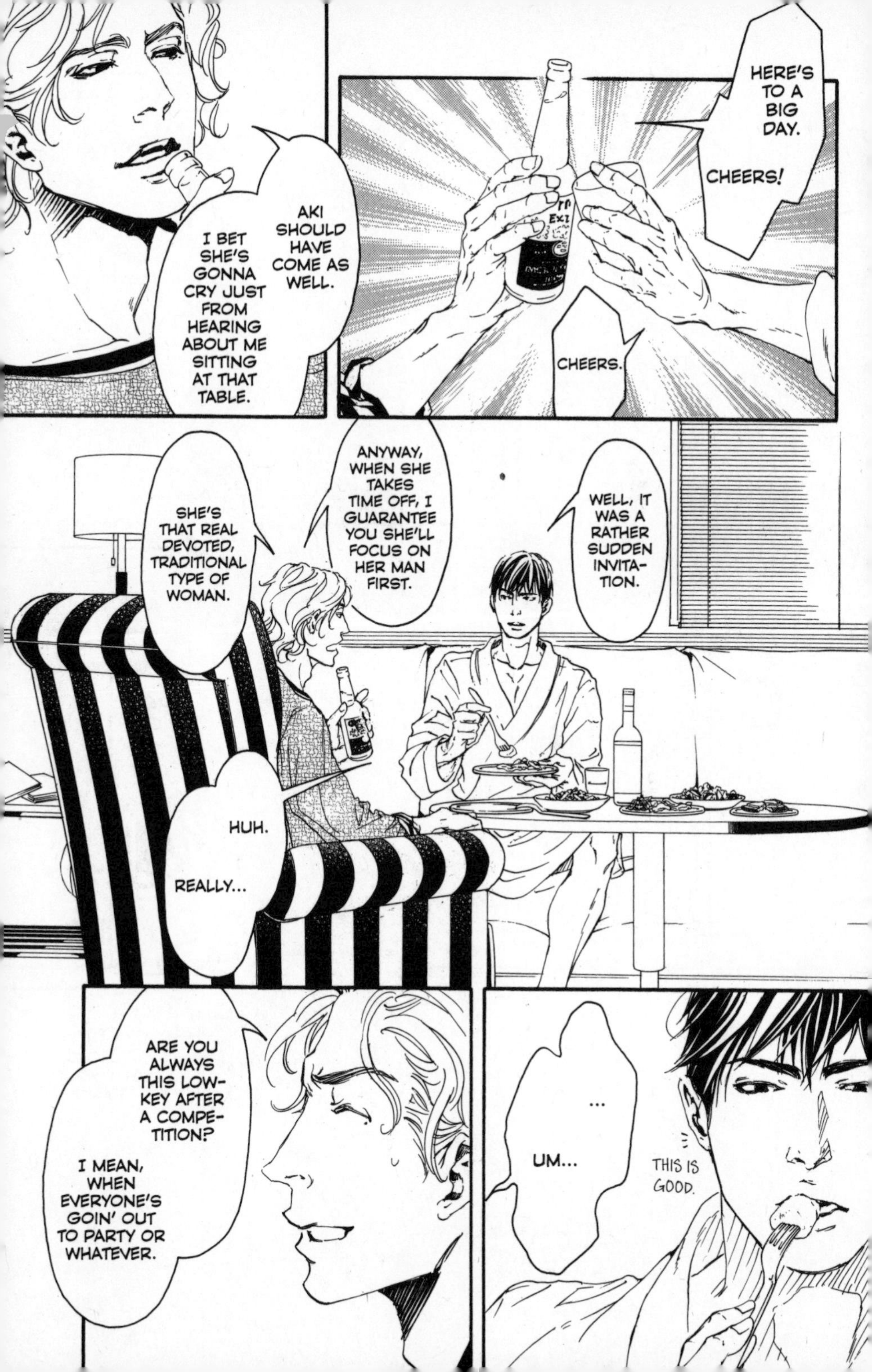
HERE'S TO A BIG DAY.
CHEERS!
CHEERS.
AKI SHOULD HAVE COME AS WELL.
I BET SHE'S GONNA CRY JUST FROM HEARING ABOUT ME SITTING AT THAT TABLE.
WELL, IT WAS A RATHER SUDDEN INVITATION.
ANYWAY, WHEN SHE TAKES TIME OFF, I GUARANTEE YOU SHE'LL FOCUS ON HER MAN FIRST.
SHE'S THAT REAL DEVOTED, TRADITIONAL TYPE OF WOMAN.
HUH.
REALLY...
...
UM...
THIS IS GOOD.
ARE YOU ALWAYS THIS LOW-KEY AFTER A COMPETITION?
I MEAN, WHEN EVERYONE'S GOIN' OUT TO PARTY OR WHATEVER.

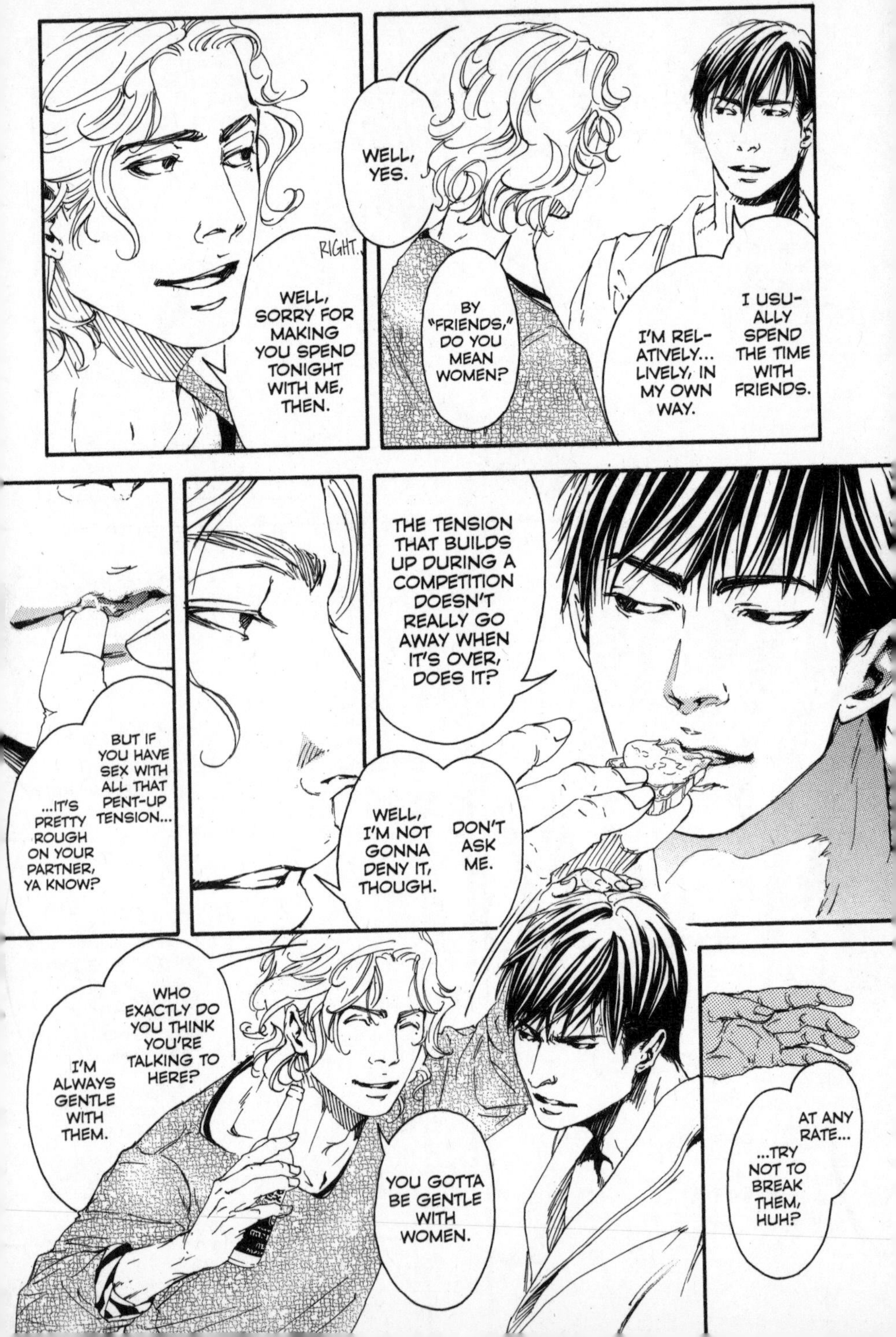
I USU-ALLY SPEND THE TIME WITH FRIENDS.
I'M REL-ATIVELY... LIVELY, IN MY OWN WAY.
BY "FRIENDS," DO YOU MEAN WOMEN?
WELL, YES.
RIGHT.
WELL, SORRY FOR MAKING YOU SPEND TONIGHT WITH ME, THEN.
THE TENSION THAT BUILDS UP DURING A COMPETITION DOESN'T REALLY GO AWAY WHEN IT'S OVER, DOES IT?
DON'T ASK ME.
WELL, I'M NOT GONNA DENY IT, THOUGH.
BUT IF YOU HAVE SEX WITH ALL THAT PENT-UP TENSION...
...IT'S PRETTY ROUGH ON YOUR PARTNER, YA KNOW?
AT ANY RATE...
...TRY NOT TO BREAK THEM, HUH?
YOU GOTTA BE GENTLE WITH WOMEN.
WHO EXACTLY DO YOU THINK YOU'RE TALKING TO HERE?
I'M ALWAYS GENTLE WITH THEM.

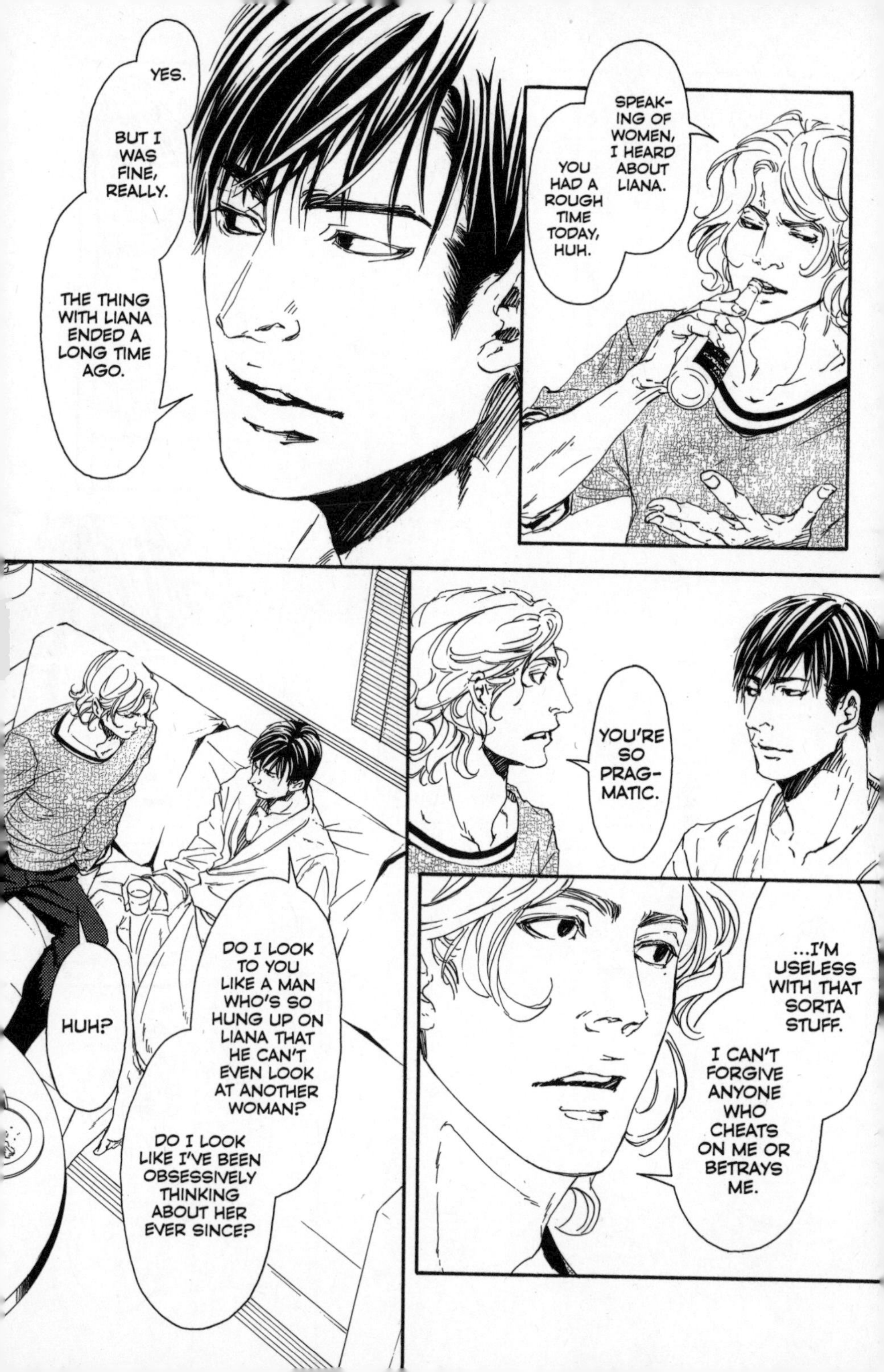
SPEAK-ING OF WOMEN, I HEARD ABOUT LIANA.
YOU HAD A ROUGH TIME TODAY, HUH.
YES.
BUT I WAS FINE, REALLY.
THE THING WITH LIANA ENDED A LONG TIME AGO.
YOU'RE SO PRAG-MATIC.
...I'M USELESS WITH THAT SORTA STUFF.
I CAN'T FORGIVE ANYONE WHO CHEATS ON ME OR BETRAYS ME.
DO I LOOK TO YOU LIKE A MAN WHO'S SO HUNG UP ON LIANA THAT HE CAN'T EVEN LOOK AT ANOTHER WOMAN?
DO I LOOK LIKE I'VE BEEN OBSESSIVELY THINKING ABOUT HER EVER SINCE?
HUH?

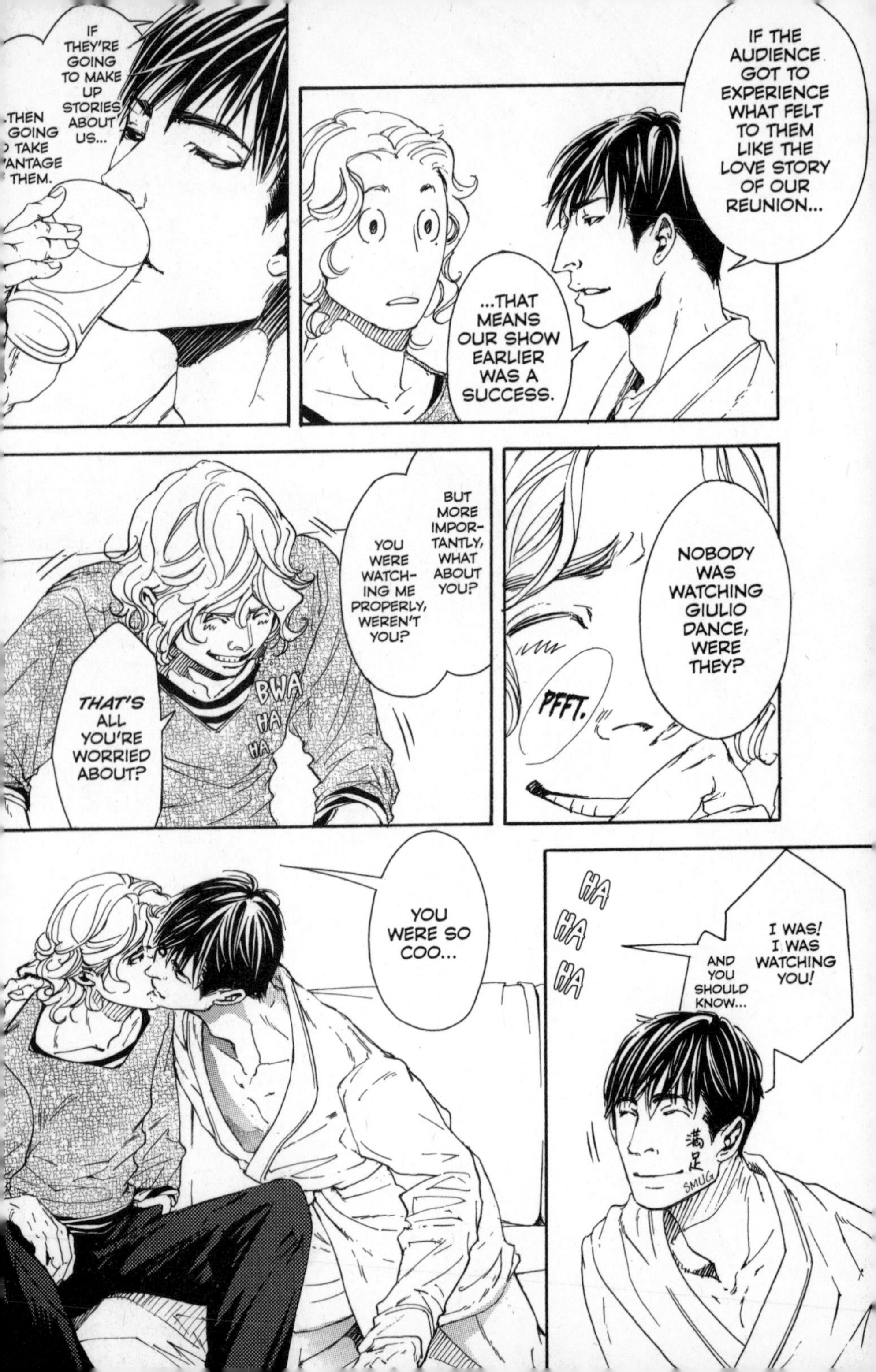
IF THE AUDIENCE GOT TO EXPERIENCE WHAT FELT TO THEM LIKE THE LOVE STORY OF OUR REUNION...
...THAT MEANS OUR SHOW EARLIER WAS A SUCCESS.
IF THEY'RE GOING TO MAKE UP STORIES ABOUT US...
.THEN GOING D TAKE VANTAGE F THEM.
NOBODY WAS WATCHING GIULIO DANCE, WERE THEY?
PFFT.
BUT MORE IMPORTANTLY, WHAT ABOUT YOU?
YOU WERE WATCHING ME PROPERLY, WEREN'T YOU?
BWA HA HA
THAT'S ALL YOU'RE WORRIED ABOUT?
HA HA HA
I WAS! I WAS WATCHING YOU!
AND YOU SHOULD KNOW...
満足
SMUG
YOU WERE SO COO...

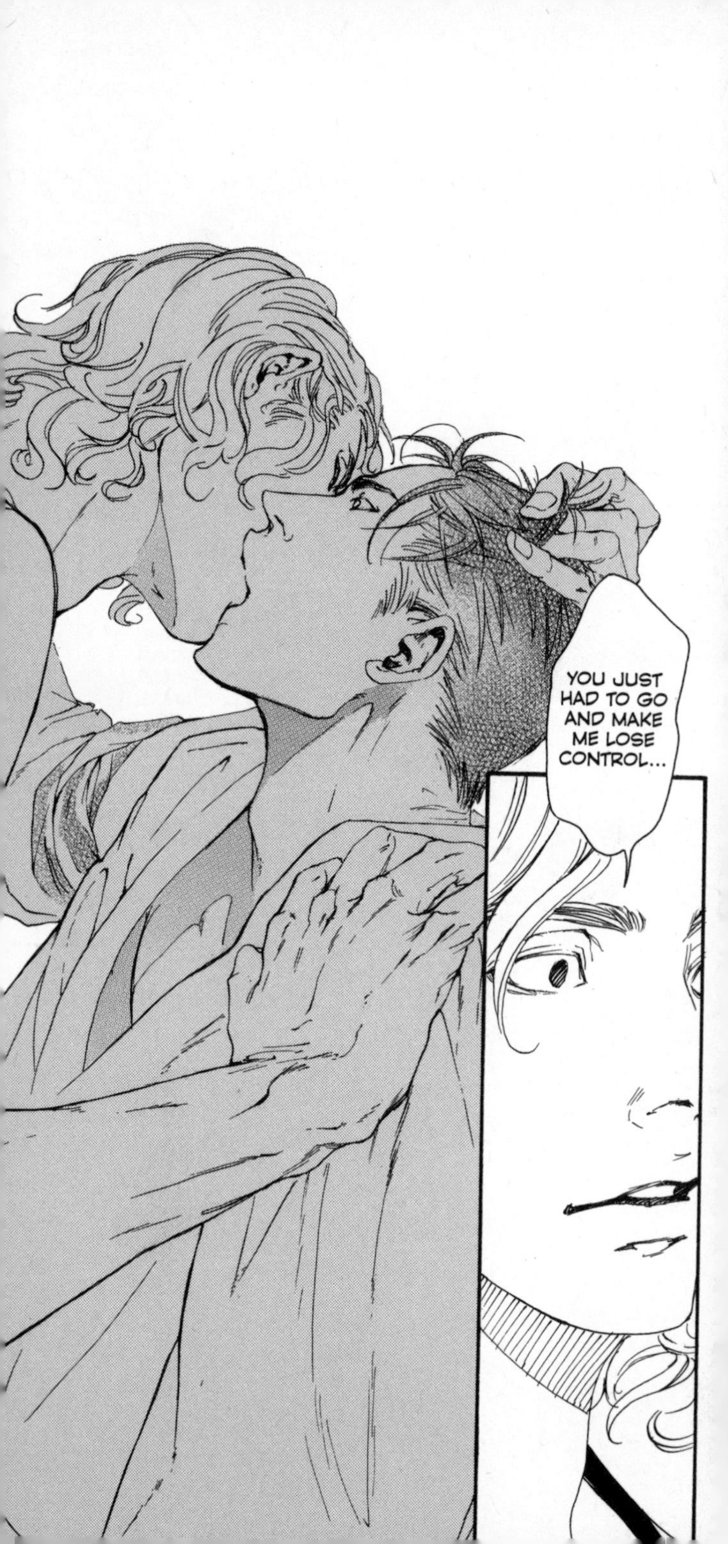
YOU JUST HAD TO GO AND MAKE ME LOSE CONTROL...

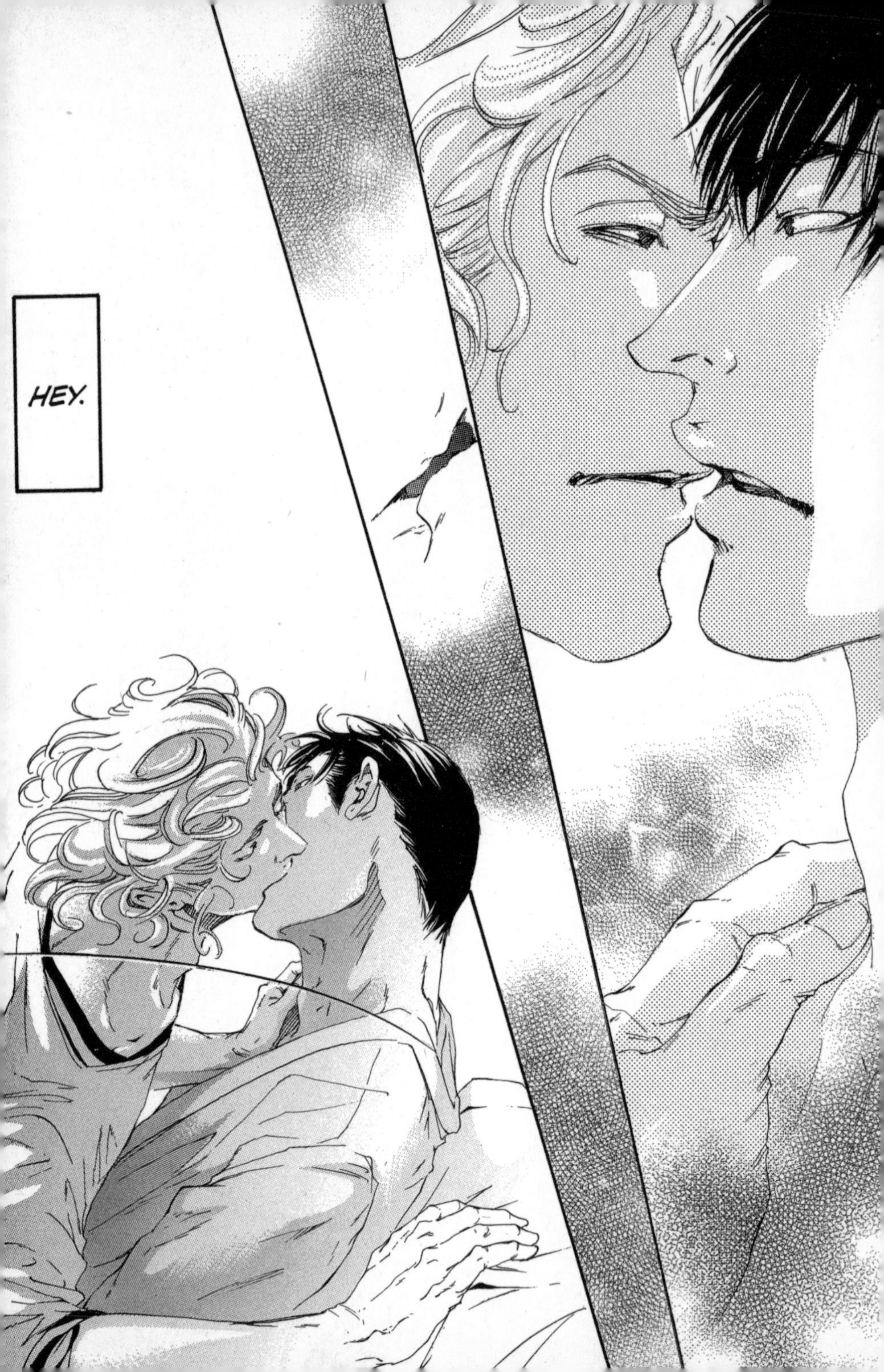
HEY.

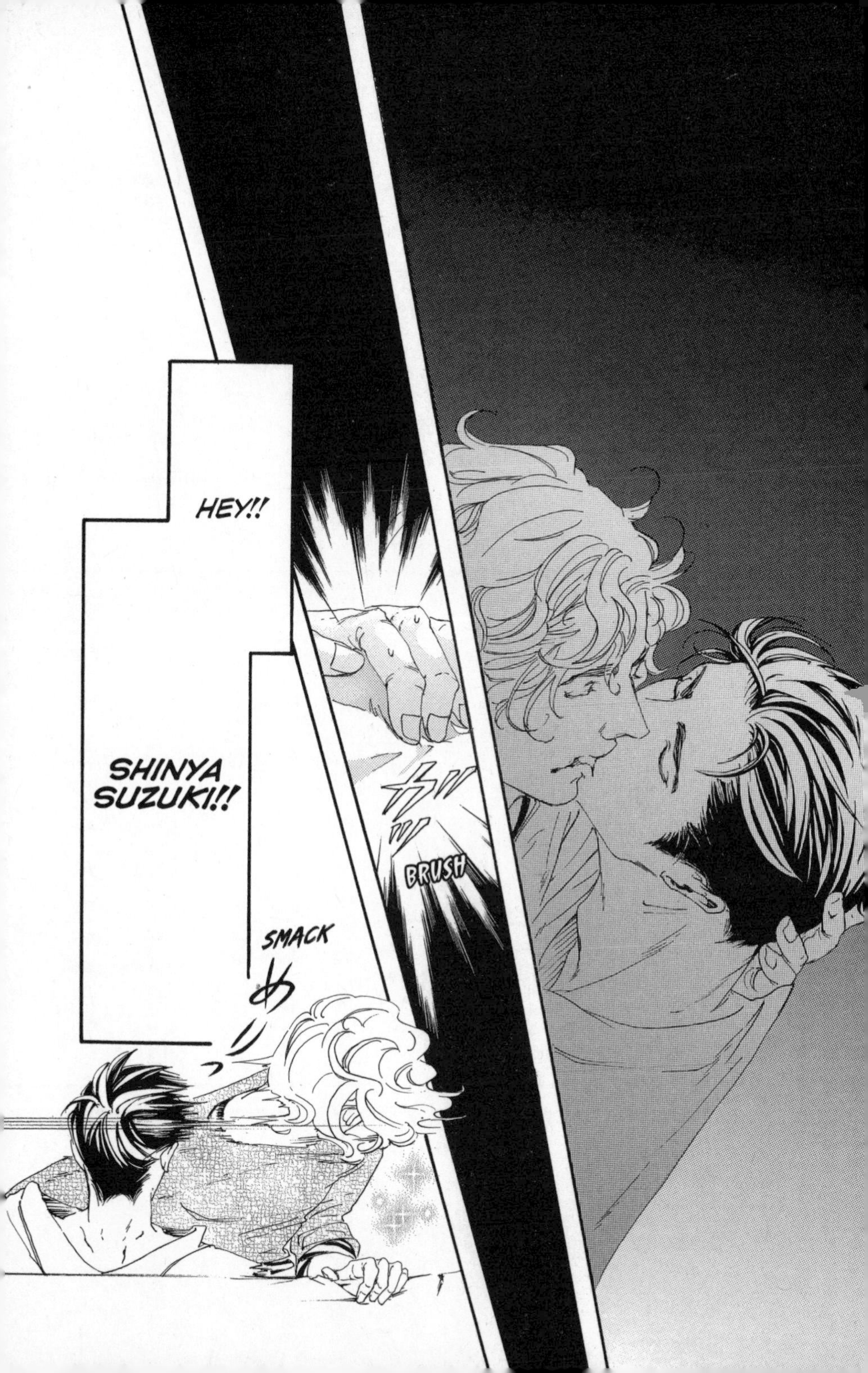
BRUSH
HEY!!
SHINYA SUZUKI!!
SMACK

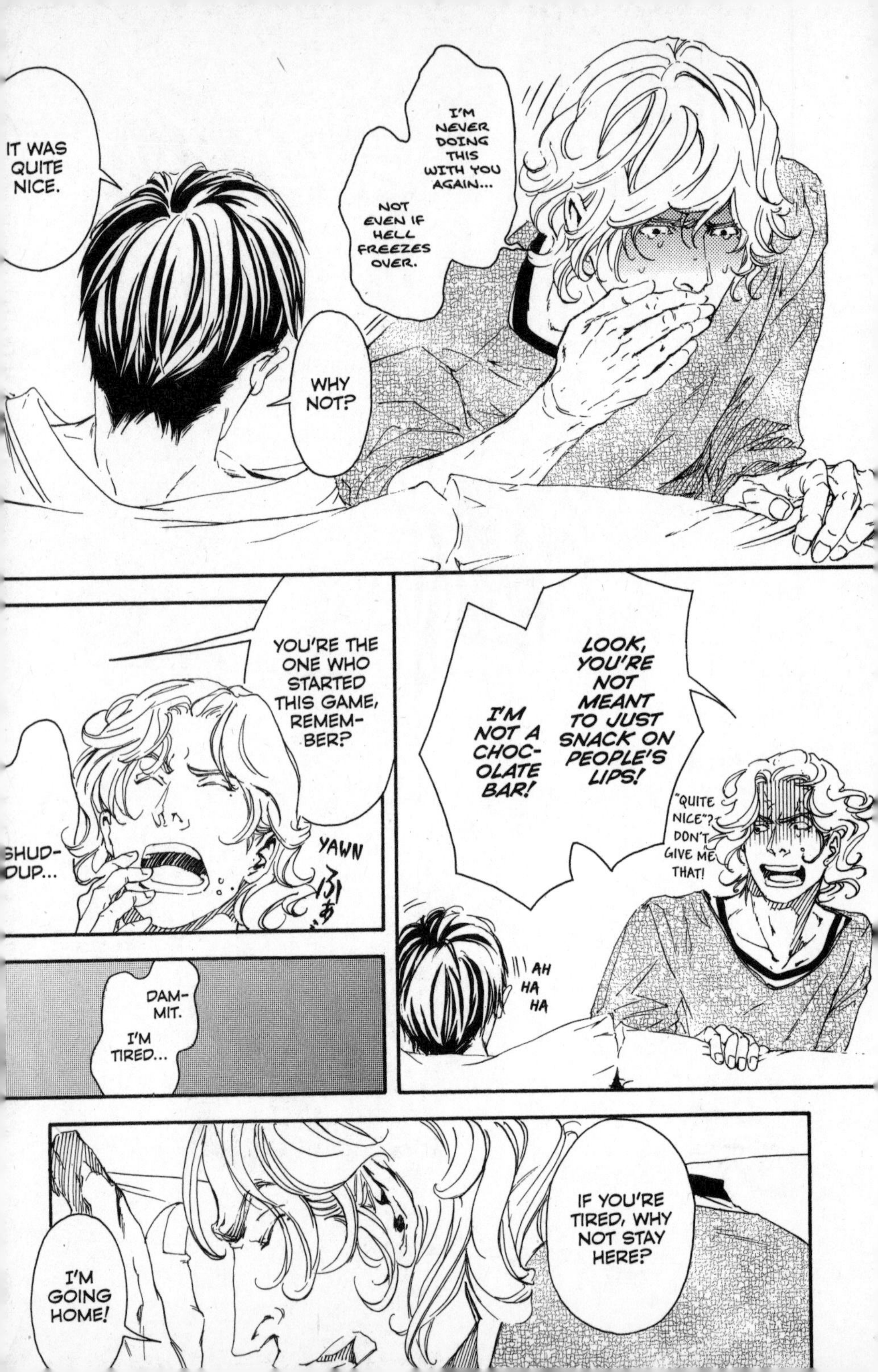
I'M NEVER DOING THIS WITH YOU AGAIN...
NOT EVEN IF HELL FREEZES OVER.
IT WAS QUITE NICE.
WHY NOT?
LOOK, YOU'RE NOT MEANT TO JUST SNACK ON PEOPLE'S LIPS!
I'M NOT A CHOC-OLATE BAR!
"QUITE NICE"? DON'T GIVE ME THAT!
AH HA HA
YOU'RE THE ONE WHO STARTED THIS GAME, REMEM-BER?
YAWN
SHUD-UP...
DAM-MIT.
I'M TIRED...
IF YOU'RE TIRED, WHY NOT STAY HERE?
I'M GOING HOME!

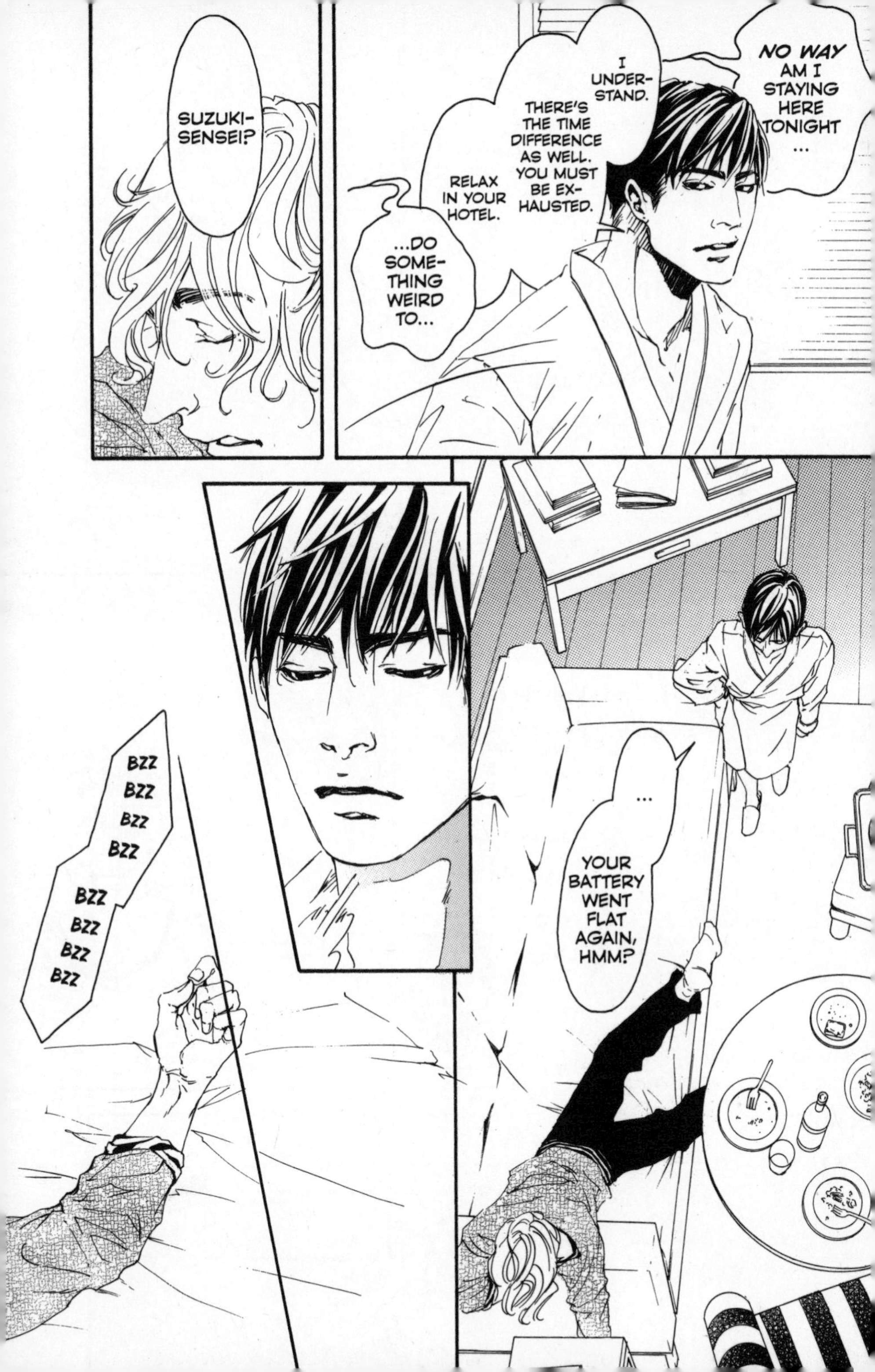
NO WAY AM I STAYING HERE TONIGHT ...
I UNDERSTAND. THERE'S THE TIME DIFFERENCE AS WELL. YOU MUST BE EXHAUSTED. RELAX IN YOUR HOTEL.
...DO SOMETHING WEIRD TO...
SUZUKI-SENSEI?
...
YOUR BATTERY WENT FLAT AGAIN, HMM?
BZZ BZZ BZZ BZZ
BZZ BZZ BZZ BZZ

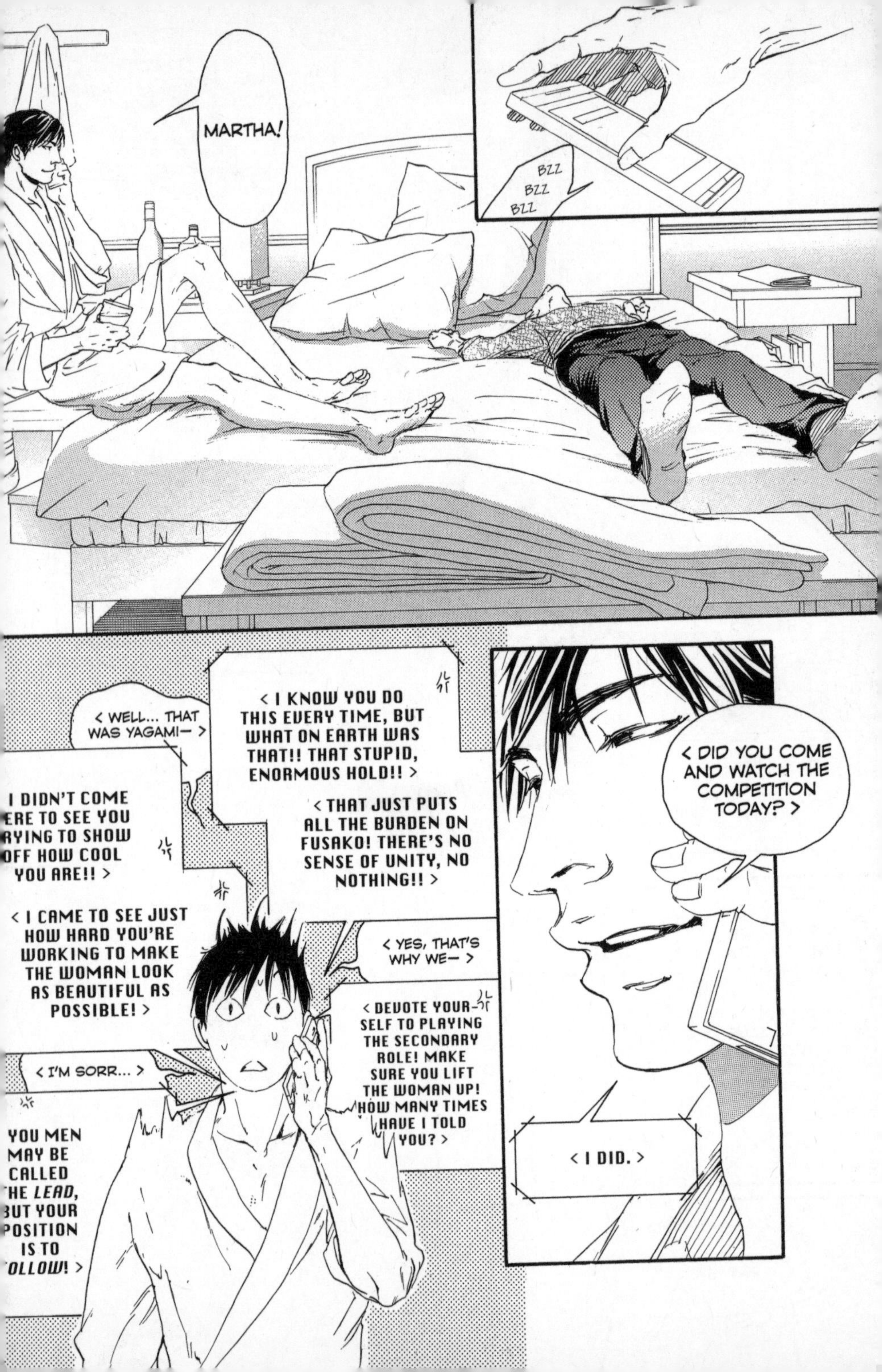
BZZ BZZ BZZ
MARTHA!
< DID YOU COME AND WATCH THE COMPETITION TODAY? >
< I DID. >
< WELL... THAT WAS YAGAMI— >
< I KNOW YOU DO THIS EVERY TIME, BUT WHAT ON EARTH WAS THAT!! THAT STUPID, ENORMOUS HOLD!! >
< THAT JUST PUTS ALL THE BURDEN ON FUSAKO! THERE'S NO SENSE OF UNITY, NO NOTHING!! >
I DIDN'T COME ERE TO SEE YOU RYING TO SHOW OFF HOW COOL YOU ARE!! >
< I CAME TO SEE JUST HOW HARD YOU'RE WORKING TO MAKE THE WOMAN LOOK AS BEAUTIFUL AS POSSIBLE! >
< YES, THAT'S WHY WE— >
< DEVOTE YOUR-SELF TO PLAYING THE SECONDARY ROLE! MAKE SURE YOU LIFT THE WOMAN UP! HOW MANY TIMES HAVE I TOLD YOU? >
< I'M SORR... >
YOU MEN MAY BE CALLED THE *LEAD*, BUT YOUR POSITION IS TO *OLLOW*! >

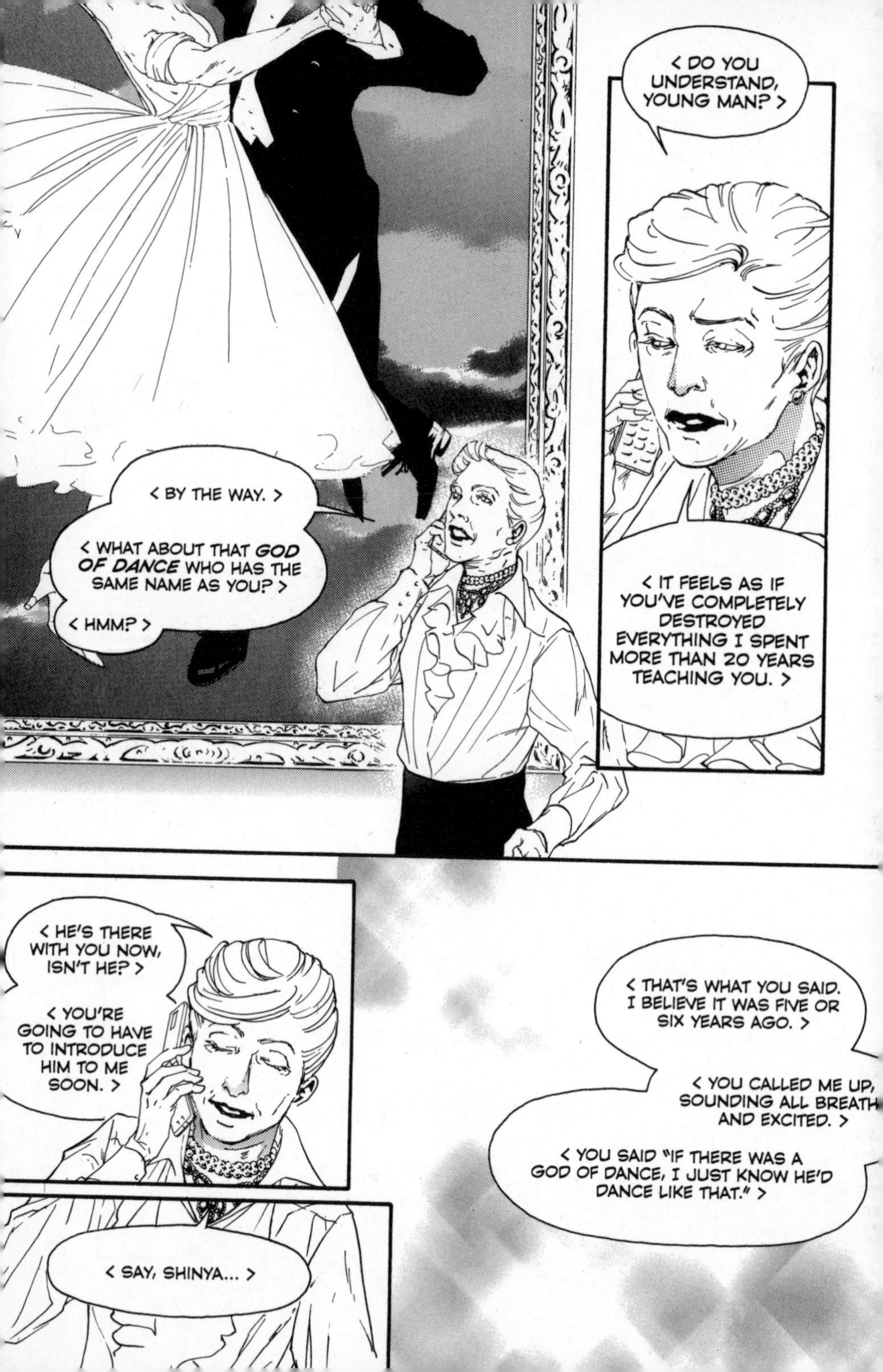
< DO YOU UNDERSTAND, YOUNG MAN? >
< IT FEELS AS IF YOU'VE COMPLETELY DESTROYED EVERYTHING I SPENT MORE THAN 20 YEARS TEACHING YOU. >
< BY THE WAY. >
< WHAT ABOUT THAT *GOD OF DANCE* WHO HAS THE SAME NAME AS YOU? >
< HMM? >
< THAT'S WHAT YOU SAID. I BELIEVE IT WAS FIVE OR SIX YEARS AGO. >
< YOU CALLED ME UP, SOUNDING ALL BREATH AND EXCITED. >
< YOU SAID "IF THERE WAS A GOD OF DANCE, I JUST KNOW HE'D DANCE LIKE THAT." >
< HE'S THERE WITH YOU NOW, ISN'T HE? >
< YOU'RE GOING TO HAVE TO INTRODUCE HIM TO ME SOON. >
< SAY, SHINYA... >

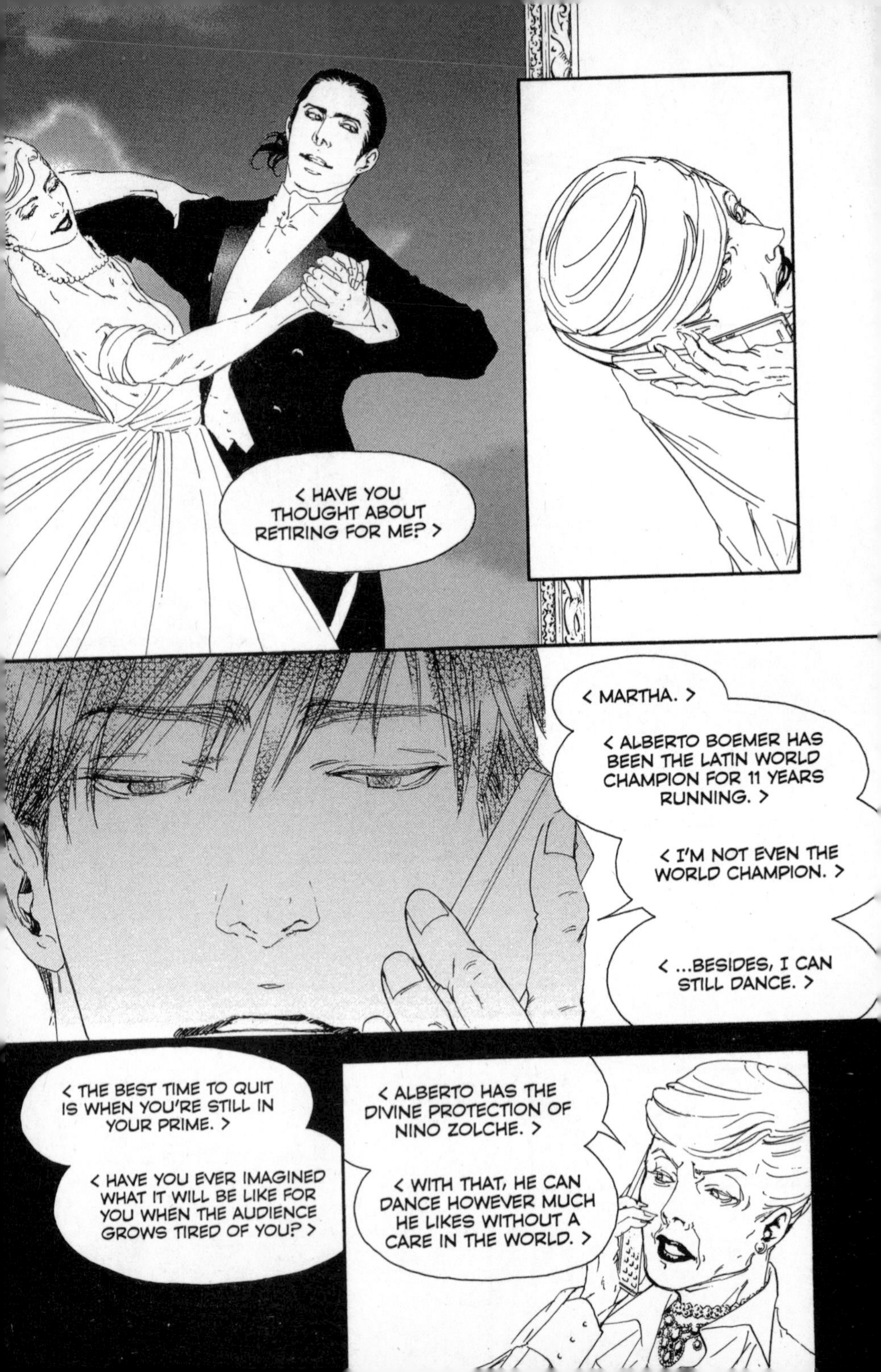
< HAVE YOU THOUGHT ABOUT RETIRING FOR ME? >
< MARTHA. >
< ALBERTO BOEMER HAS BEEN THE LATIN WORLD CHAMPION FOR 11 YEARS RUNNING. >
< I'M NOT EVEN THE WORLD CHAMPION. >
< ...BESIDES, I CAN STILL DANCE. >
< ALBERTO HAS THE DIVINE PROTECTION OF NINO ZOLCHE. >
< WITH THAT, HE CAN DANCE HOWEVER MUCH HE LIKES WITHOUT A CARE IN THE WORLD. >
< THE BEST TIME TO QUIT IS WHEN YOU'RE STILL IN YOUR PRIME. >
< HAVE YOU EVER IMAGINED WHAT IT WILL BE LIKE FOR YOU WHEN THE AUDIENCE GROWS TIRED OF YOU? >

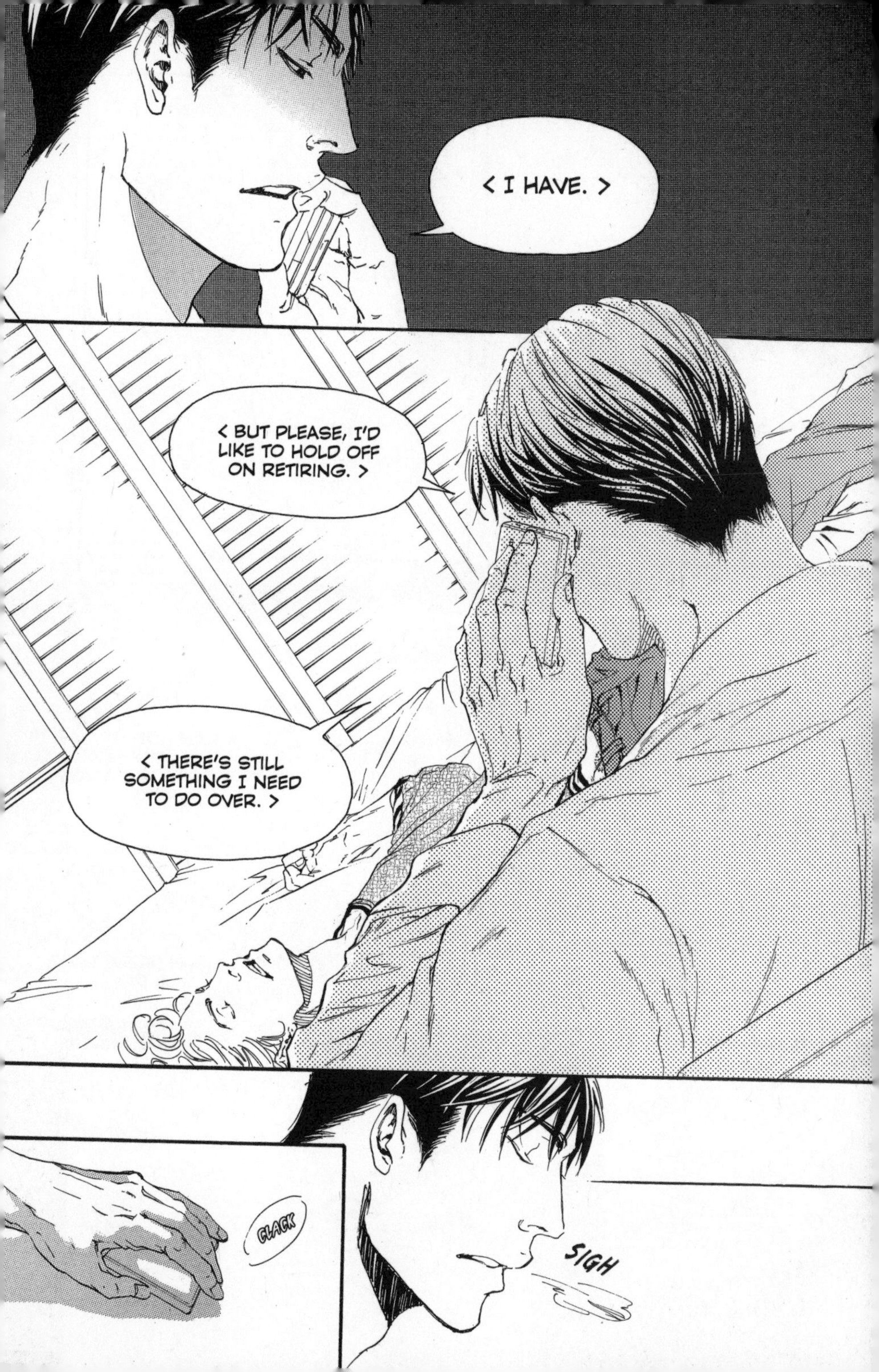
< I HAVE. >
< BUT PLEASE, I'D LIKE TO HOLD OFF ON RETIRING. >
< THERE'S STILL SOMETHING I NEED TO DO OVER. >
SIGH
CLACK

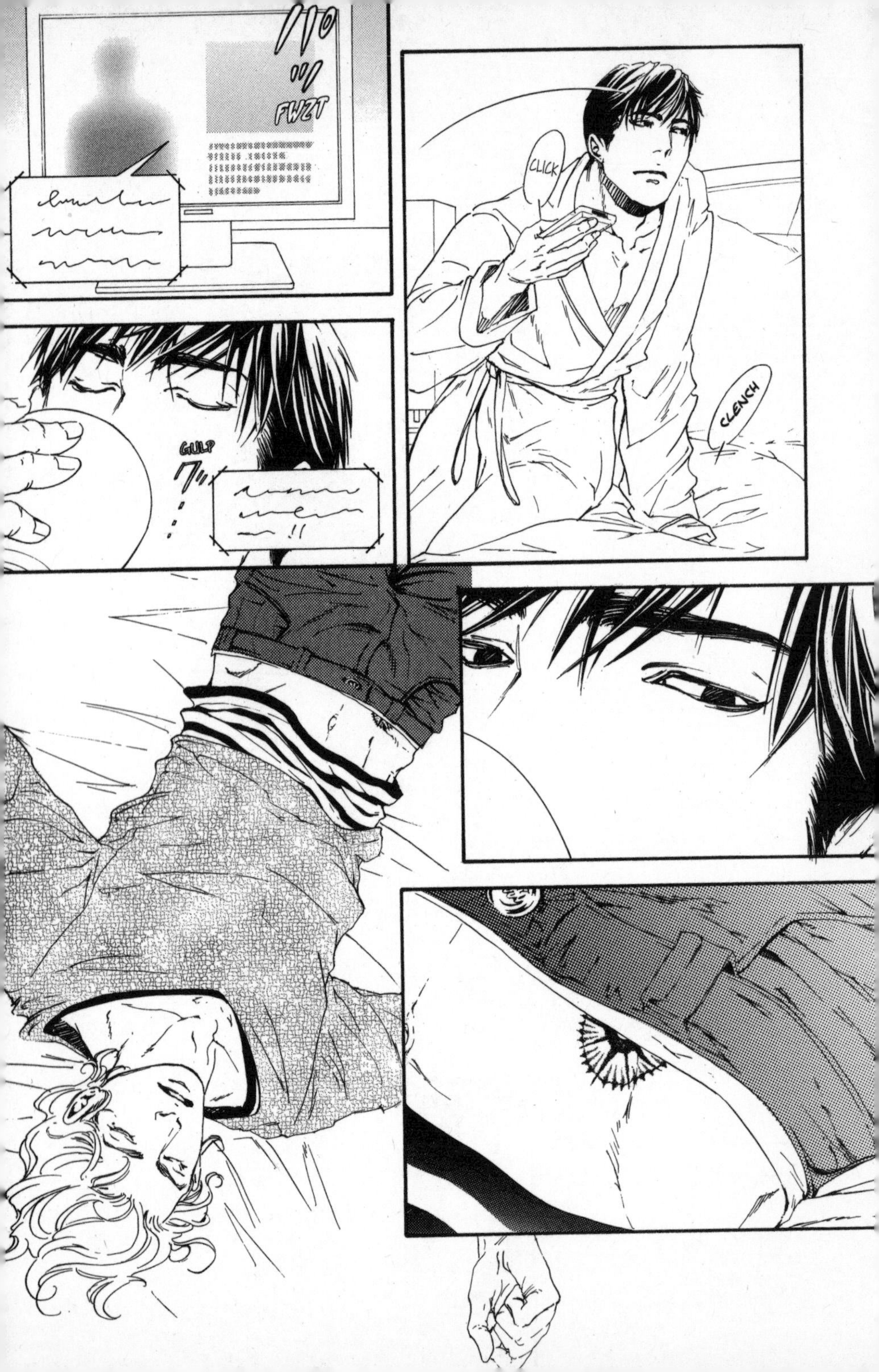
CLICK
CLENCH
FWZT
GULP

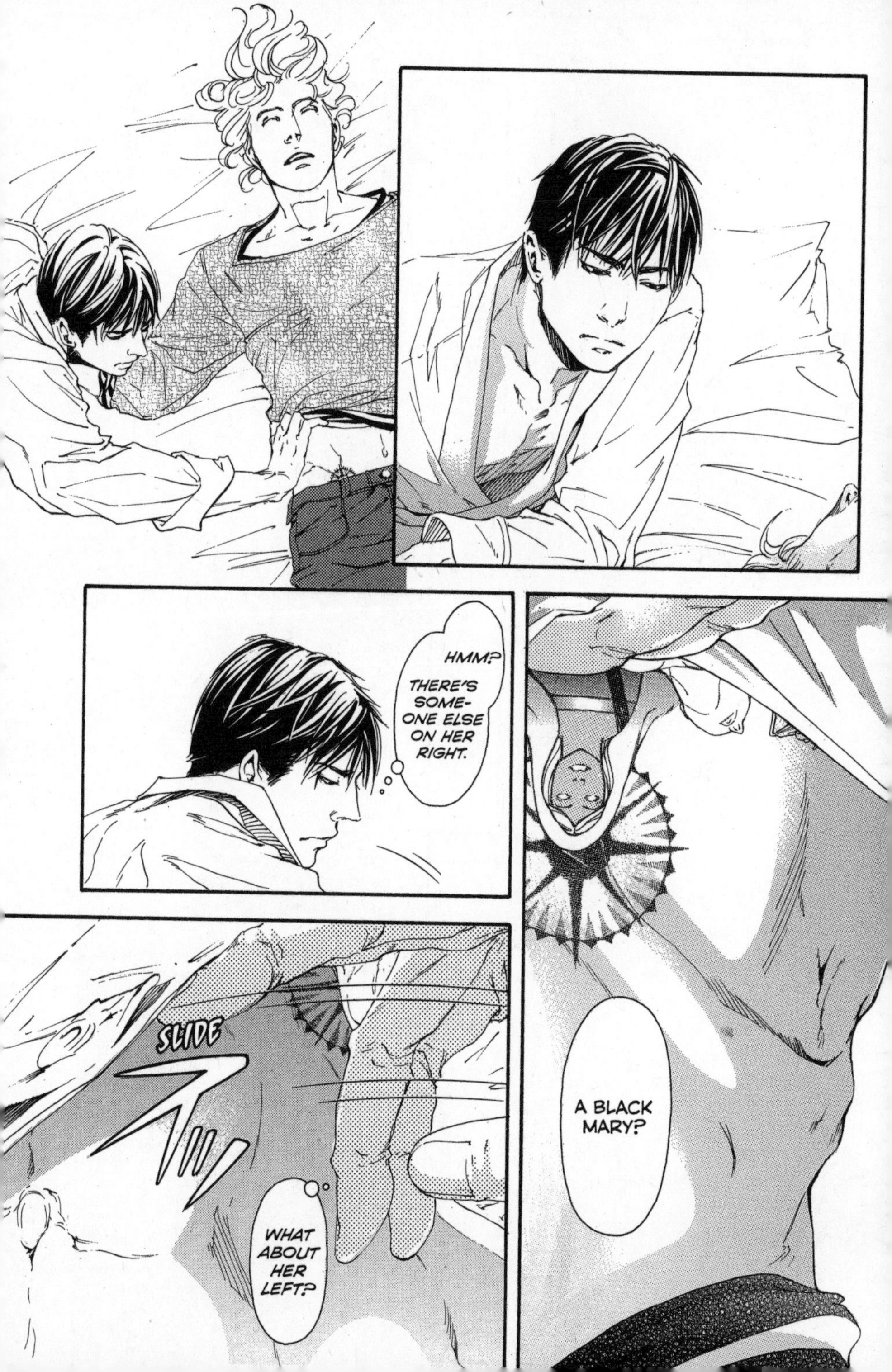
A BLACK MARY?
HMM?
THERE'S SOME-ONE ELSE ON HER RIGHT.
SLIDE
WHAT ABOUT HER LEFT?

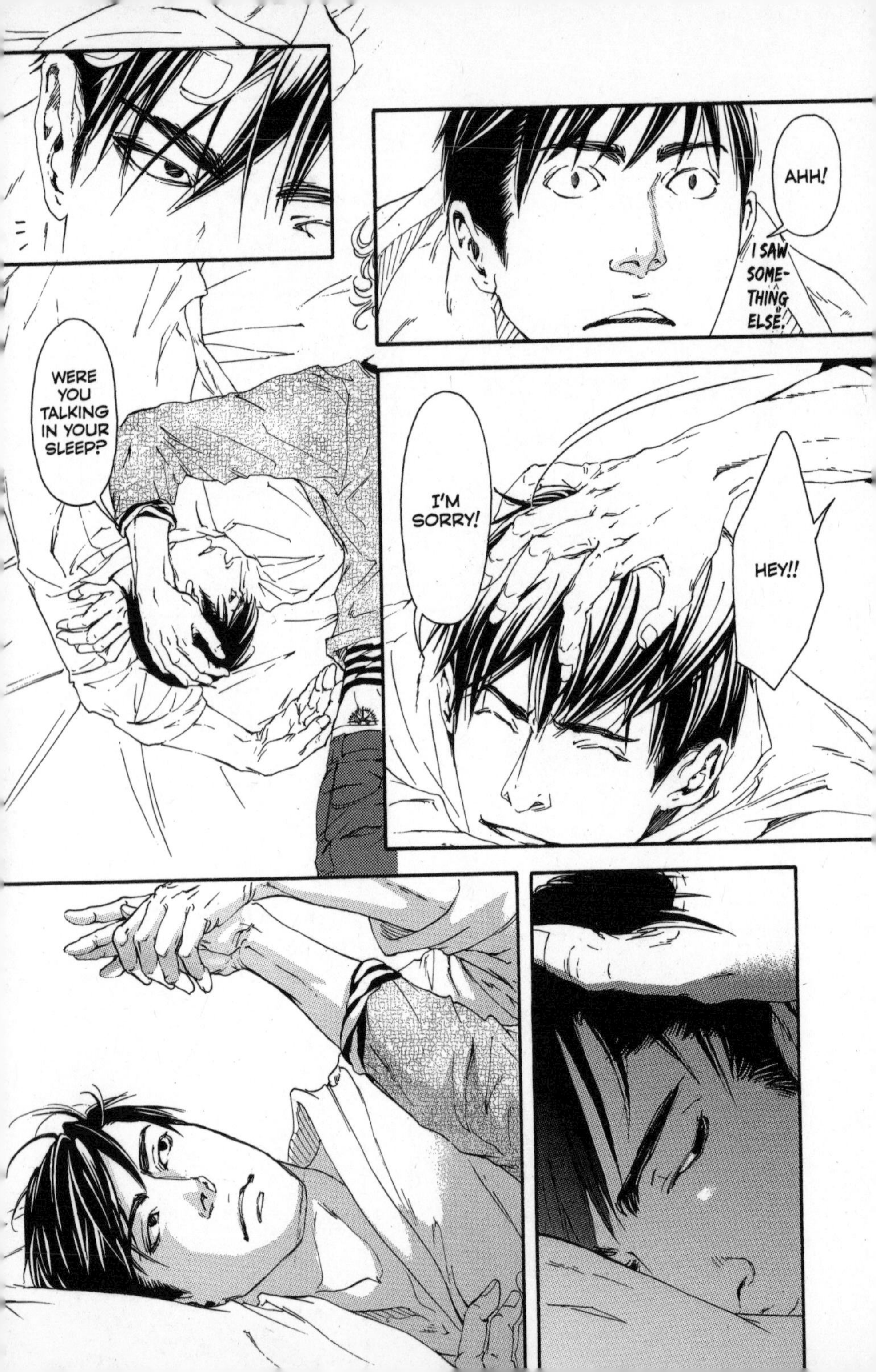
AHH!
I SAW SOMETHING ELSE!
HEY!!
I'M SORRY!
WERE YOU TALKING IN YOUR SLEEP?

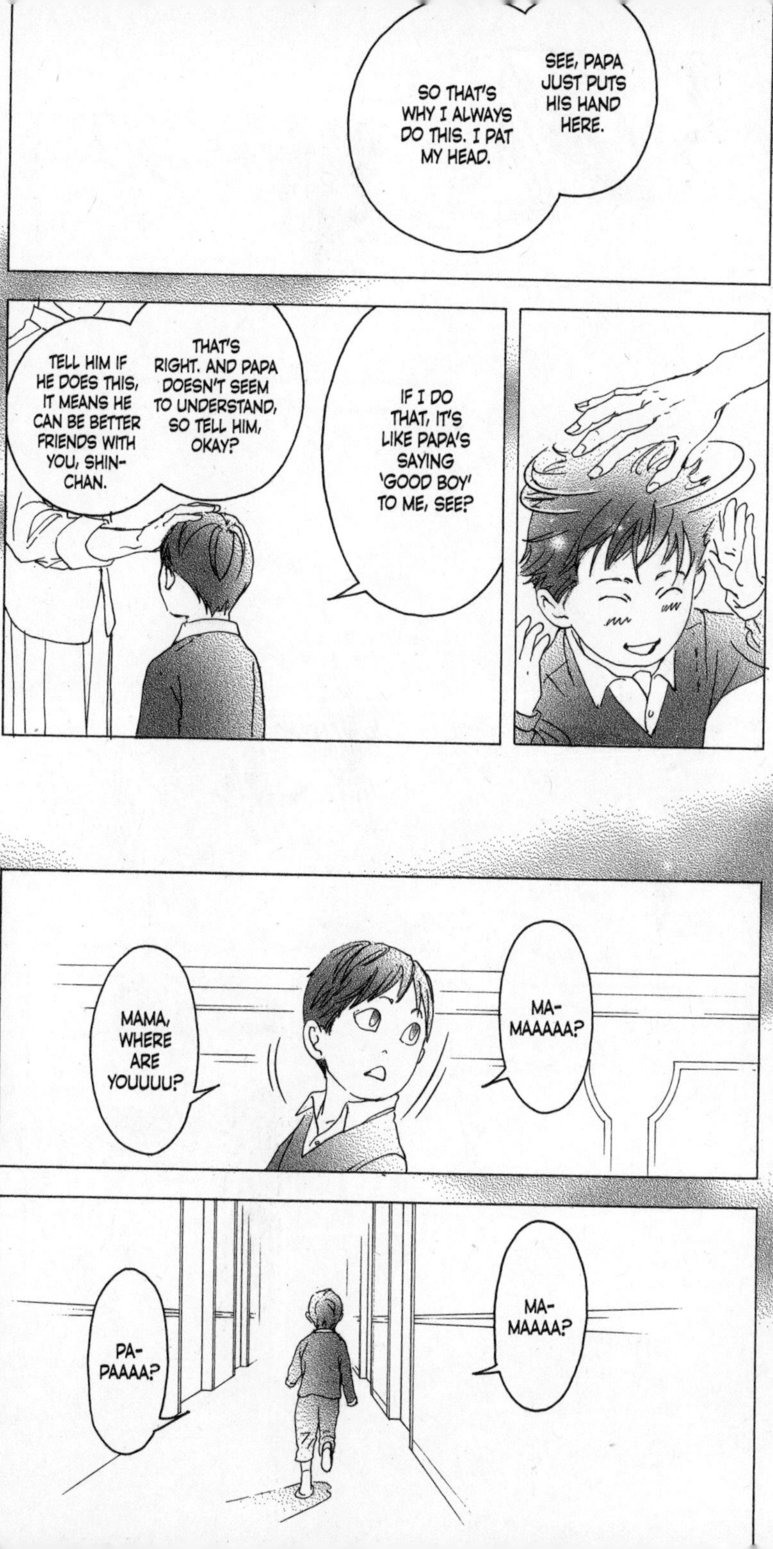
SEE, PAPA JUST PUTS HIS HAND HERE.
SO THAT'S WHY I ALWAYS DO THIS. I PAT MY HEAD.
IF I DO THAT, IT'S LIKE PAPA'S SAYING 'GOOD BOY' TO ME, SEE?
THAT'S RIGHT. AND PAPA DOESN'T SEEM TO UNDERSTAND, SO TELL HIM, OKAY?
TELL HIM IF HE DOES THIS, IT MEANS HE CAN BE BETTER FRIENDS WITH YOU, SHIN-CHAN.
MA-MAAAAA?
MAMA, WHERE ARE YOUUUU?
MA-MAAAA?
PA-PAAAA?

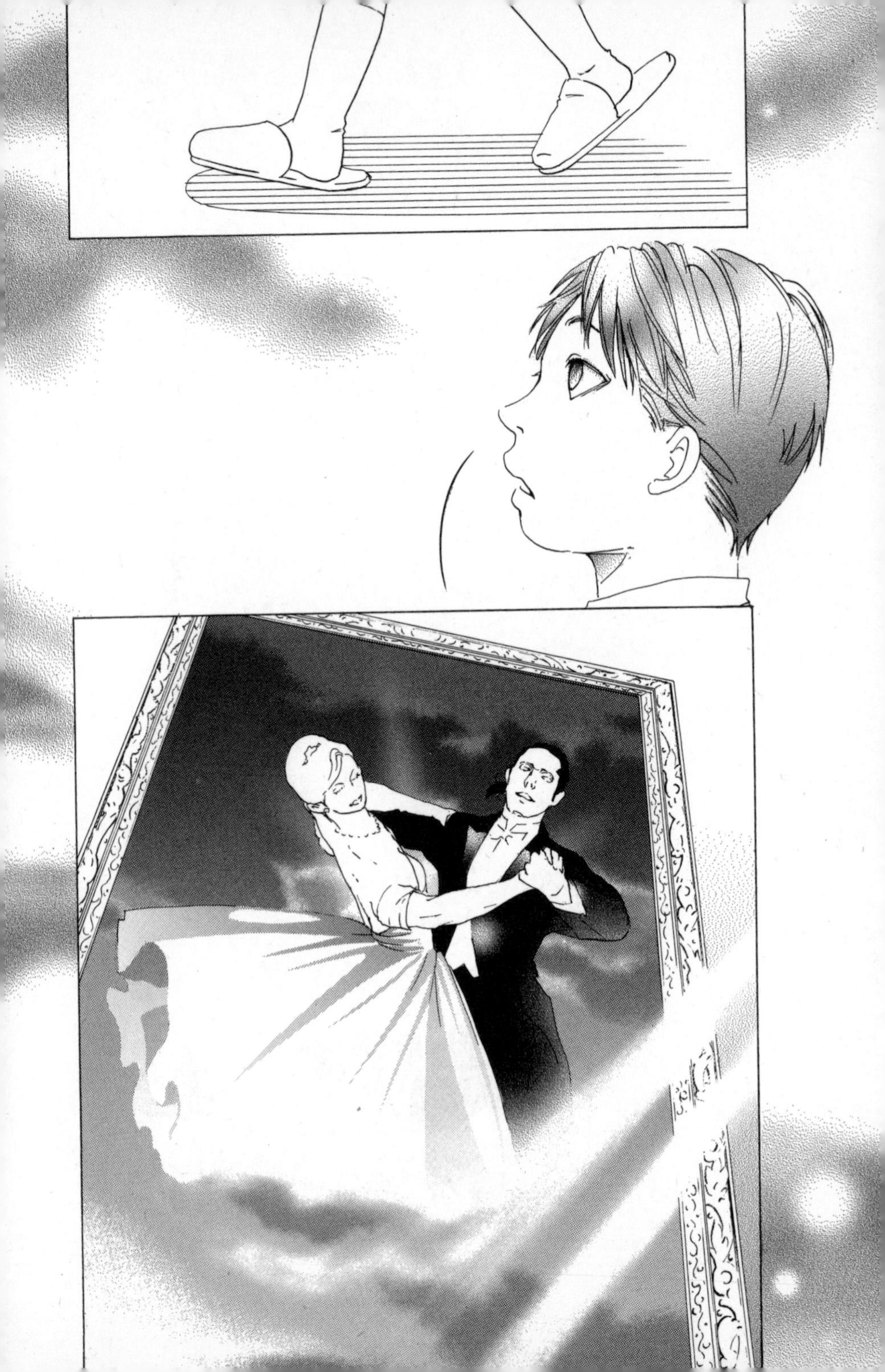

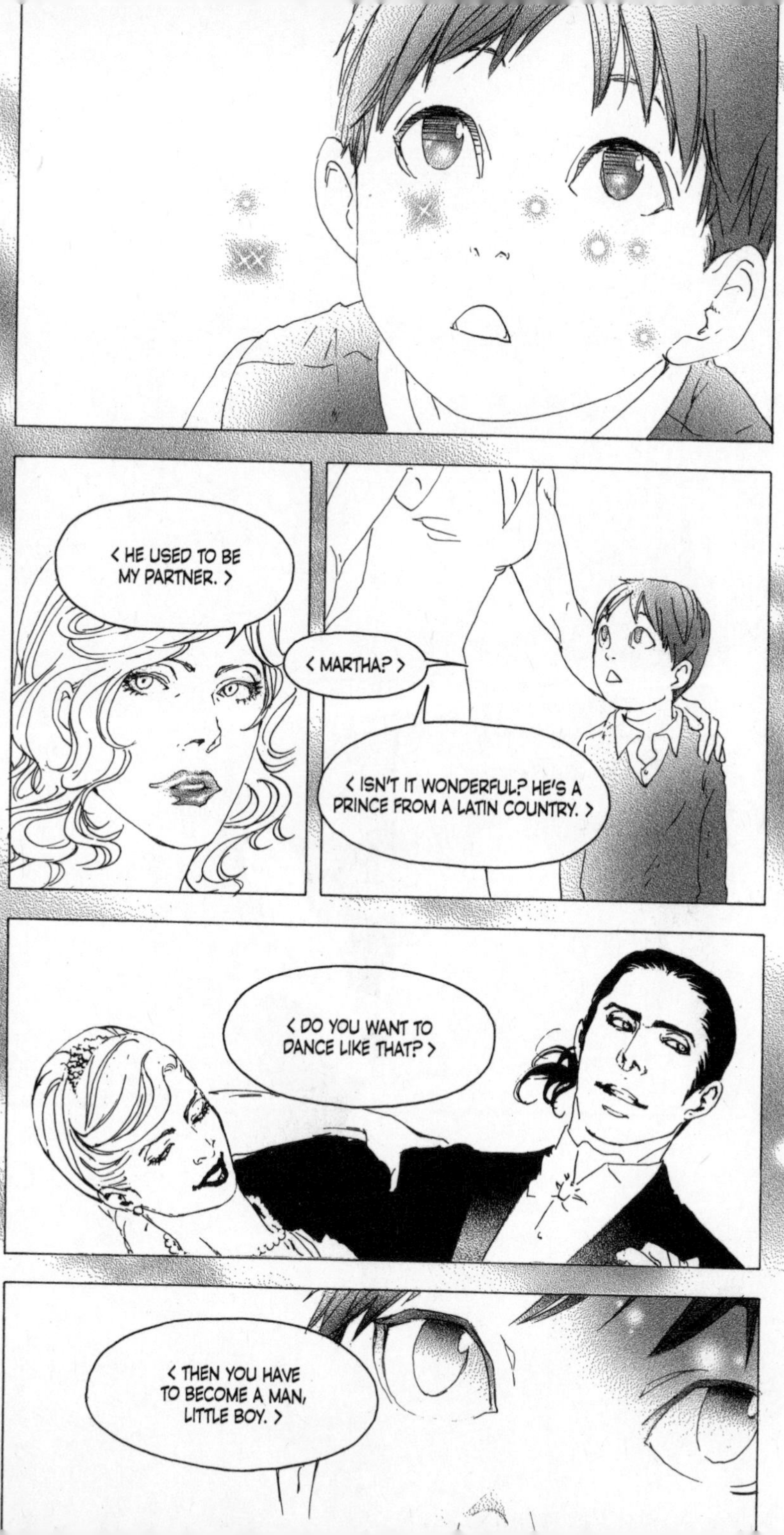
< MARTHA? >
< ISN'T IT WONDERFUL? HE'S A PRINCE FROM A LATIN COUNTRY. >
< HE USED TO BE MY PARTNER. >
< DO YOU WANT TO DANCE LIKE THAT? >
< THEN YOU HAVE TO BECOME A MAN, LITTLE BOY. >

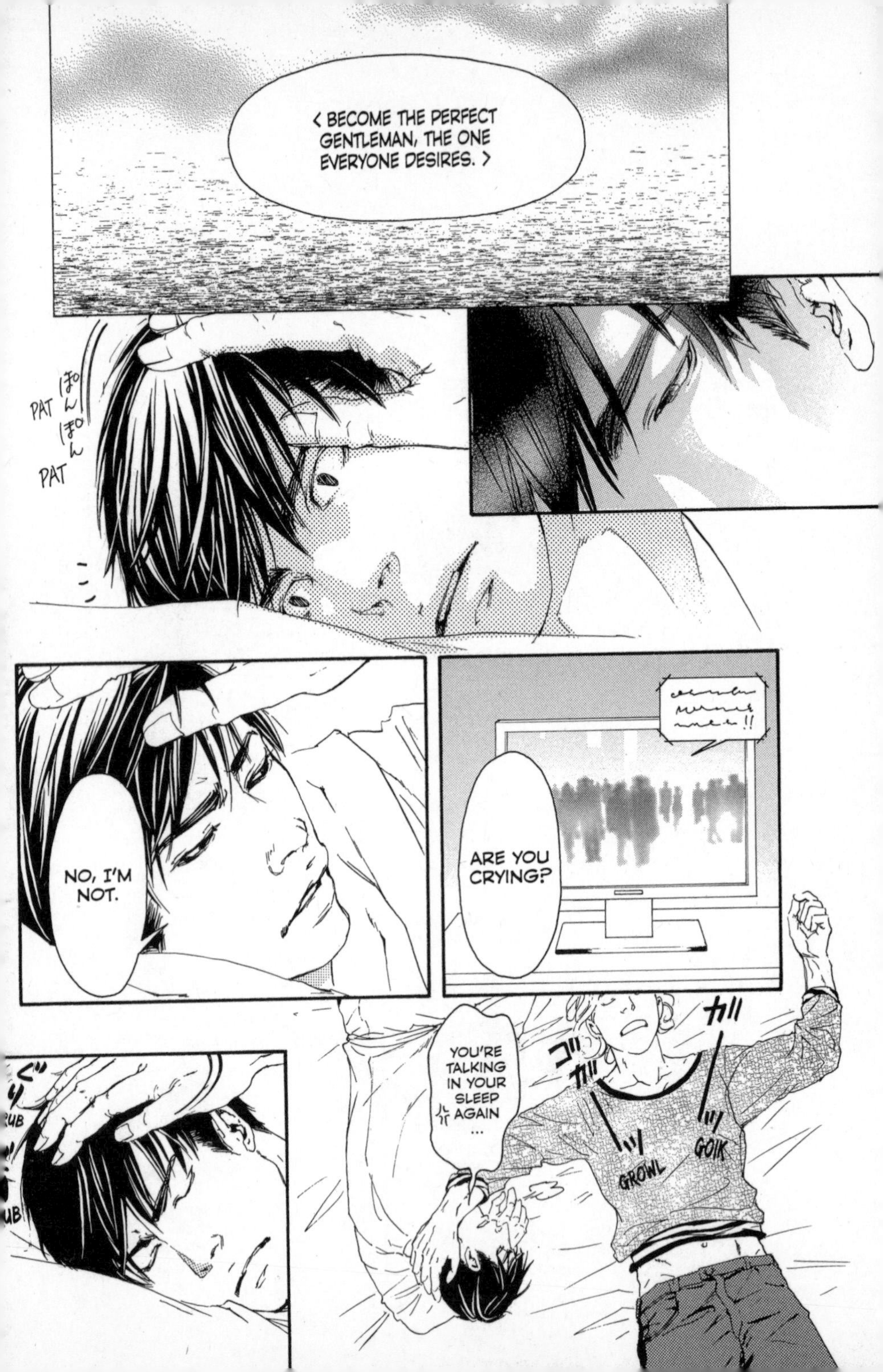
< BECOME THE PERFECT GENTLEMAN, THE ONE EVERYONE DESIRES. >
PAT
PAT
ARE YOU CRYING?
NO, I'M NOT.
YOU'RE TALKING IN YOUR SLEEP AGAIN ...
GOIK
GROWL

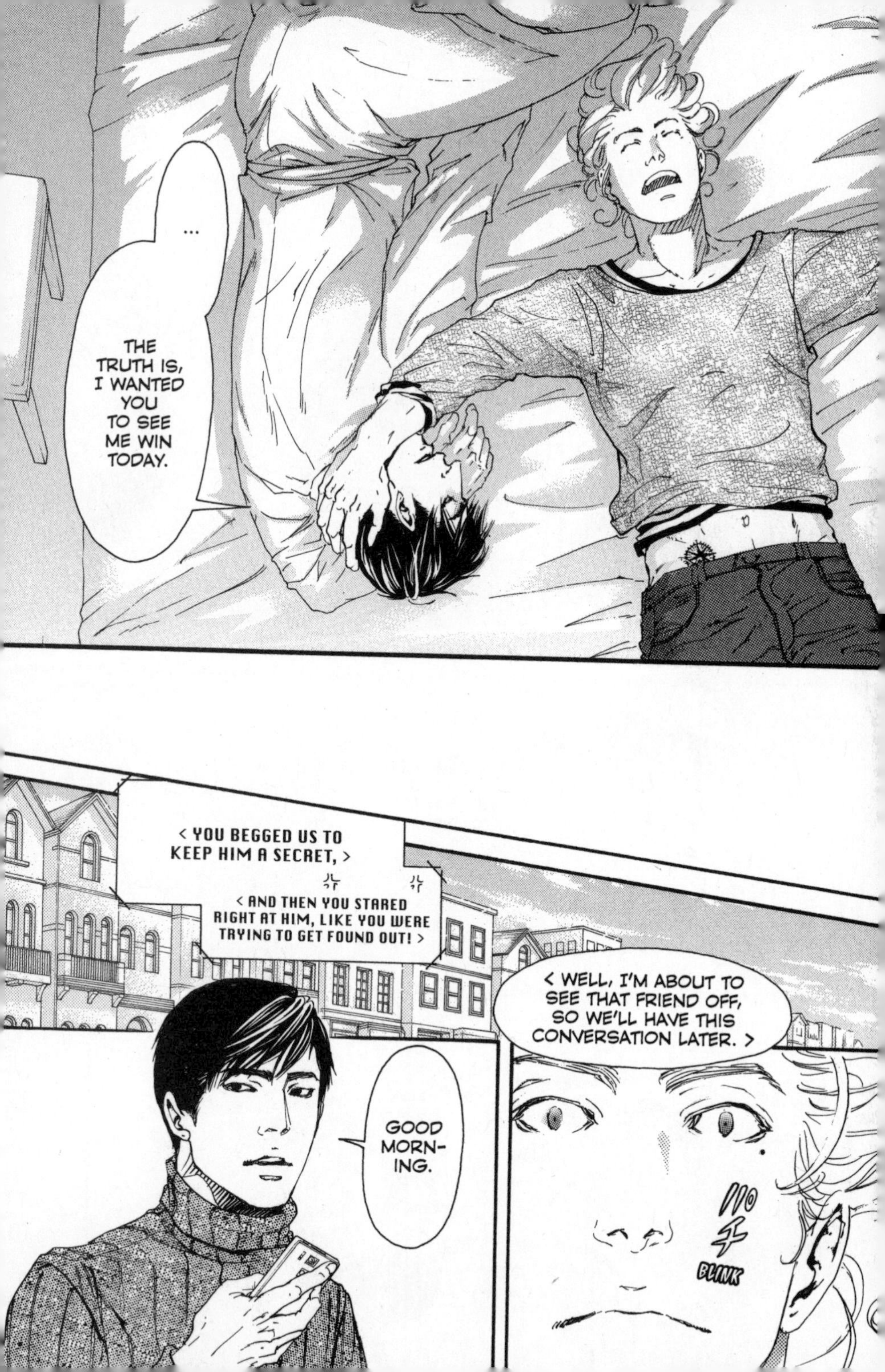
...
THE TRUTH IS, I WANTED YOU TO SEE ME WIN TODAY.
< YOU BEGGED US TO KEEP HIM A SECRET, >
< AND THEN YOU STARED RIGHT AT HIM, LIKE YOU WERE TRYING TO GET FOUND OUT! >
< WELL, I'M ABOUT TO SEE THAT FRIEND OFF, SO WE'LL HAVE THIS CONVERSATION LATER. >
パチ
BLINK
GOOD MORN-ING.

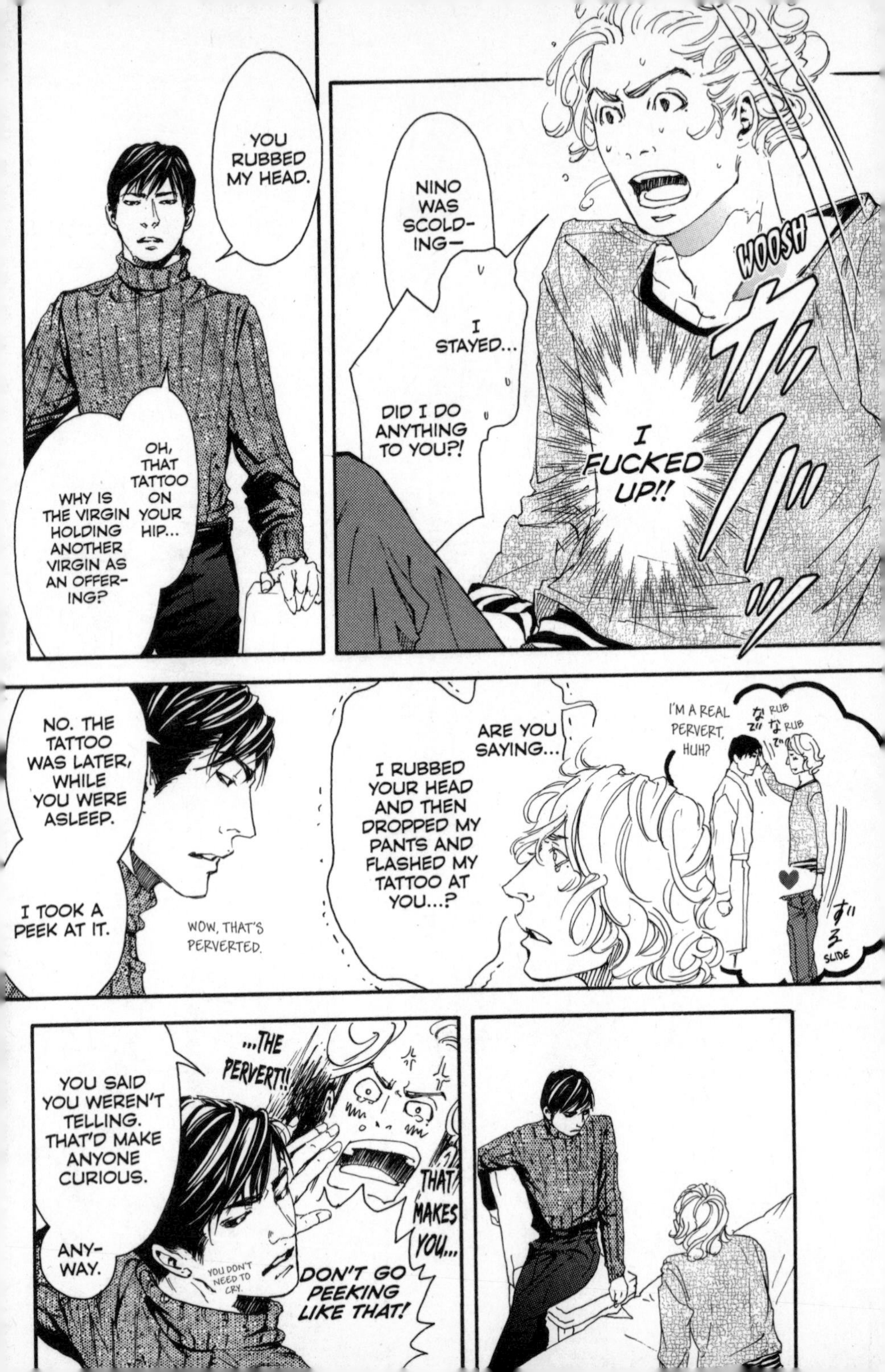
NINO WAS SCOLDING—
I STAYED...
DID I DO ANYTHING TO YOU?!
WOOSH
I FUCKED UP!!
YOU RUBBED MY HEAD.
OH, THAT TATTOO ON YOUR HIP...
WHY IS THE VIRGIN HOLDING ANOTHER VIRGIN AS AN OFFERING?
ARE YOU SAYING...
I RUBBED YOUR HEAD AND THEN DROPPED MY PANTS AND FLASHED MY TATTOO AT YOU...?
I'M A REAL PERVERT, HUH?
なで RUB
なで RUB
ずる SLIDE
NO. THE TATTOO WAS LATER, WHILE YOU WERE ASLEEP.
I TOOK A PEEK AT IT.
WOW, THAT'S PERVERTED.
...THE PERVERT!!
YOU SAID YOU WEREN'T TELLING. THAT'D MAKE ANYONE CURIOUS.
THAT MAKES YOU...
DON'T GO PEEKING LIKE THAT!
ANY-WAY.
YOU DON'T NEED TO CRY.

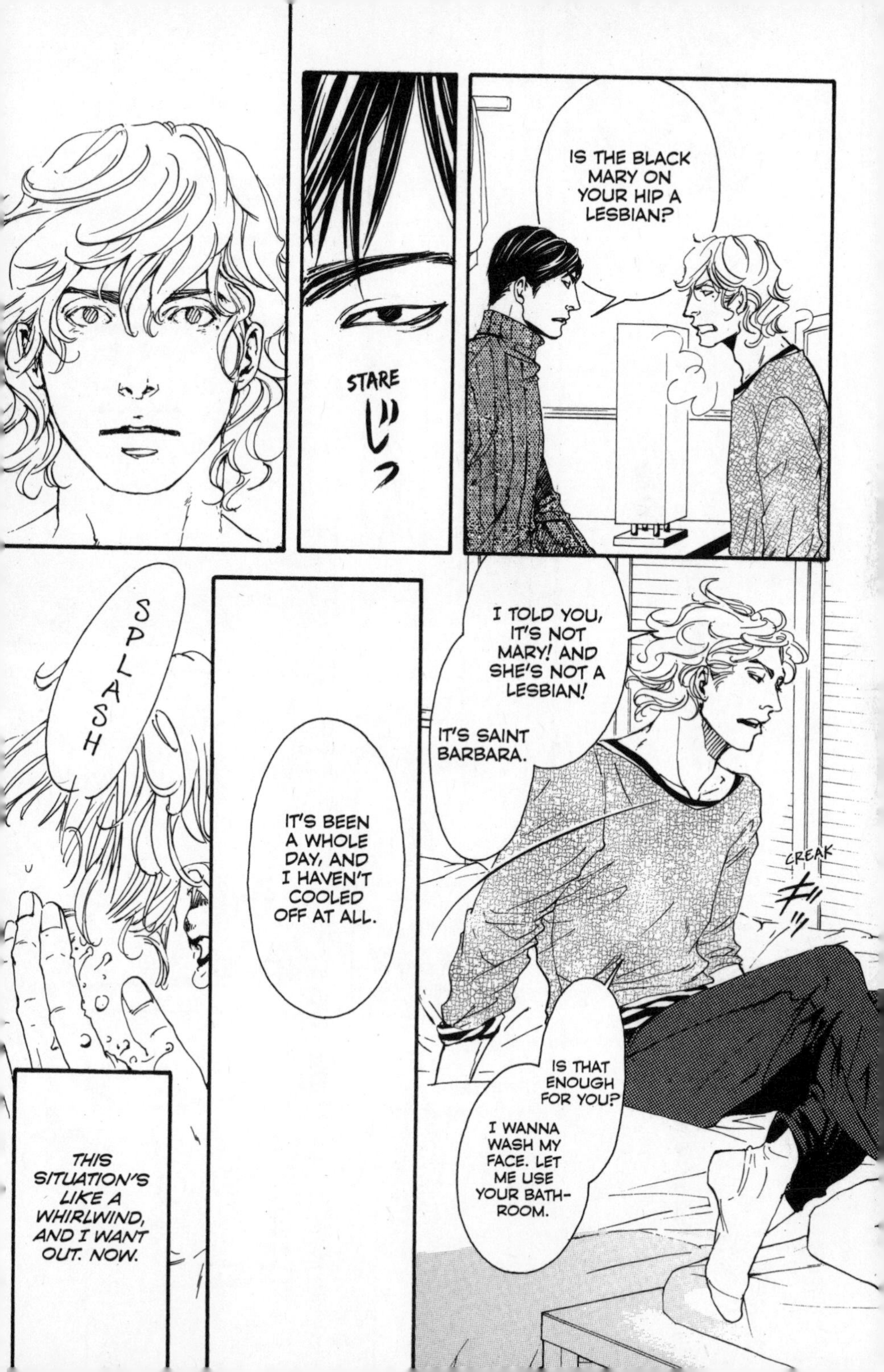
IS THE BLACK MARY ON YOUR HIP A LESBIAN?
STARE
じっ
I TOLD YOU, IT'S NOT MARY! AND SHE'S NOT A LESBIAN!
IT'S SAINT BARBARA.
CREAK
ギッ
IS THAT ENOUGH FOR YOU?
I WANNA WASH MY FACE. LET ME USE YOUR BATH-ROOM.
IT'S BEEN A WHOLE DAY, AND I HAVEN'T COOLED OFF AT ALL.
SPLASH
THIS SITUATION'S LIKE A WHIRLWIND, AND I WANT OUT. NOW.

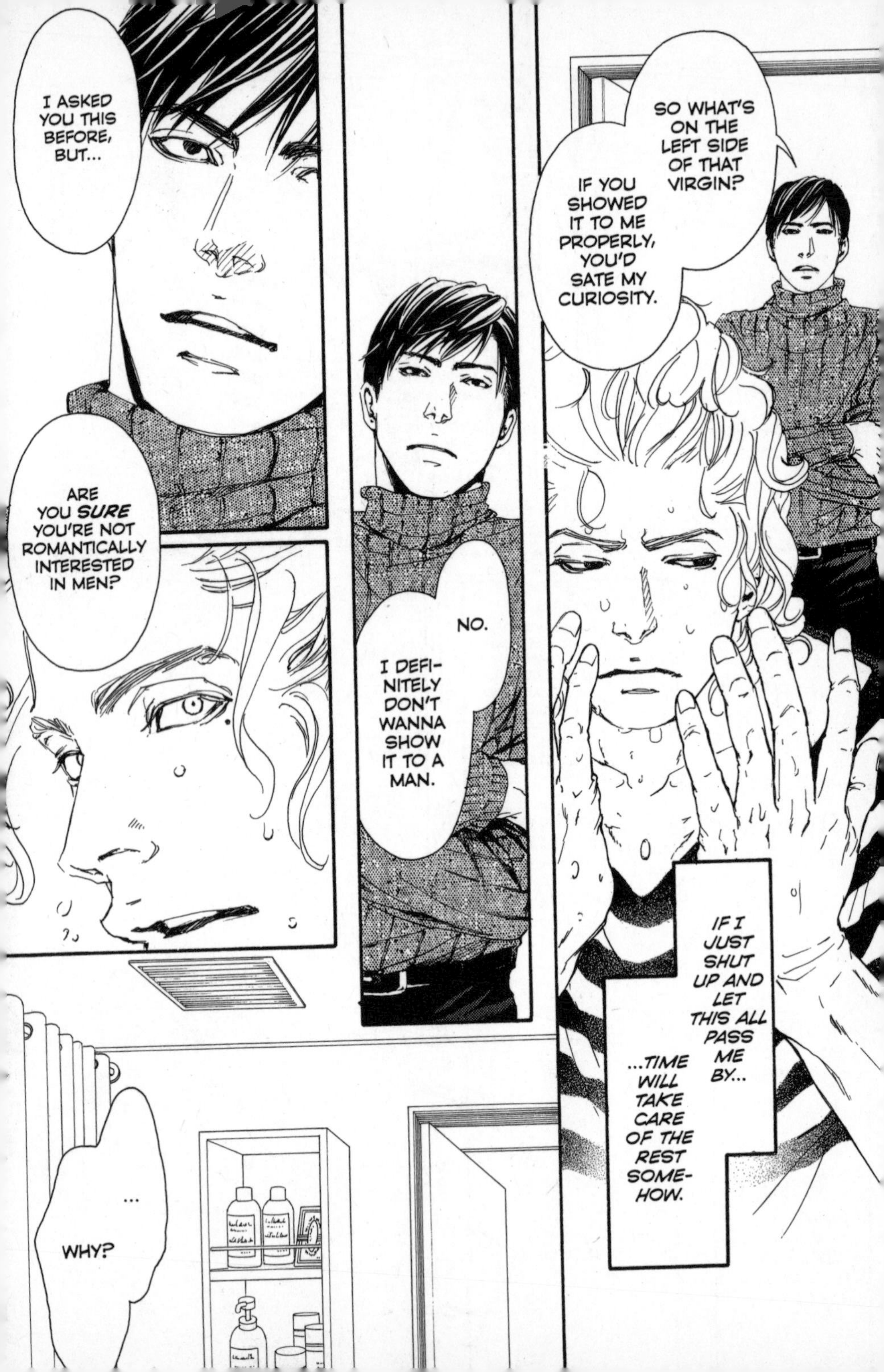
SO WHAT'S ON THE LEFT SIDE OF THAT VIRGIN?
IF YOU SHOWED IT TO ME PROPERLY, YOU'D SATE MY CURIOSITY.
IF I JUST SHUT UP AND LET THIS ALL PASS ME BY...
...TIME WILL TAKE CARE OF THE REST SOME-HOW.
NO.
I DEFI-NITELY DON'T WANNA SHOW IT TO A MAN.
I ASKED YOU THIS BEFORE, BUT...
ARE YOU SURE YOU'RE NOT ROMANTICALLY INTERESTED IN MEN?
...
WHY?

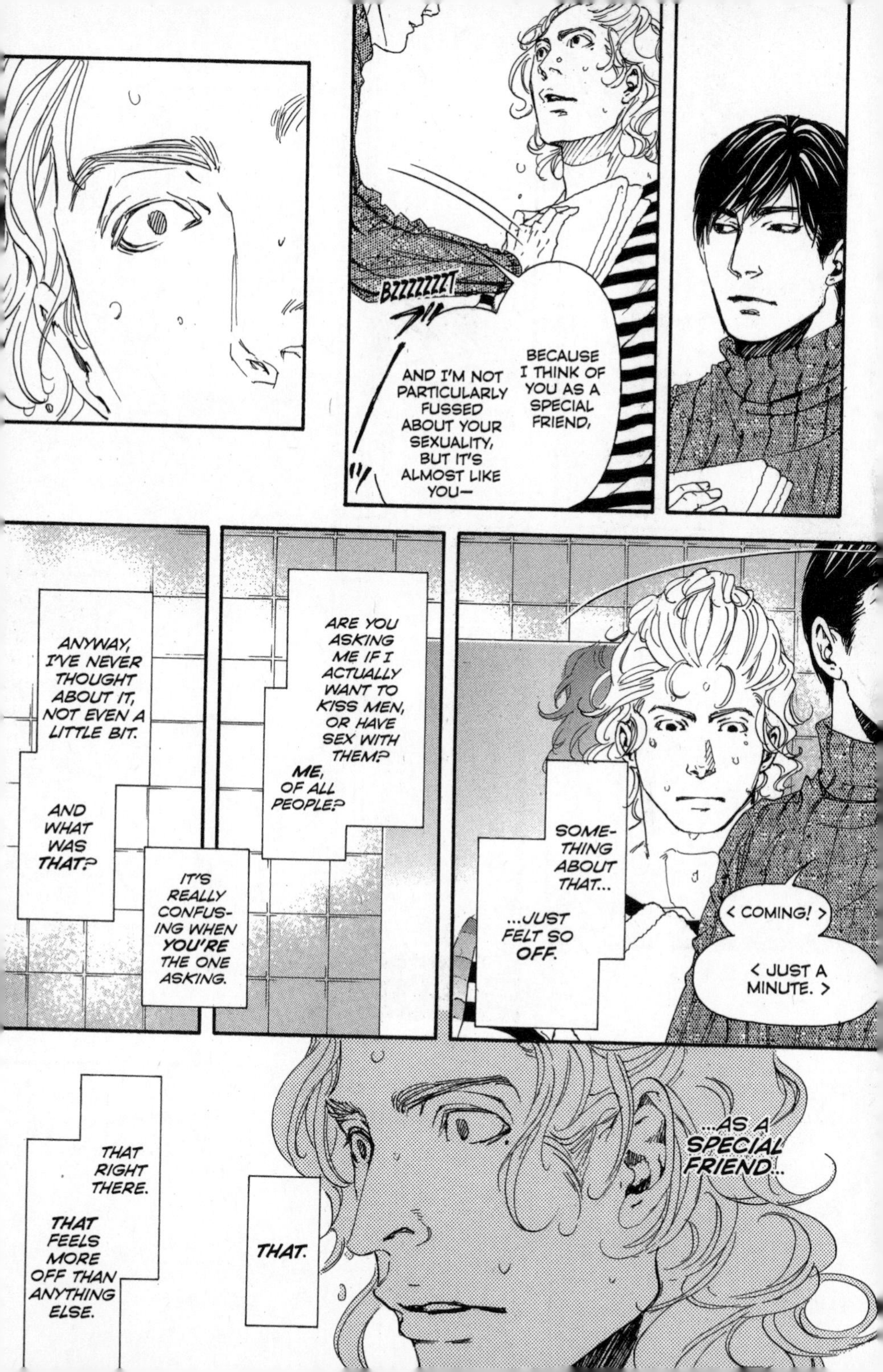
BECAUSE I THINK OF YOU AS A SPECIAL FRIEND,
AND I'M NOT PARTICULARLY FUSSED ABOUT YOUR SEXUALITY, BUT IT'S ALMOST LIKE YOU—
BZZZZZZZZT
SOMETHING ABOUT THAT...
...JUST FELT SO OFF.
< COMING! >
< JUST A MINUTE. >
ARE YOU ASKING ME IF I ACTUALLY WANT TO KISS MEN, OR HAVE SEX WITH THEM?
ME, OF ALL PEOPLE?
IT'S REALLY CONFUSING WHEN YOU'RE THE ONE ASKING.
ANYWAY, I'VE NEVER THOUGHT ABOUT IT, NOT EVEN A LITTLE BIT.
AND WHAT WAS THAT?
...AS A SPECIAL FRIEND...
THAT.
THAT RIGHT THERE.
THAT FEELS MORE OFF THAN ANYTHING ELSE.

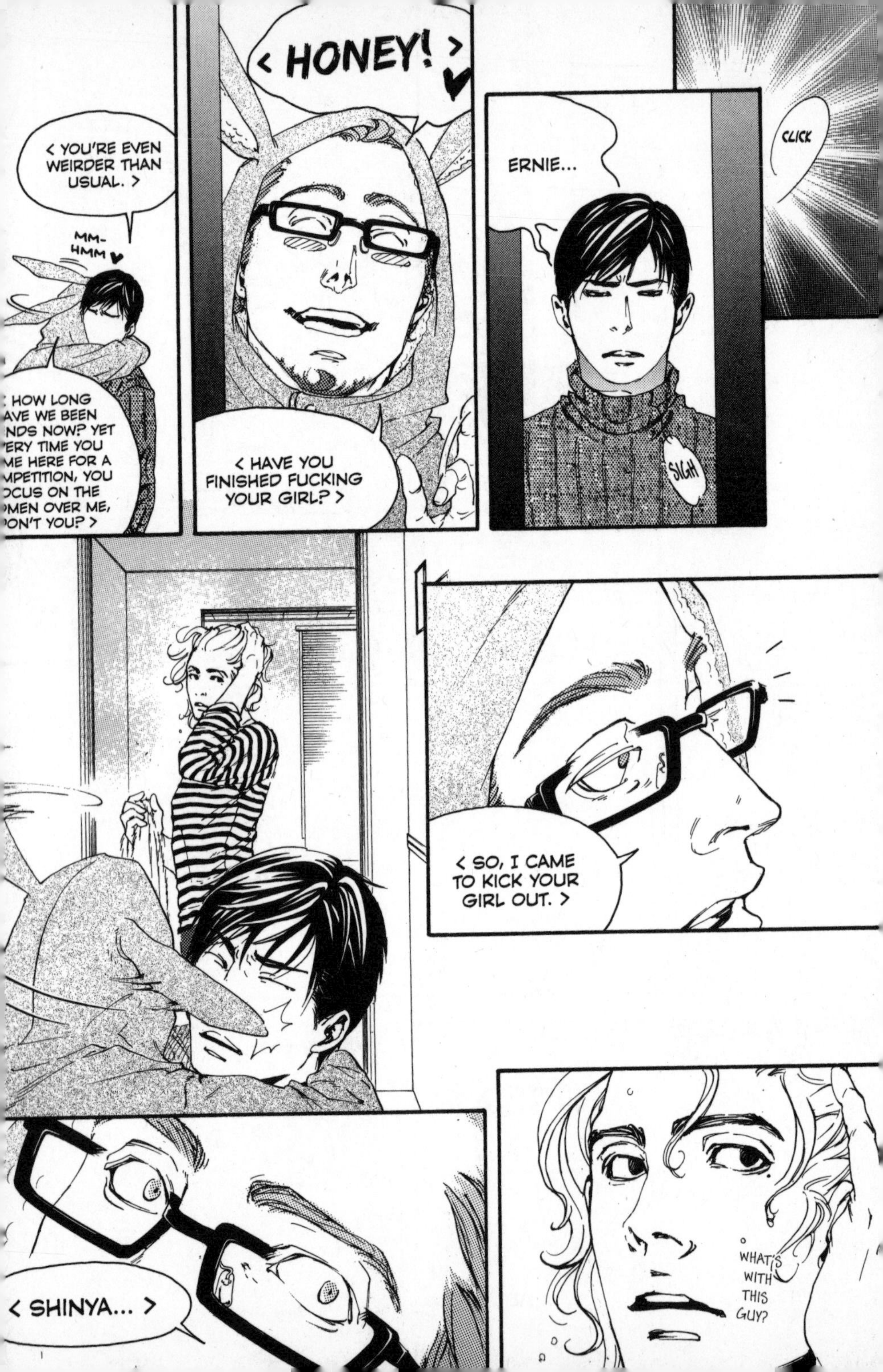
CLICK
ERNIE...
SIGH
< HONEY! >
< HAVE YOU FINISHED FUCKING YOUR GIRL? >
< YOU'RE EVEN WEIRDER THAN USUAL. >
MM-HMM
HOW LONG AVE WE BEEN NDS NOW? YET ERY TIME YOU ME HERE FOR A MPETITION, YOU OCUS ON THE OMEN OVER ME, ON'T YOU? >
< SO, I CAME TO KICK YOUR GIRL OUT. >
WHAT'S WITH THIS GUY?
< SHINYA... >

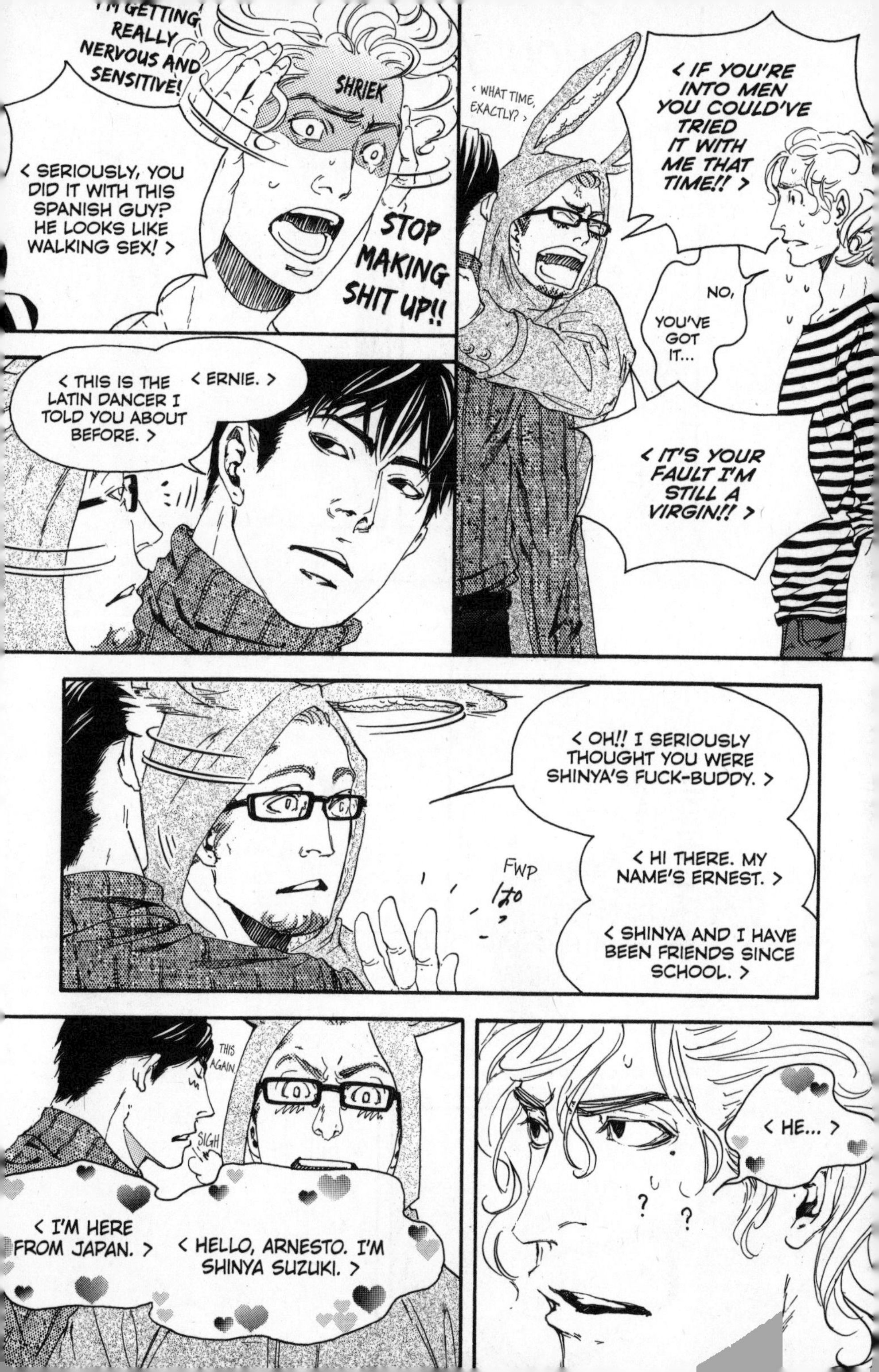
< WHAT TIME, EXACTLY? >
< IF YOU'RE INTO MEN YOU COULD'VE TRIED IT WITH ME THAT TIME!! >
NO, YOU'VE GOT IT...
< IT'S YOUR FAULT I'M STILL A VIRGIN!! >
I'M GETTING REALLY NERVOUS AND SENSITIVE!
SHRIEK
STOP MAKING SHIT UP!!
< SERIOUSLY, YOU DID IT WITH THIS SPANISH GUY? HE LOOKS LIKE WALKING SEX! >
< ERNIE. >
< THIS IS THE LATIN DANCER I TOLD YOU ABOUT BEFORE. >
< OH!! I SERIOUSLY THOUGHT YOU WERE SHINYA'S FUCK-BUDDY. >
< HI THERE. MY NAME'S ERNEST. >
< SHINYA AND I HAVE BEEN FRIENDS SINCE SCHOOL. >
FWP
< HE... >
THIS AGAIN.
SIGH
< HELLO, ARNESTO. I'M SHINYA SUZUKI. >
< I'M HERE FROM JAPAN. >

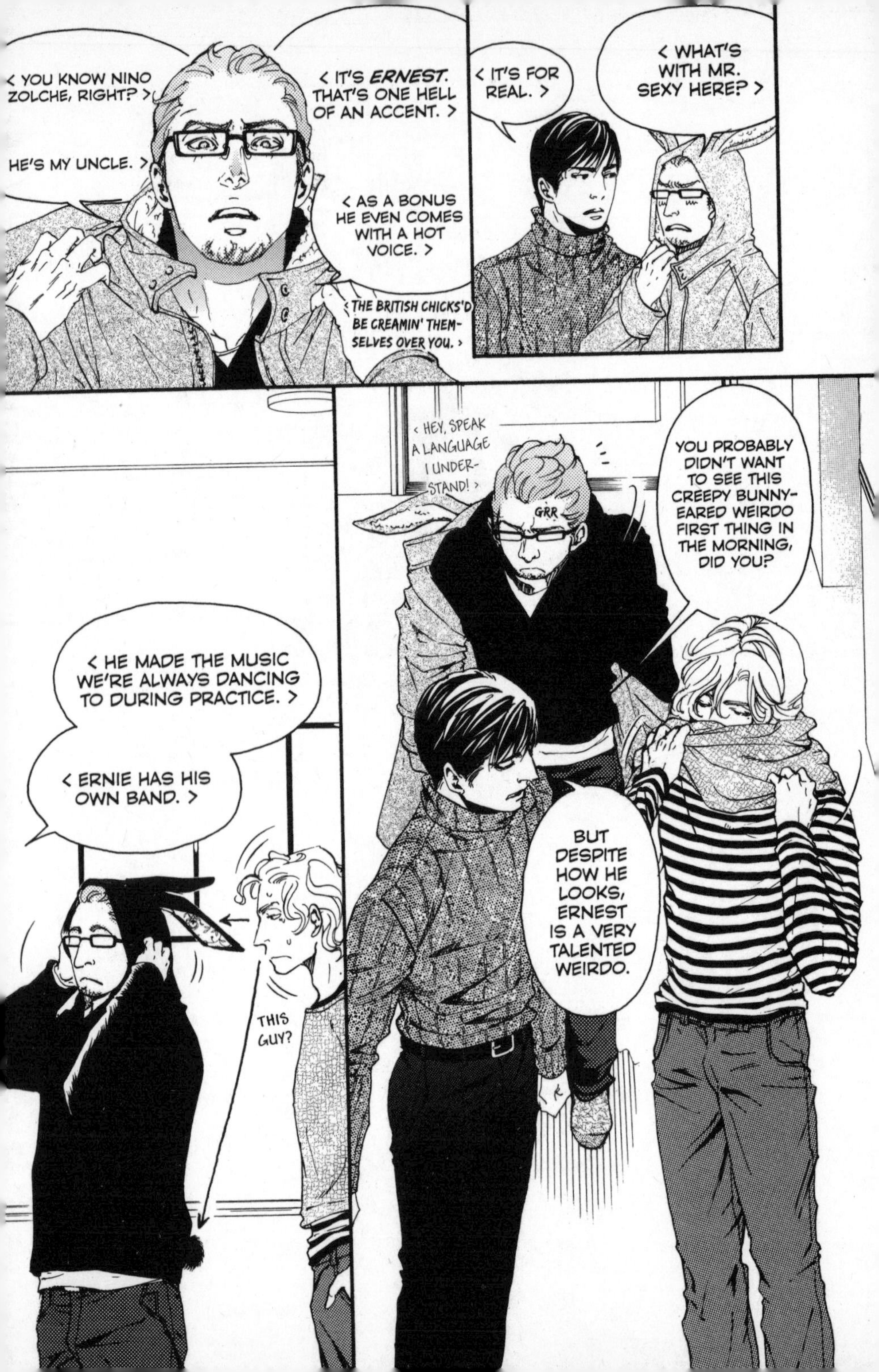
< WHAT'S WITH MR. SEXY HERE? >
< IT'S FOR REAL. >
< IT'S *ERNEST*. THAT'S ONE HELL OF AN ACCENT. >
< YOU KNOW NINO ZOLCHE, RIGHT?
HE'S MY UNCLE. >
< AS A BONUS HE EVEN COMES WITH A HOT VOICE. >
< THE BRITISH CHICKS'D BE CREAMIN' THEMSELVES OVER YOU. >
YOU PROBABLY DIDN'T WANT TO SEE THIS CREEPY BUNNY-EARED WEIRDO FIRST THING IN THE MORNING, DID YOU?
< HEY, SPEAK A LANGUAGE I UNDERSTAND! >
GRR
BUT DESPITE HOW HE LOOKS, ERNEST IS A VERY TALENTED WEIRDO.
< HE MADE THE MUSIC WE'RE ALWAYS DANCING TO DURING PRACTICE. >
< ERNIE HAS HIS OWN BAND. >
THIS GUY?

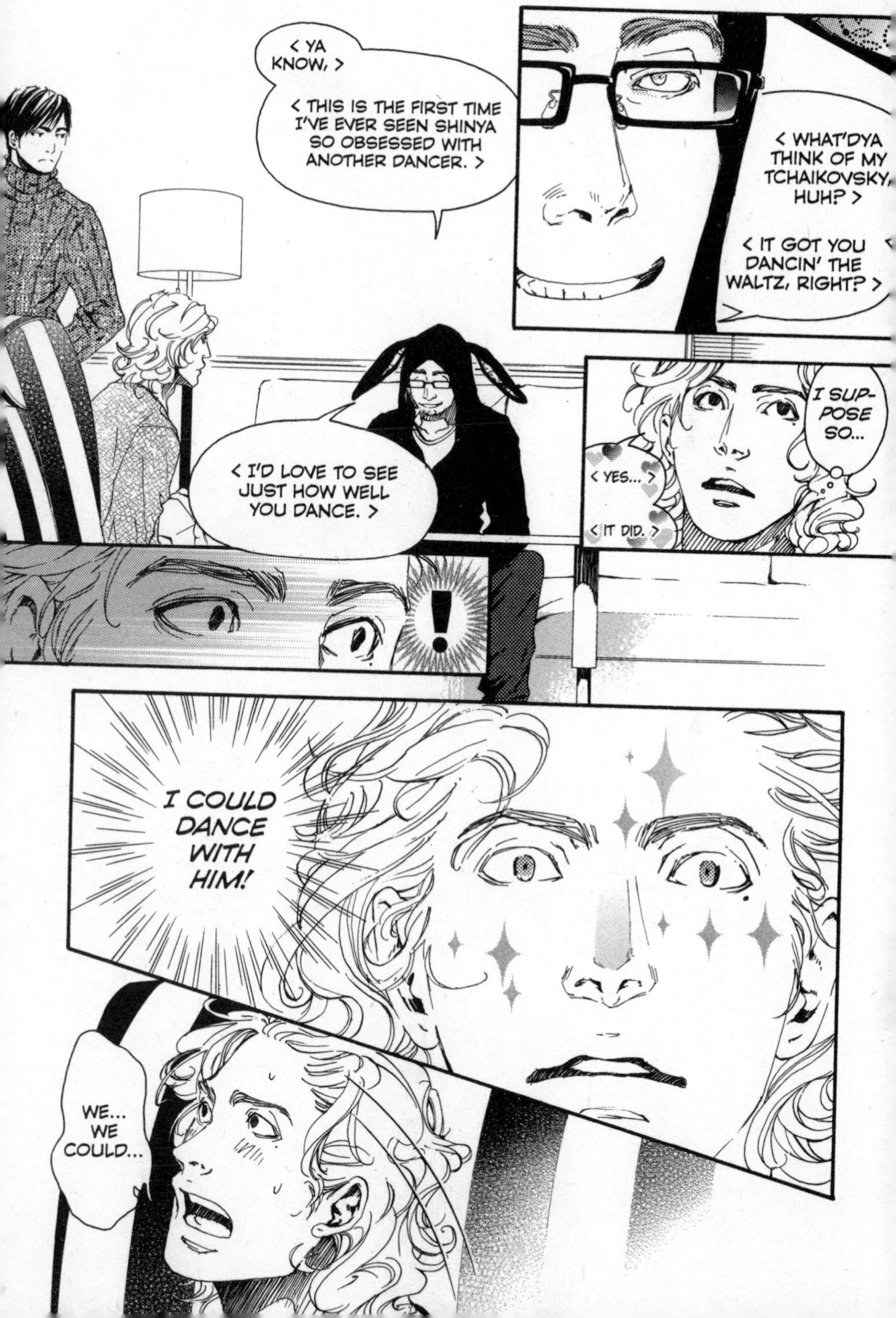
< WHAT'DYA THINK OF MY TCHAIKOVSKY, HUH? >
< IT GOT YOU DANCIN' THE WALTZ, RIGHT? >
I SUP-POSE SO...
< YES... >
< IT DID. >
< YA KNOW, >
< THIS IS THE FIRST TIME I'VE EVER SEEN SHINYA SO OBSESSED WITH ANOTHER DANCER. >
< I'D LOVE TO SEE JUST HOW WELL YOU DANCE. >
!
I COULD DANCE WITH HIM!
WE... WE COULD...

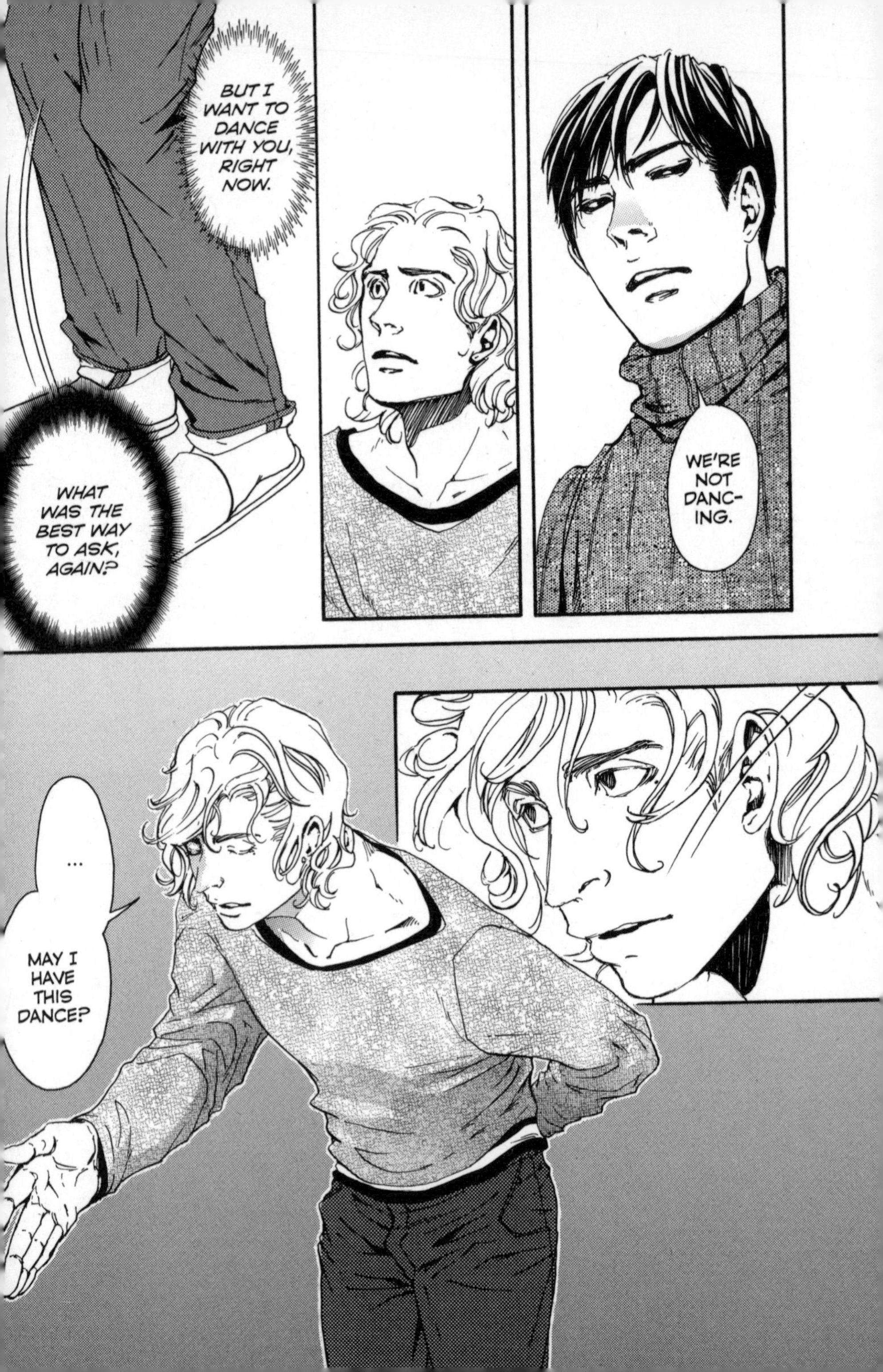
WE'RE NOT DANCING.
BUT I WANT TO DANCE WITH YOU, RIGHT NOW.
WHAT WAS THE BEST WAY TO ASK, AGAIN?
...
MAY I HAVE THIS DANCE?

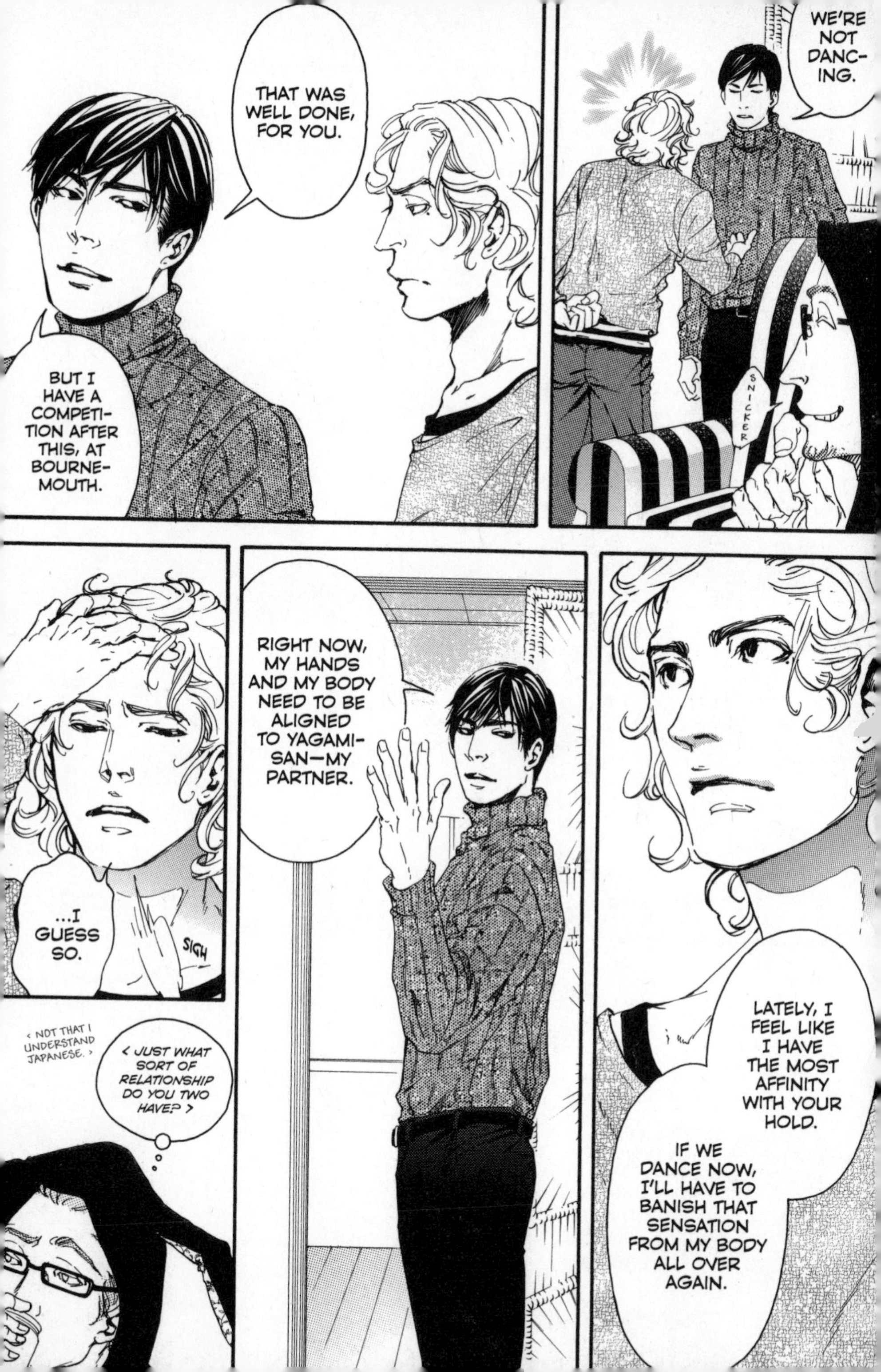
WE'RE NOT DANCING.
SNICKER
THAT WAS WELL DONE, FOR YOU.
BUT I HAVE A COMPETITION AFTER THIS, AT BOURNEMOUTH.
LATELY, I FEEL LIKE I HAVE THE MOST AFFINITY WITH YOUR HOLD.
IF WE DANCE NOW, I'LL HAVE TO BANISH THAT SENSATION FROM MY BODY ALL OVER AGAIN.
RIGHT NOW, MY HANDS AND MY BODY NEED TO BE ALIGNED TO YAGAMI-SAN—MY PARTNER.
...I GUESS SO.
SIGH
< JUST WHAT SORT OF RELATIONSHIP DO YOU TWO HAVE? >
< NOT THAT I UNDERSTAND JAPANESE. >

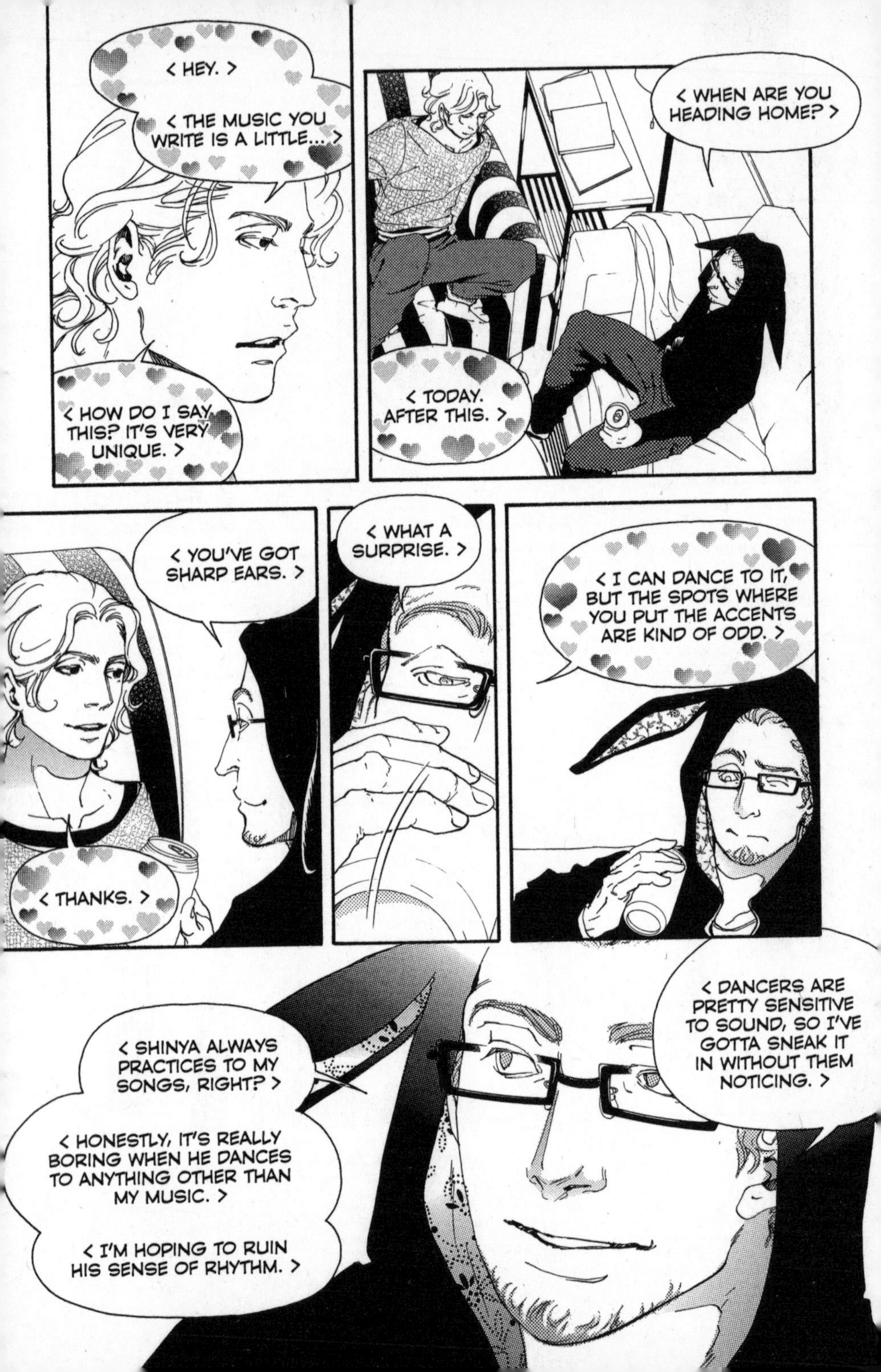
< WHEN ARE YOU HEADING HOME? >
< TODAY. AFTER THIS. >
< HEY. >
< THE MUSIC YOU WRITE IS A LITTLE... >
< HOW DO I SAY THIS? IT'S VERY UNIQUE. >
< I CAN DANCE TO IT, BUT THE SPOTS WHERE YOU PUT THE ACCENTS ARE KIND OF ODD. >
< WHAT A SURPRISE. >
< YOU'VE GOT SHARP EARS. >
< THANKS. >
< DANCERS ARE PRETTY SENSITIVE TO SOUND, SO I'VE GOTTA SNEAK IT IN WITHOUT THEM NOTICING. >
< SHINYA ALWAYS PRACTICES TO MY SONGS, RIGHT? >
< HONESTLY, IT'S REALLY BORING WHEN HE DANCES TO ANYTHING OTHER THAN MY MUSIC. >
< I'M HOPING TO RUIN HIS SENSE OF RHYTHM. >

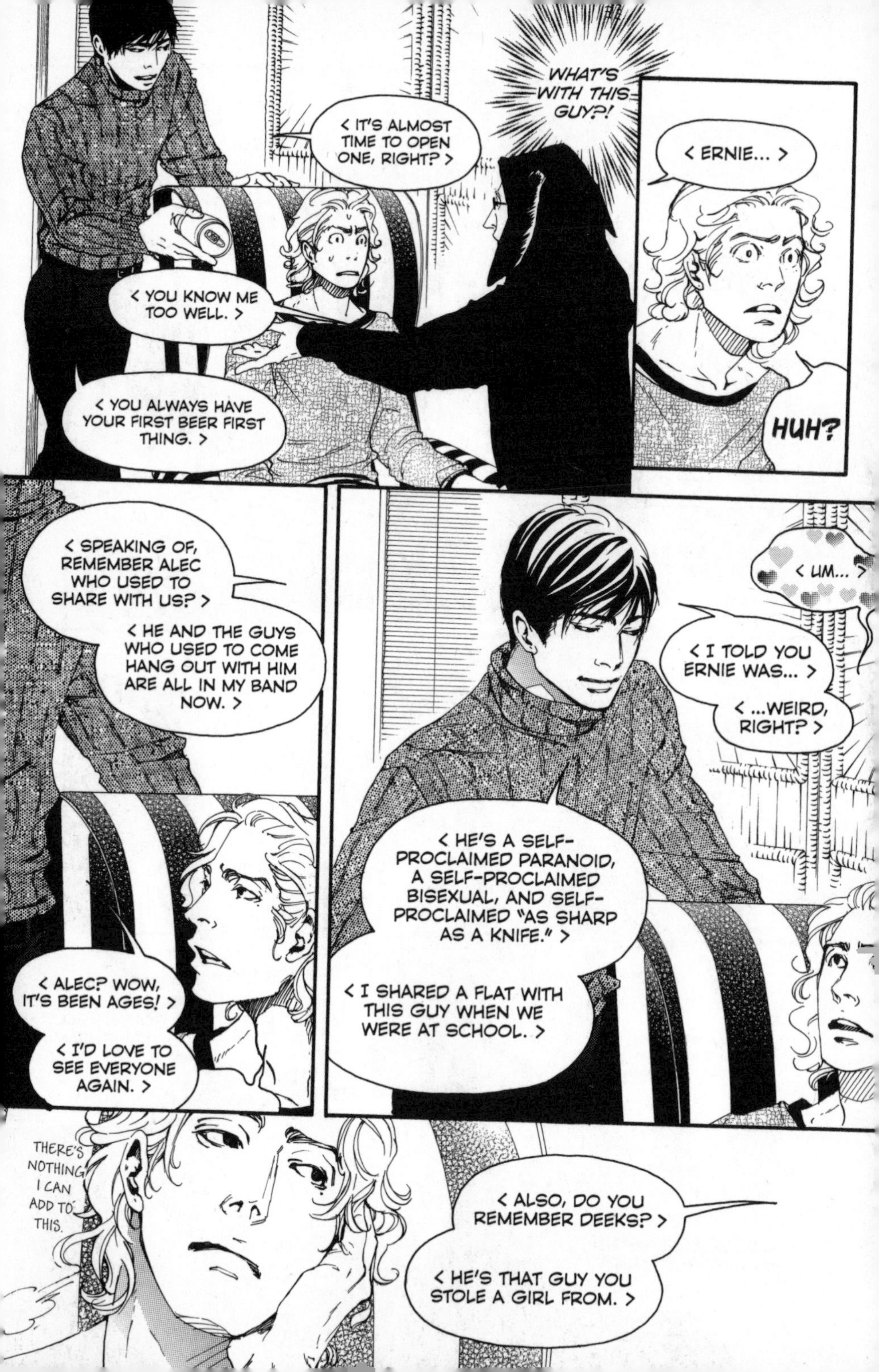
< ERNIE... >
HUH?
WHAT'S WITH THIS GUY?!
< IT'S ALMOST TIME TO OPEN ONE, RIGHT? >
< YOU KNOW ME TOO WELL. >
< YOU ALWAYS HAVE YOUR FIRST BEER FIRST THING. >
< UM... >
< I TOLD YOU ERNIE WAS... >
< ...WEIRD, RIGHT? >
< HE'S A SELF-PROCLAIMED PARANOID, A SELF-PROCLAIMED BISEXUAL, AND SELF-PROCLAIMED "AS SHARP AS A KNIFE." >
< I SHARED A FLAT WITH THIS GUY WHEN WE WERE AT SCHOOL. >
< SPEAKING OF, REMEMBER ALEC WHO USED TO SHARE WITH US? >
< HE AND THE GUYS WHO USED TO COME HANG OUT WITH HIM ARE ALL IN MY BAND NOW. >
< ALEC? WOW, IT'S BEEN AGES! >
< I'D LOVE TO SEE EVERYONE AGAIN. >
< ALSO, DO YOU REMEMBER DEEKS? >
< HE'S THAT GUY YOU STOLE A GIRL FROM. >
THERE'S NOTHING I CAN ADD TO THIS.

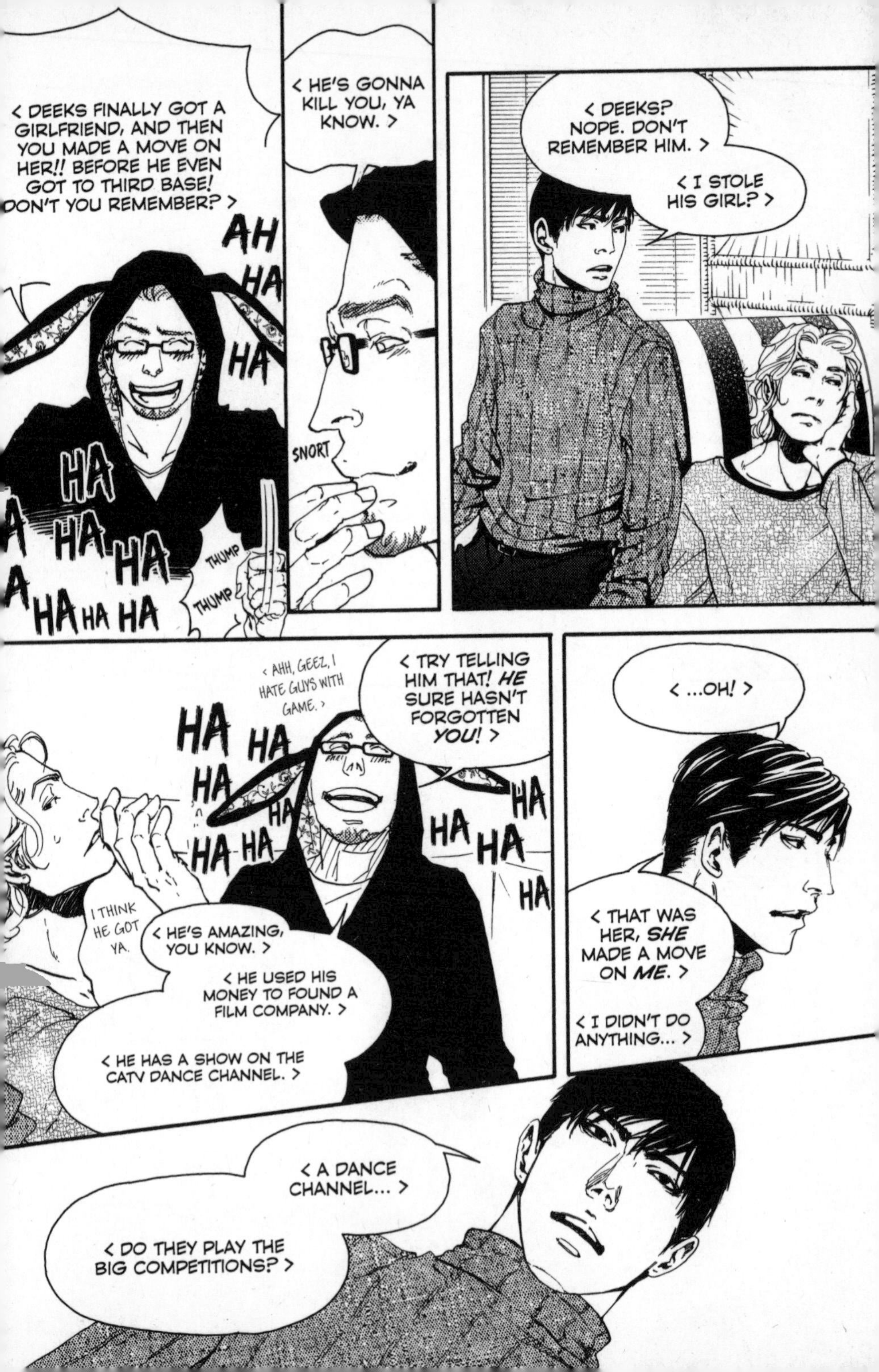
< DEEKS? NOPE. DON'T REMEMBER HIM. >
< I STOLE HIS GIRL? >
< HE'S GONNA KILL YOU, YA KNOW. >
SNORT
< DEEKS FINALLY GOT A GIRLFRIEND, AND THEN YOU MADE A MOVE ON HER!! BEFORE HE EVEN GOT TO THIRD BASE! DON'T YOU REMEMBER? >
AH HA HA
HA HA HA HA HA HA HA HA HA
THUMP THUMP
< ...OH! >
< THAT WAS HER, *SHE* MADE A MOVE ON *ME*. >
< I DIDN'T DO ANYTHING... >
< TRY TELLING HIM THAT! *HE* SURE HASN'T FORGOTTEN *YOU*! >
< AHH, GEEZ, I HATE GUYS WITH GAME. >
HA HA HA HA HA HA HA HA HA HA HA
I THINK HE GOT YA.
< HE'S AMAZING, YOU KNOW. >
< HE USED HIS MONEY TO FOUND A FILM COMPANY. >
< HE HAS A SHOW ON THE CATV DANCE CHANNEL. >
< A DANCE CHANNEL... >
< DO THEY PLAY THE BIG COMPETITIONS? >

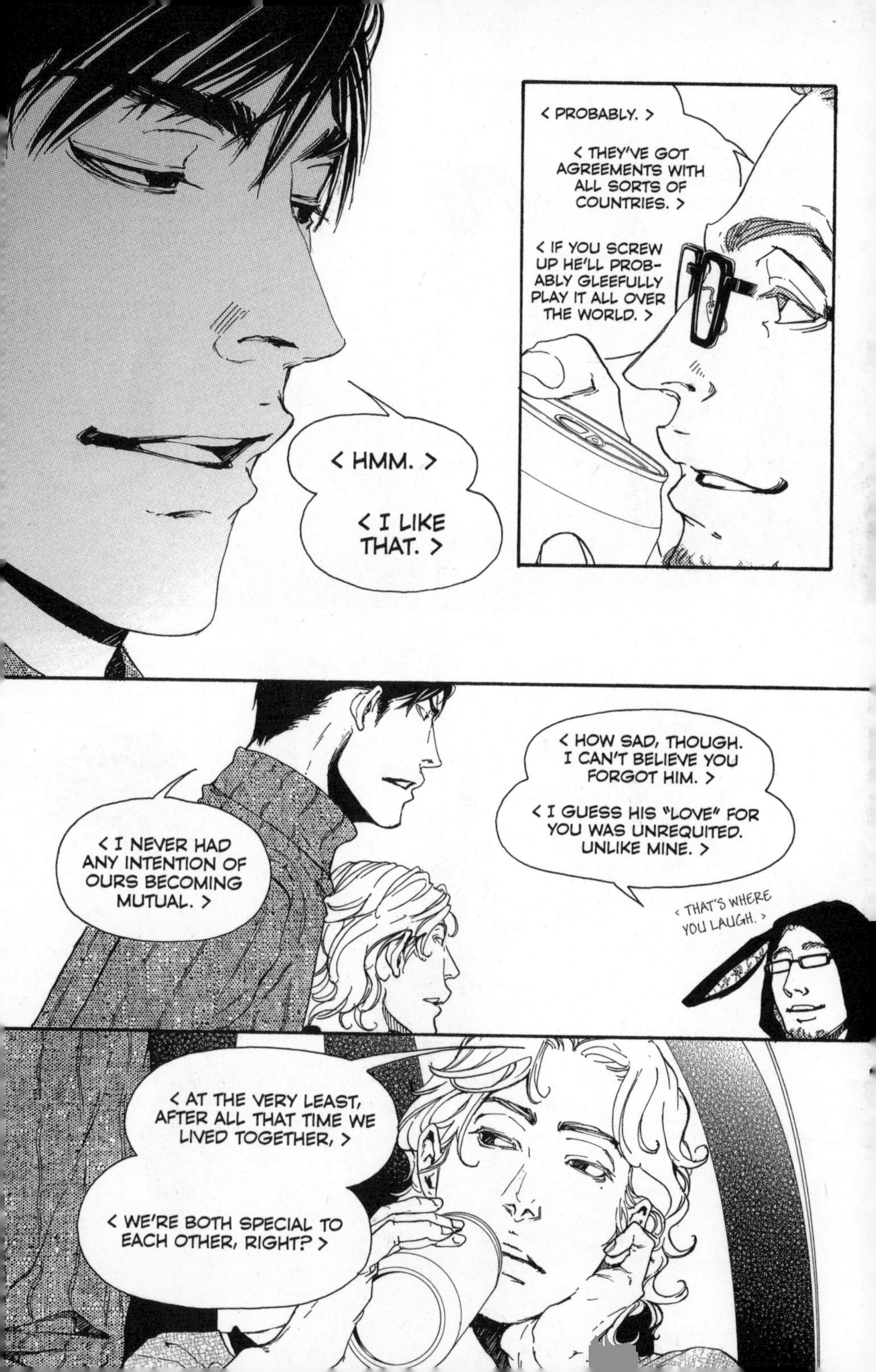
< PROBABLY. >
< THEY'VE GOT AGREEMENTS WITH ALL SORTS OF COUNTRIES. >
< IF YOU SCREW UP HE'LL PROBABLY GLEEFULLY PLAY IT ALL OVER THE WORLD. >
< HMM. >
< I LIKE THAT. >
< HOW SAD, THOUGH. I CAN'T BELIEVE YOU FORGOT HIM. >
< I GUESS HIS "LOVE" FOR YOU WAS UNREQUITED. UNLIKE MINE. >
< I NEVER HAD ANY INTENTION OF OURS BECOMING MUTUAL. >
< THAT'S WHERE YOU LAUGH. >
< AT THE VERY LEAST, AFTER ALL THAT TIME WE LIVED TOGETHER, >
< WE'RE BOTH SPECIAL TO EACH OTHER, RIGHT? >

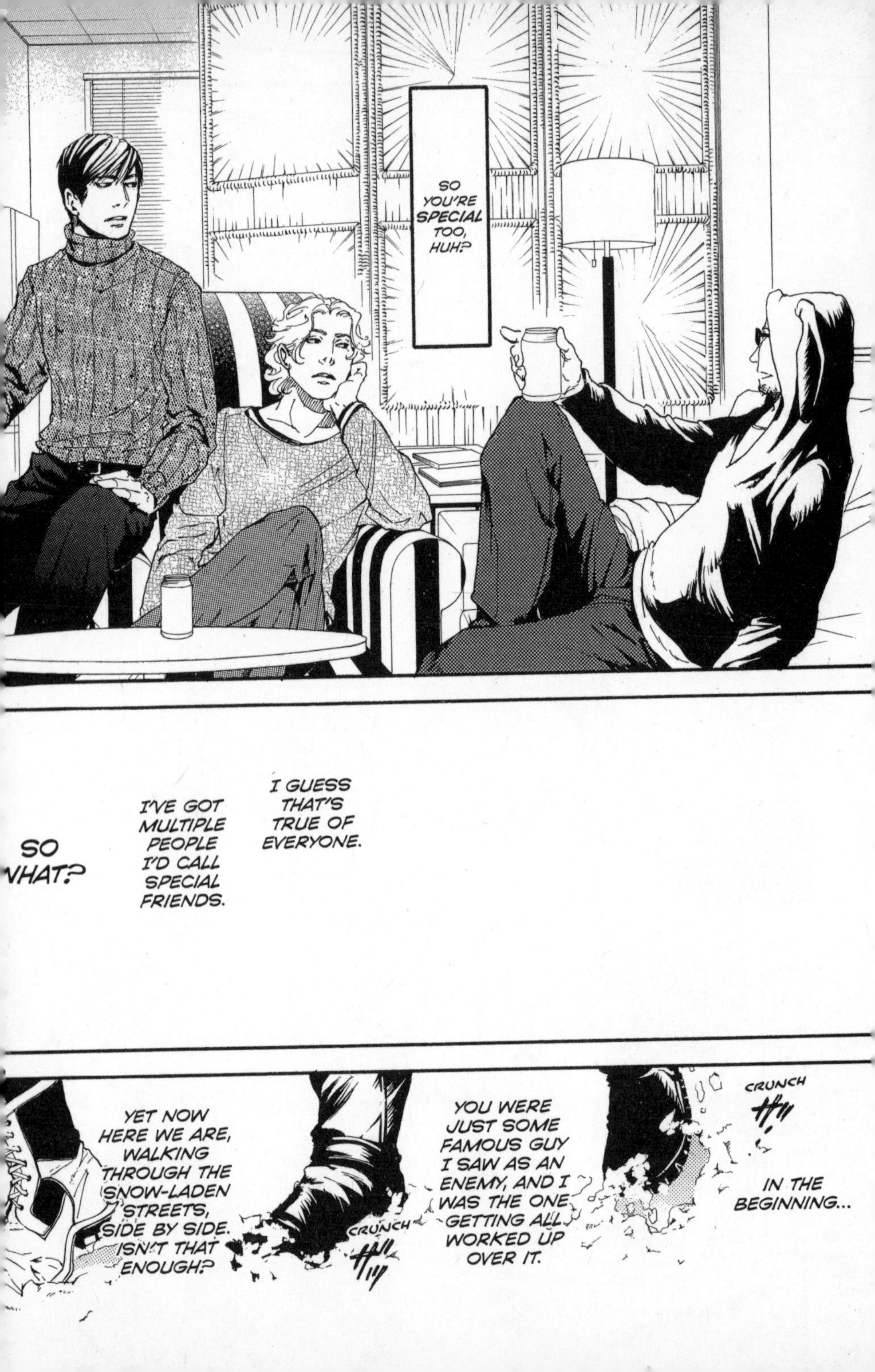
SO YOU'RE SPECIAL TOO, HUH?
I GUESS THAT'S TRUE OF EVERYONE.
I'VE GOT MULTIPLE PEOPLE I'D CALL SPECIAL FRIENDS.
SO WHAT?
CRUNCH
IN THE BEGINNING...
YOU WERE JUST SOME FAMOUS GUY I SAW AS AN ENEMY, AND I WAS THE ONE GETTING ALL WORKED UP OVER IT.
CRUNCH
YET NOW HERE WE ARE, WALKING THROUGH THE SNOW-LADEN STREETS, SIDE BY SIDE. ISN'T THAT ENOUGH?

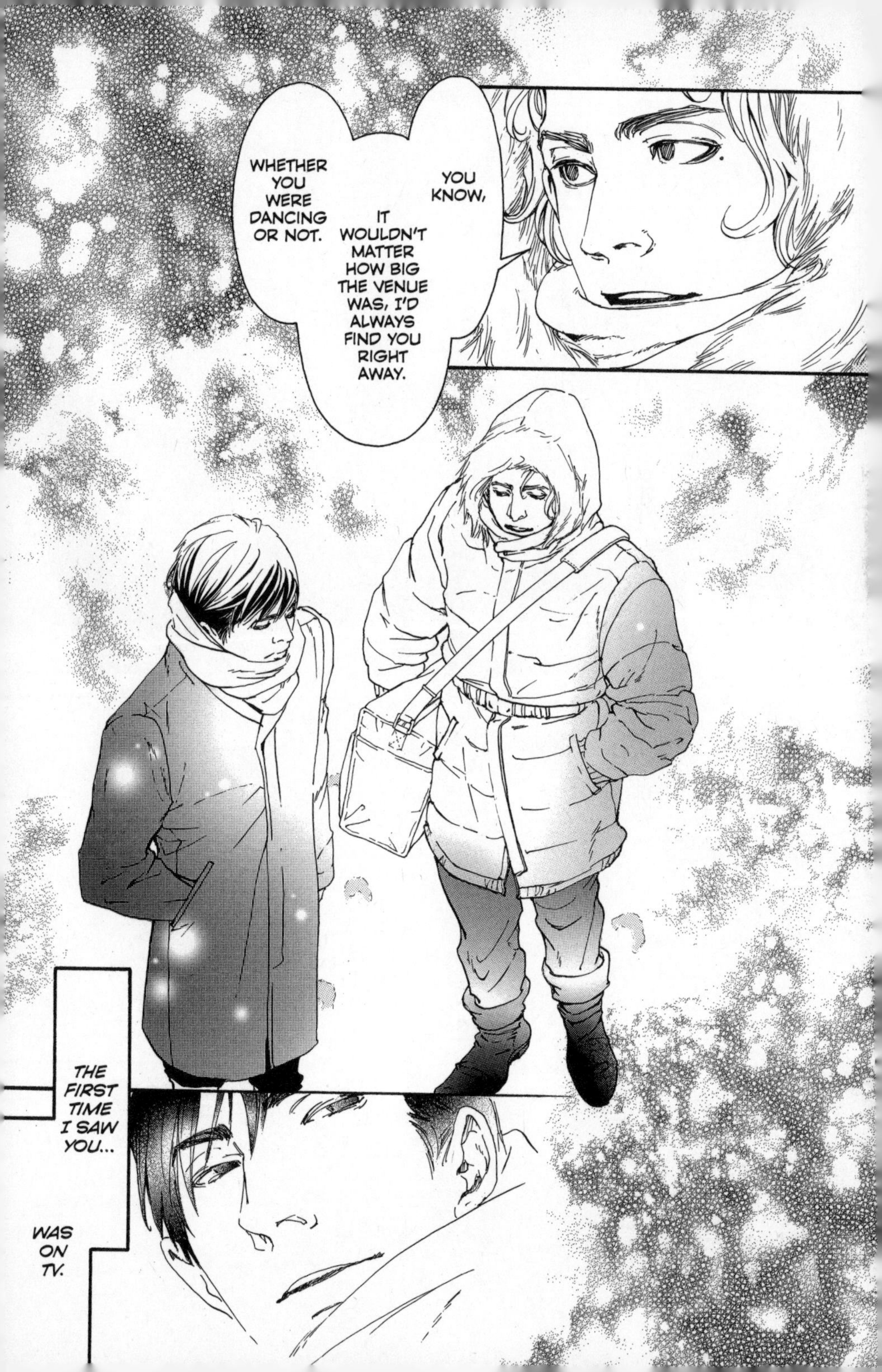
YOU KNOW,
IT WOULDN'T MATTER HOW BIG THE VENUE WAS, I'D ALWAYS FIND YOU RIGHT AWAY.
WHETHER YOU WERE DANCING OR NOT.
THE FIRST TIME I SAW YOU...
WAS ON TV.

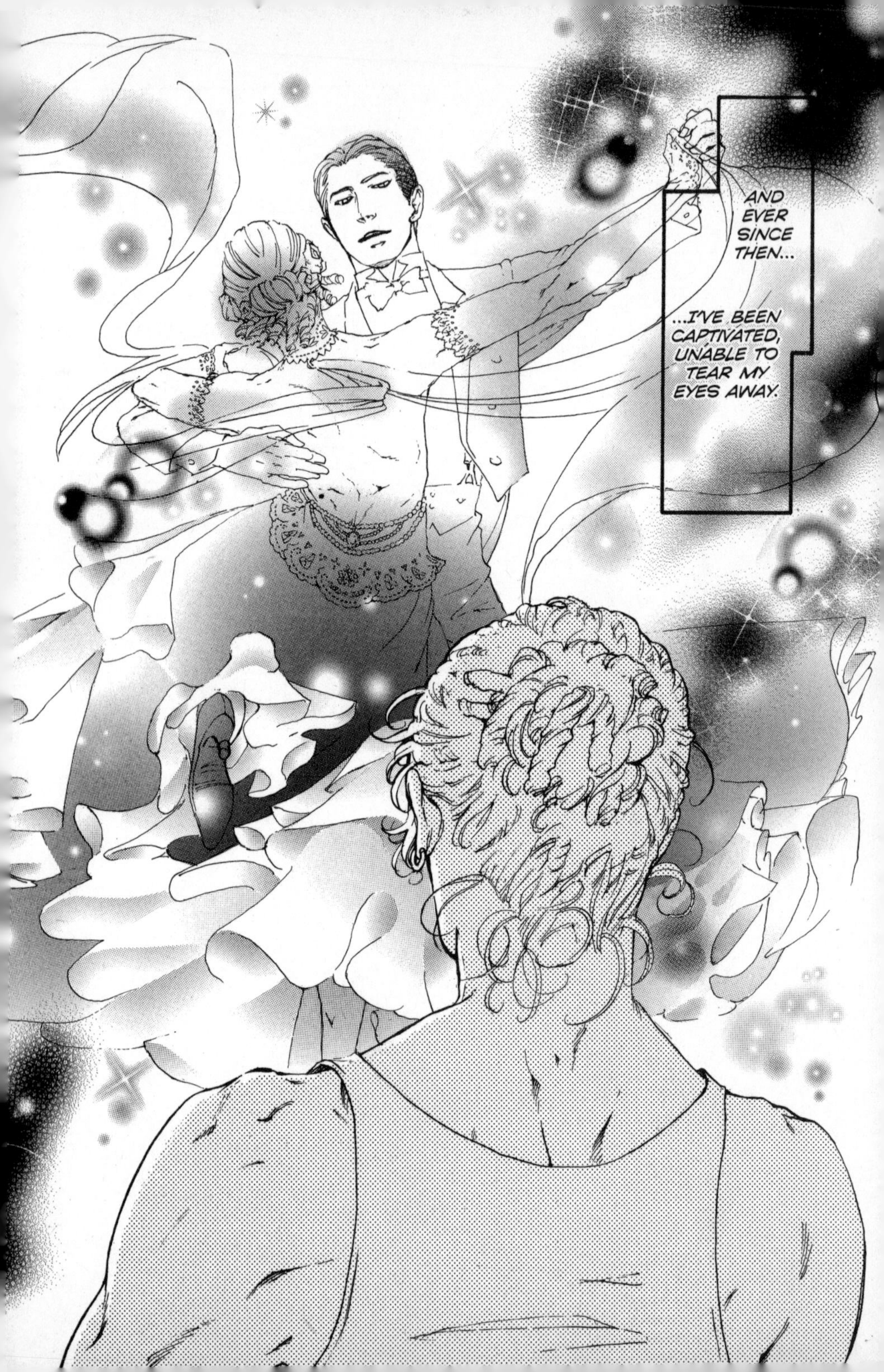
AND EVER SINCE THEN...
...I'VE BEEN CAPTIVATED, UNABLE TO TEAR MY EYES AWAY.

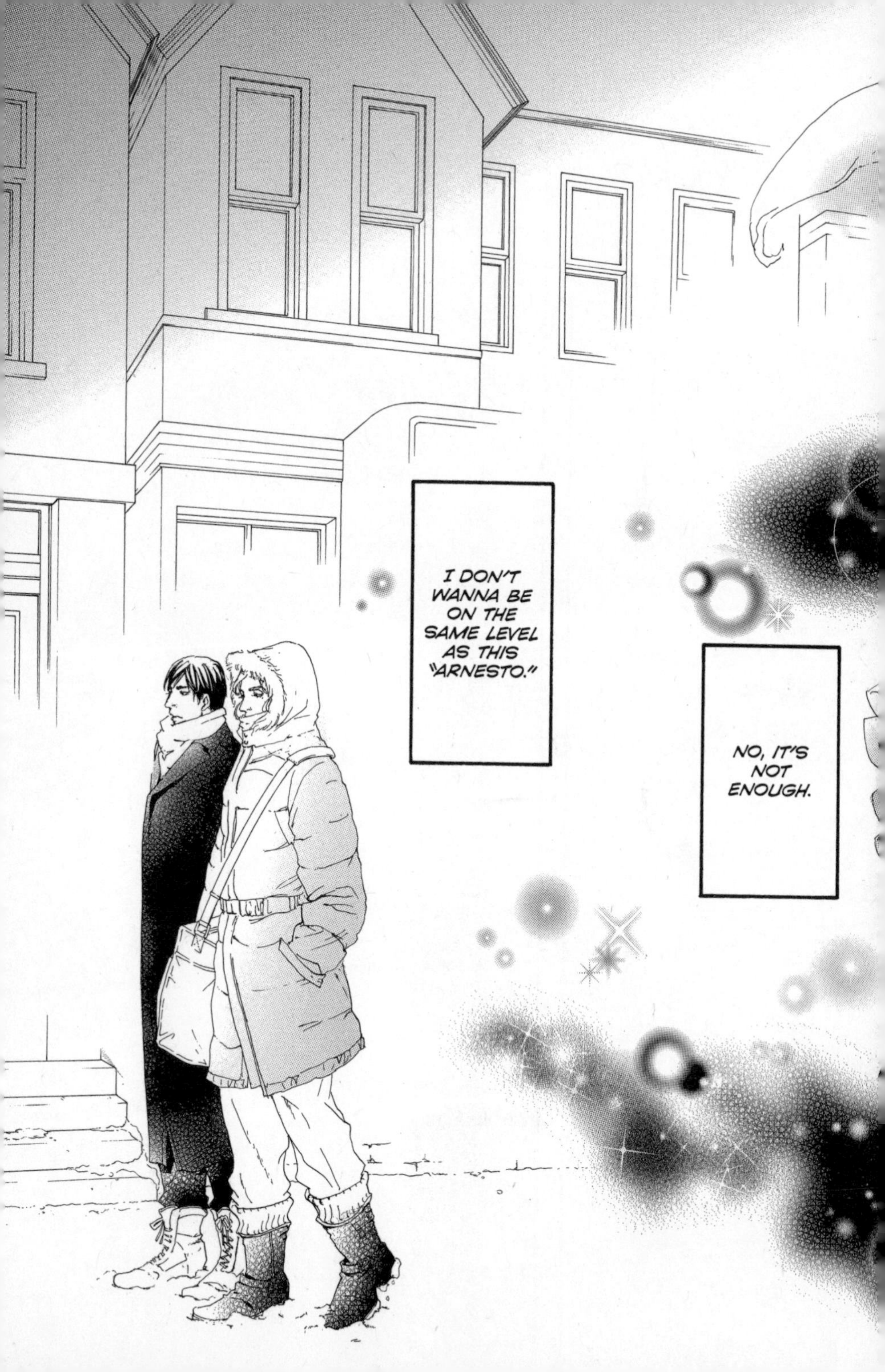
I DON'T WANNA BE ON THE SAME LEVEL AS THIS "ARNESTO."
NO, IT'S NOT ENOUGH.

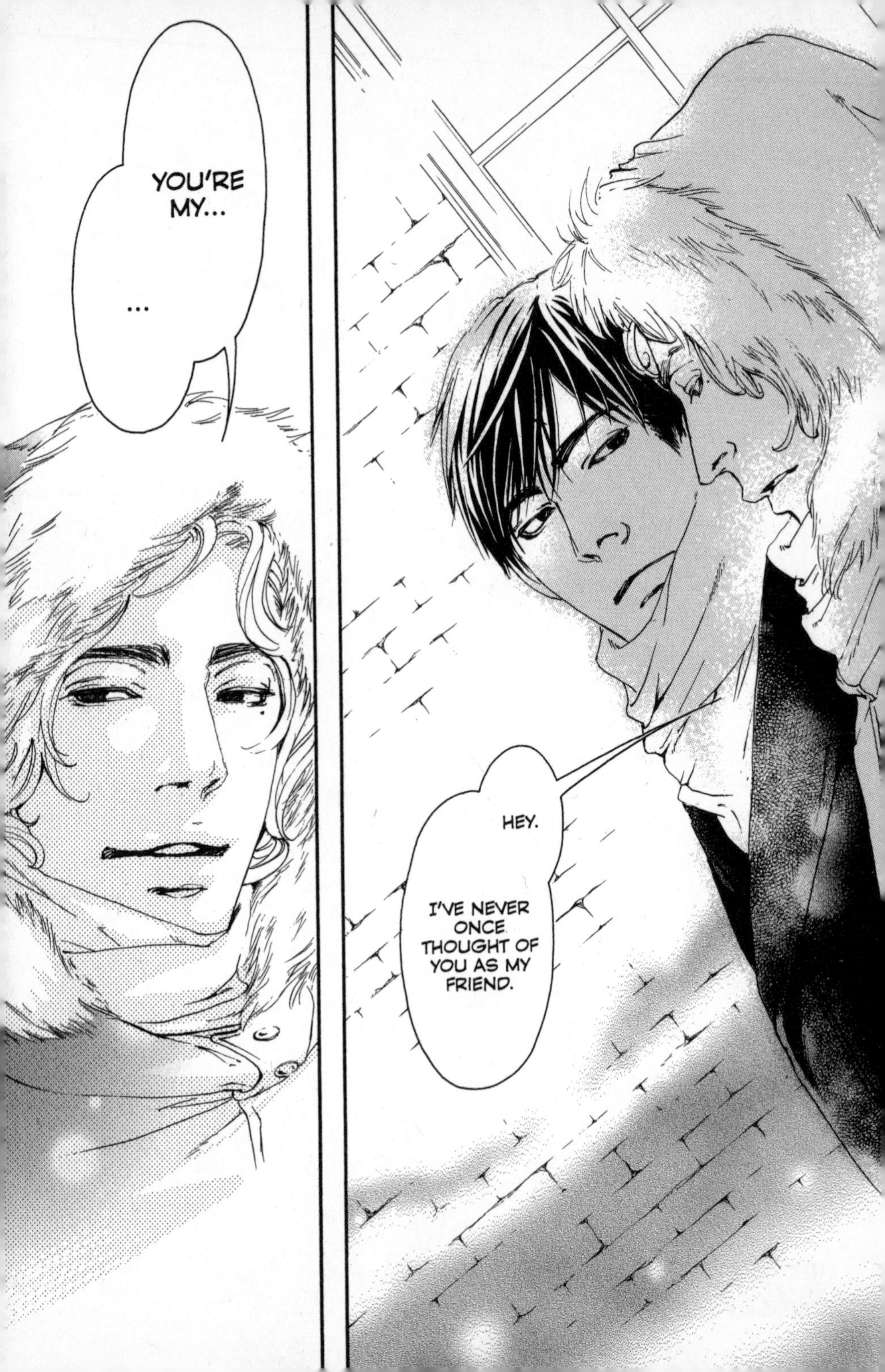
HEY.
I'VE NEVER ONCE THOUGHT OF YOU AS MY FRIEND.
YOU'RE MY...
...

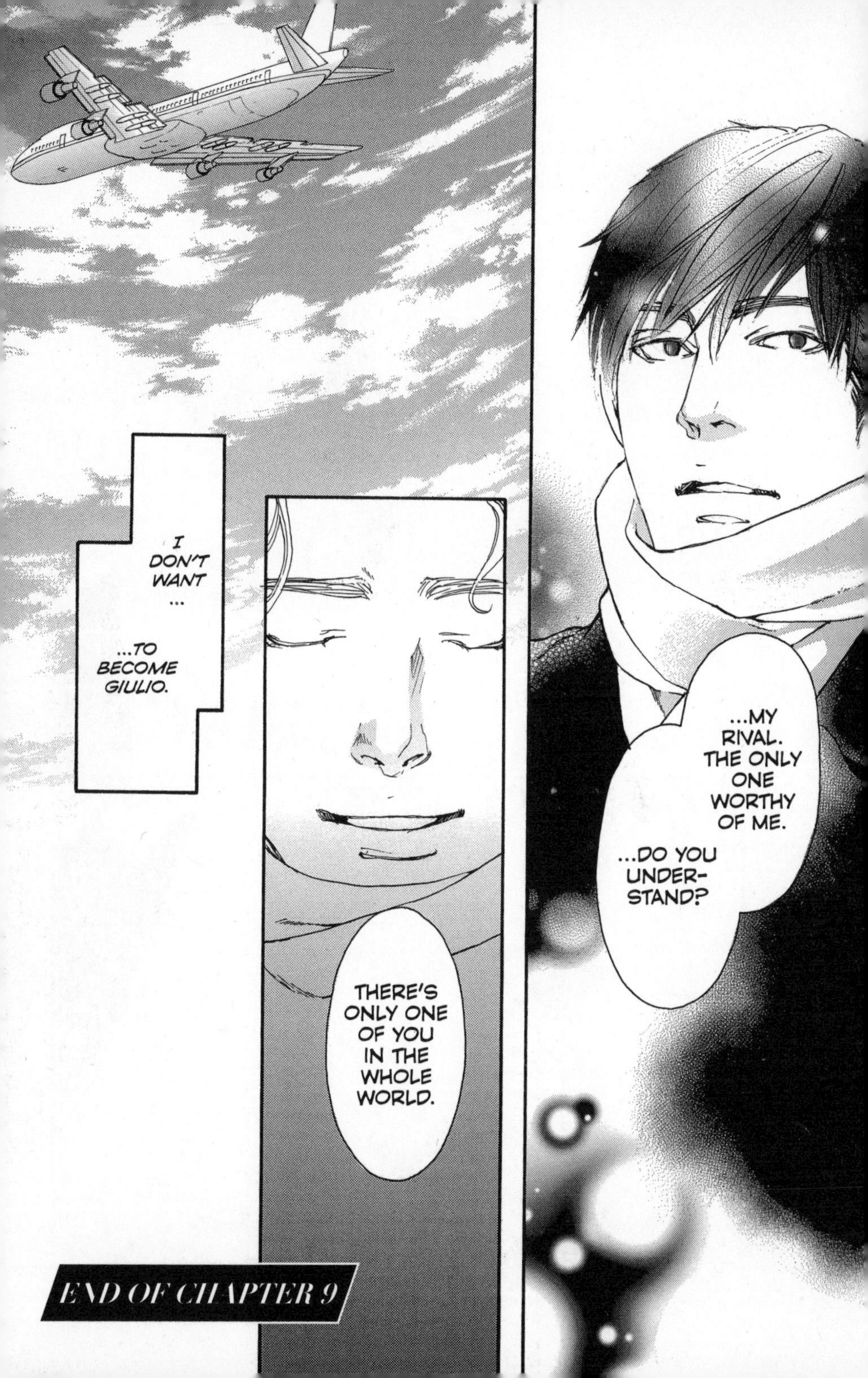
...MY RIVAL. THE ONLY ONE WORTHY OF ME.
...DO YOU UNDER-STAND?
THERE'S ONLY ONE OF YOU IN THE WHOLE WORLD.
I DON'T WANT ...
...TO BECOME GIULIO.
END OF CHAPTER 9

10 DANCE

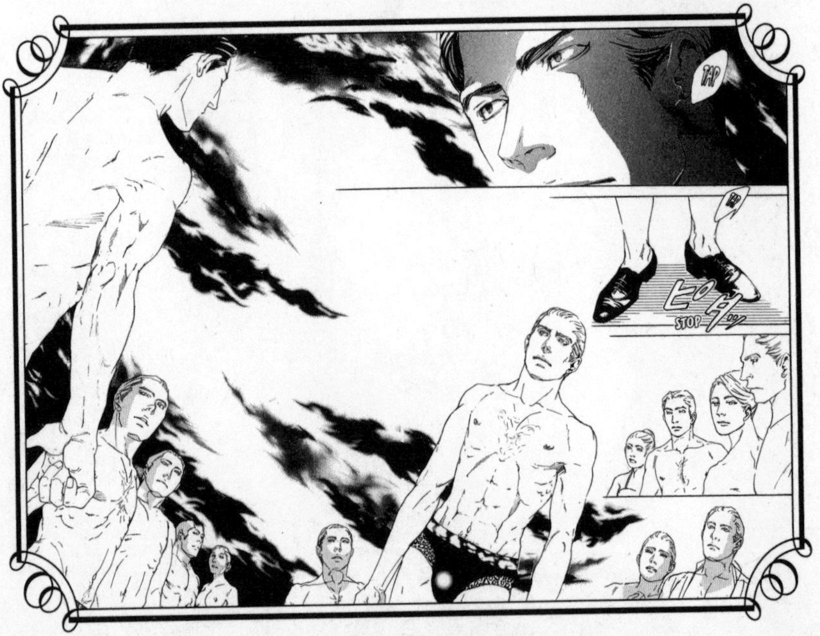
TAP
TAP
STOP

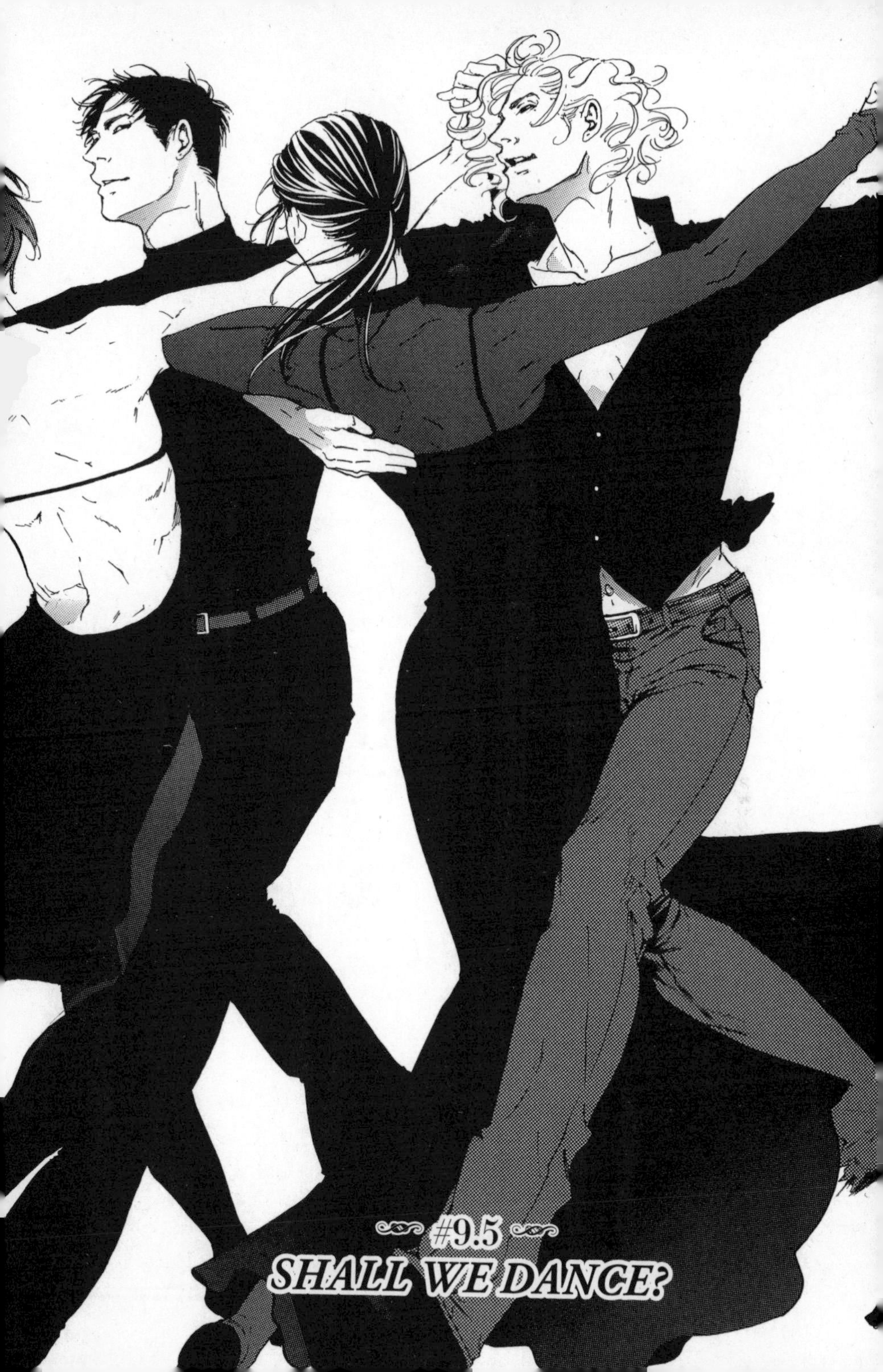
#9.5
SHALL WE DANCE?

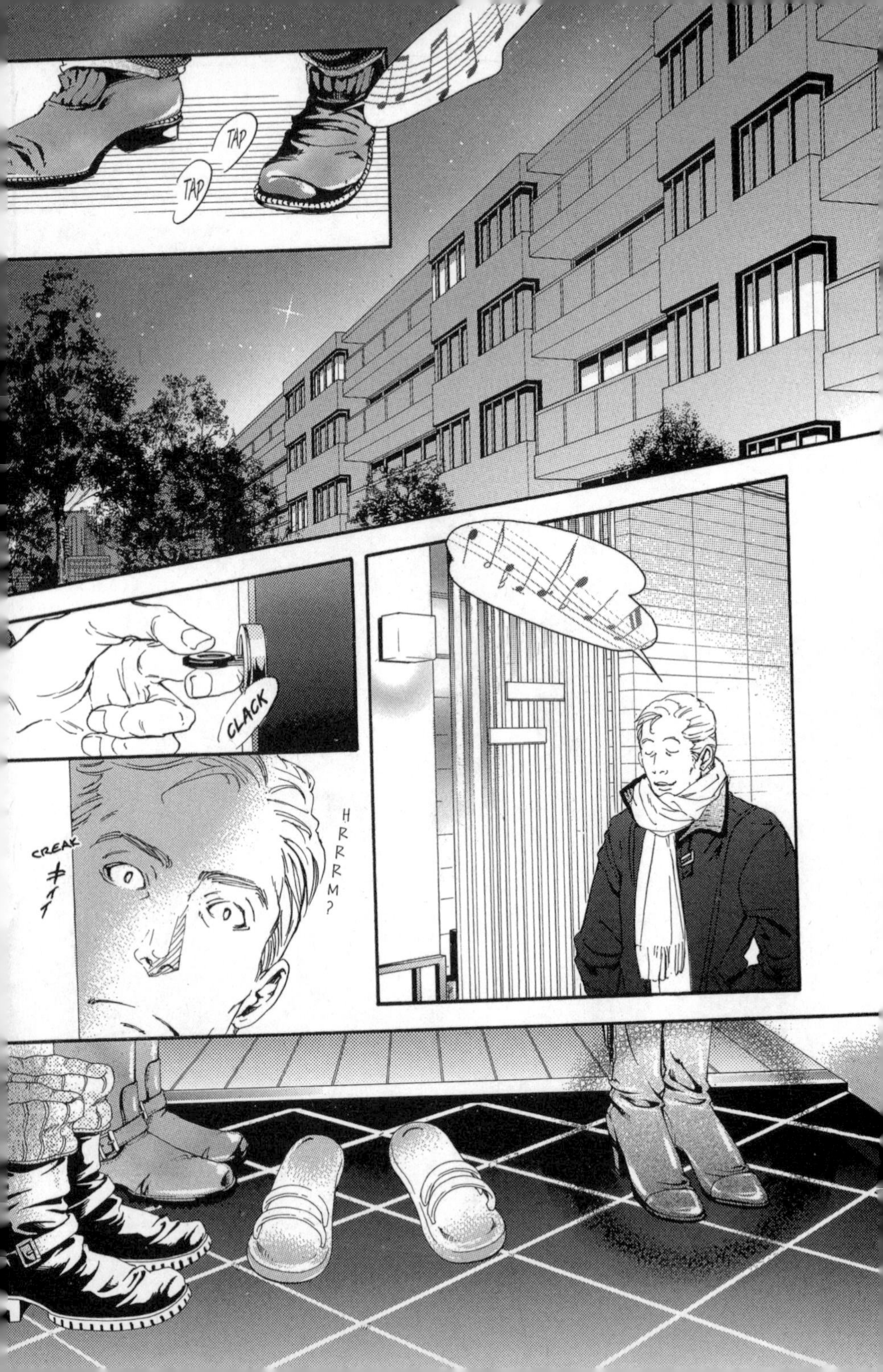
TAP
TAP
CLACK
HRRRM?
CREAK

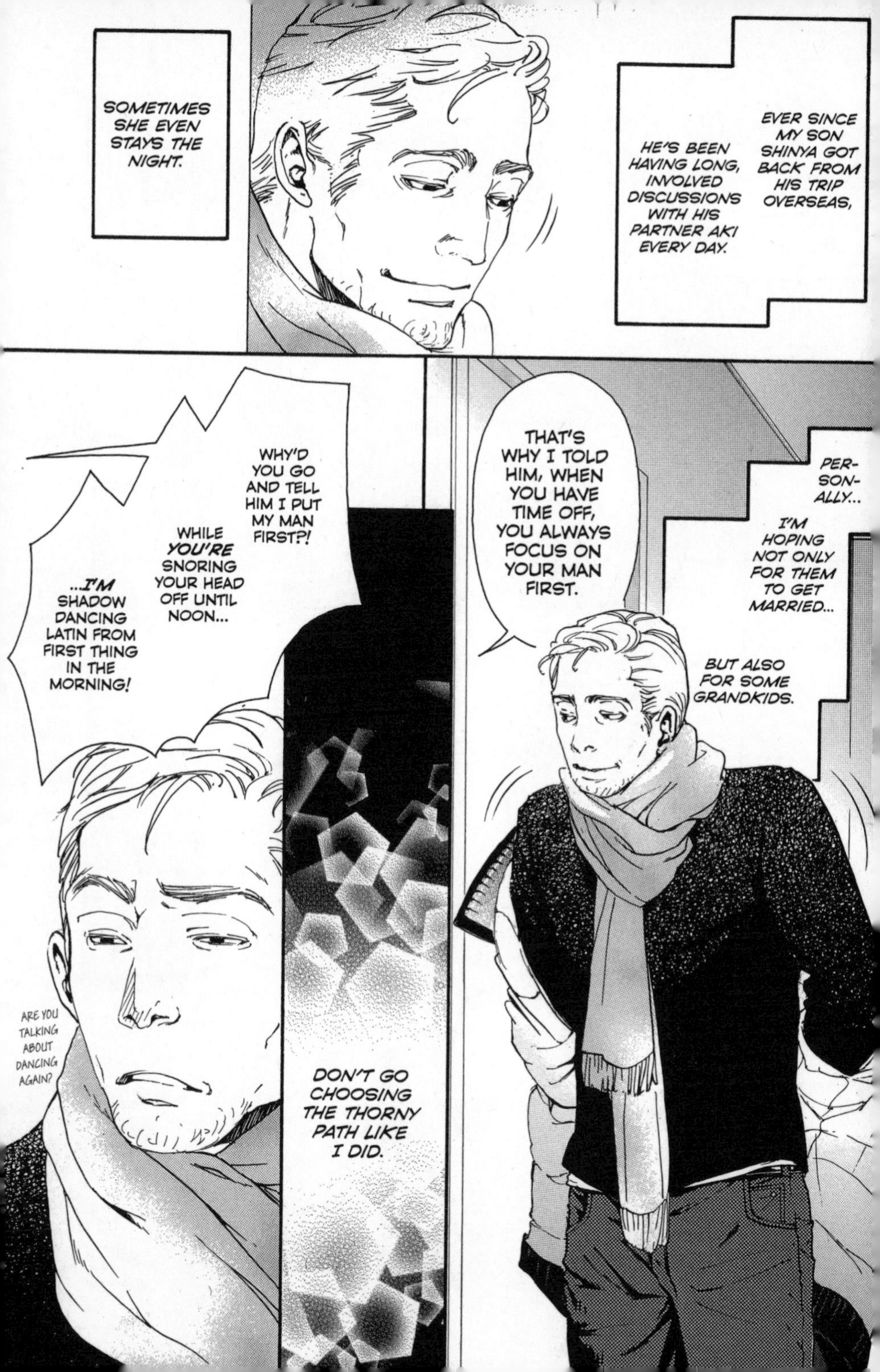
EVER SINCE MY SON SHINYA GOT BACK FROM HIS TRIP OVERSEAS,
HE'S BEEN HAVING LONG, INVOLVED DISCUSSIONS WITH HIS PARTNER AKI EVERY DAY.
SOMETIMES SHE EVEN STAYS THE NIGHT.
PER-SON-ALLY...
I'M HOPING NOT ONLY FOR THEM TO GET MARRIED...
BUT ALSO FOR SOME GRANDKIDS.
THAT'S WHY I TOLD HIM, WHEN YOU HAVE TIME OFF, YOU ALWAYS FOCUS ON YOUR MAN FIRST.
DON'T GO CHOOSING THE THORNY PATH LIKE I DID.
WHY'D YOU GO AND TELL HIM I PUT MY MAN FIRST?!
WHILE *YOU'RE* SNORING YOUR HEAD OFF UNTIL NOON...
...*I'M* SHADOW DANCING LATIN FROM FIRST THING IN THE MORNING!
ARE YOU TALKING ABOUT DANCING AGAIN?

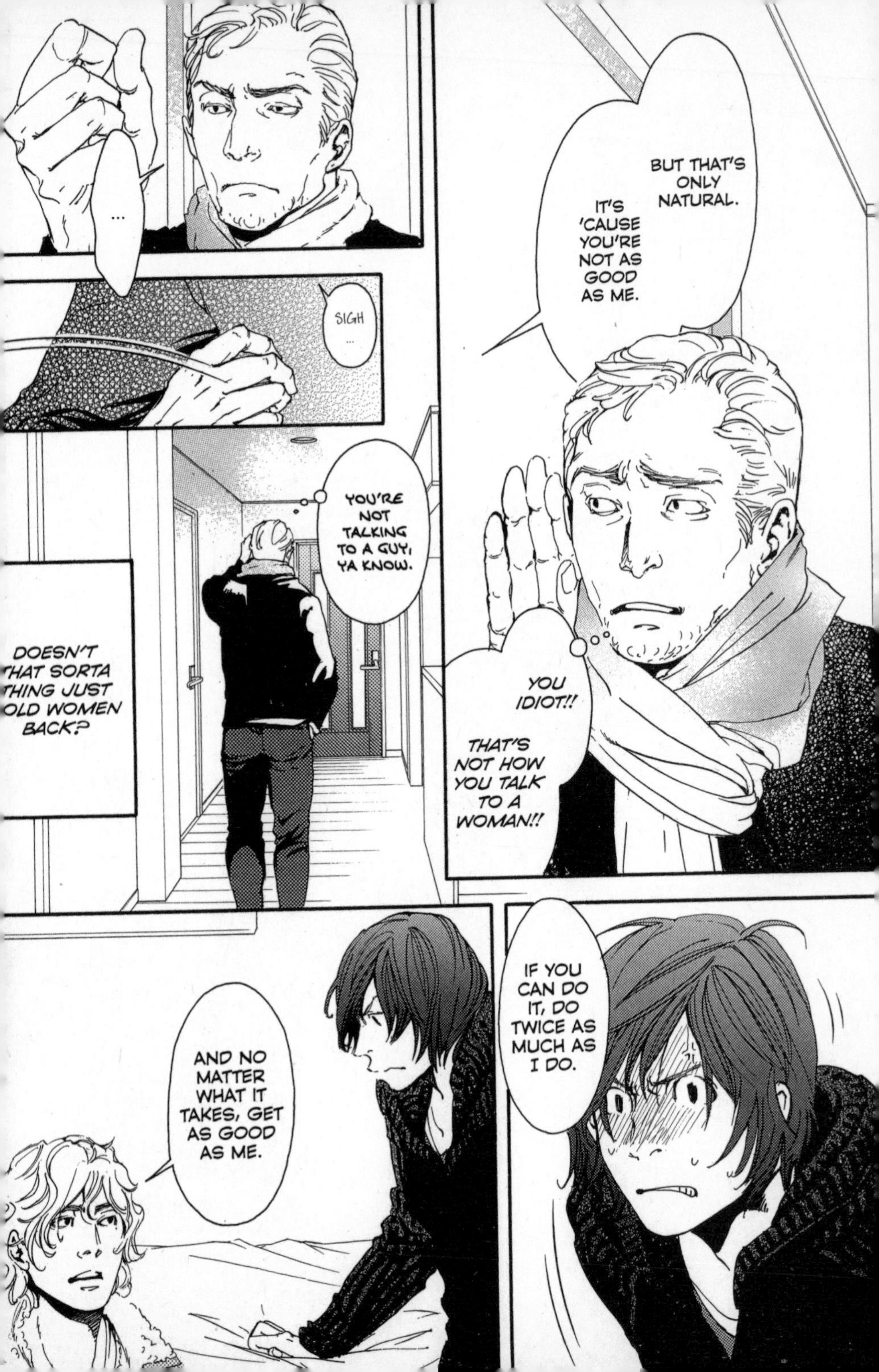
BUT THAT'S ONLY NATURAL.
IT'S 'CAUSE YOU'RE NOT AS GOOD AS ME.
YOU IDIOT!!
THAT'S NOT HOW YOU TALK TO A WOMAN!!
...
SIGH ...
YOU'RE NOT TALKING TO A GUY, YA KNOW.
DOESN'T THAT SORTA THING JUST OLD WOMEN BACK?
IF YOU CAN DO IT, DO TWICE AS MUCH AS I DO.
AND NO MATTER WHAT IT TAKES, GET AS GOOD AS ME.

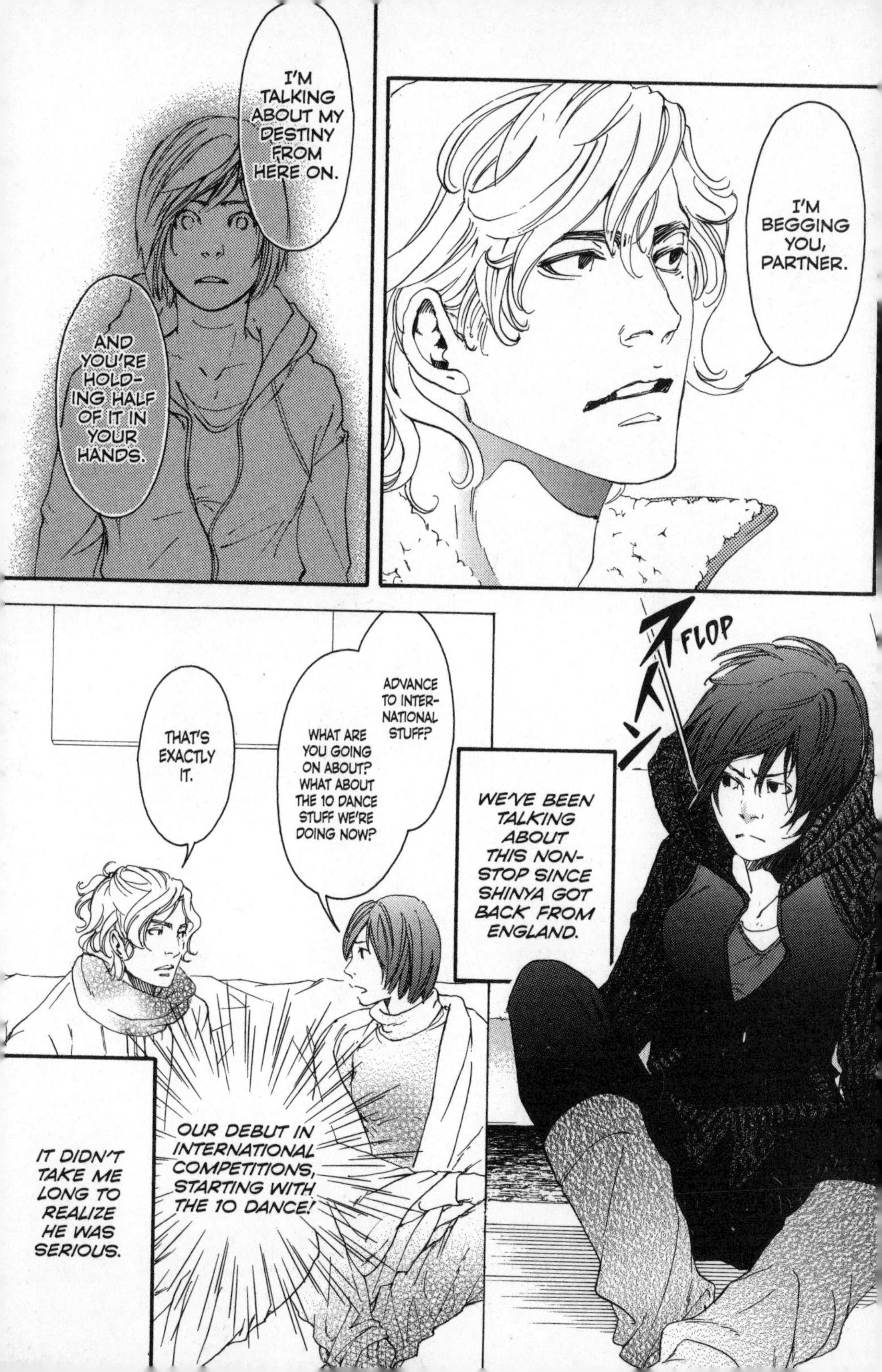
I'M BEGGING YOU, PARTNER.
I'M TALKING ABOUT MY DESTINY FROM HERE ON.
AND YOU'RE HOLD-ING HALF OF IT IN YOUR HANDS.
FLOP
WE'VE BEEN TALKING ABOUT THIS NON-STOP SINCE SHINYA GOT BACK FROM ENGLAND.
ADVANCE TO INTER-NATIONAL STUFF?
WHAT ARE YOU GOING ON ABOUT? WHAT ABOUT THE 10 DANCE STUFF WE'RE DOING NOW?
THAT'S EXACTLY IT.
OUR DEBUT IN INTERNATIONAL COMPETITIONS, STARTING WITH THE 10 DANCE!
IT DIDN'T TAKE ME LONG TO REALIZE HE WAS SERIOUS.

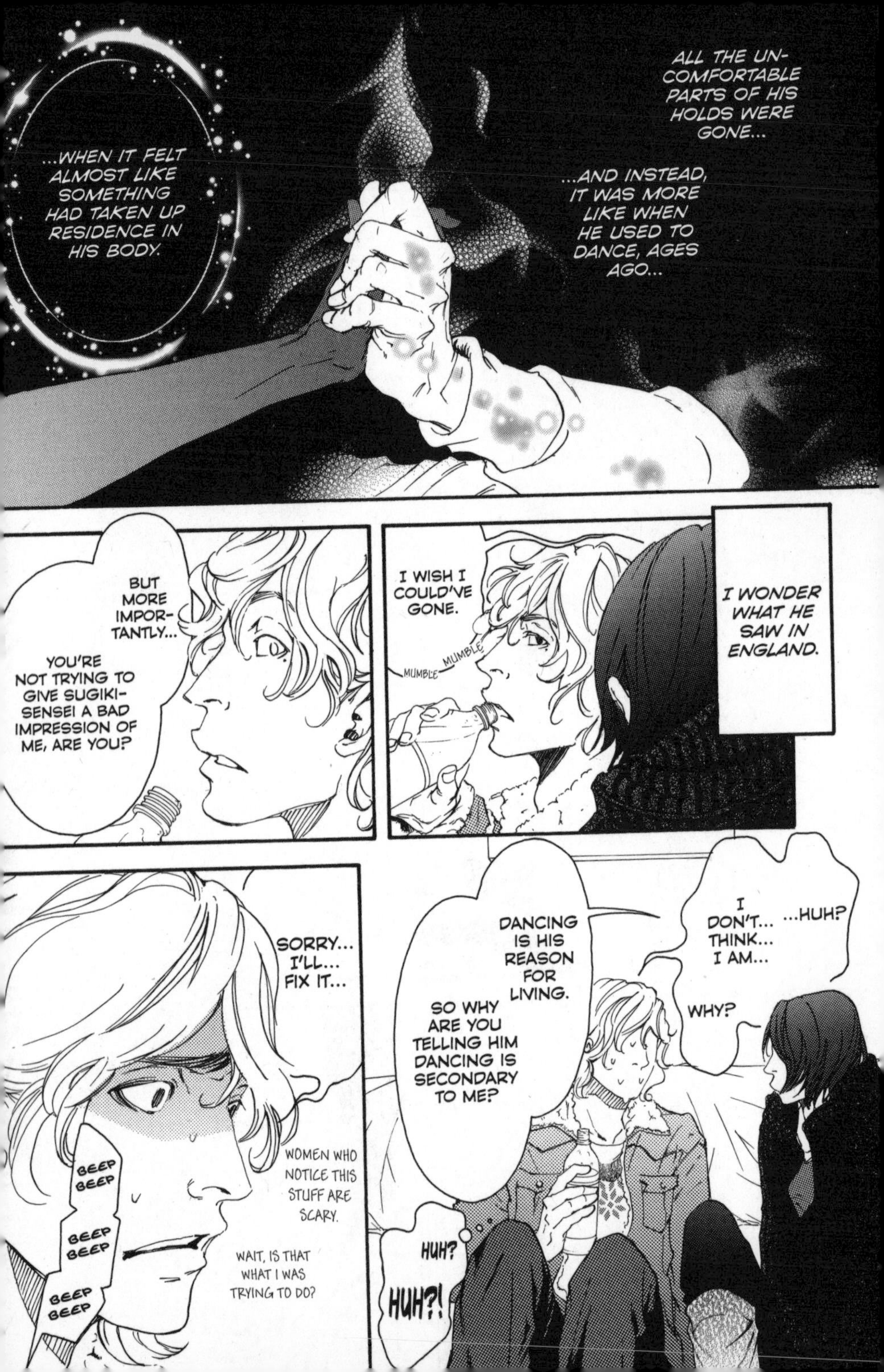
ALL THE UN-COMFORTABLE PARTS OF HIS HOLDS WERE GONE...
...AND INSTEAD, IT WAS MORE LIKE WHEN HE USED TO DANCE, AGES AGO...
...WHEN IT FELT ALMOST LIKE SOMETHING HAD TAKEN UP RESIDENCE IN HIS BODY.
I WONDER WHAT HE SAW IN ENGLAND.
I WISH I COULD'VE GONE.
MUMBLE MUMBLE
BUT MORE IMPOR-TANTLY...
YOU'RE NOT TRYING TO GIVE SUGIKI-SENSEI A BAD IMPRESSION OF ME, ARE YOU?
...HUH?
I DON'T... THINK... I AM...
WHY?
DANCING IS HIS REASON FOR LIVING.
SO WHY ARE YOU TELLING HIM DANCING IS SECONDARY TO ME?
HUH?
HUH?!
SORRY... I'LL... FIX IT...
WOMEN WHO NOTICE THIS STUFF ARE SCARY.
WAIT, IS THAT WHAT I WAS TRYING TO DO?
BEEP BEEP
BEEP BEEP
BEEP BEEP

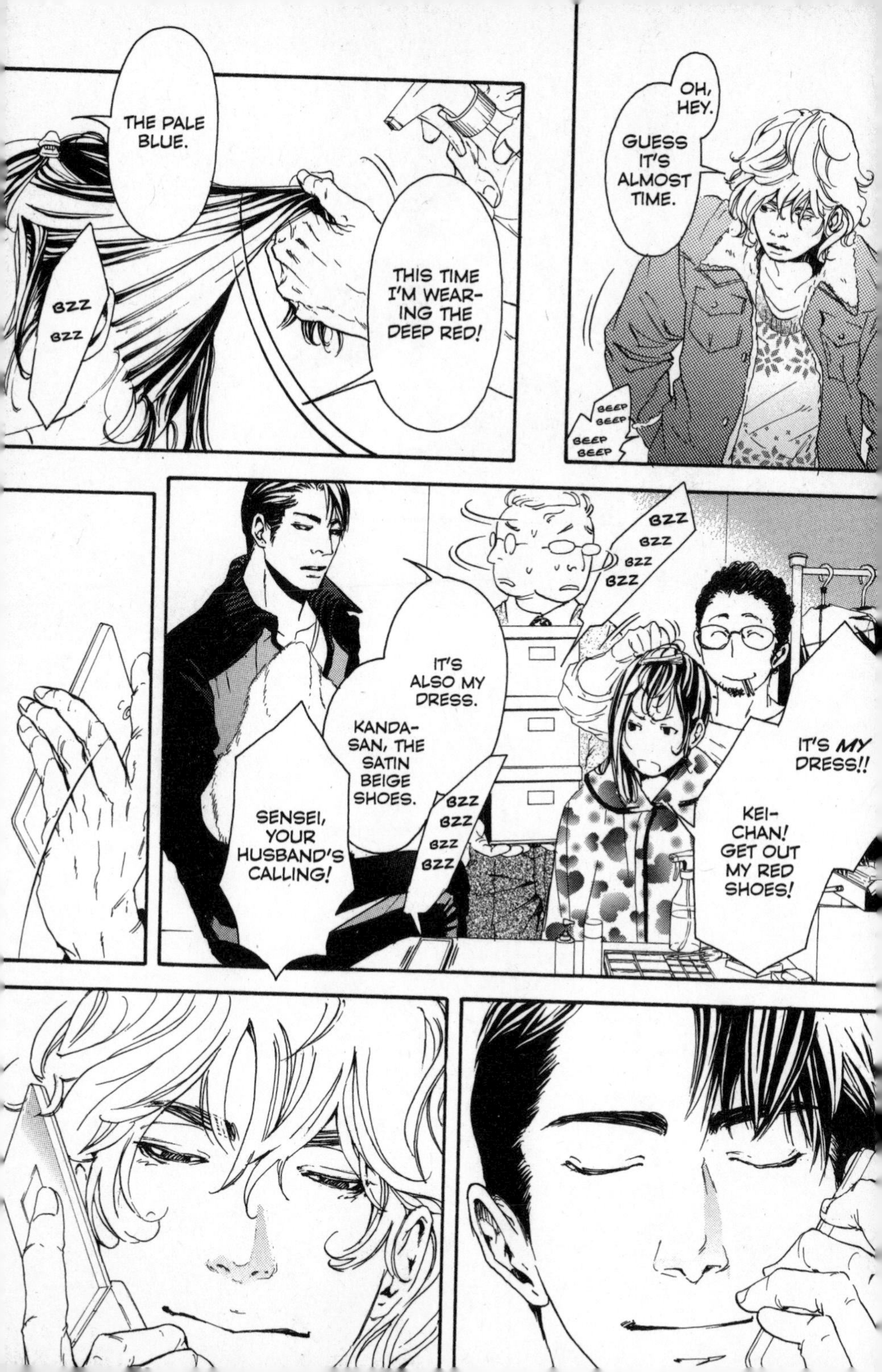
OH, HEY.
GUESS IT'S ALMOST TIME.
BEEP BEEP
BEEP BEEP
THIS TIME I'M WEAR-ING THE DEEP RED!
THE PALE BLUE.
BZZ
BZZ
IT'S *MY* DRESS!!
KEI-CHAN! GET OUT MY RED SHOES!
BZZ
BZZ
BZZ
BZZ
IT'S ALSO MY DRESS.
KANDA-SAN, THE SATIN BEIGE SHOES.
BZZ
BZZ
BZZ
BZZ
SENSEI, YOUR HUSBAND'S CALLING!

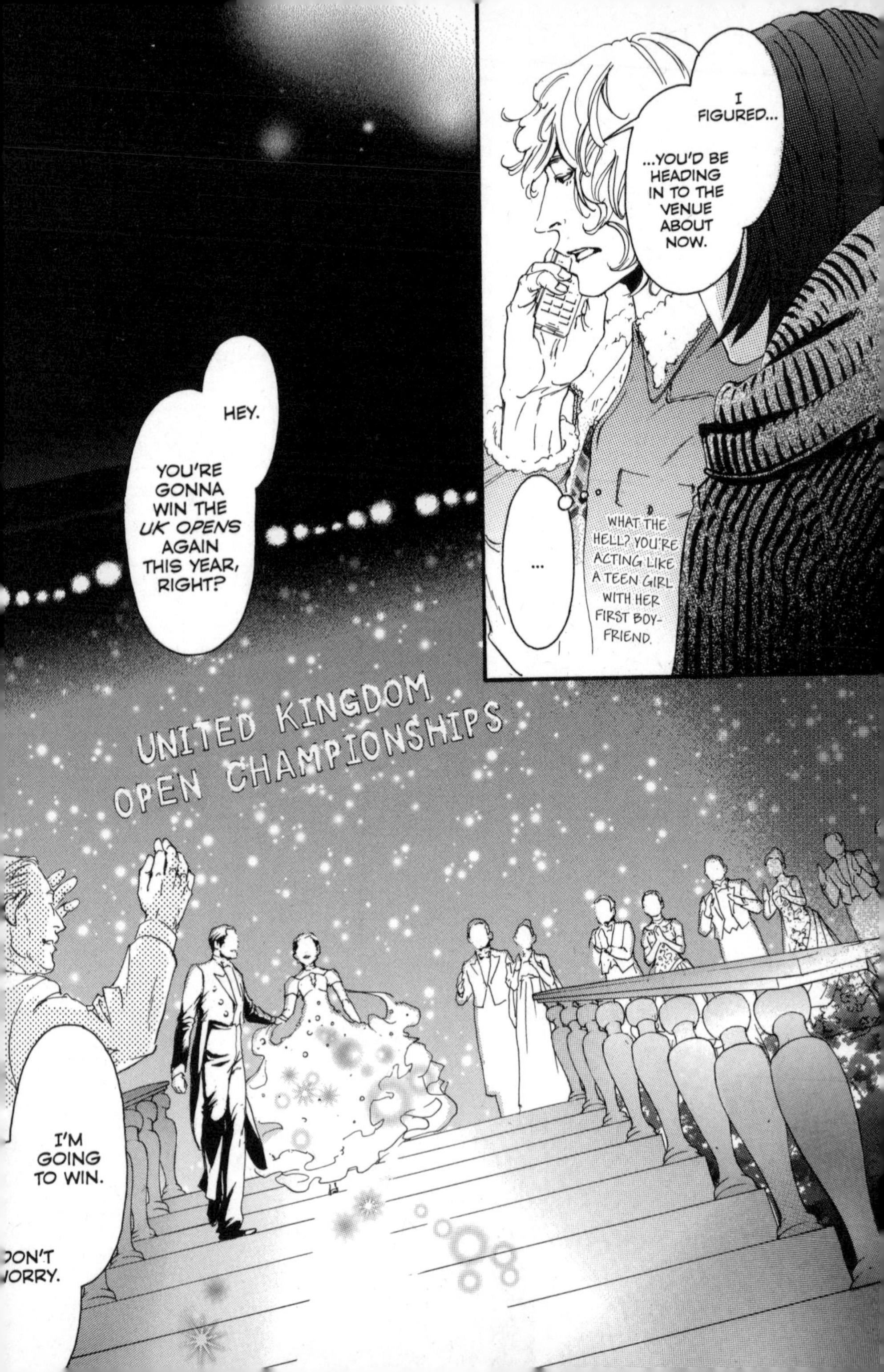
I FIGURED...
...YOU'D BE HEADING IN TO THE VENUE ABOUT NOW.
...
WHAT THE HELL? YOU'RE ACTING LIKE A TEEN GIRL WITH HER FIRST BOY-FRIEND.
HEY.
YOU'RE GONNA WIN THE *UK OPENS* AGAIN THIS YEAR, RIGHT?
UNITED KINGDOM OPEN CHAMPIONSHIPS
I'M GOING TO WIN.
DON'T WORRY.

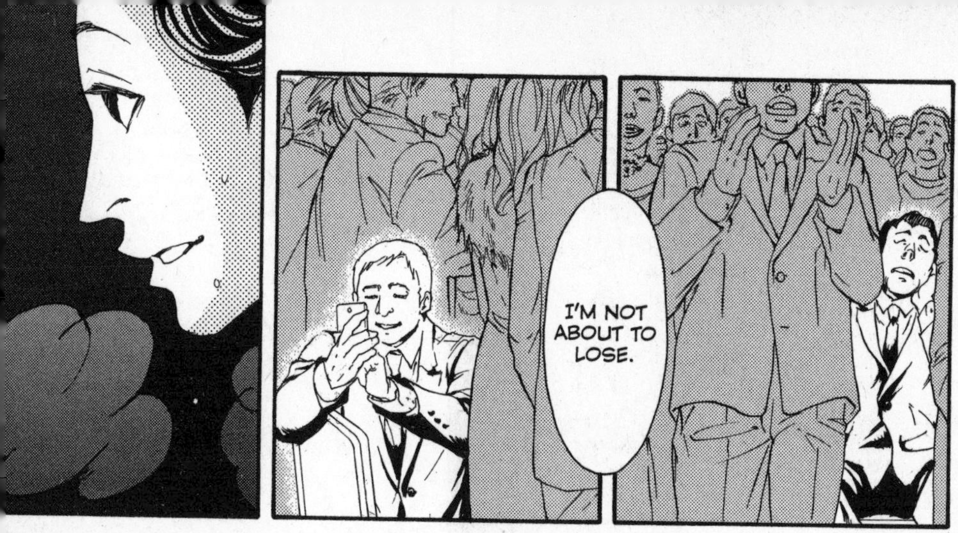
I'M NOT ABOUT TO LOSE.

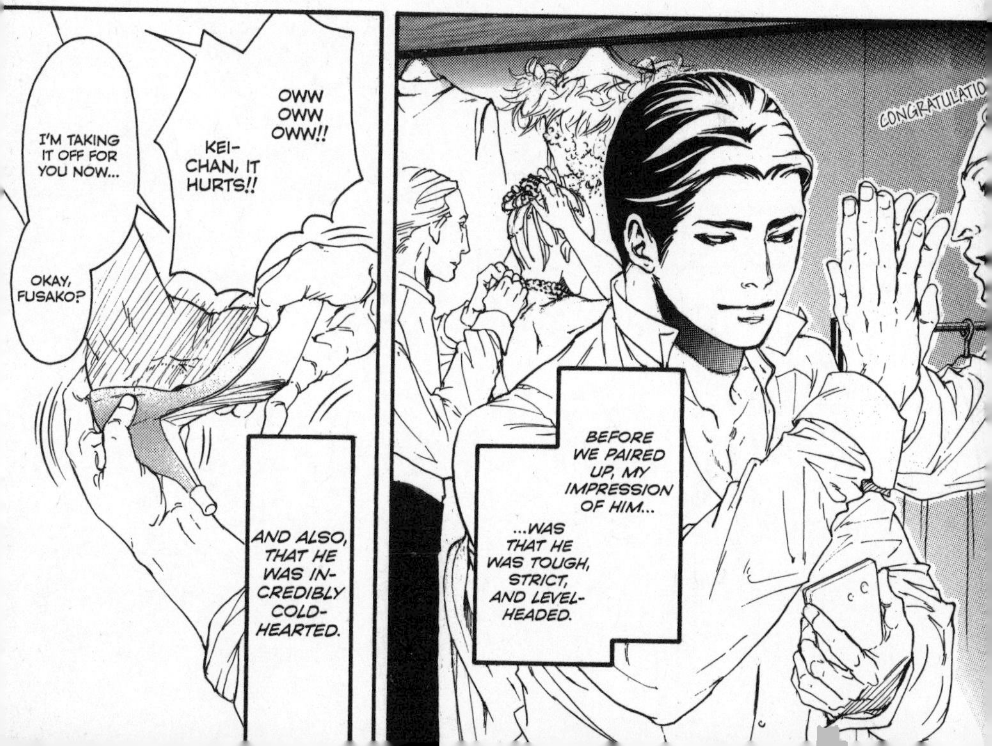
CONGRATULATIO
BEFORE WE PAIRED UP, MY IMPRESSION OF HIM...
...WAS THAT HE WAS TOUGH, STRICT, AND LEVEL-HEADED.
OWW OWW OWW!!
KEI-CHAN, IT HURTS!!
I'M TAKING IT OFF FOR YOU NOW...
OKAY, FUSAKO?
AND ALSO, THAT HE WAS IN-CREDIBLY COLD-HEARTED.

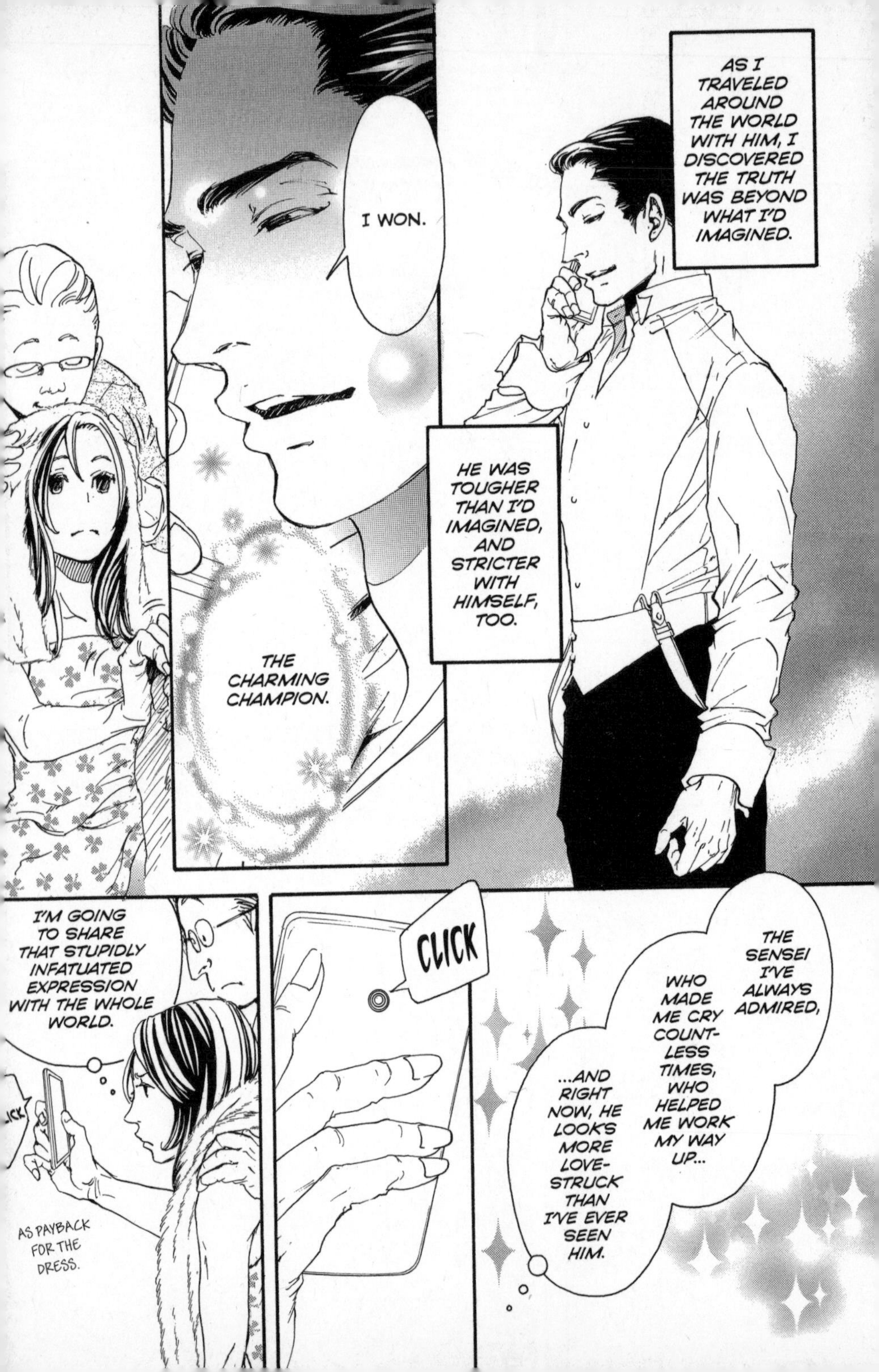
AS I TRAVELED AROUND THE WORLD WITH HIM, I DISCOVERED THE TRUTH WAS BEYOND WHAT I'D IMAGINED.
HE WAS TOUGHER THAN I'D IMAGINED, AND STRICTER WITH HIMSELF, TOO.
I WON.
THE CHARMING CHAMPION.
THE SENSEI I'VE ALWAYS ADMIRED,
WHO MADE ME CRY COUNTLESS TIMES, WHO HELPED ME WORK MY WAY UP...
...AND RIGHT NOW, HE LOOKS MORE LOVE-STRUCK THAN I'VE EVER SEEN HIM.
CLICK
I'M GOING TO SHARE THAT STUPIDLY INFATUATED EXPRESSION WITH THE WHOLE WORLD.
AS PAYBACK FOR THE DRESS.

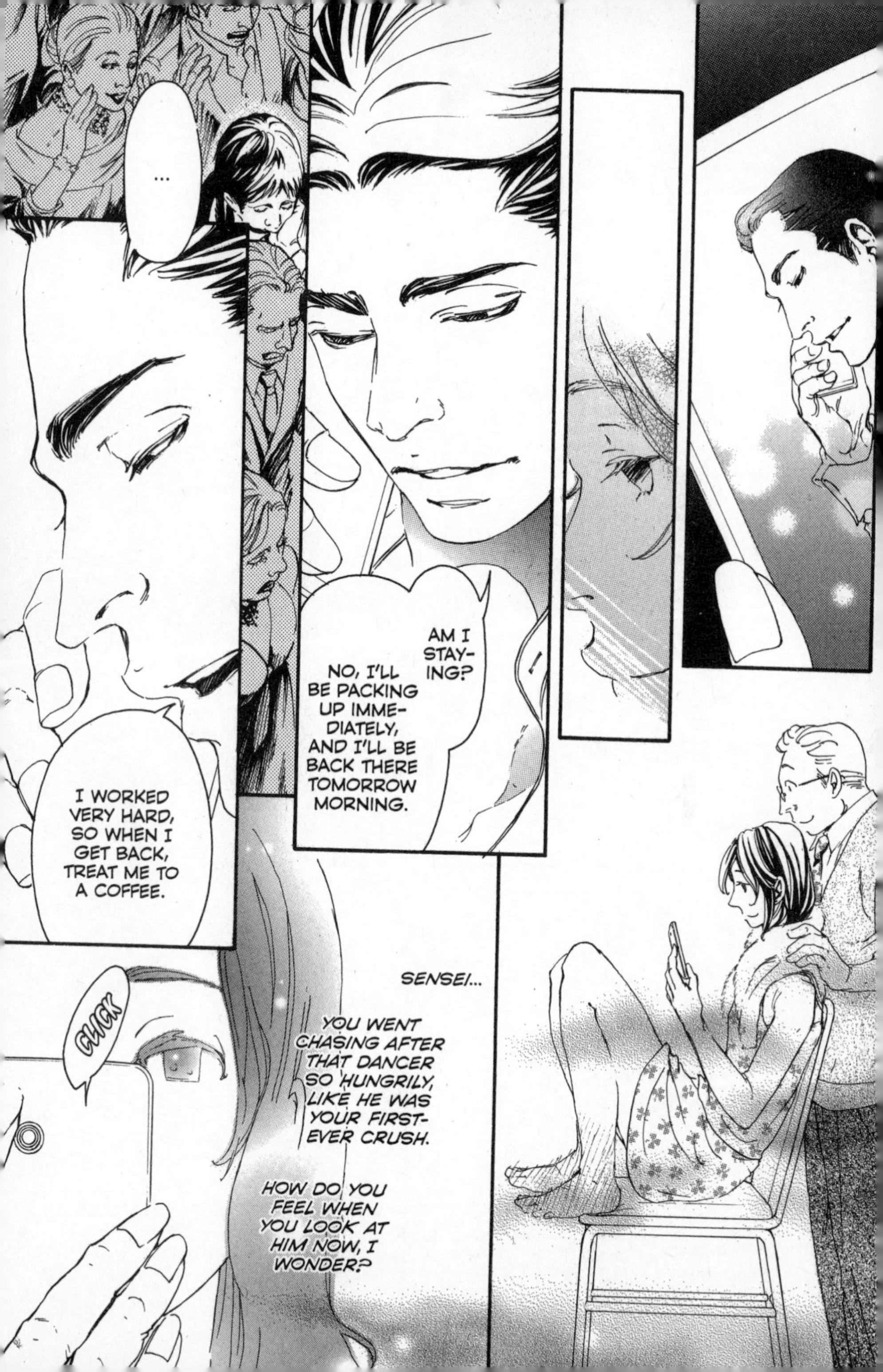
AM I STAYING? NO, I'LL BE PACKING UP IMMEDIATELY, AND I'LL BE BACK THERE TOMORROW MORNING.
...
I WORKED VERY HARD, SO WHEN I GET BACK, TREAT ME TO A COFFEE.
SENSEI...
YOU WENT CHASING AFTER THAT DANCER SO HUNGRILY, LIKE HE WAS YOUR FIRST-EVER CRUSH.
HOW DO YOU FEEL WHEN YOU LOOK AT HIM NOW, I WONDER?
CLICK

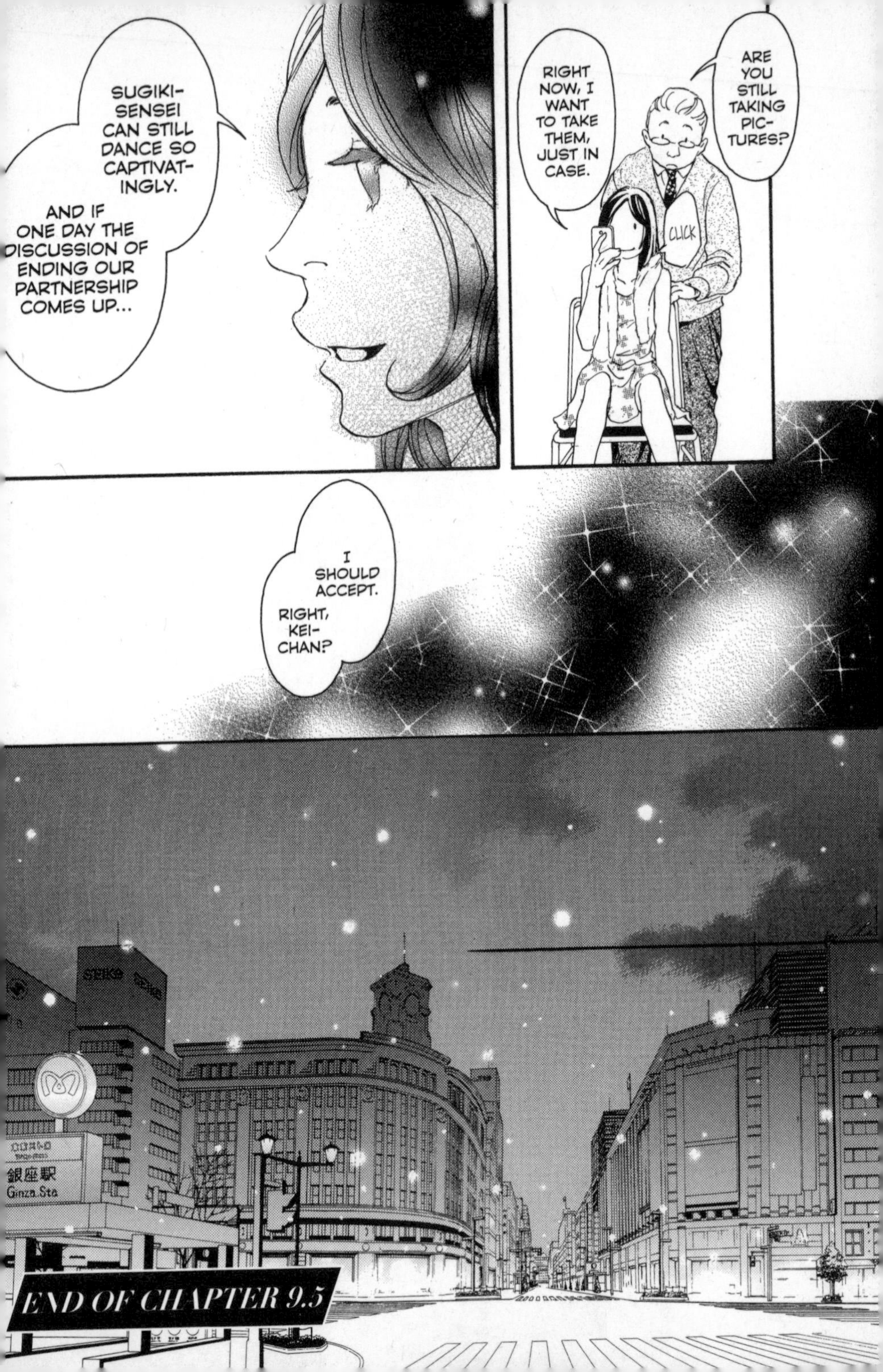
ARE YOU STILL TAKING PICTURES?
RIGHT NOW, I WANT TO TAKE THEM, JUST IN CASE.
CLICK
SUGIKI-SENSEI CAN STILL DANCE SO CAPTIVATINGLY.
AND IF ONE DAY THE DISCUSSION OF ENDING OUR PARTNERSHIP COMES UP...
I SHOULD ACCEPT.
RIGHT, KEI-CHAN?
SEIKO
銀座駅
Ginza.Sta
END OF CHAPTER 9.5

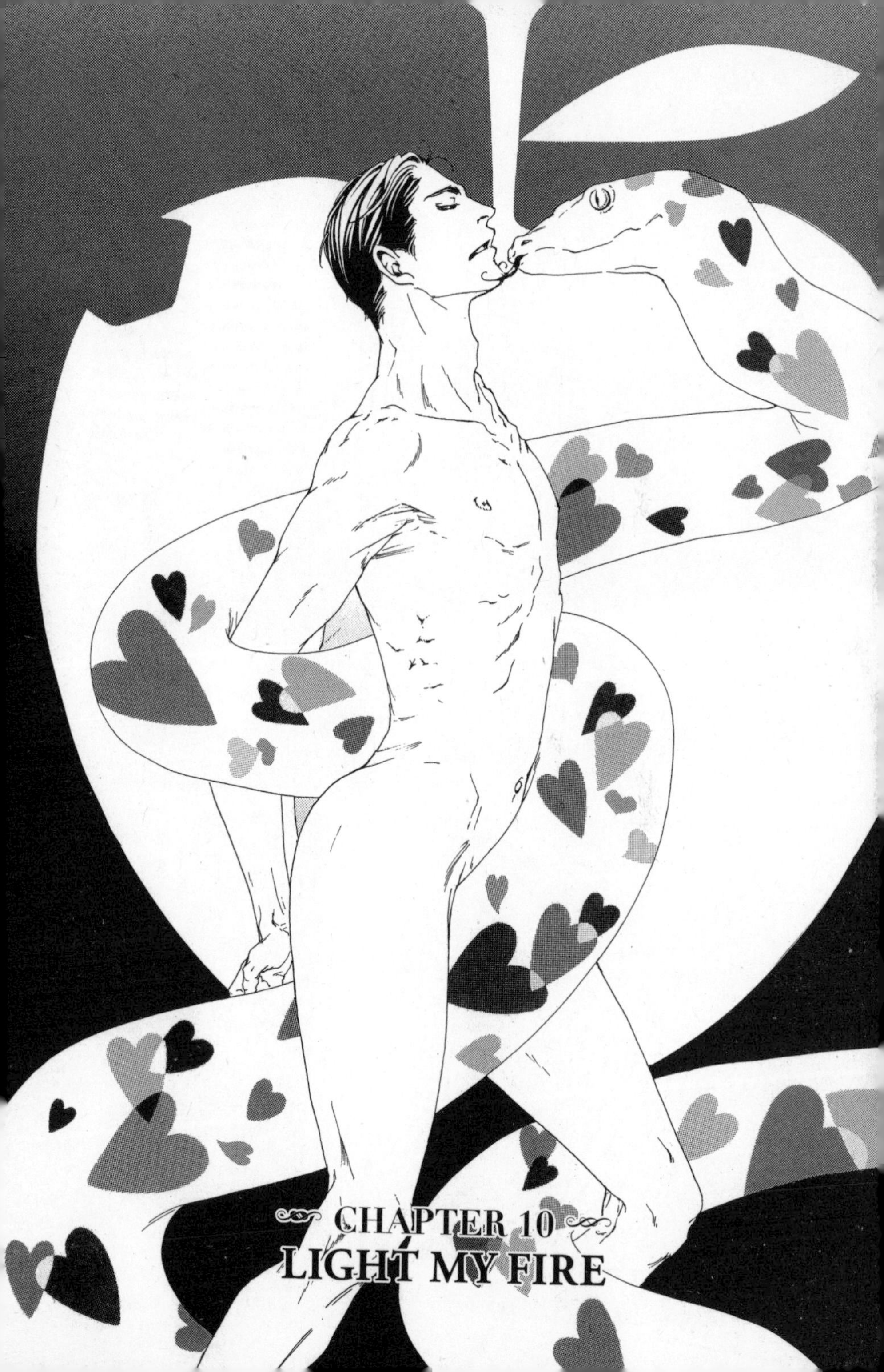

CHAPTER 10
LIGHT MY FIRE

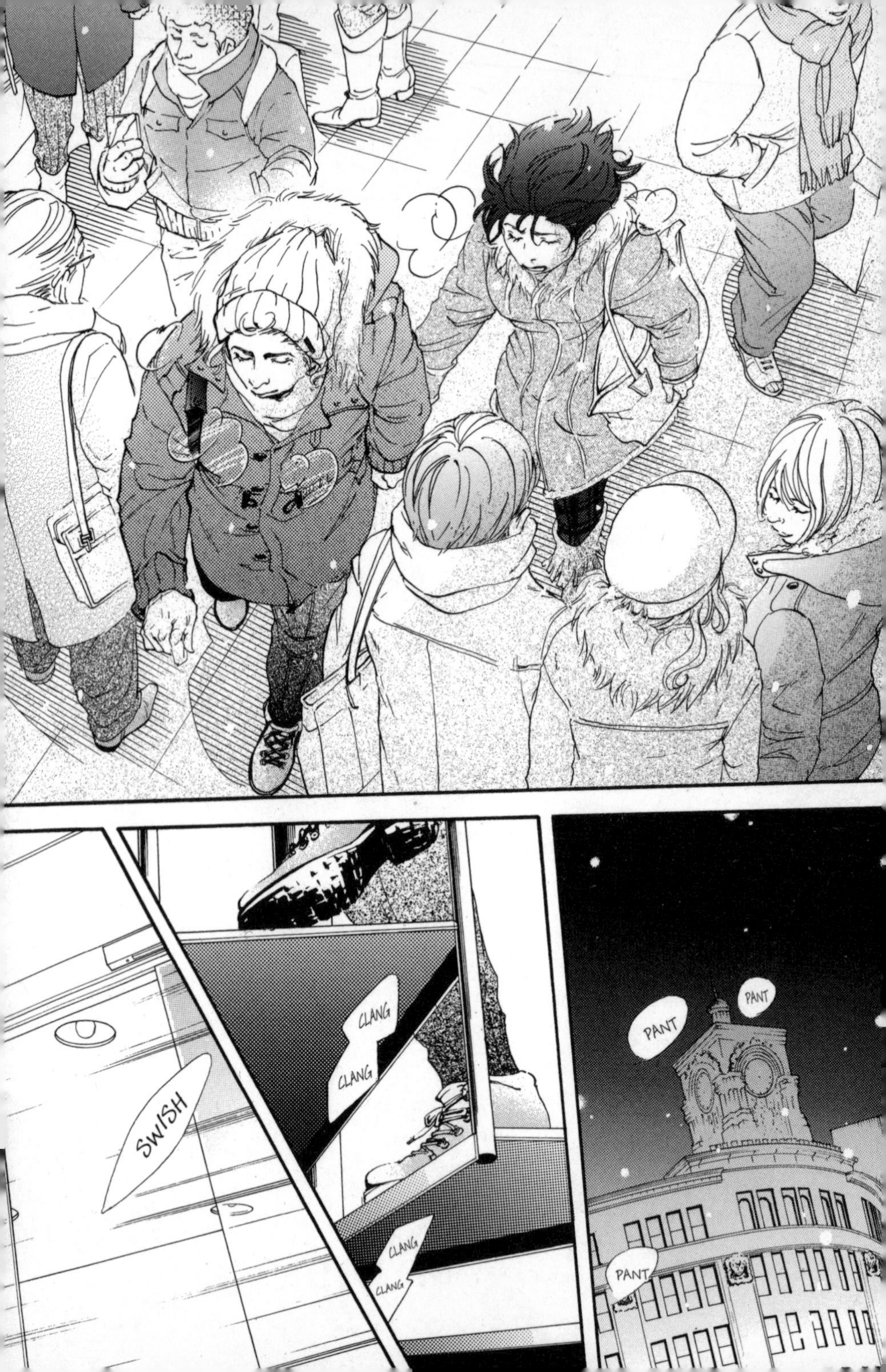
PANT
PANT
PANT
CLANG
CLANG
CLANG
CLANG
SWISH

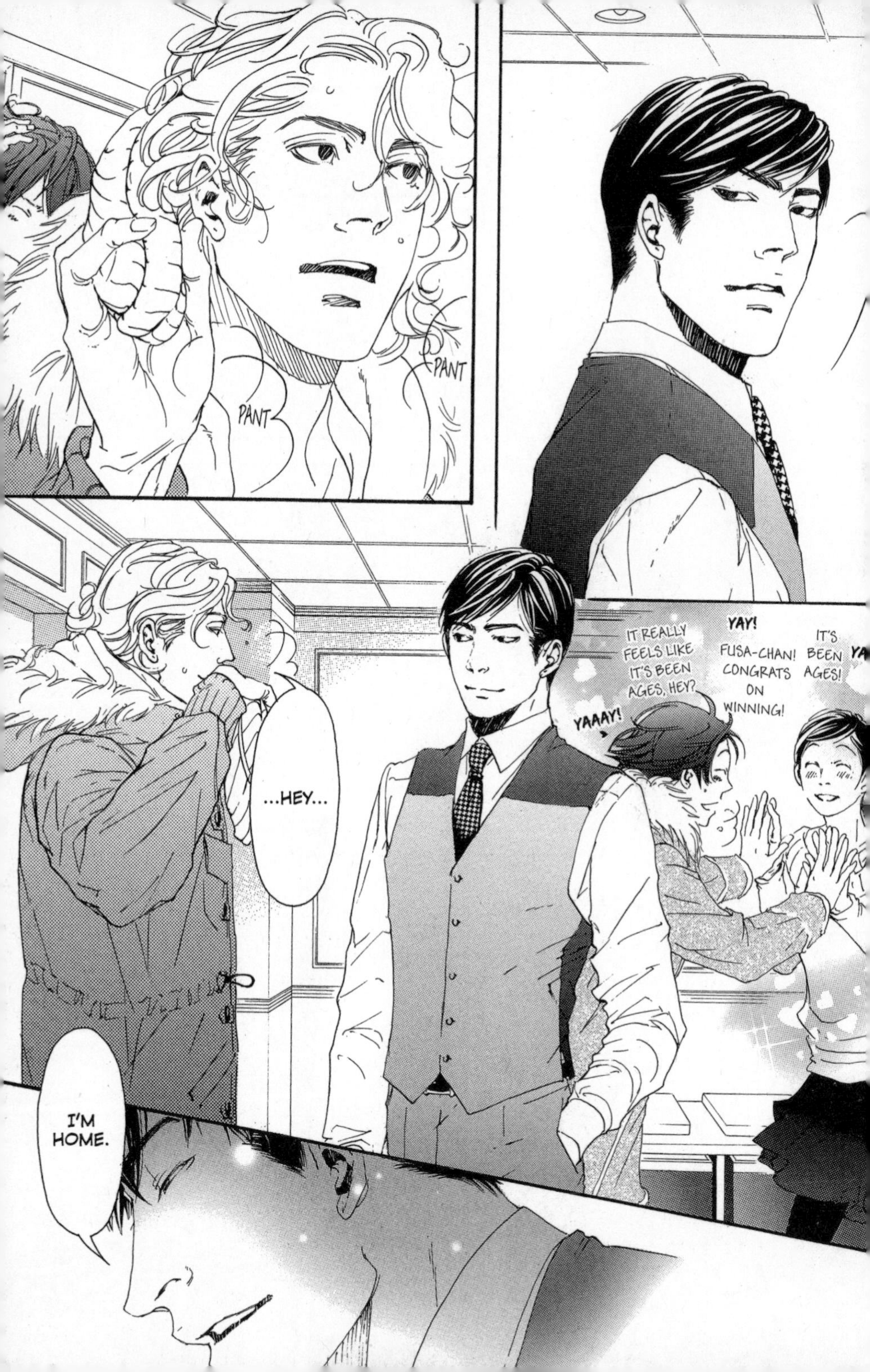
PANT
PANT
IT'S BEEN AGES!
YAY!
FUSA-CHAN! CONGRATS ON WINNING!
IT REALLY FEELS LIKE IT'S BEEN AGES, HEY?
YAAAY!
...HEY...
I'M HOME.

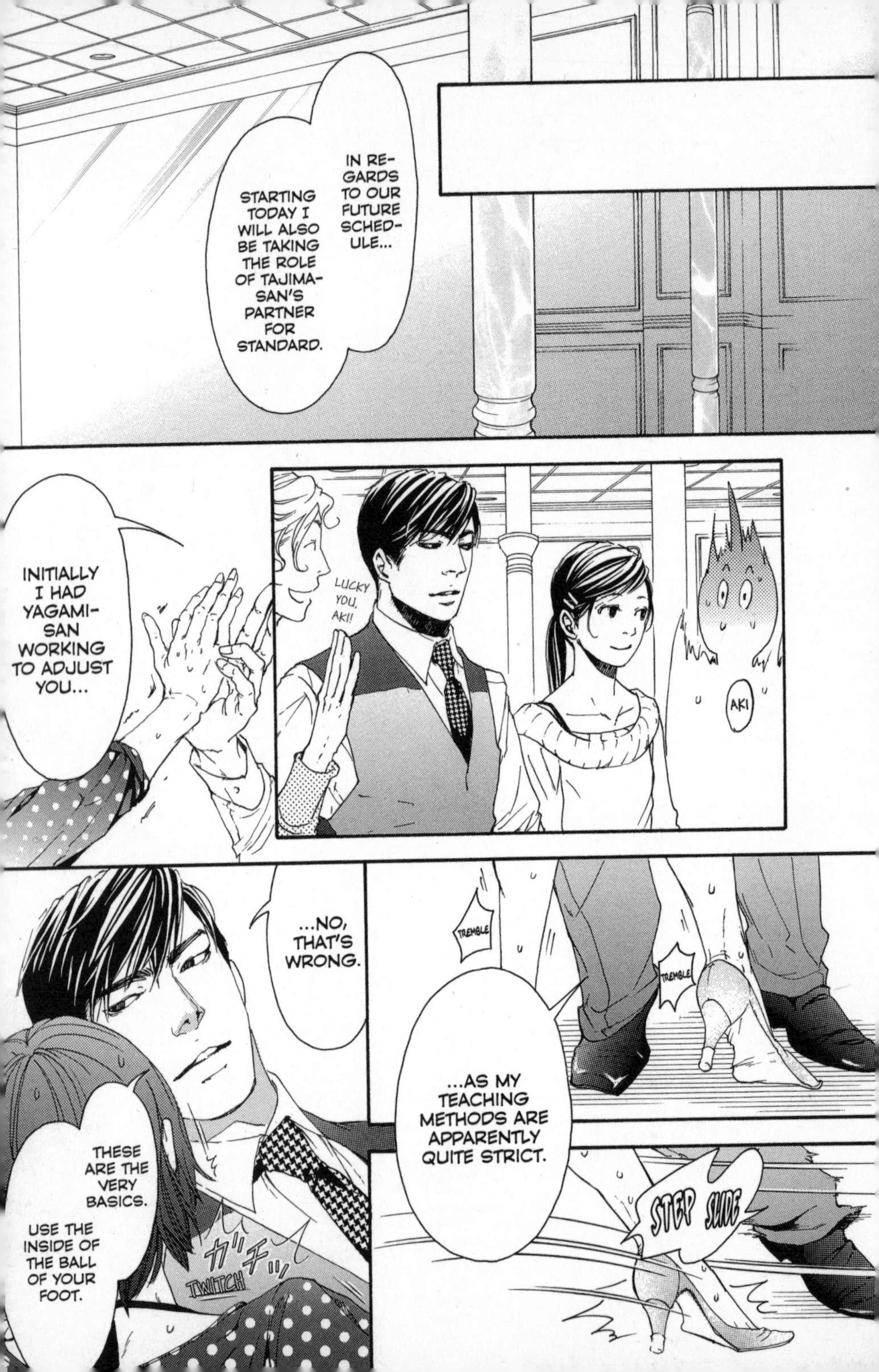
IN REGARDS TO OUR FUTURE SCHEDULE...
STARTING TODAY I WILL ALSO BE TAKING THE ROLE OF TAJIMA-SAN'S PARTNER FOR STANDARD.
AKI
LUCKY YOU, AKI!
INITIALLY I HAD YAGAMI-SAN WORKING TO ADJUST YOU...
TREMBLE
TREMBLE
...AS MY TEACHING METHODS ARE APPARENTLY QUITE STRICT.
STEP SLIDE
...NO, THAT'S WRONG.
THESE ARE THE VERY BASICS.
USE THE INSIDE OF THE BALL OF YOUR FOOT.
TWITCH

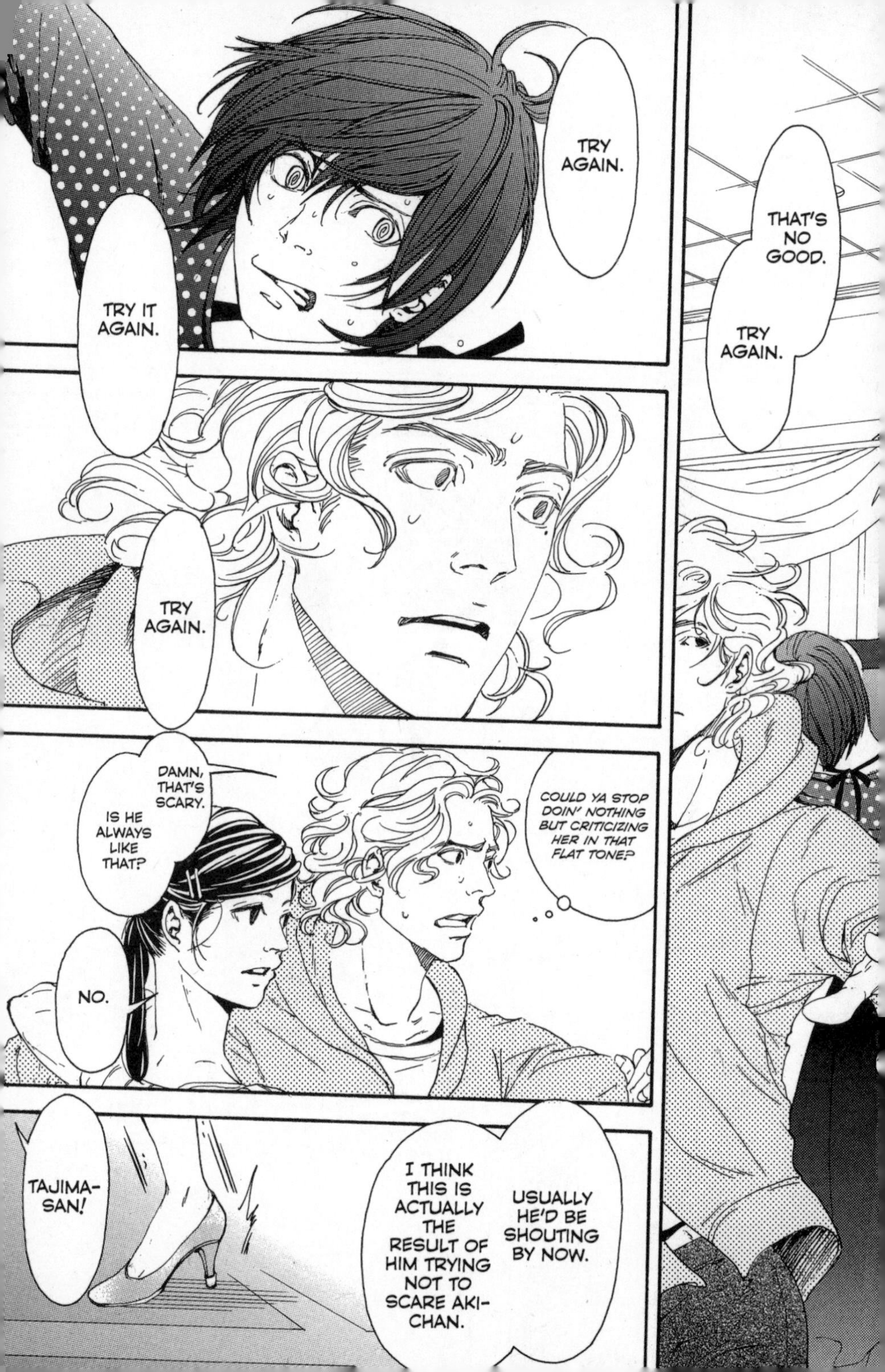
THAT'S NO GOOD.
TRY AGAIN.
TRY AGAIN.
TRY IT AGAIN.
TRY AGAIN.
COULD YA STOP DOIN' NOTHING BUT CRITICIZING HER IN THAT FLAT TONE?
DAMN, THAT'S SCARY.
IS HE ALWAYS LIKE THAT?
NO.
USUALLY HE'D BE SHOUTING BY NOW.
I THINK THIS IS ACTUALLY THE RESULT OF HIM TRYING NOT TO SCARE AKI-CHAN.
TAJIMA-SAN!

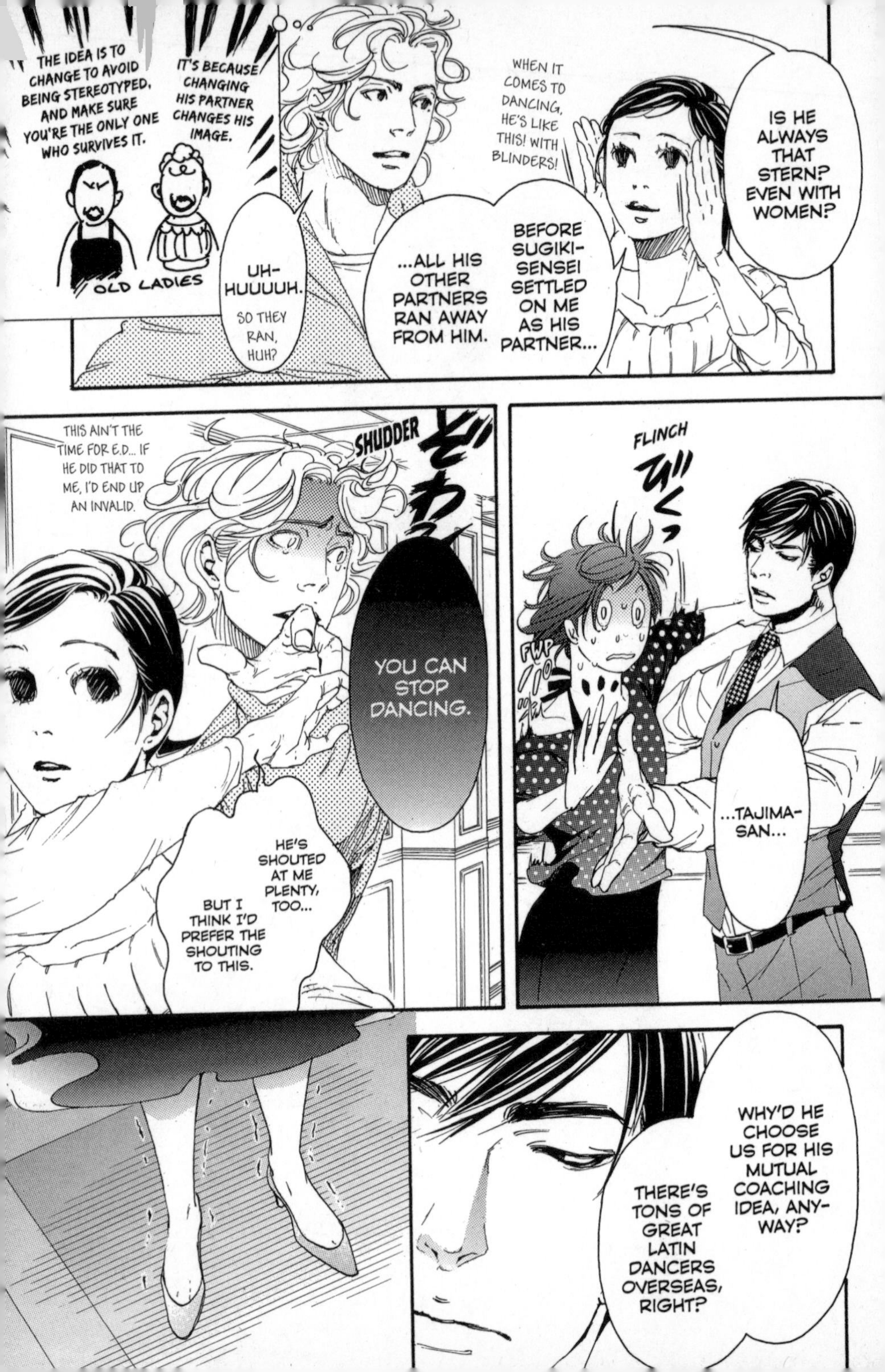
IS HE ALWAYS THAT STERN? EVEN WITH WOMEN?
WHEN IT COMES TO DANCING, HE'S LIKE THIS! WITH BLINDERS!
BEFORE SUGIKI-SENSEI SETTLED ON ME AS HIS PARTNER...
...ALL HIS OTHER PARTNERS RAN AWAY FROM HIM.
UH-HUUUUH.
SO THEY RAN, HUH?
IT'S BECAUSE CHANGING HIS PARTNER CHANGES HIS IMAGE.
THE IDEA IS TO CHANGE TO AVOID BEING STEREOTYPED, AND MAKE SURE YOU'RE THE ONLY ONE WHO SURVIVES IT.
OLD LADIES
FLINCH
FWP
...TAJIMA-SAN...
SHUDDER
YOU CAN STOP DANCING.
THIS AIN'T THE TIME FOR E.D... IF HE DID THAT TO ME, I'D END UP AN INVALID.
HE'S SHOUTED AT ME PLENTY, TOO...
BUT I THINK I'D PREFER THE SHOUTING TO THIS.
WHY'D HE CHOOSE US FOR HIS MUTUAL COACHING IDEA, ANYWAY?
THERE'S TONS OF GREAT LATIN DANCERS OVERSEAS, RIGHT?

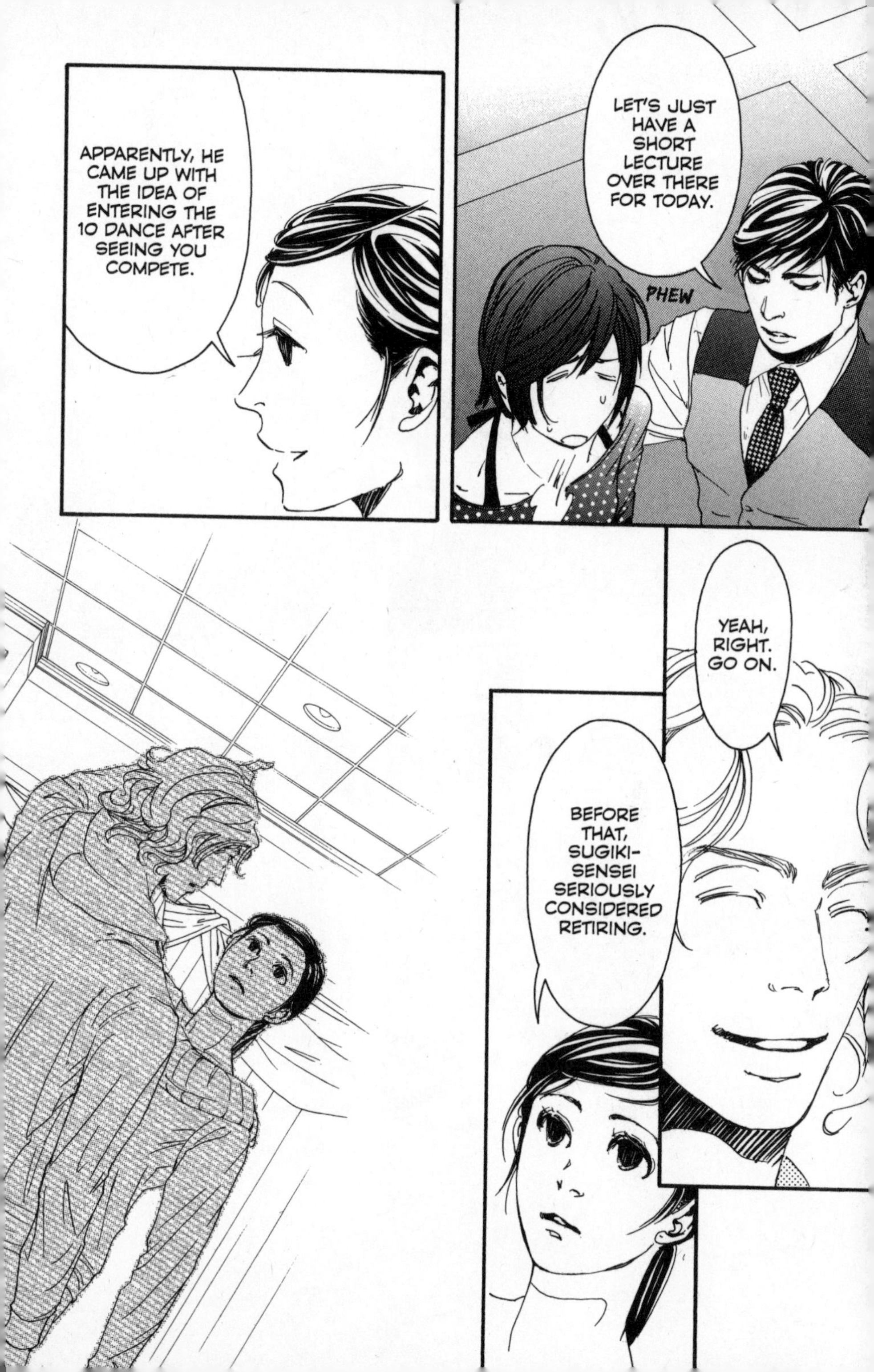
LET'S JUST HAVE A SHORT LECTURE OVER THERE FOR TODAY.
PHEW
APPARENTLY, HE CAME UP WITH THE IDEA OF ENTERING THE 10 DANCE AFTER SEEING YOU COMPETE.
YEAH, RIGHT. GO ON.
BEFORE THAT, SUGIKI-SENSEI SERIOUSLY CONSIDERED RETIRING.

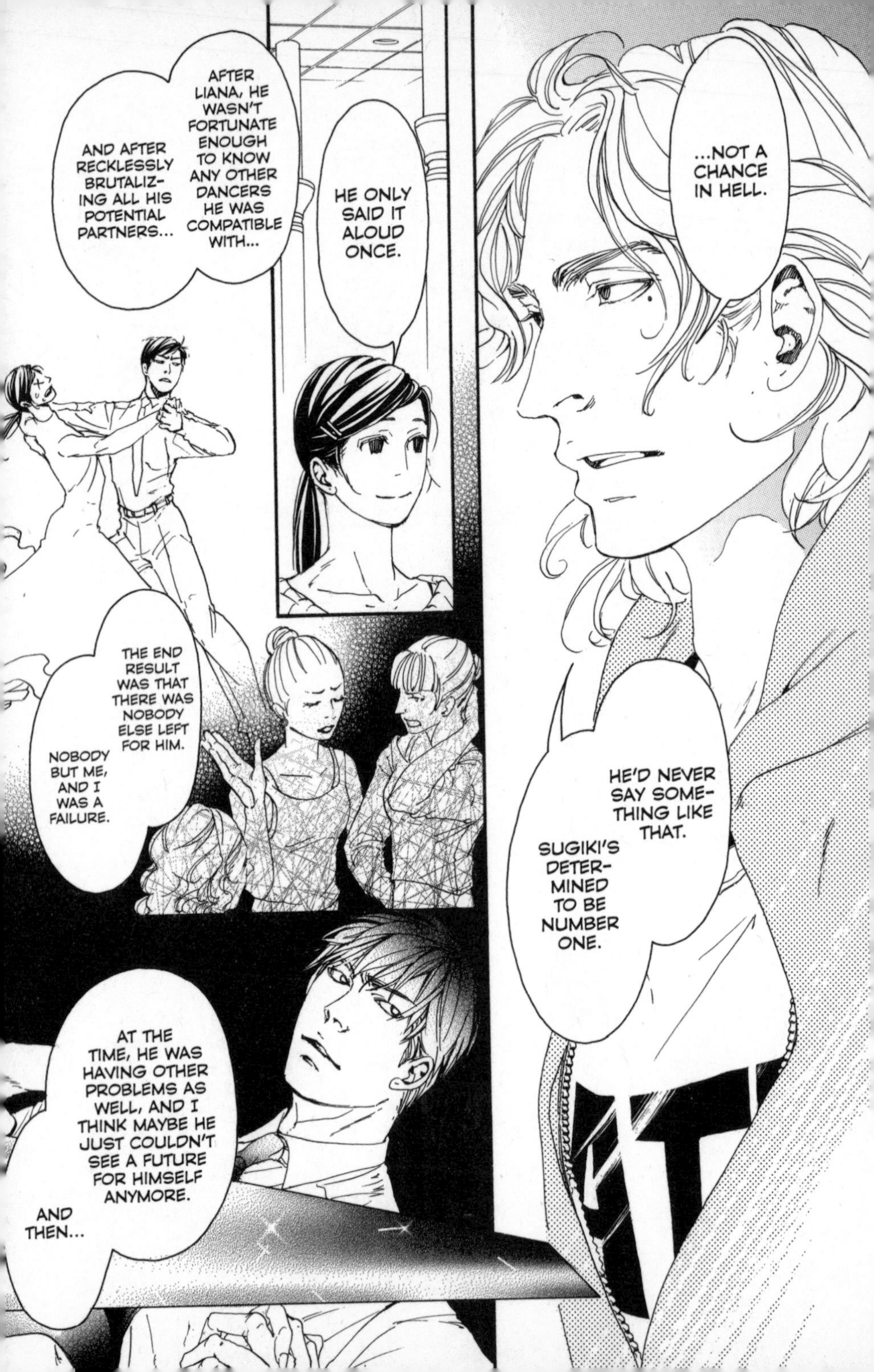
...NOT A CHANCE IN HELL.
HE'D NEVER SAY SOMETHING LIKE THAT.
SUGIKI'S DETERMINED TO BE NUMBER ONE.
HE ONLY SAID IT ALOUD ONCE.
AFTER LIANA, HE WASN'T FORTUNATE ENOUGH TO KNOW ANY OTHER DANCERS HE WAS COMPATIBLE WITH...
AND AFTER RECKLESSLY BRUTALIZING ALL HIS POTENTIAL PARTNERS...
THE END RESULT WAS THAT THERE WAS NOBODY ELSE LEFT FOR HIM.
NOBODY BUT ME, AND I WAS A FAILURE.
AT THE TIME, HE WAS HAVING OTHER PROBLEMS AS WELL, AND I THINK MAYBE HE JUST COULDN'T SEE A FUTURE FOR HIMSELF ANYMORE.
AND THEN...

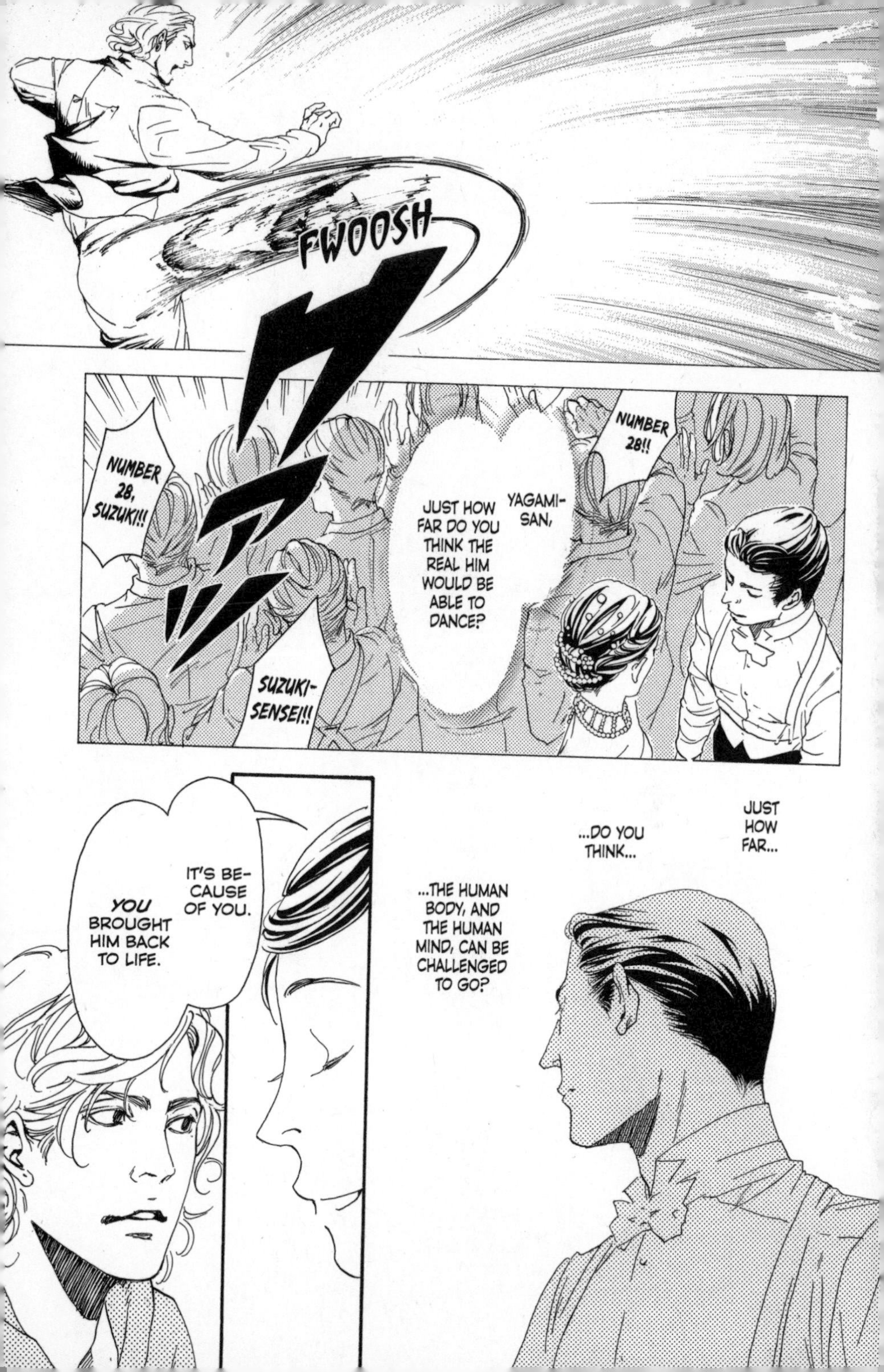
FWOOSH
NUMBER 28!!
YAGAMI-SAN,
JUST HOW FAR DO YOU THINK THE REAL HIM WOULD BE ABLE TO DANCE?
NUMBER 28, SUZUKI!!!
SUZUKI-SENSEI!!!
JUST HOW FAR...
...DO YOU THINK...
...THE HUMAN BODY, AND THE HUMAN MIND, CAN BE CHALLENGED TO GO?
IT'S BECAUSE OF YOU.
YOU BROUGHT HIM BACK TO LIFE.

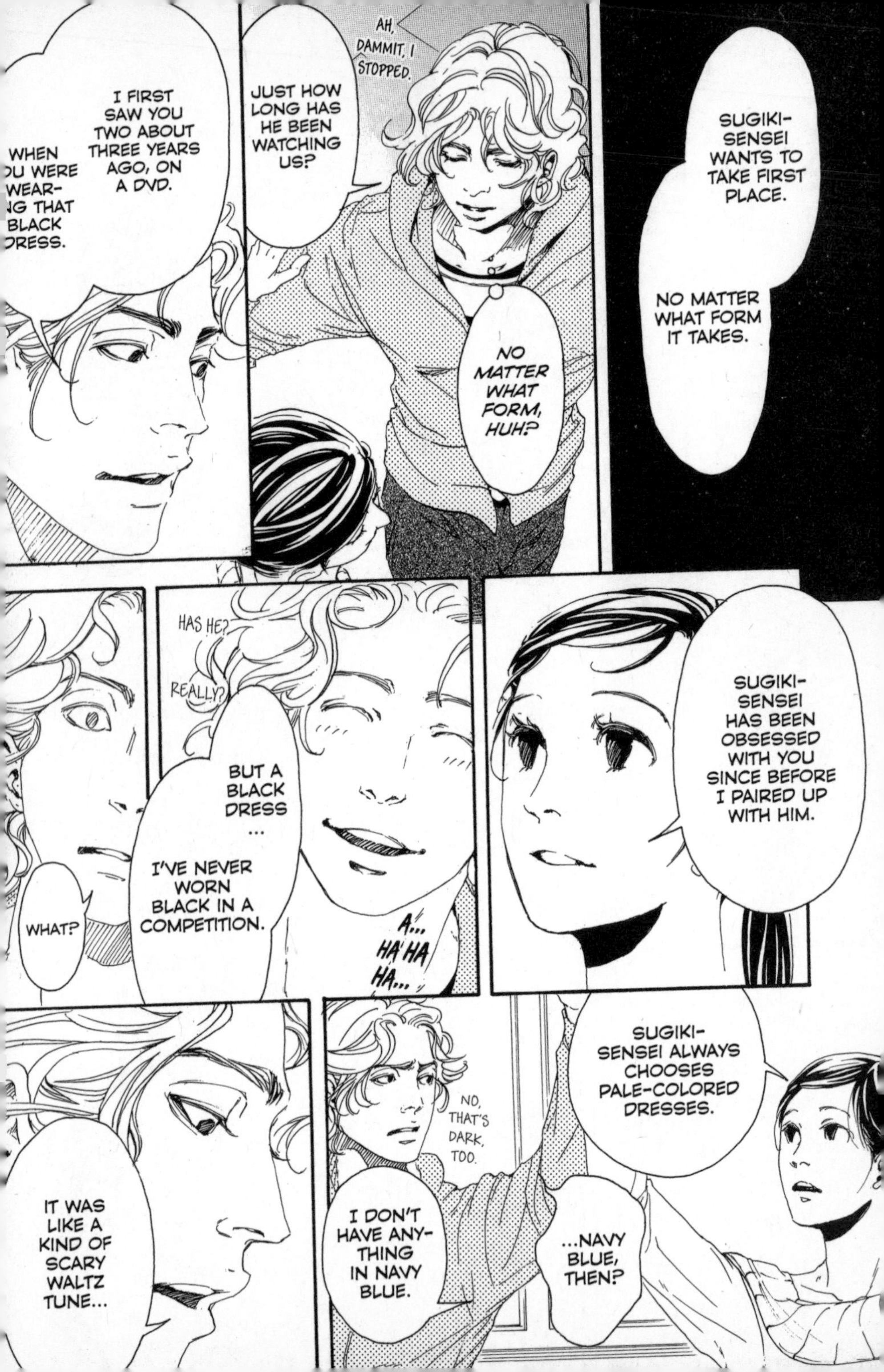
SUGIKI-SENSEI WANTS TO TAKE FIRST PLACE.
NO MATTER WHAT FORM IT TAKES.
AH, DAMMIT, I STOPPED.
JUST HOW LONG HAS HE BEEN WATCHING US?
NO MATTER WHAT FORM, HUH?
I FIRST SAW YOU TWO ABOUT THREE YEARS AGO, ON A DVD.
WHEN OU WERE WEAR- NG THAT BLACK RESS.
SUGIKI-SENSEI HAS BEEN OBSESSED WITH YOU SINCE BEFORE I PAIRED UP WITH HIM.
HAS HE?
REALLY?
BUT A BLACK DRESS ...
I'VE NEVER WORN BLACK IN A COMPETITION.
A... HA HA HA...
WHAT?
SUGIKI-SENSEI ALWAYS CHOOSES PALE-COLORED DRESSES.
...NAVY BLUE, THEN?
NO, THAT'S DARK, TOO.
I DON'T HAVE ANY- THING IN NAVY BLUE.
IT WAS LIKE A KIND OF SCARY WALTZ TUNE...

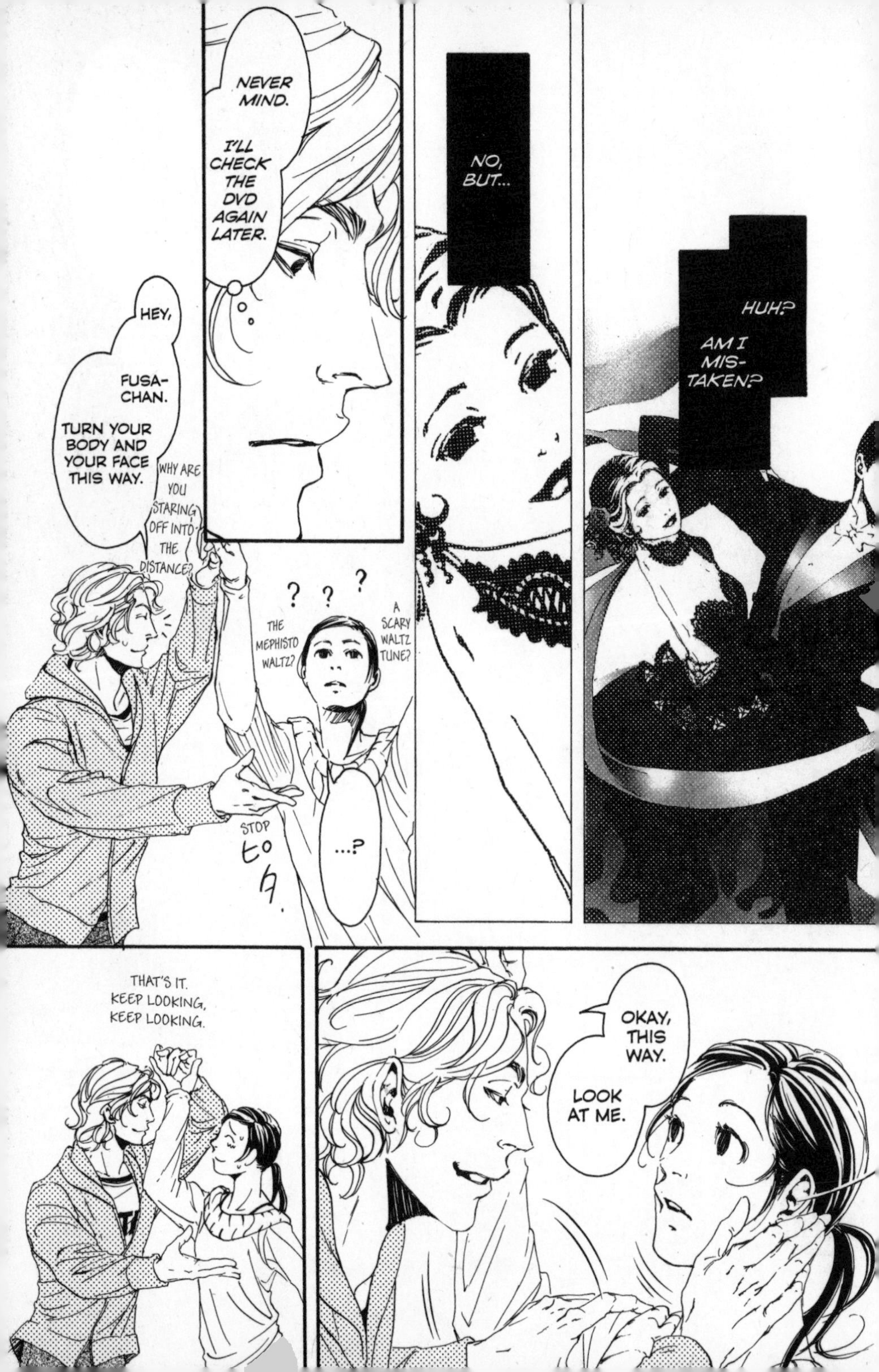
HUH?
AM I MISTAKEN?
NO, BUT...
NEVER MIND.
I'LL CHECK THE DVD AGAIN LATER.
HEY,
FUSA-CHAN.
TURN YOUR BODY AND YOUR FACE THIS WAY.
WHY ARE YOU STARING OFF INTO THE DISTANCE?
? ? ?
A SCARY WALTZ TUNE?
THE MEPHISTO WALTZ?
STOP
ヒク
...?
OKAY, THIS WAY.
LOOK AT ME.
THAT'S IT. KEEP LOOKING, KEEP LOOKING.

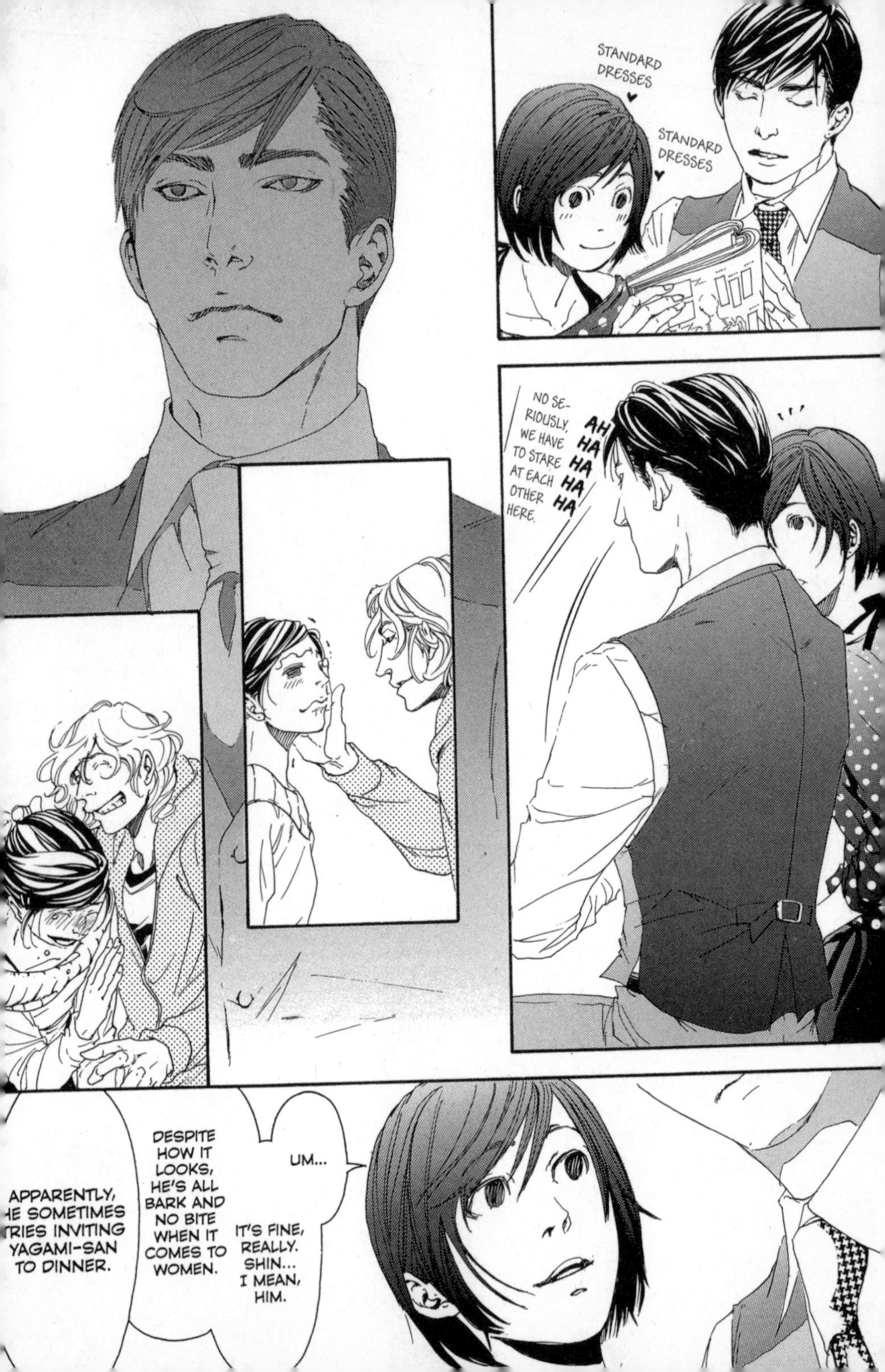
STANDARD DRESSES ♥
STANDARD DRESSES ♥
NO SERIOUSLY, WE HAVE TO STARE AT EACH OTHER HERE.
AH HA HA HA HA
UM...
IT'S FINE, REALLY. SHIN... I MEAN, HIM.
DESPITE HOW IT LOOKS, HE'S ALL BARK AND NO BITE WHEN IT COMES TO WOMEN.
APPARENTLY, HE SOMETIMES TRIES INVITING YAGAMI-SAN TO DINNER.

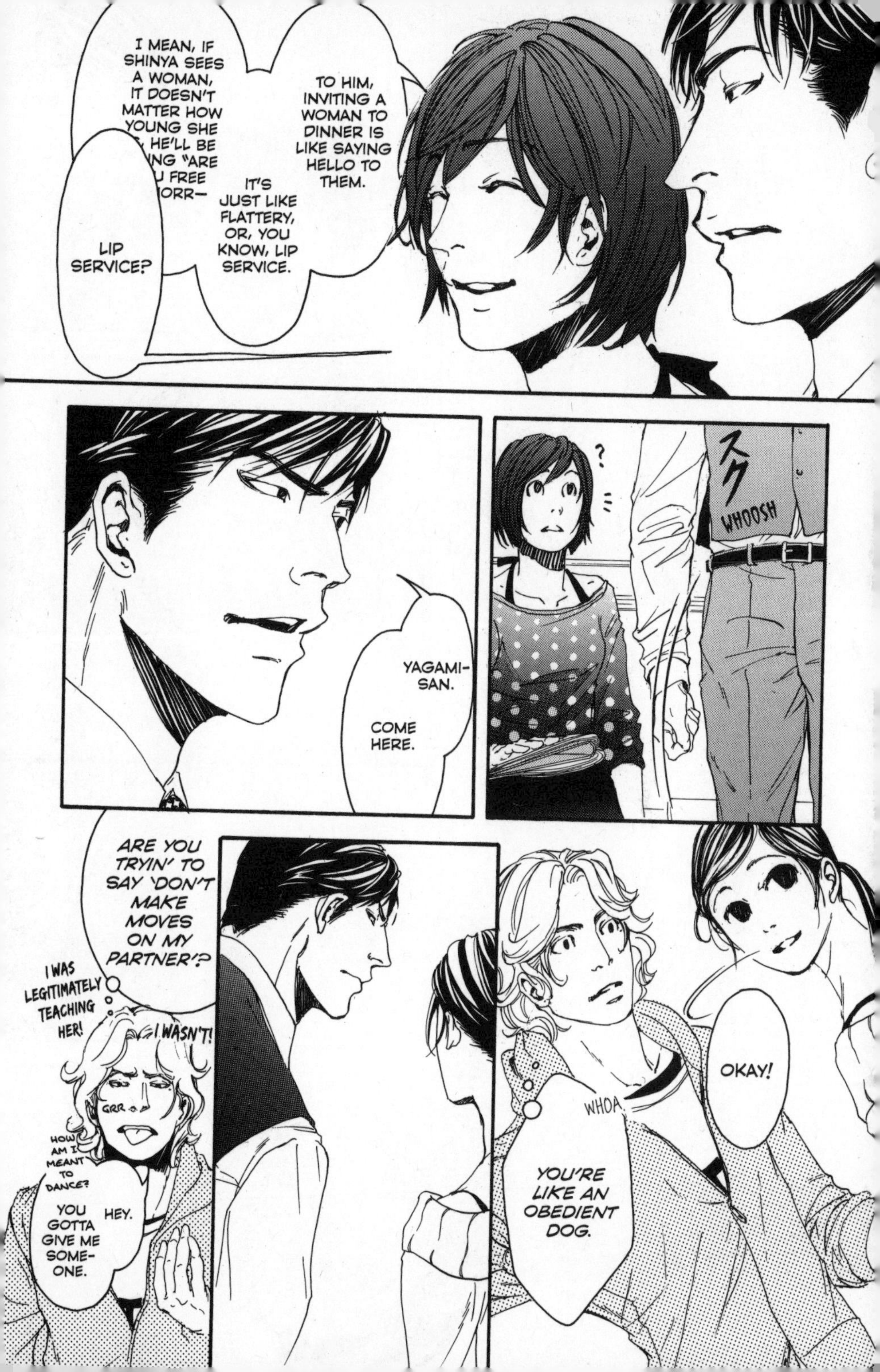

TO HIM, INVITING A WOMAN TO DINNER IS LIKE SAYING HELLO TO THEM.
IT'S JUST LIKE FLATTERY, OR, YOU KNOW, LIP SERVICE.
I MEAN, IF SHINYA SEES A WOMAN, IT DOESN'T MATTER HOW YOUNG SHE
HE'LL BE
NG "ARE
U FREE
ORR—
LIP SERVICE?
?
スク
WHOOSH
YAGAMI-SAN.
COME HERE.
OKAY!
WHOA
YOU'RE LIKE AN OBEDIENT DOG.
ARE YOU TRYIN' TO SAY 'DON'T MAKE MOVES ON MY PARTNER'?
I WAS LEGITIMATELY TEACHING HER!
I WASN'T!
GRR
HEY.
YOU GOTTA GIVE ME SOMEONE.
HOW AM I MEANT TO DANCE?

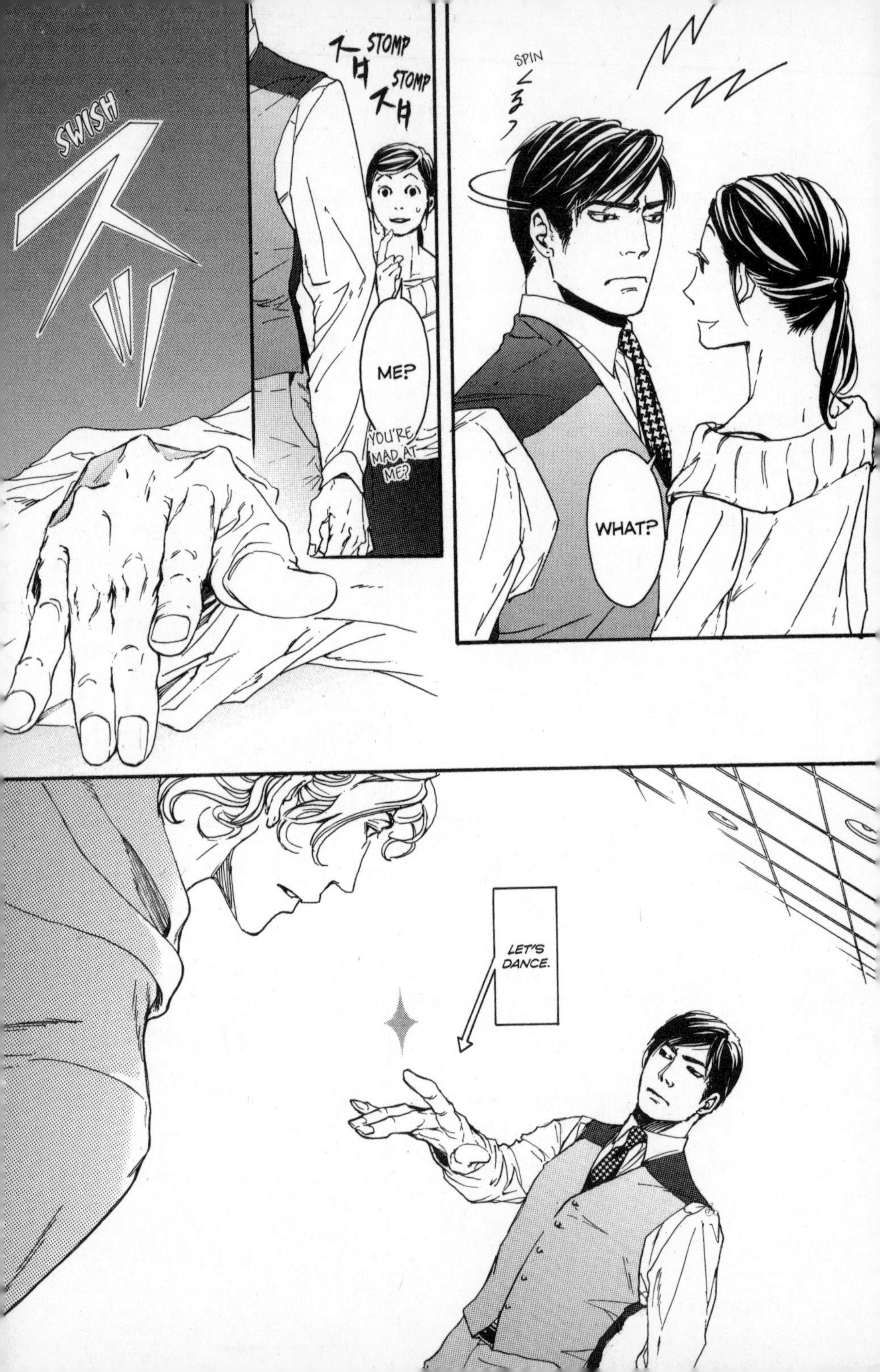
SPIN
WHAT?
STOMP
STOMP
ME?
YOU'RE MAD AT ME?
SWISH
LET'S DANCE.

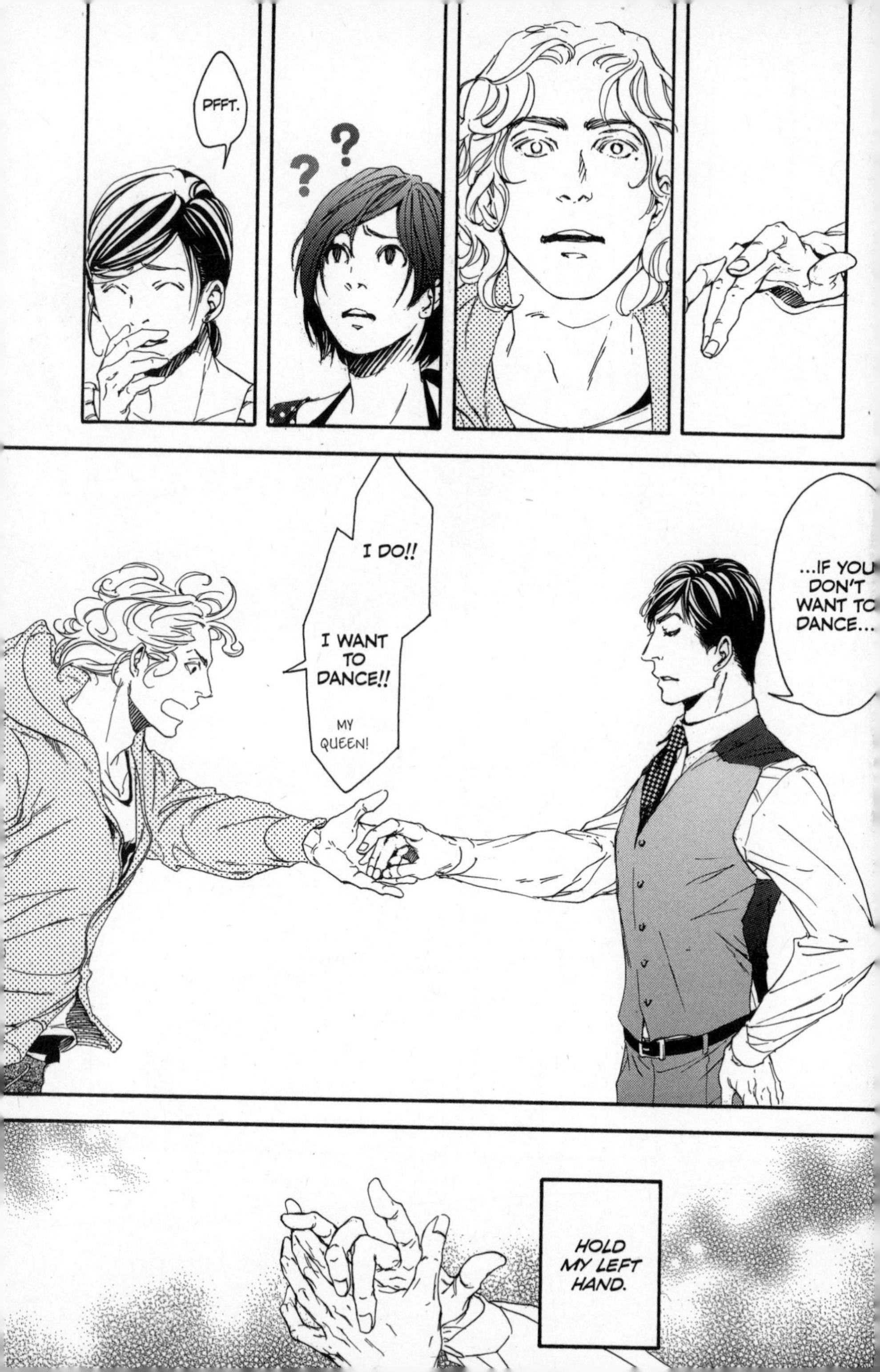
??
PFFT.
...IF YOU DON'T WANT TO DANCE...
I DO!!
I WANT TO DANCE!!
MY QUEEN!
HOLD MY LEFT HAND.

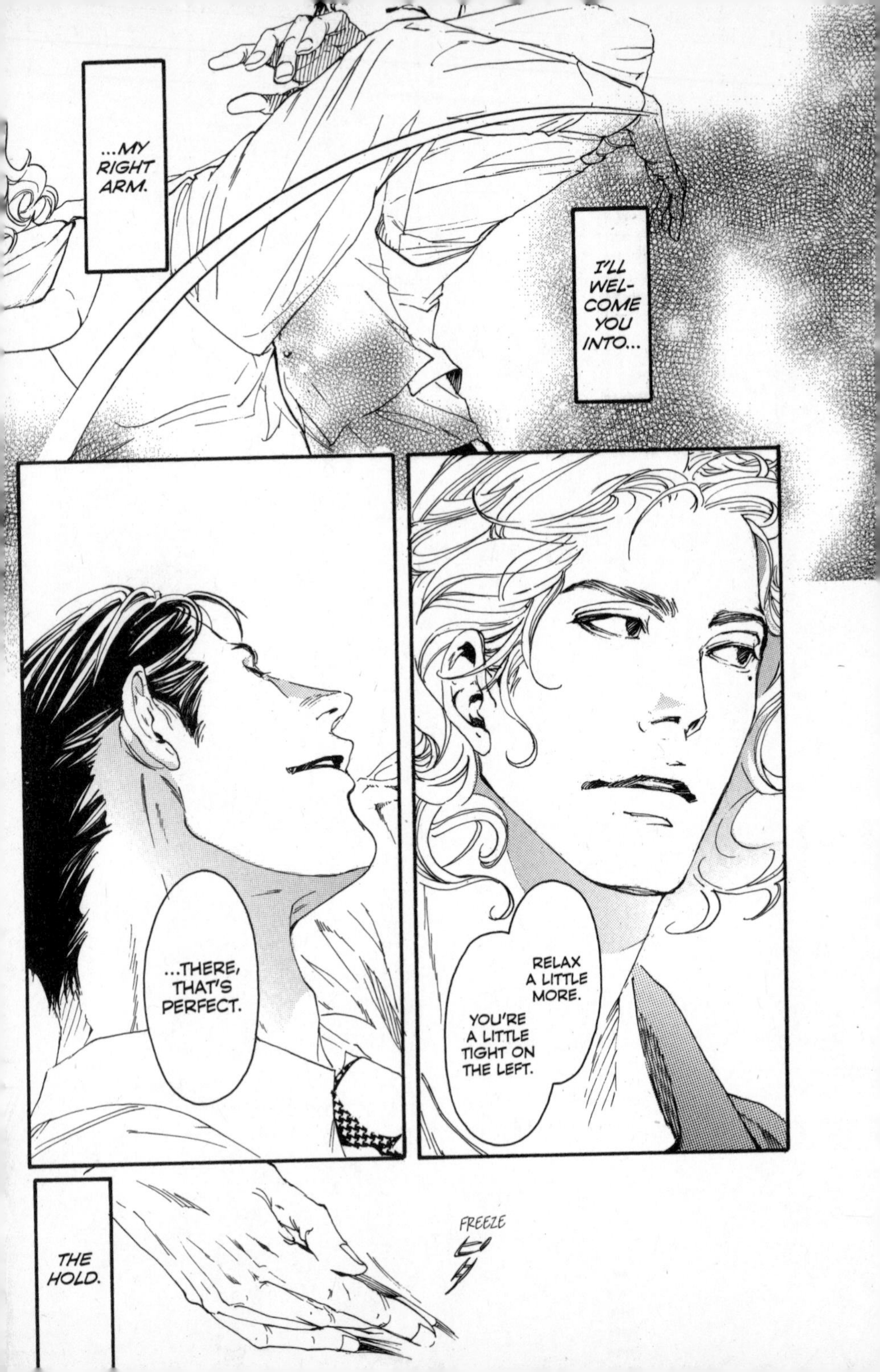
I'LL WEL-COME YOU INTO...
...MY RIGHT ARM.
RELAX A LITTLE MORE.
YOU'RE A LITTLE TIGHT ON THE LEFT.
...THERE, THAT'S PERFECT.
FREEZE
THE HOLD.

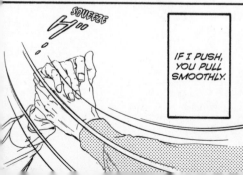

SQUEEZE

IF I PUSH,
YOU PULL
SMOOTHLY.

IT'S
HUGE...!

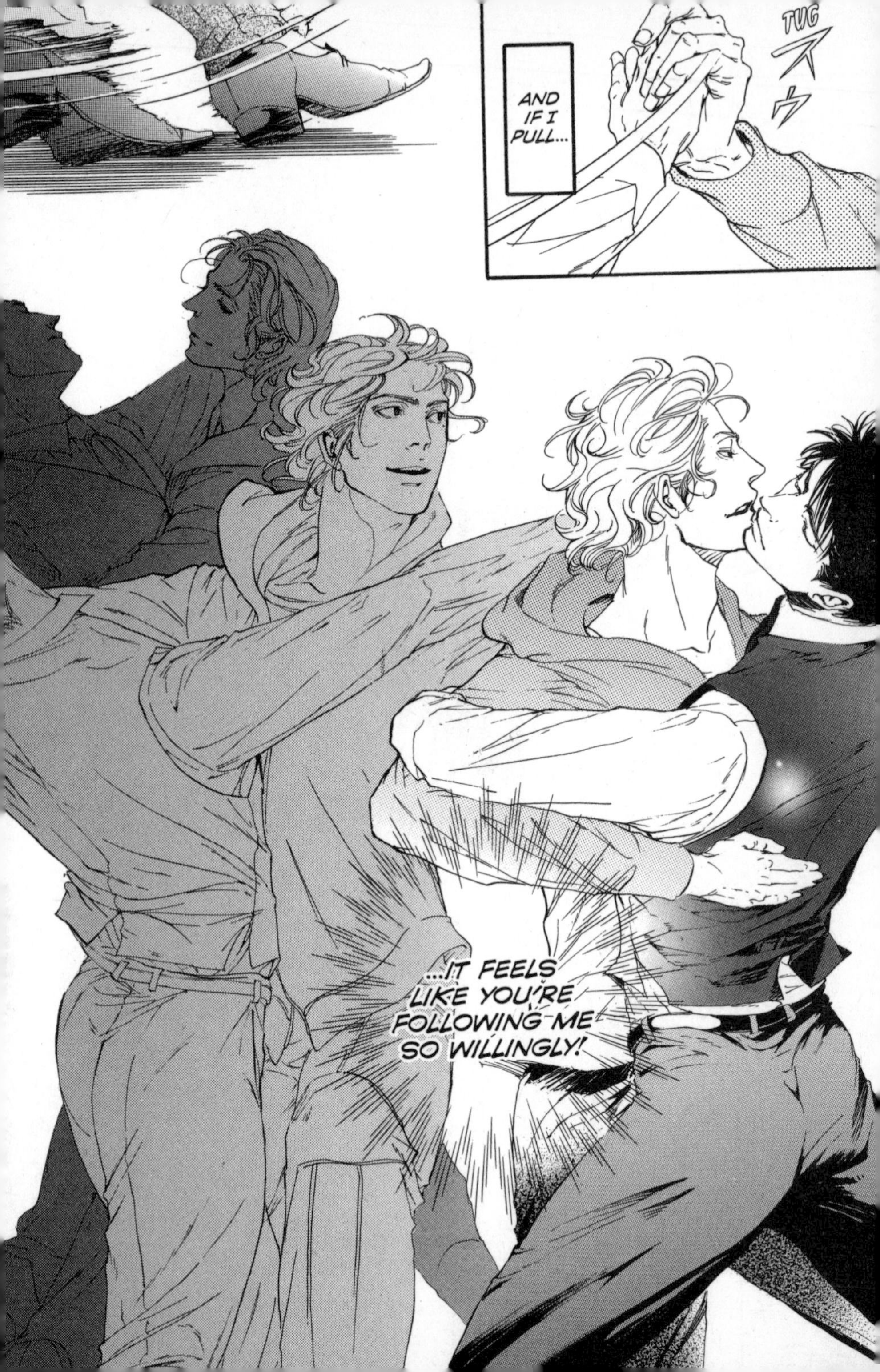
TUG
スゥ
AND IF I PULL...
...IT FEELS LIKE YOU'RE FOLLOWING ME SO WILLINGLY!

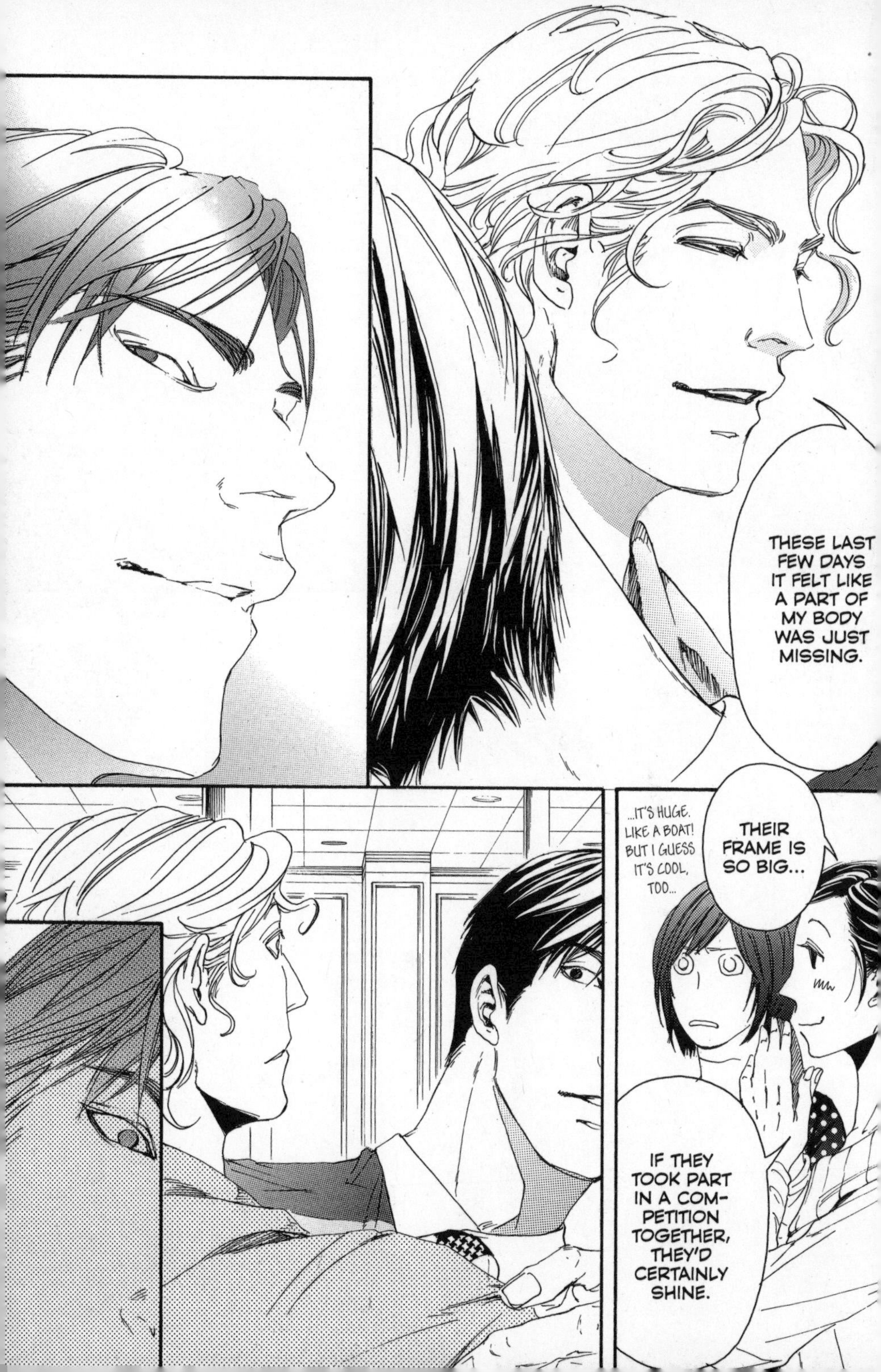
THESE LAST FEW DAYS IT FELT LIKE A PART OF MY BODY WAS JUST MISSING.
THEIR FRAME IS SO BIG...
...IT'S HUGE. LIKE A BOAT! BUT I GUESS IT'S COOL, TOO...
IF THEY TOOK PART IN A COM-PETITION TOGETHER, THEY'D CERTAINLY SHINE.

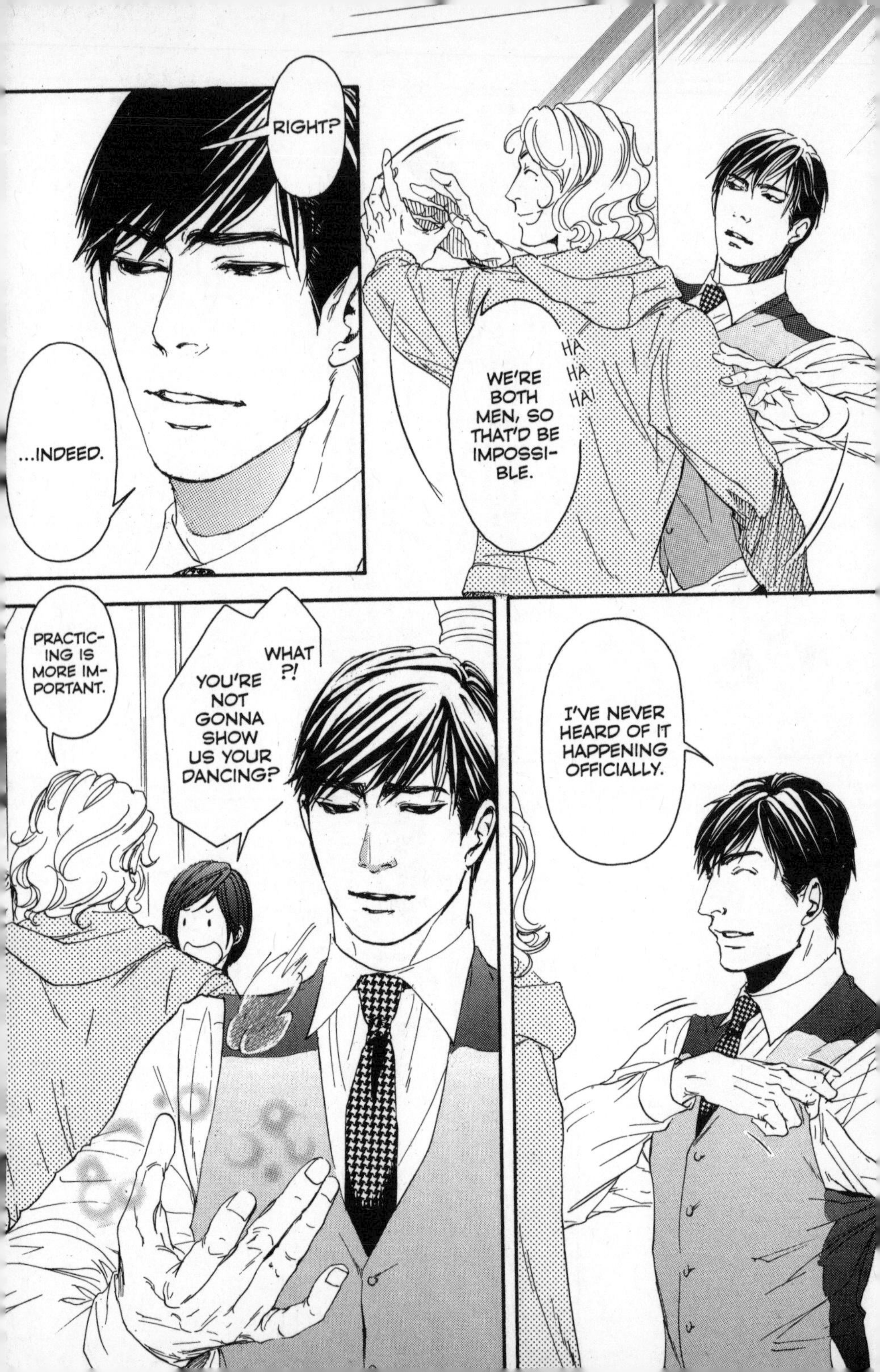
WE'RE BOTH MEN, SO THAT'D BE IMPOSSIBLE.
HA HA HA!
RIGHT?
...INDEED.
I'VE NEVER HEARD OF IT HAPPENING OFFICIALLY.
PRACTICING IS MORE IMPORTANT.
WHAT ?!
YOU'RE NOT GONNA SHOW US YOUR DANCING?

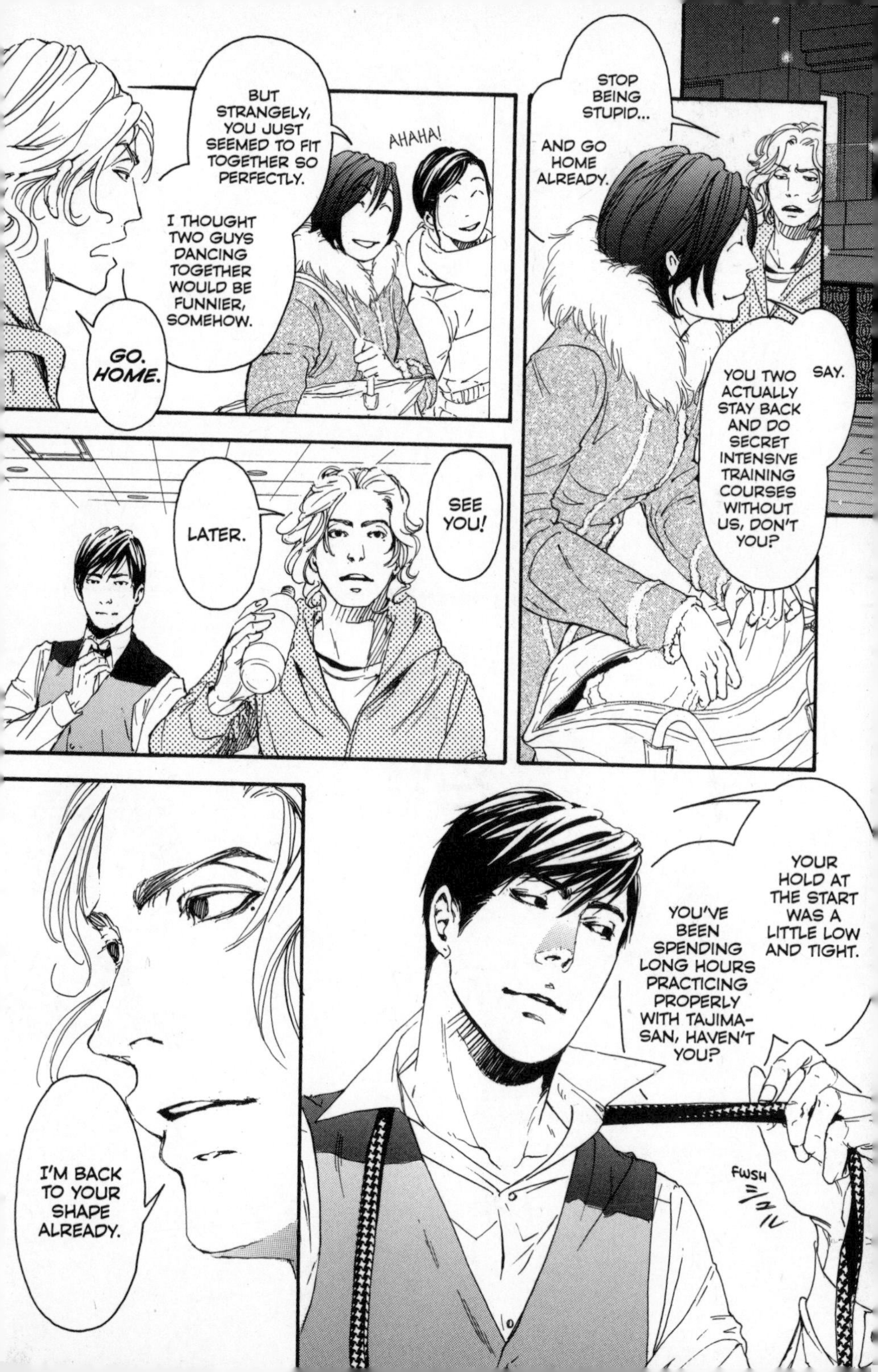
STOP BEING STUPID...
AND GO HOME ALREADY.
SAY.
YOU TWO ACTUALLY STAY BACK AND DO SECRET INTENSIVE TRAINING COURSES WITHOUT US, DON'T YOU?
BUT STRANGELY, YOU JUST SEEMED TO FIT TOGETHER SO PERFECTLY.
AHAHA!
I THOUGHT TWO GUYS DANCING TOGETHER WOULD BE FUNNIER, SOMEHOW.
GO. HOME.
SEE YOU!
LATER.
YOUR HOLD AT THE START WAS A LITTLE LOW AND TIGHT.
YOU'VE BEEN SPENDING LONG HOURS PRACTICING PROPERLY WITH TAJIMA-SAN, HAVEN'T YOU?
FWSH
I'M BACK TO YOUR SHAPE ALREADY.

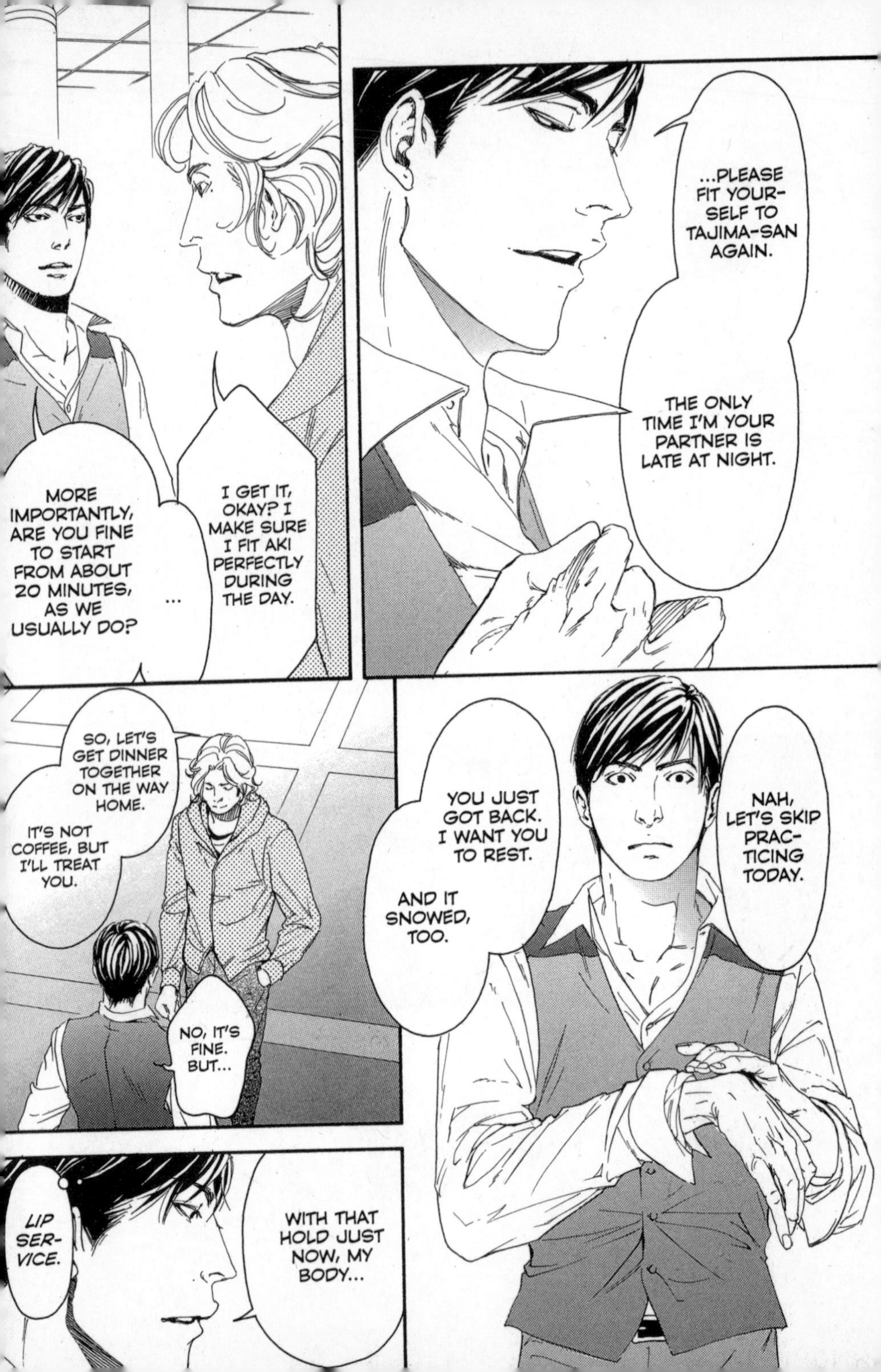
...PLEASE FIT YOUR-SELF TO TAJIMA-SAN AGAIN.
THE ONLY TIME I'M YOUR PARTNER IS LATE AT NIGHT.
I GET IT, OKAY? I MAKE SURE I FIT AKI PERFECTLY DURING THE DAY.
...
MORE IMPORTANTLY, ARE YOU FINE TO START FROM ABOUT 20 MINUTES, AS WE USUALLY DO?
NAH, LET'S SKIP PRAC-TICING TODAY.
YOU JUST GOT BACK. I WANT YOU TO REST.
AND IT SNOWED, TOO.
SO, LET'S GET DINNER TOGETHER ON THE WAY HOME.
IT'S NOT COFFEE, BUT I'LL TREAT YOU.
NO, IT'S FINE. BUT...
WITH THAT HOLD JUST NOW, MY BODY...
LIP SER-VICE.

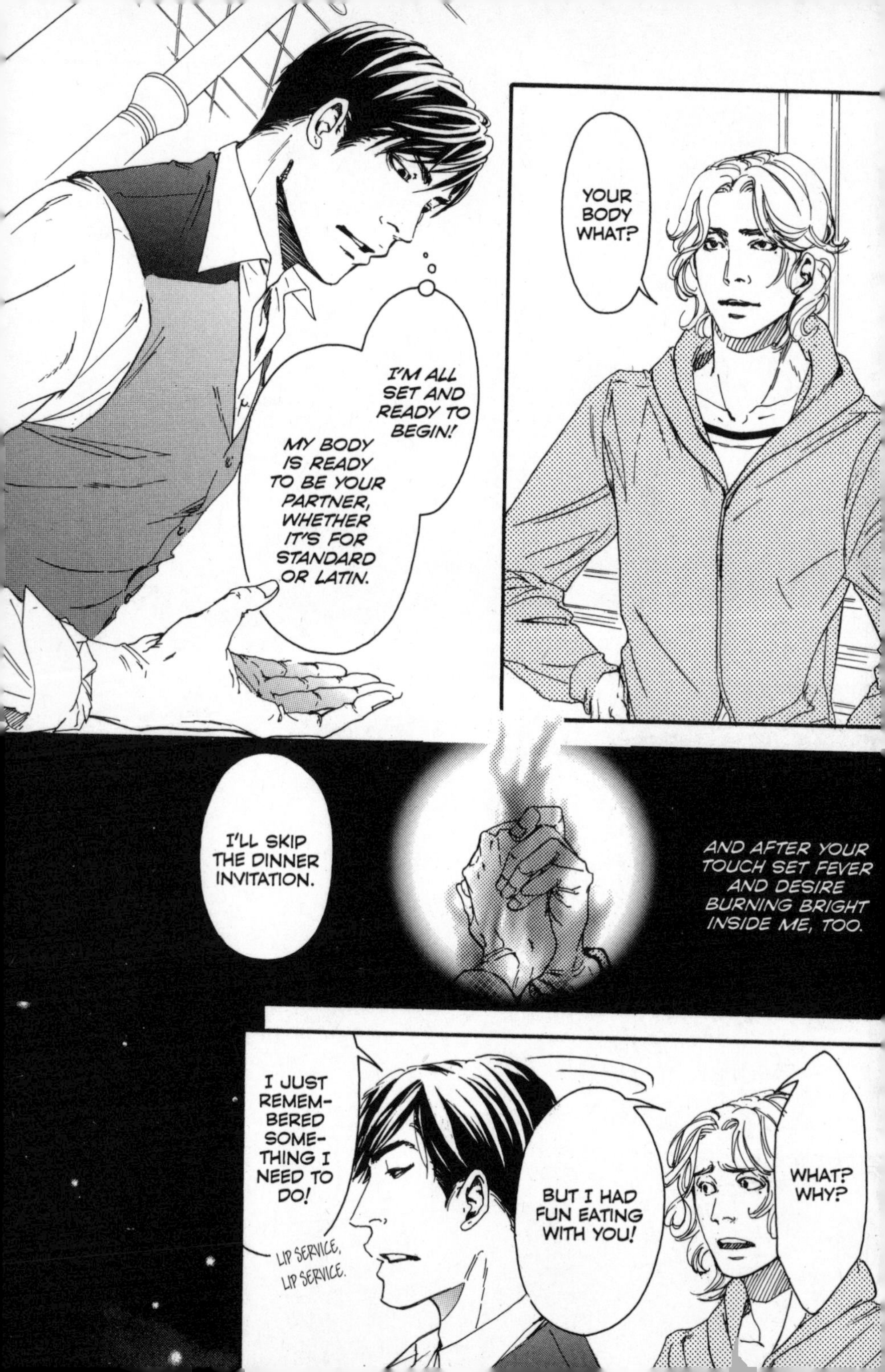
YOUR BODY WHAT?
I'M ALL SET AND READY TO BEGIN!
MY BODY IS READY TO BE YOUR PARTNER, WHETHER IT'S FOR STANDARD OR LATIN.
AND AFTER YOUR TOUCH SET FEVER AND DESIRE BURNING BRIGHT INSIDE ME, TOO.
I'LL SKIP THE DINNER INVITATION.
WHAT? WHY?
BUT I HAD FUN EATING WITH YOU!
I JUST REMEMBERED SOMETHING I NEED TO DO!
LIP SERVICE, LIP SERVICE.

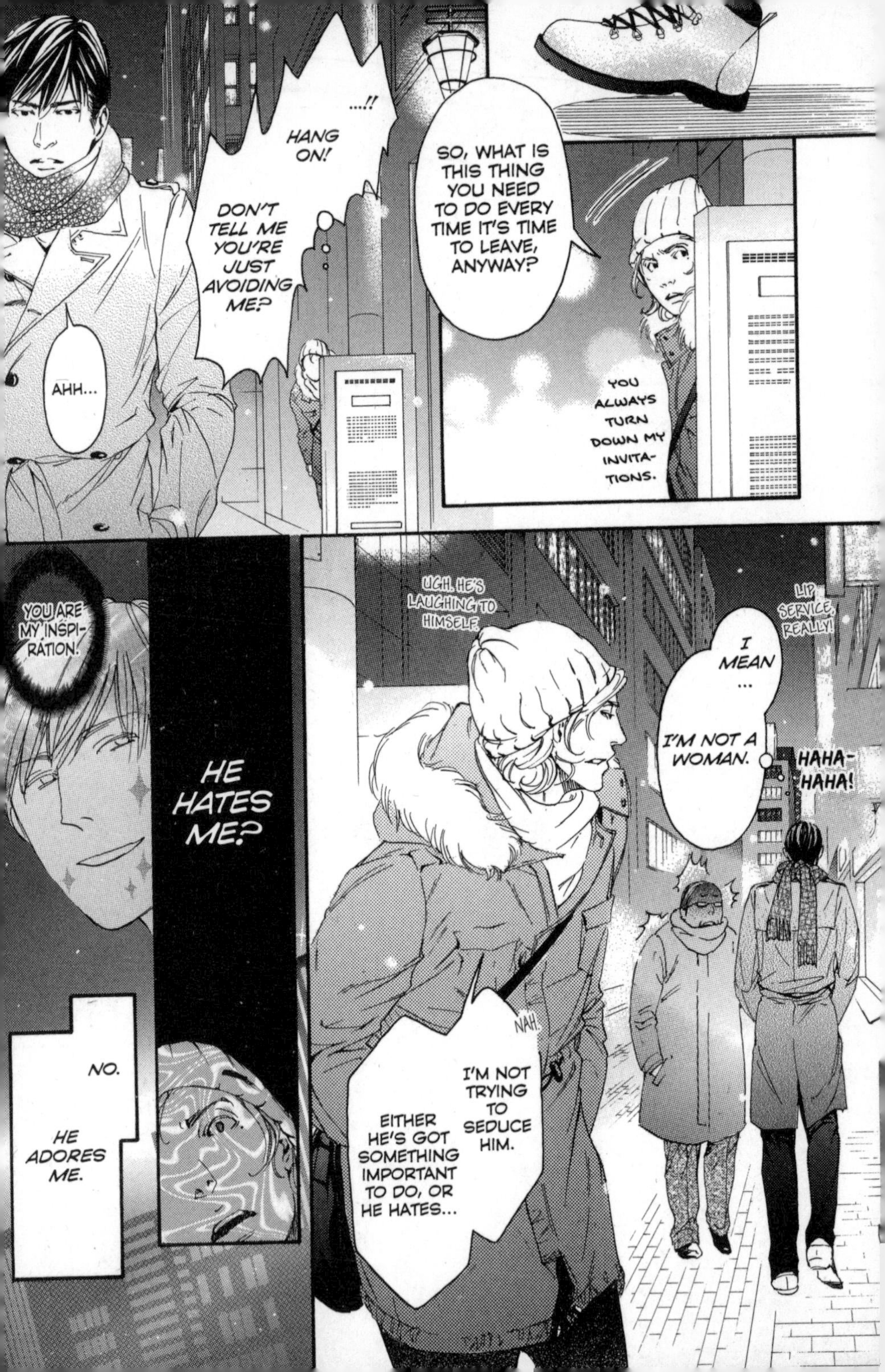
SO, WHAT IS THIS THING YOU NEED TO DO EVERY TIME IT'S TIME TO LEAVE, ANYWAY?
YOU ALWAYS TURN DOWN MY INVITA-TIONS.
...!!
HANG ON!
DON'T TELL ME YOU'RE JUST AVOIDING ME?
AHH...
LIP SERVICE, REALLY!
I MEAN ...
I'M NOT A WOMAN.
HAHA-HAHA!
UGH. HE'S LAUGHING TO HIMSELF.
NAH.
I'M NOT TRYING TO SEDUCE HIM.
EITHER HE'S GOT SOMETHING IMPORTANT TO DO, OR HE HATES...
HE HATES ME?
YOU ARE MY INSPI-RATION!
NO.
HE ADORES ME.

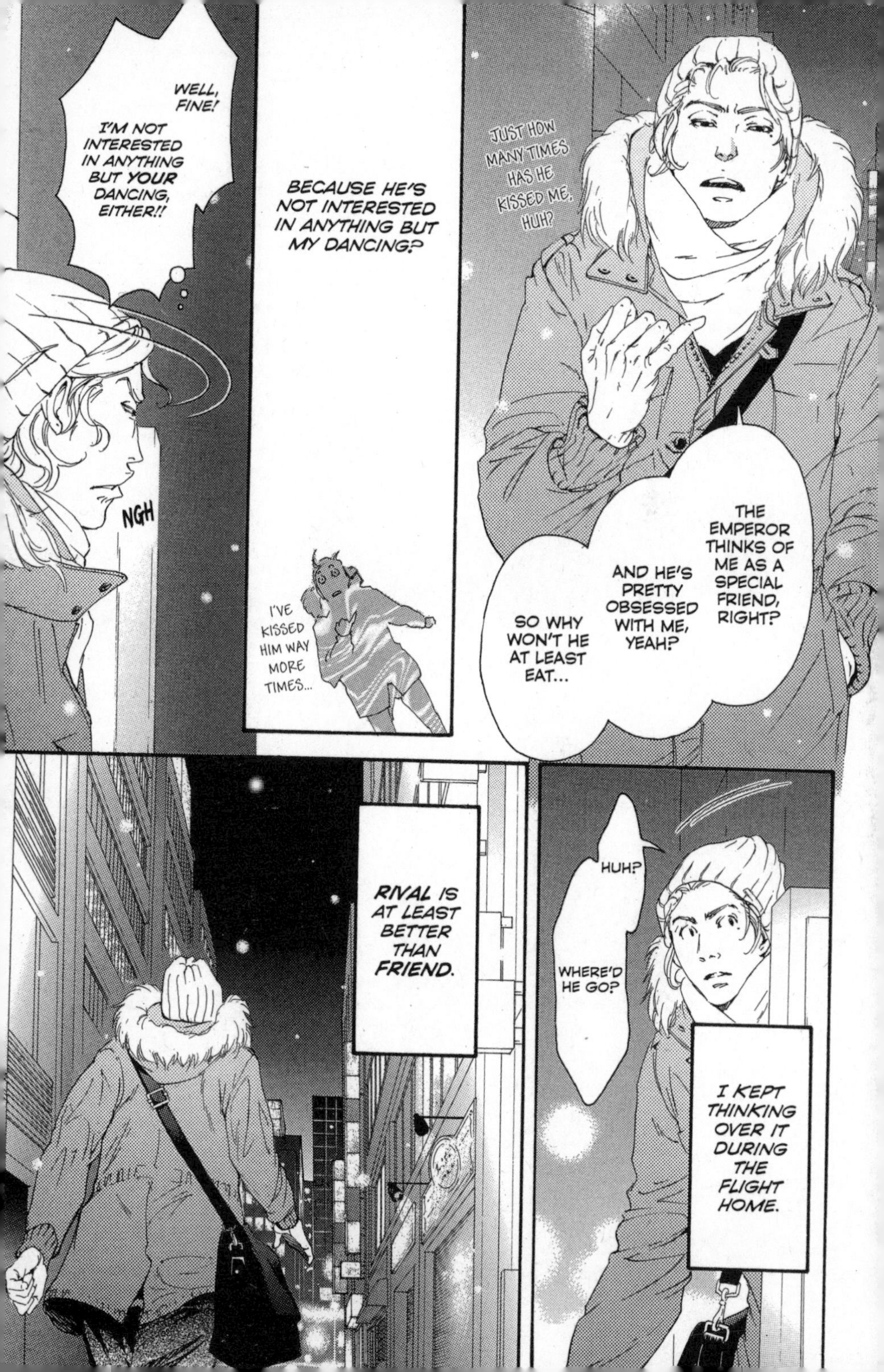

JUST HOW MANY TIMES HAS HE KISSED ME, HUH?
THE EMPEROR THINKS OF ME AS A SPECIAL FRIEND, RIGHT?
AND HE'S PRETTY OBSESSED WITH ME, YEAH?
SO WHY WON'T HE AT LEAST EAT...
BECAUSE HE'S NOT INTERESTED IN ANYTHING BUT MY DANCING?
I'VE KISSED HIM WAY MORE TIMES...
WELL, FINE!
I'M NOT INTERESTED IN ANYTHING BUT YOUR DANCING, EITHER!!
NGH
HUH?
WHERE'D HE GO?
I KEPT THINKING OVER IT DURING THE FLIGHT HOME.
RIVAL IS AT LEAST BETTER THAN FRIEND.

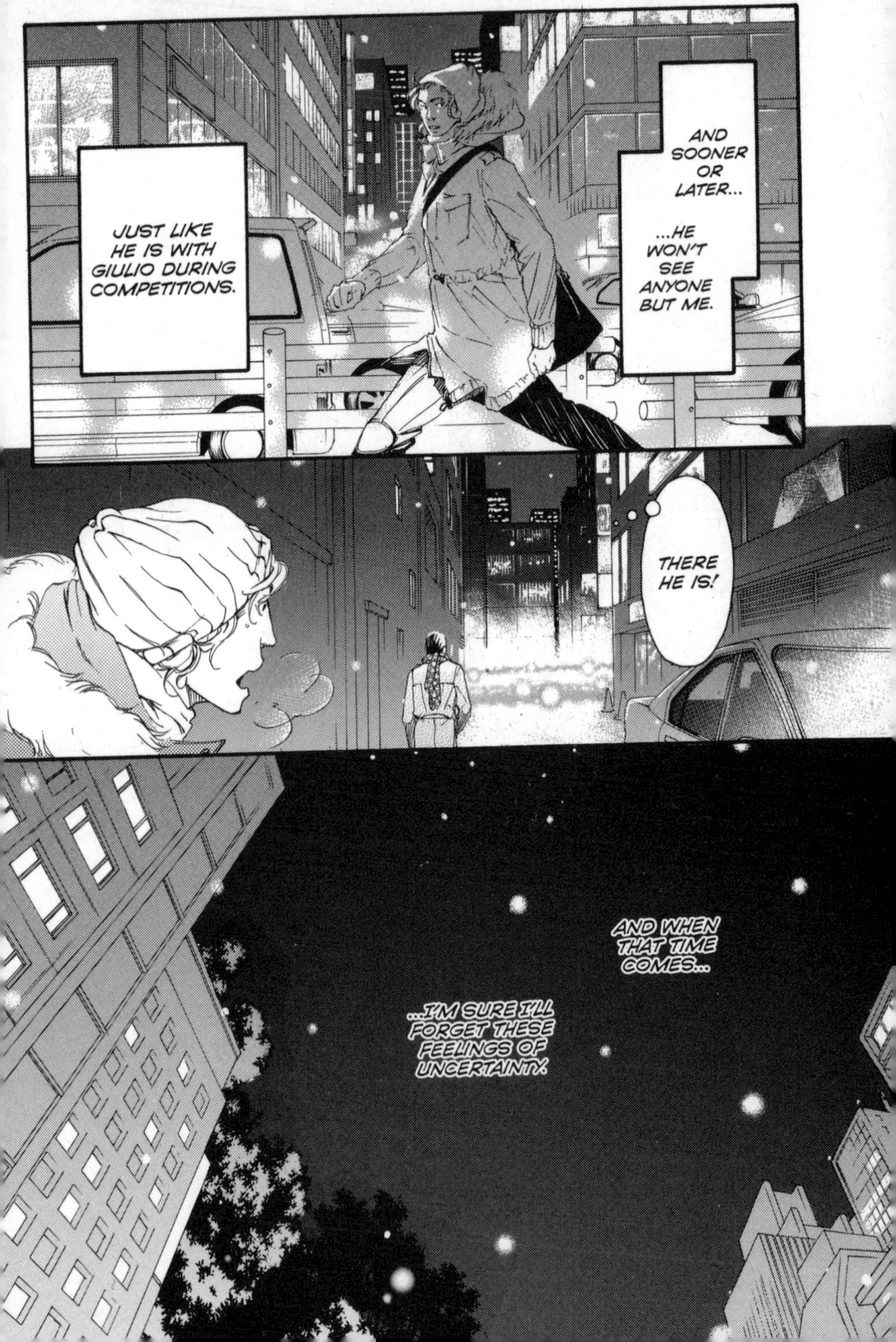
AND SOONER OR LATER...
...HE WON'T SEE ANYONE BUT ME.
JUST LIKE HE IS WITH GIULIO DURING COMPETITIONS.
THERE HE IS!
AND WHEN THAT TIME COMES...
...I'M SURE I'LL FORGET THESE FEELINGS OF UNCERTAINTY.

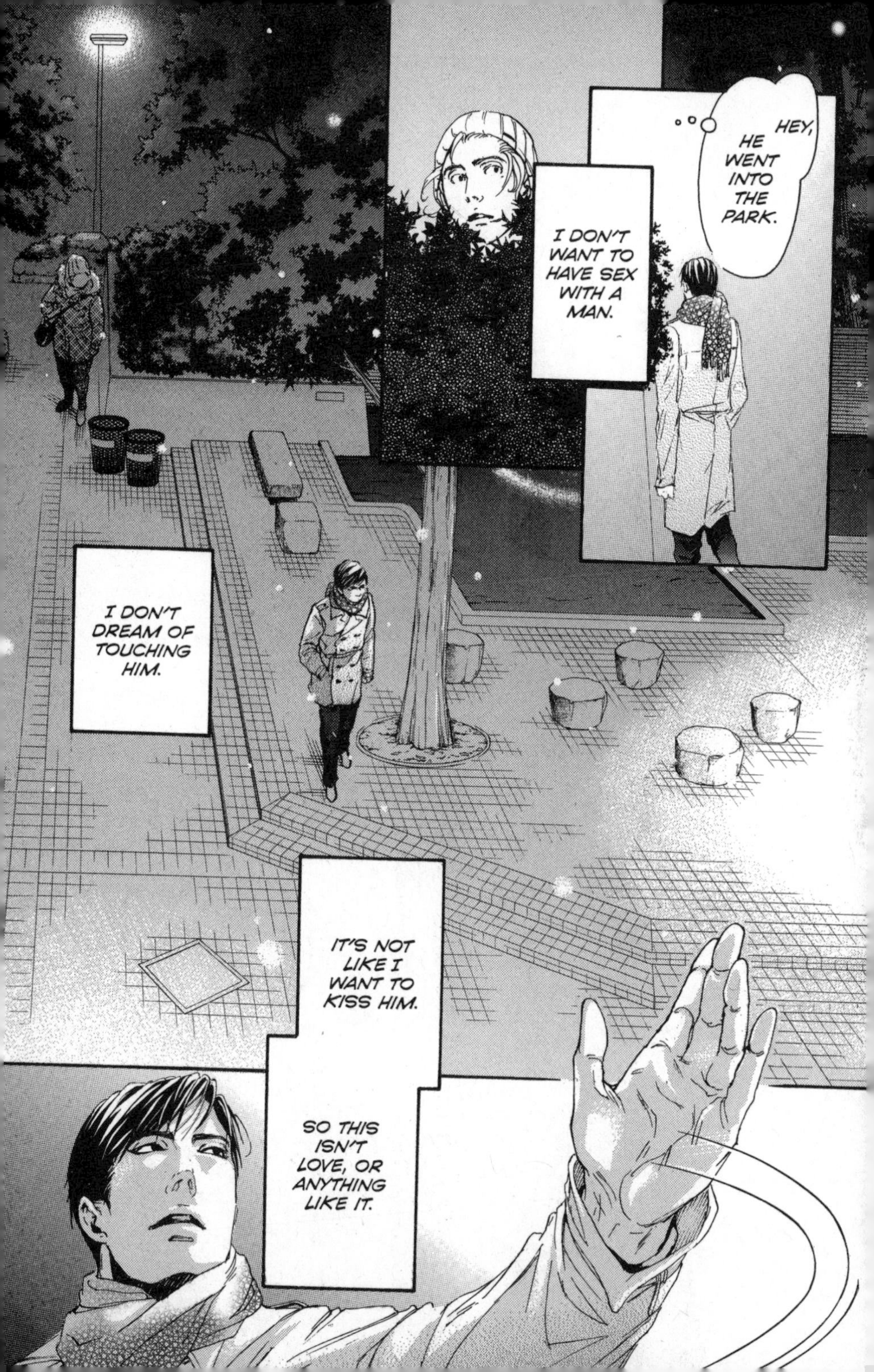
HEY, HE WENT INTO THE PARK.
I DON'T WANT TO HAVE SEX WITH A MAN.
I DON'T DREAM OF TOUCHING HIM.
IT'S NOT LIKE I WANT TO KISS HIM.
SO THIS ISN'T LOVE, OR ANYTHING LIKE IT.

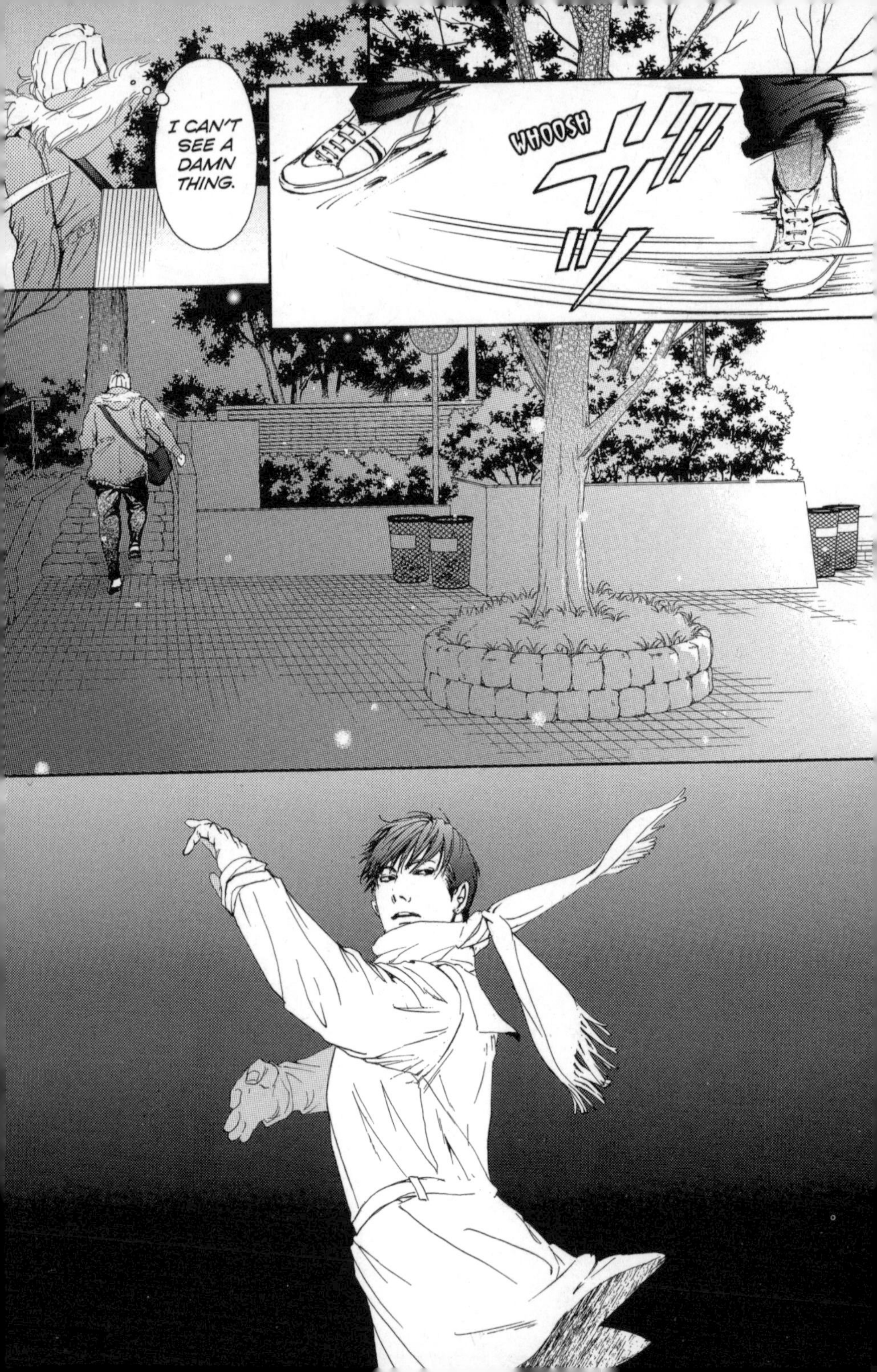
WHOOSH
I CAN'T SEE A DAMN THING.

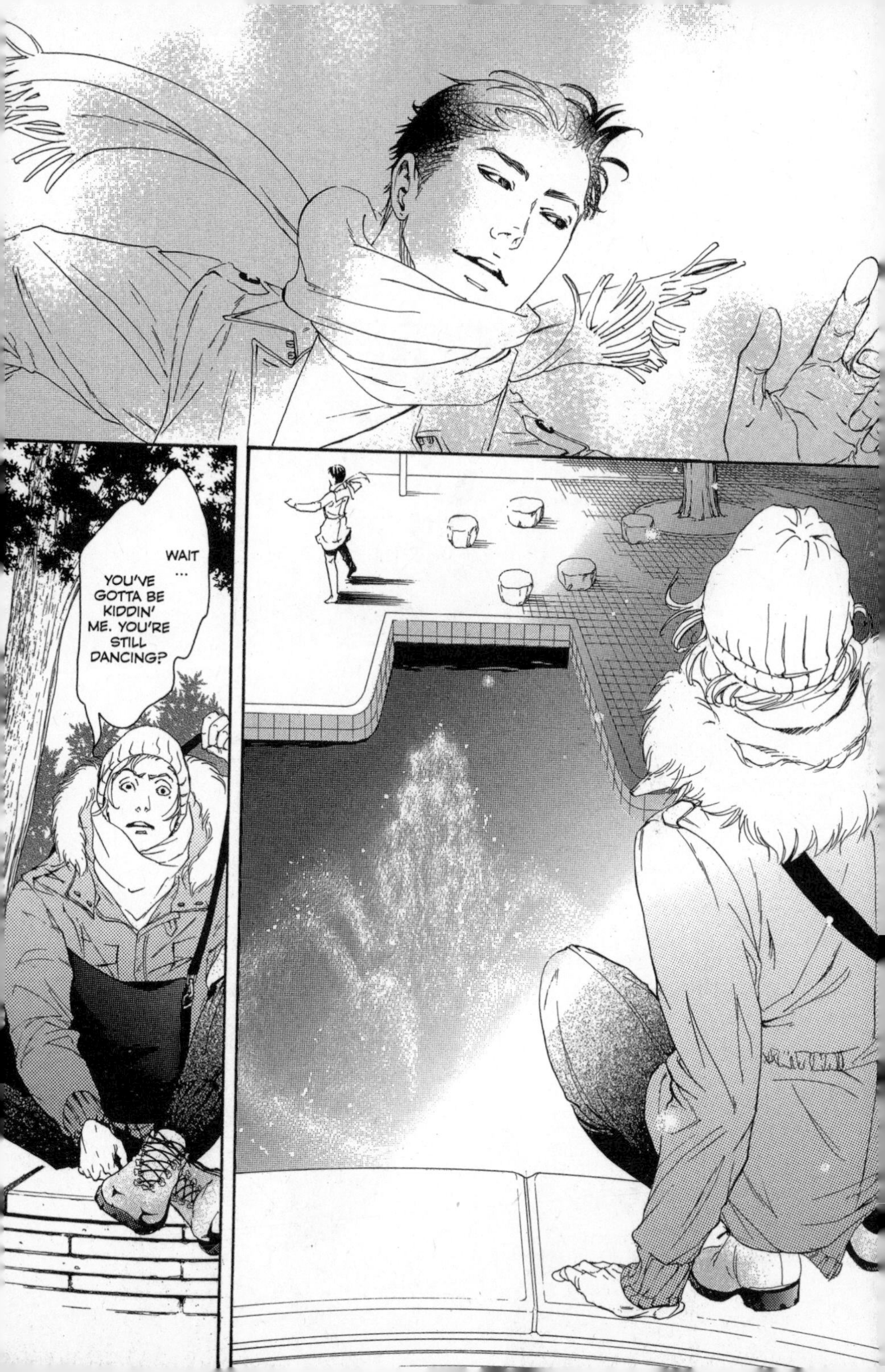
WAIT ...
YOU'VE GOTTA BE KIDDIN' ME. YOU'RE STILL DANCING?

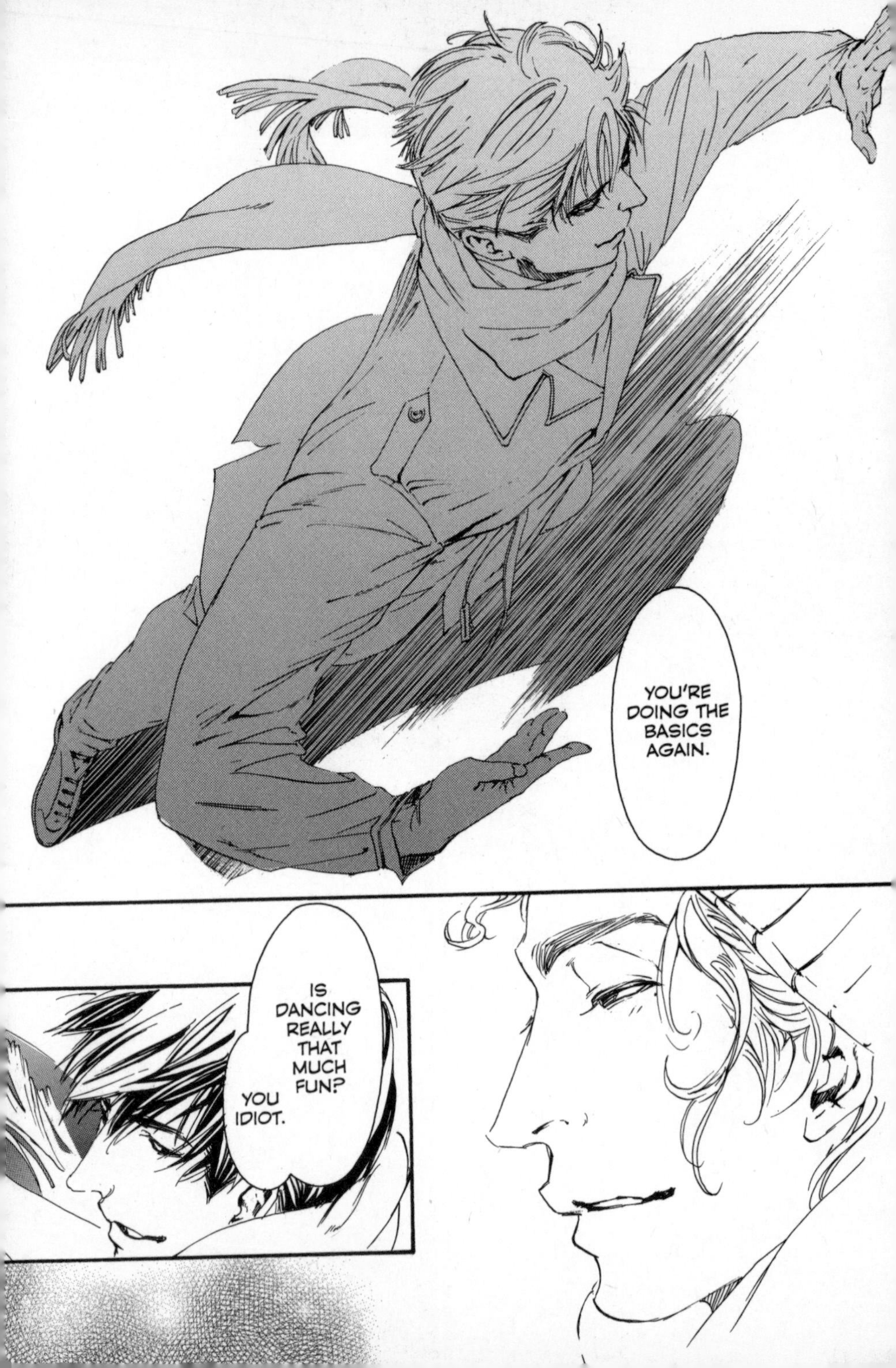
YOU'RE DOING THE BASICS AGAIN.
IS DANCING REALLY THAT MUCH FUN?
YOU IDIOT.

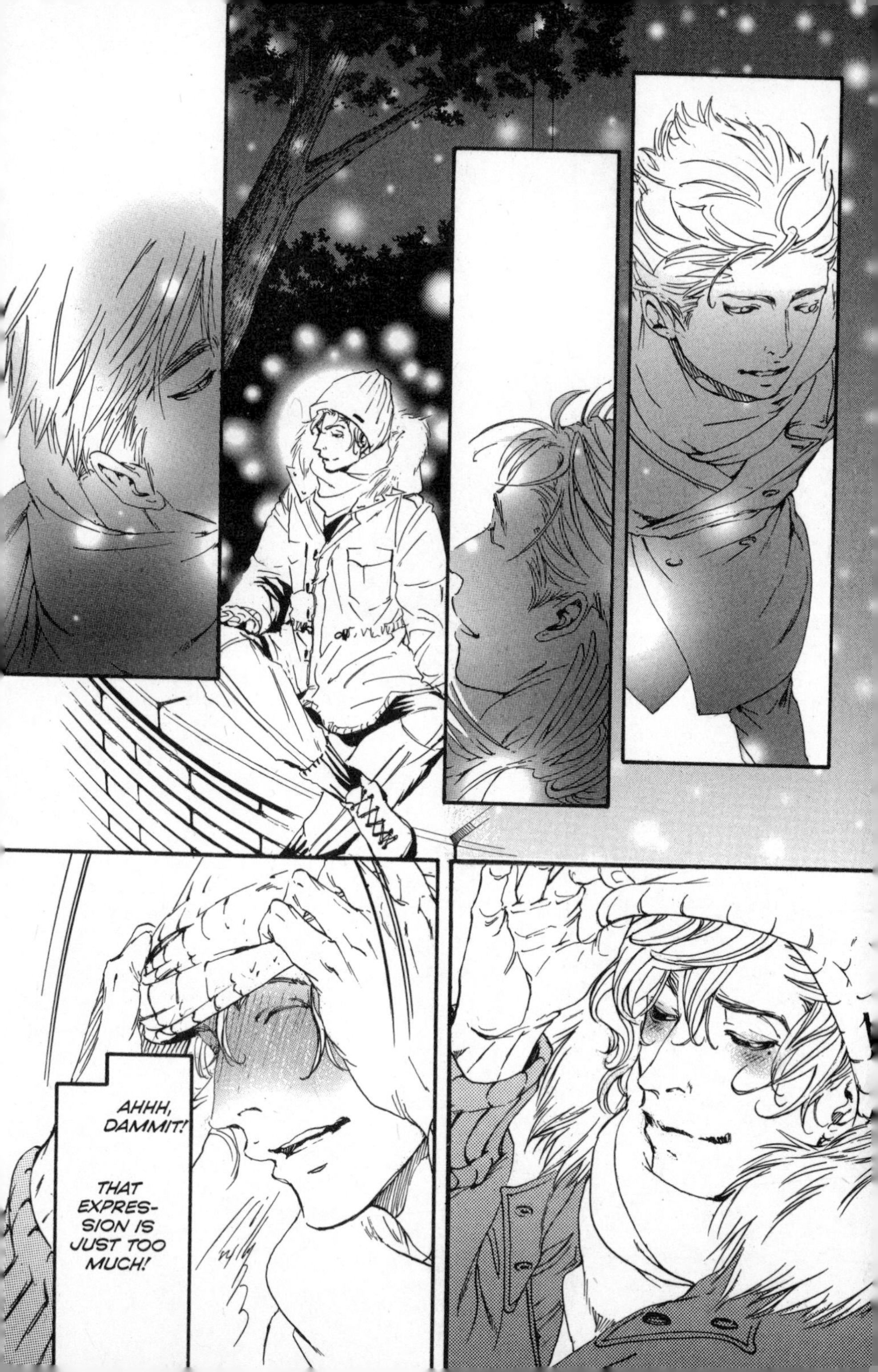
AHHH, DAMMIT!
THAT EXPRES-SION IS JUST TOO MUCH!

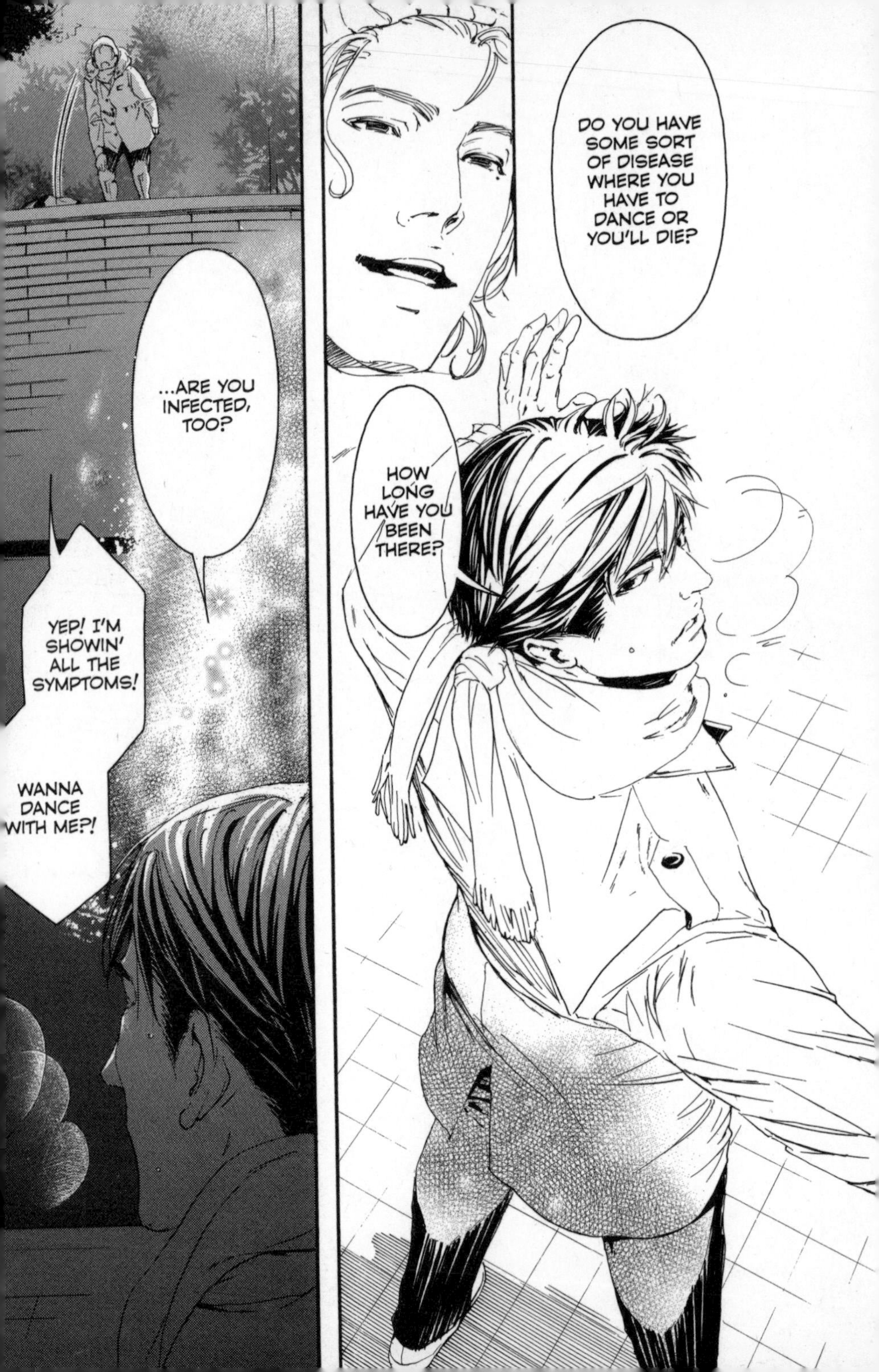
DO YOU HAVE SOME SORT OF DISEASE WHERE YOU HAVE TO DANCE OR YOU'LL DIE?
HOW LONG HAVE YOU BEEN THERE?
...ARE YOU INFECTED, TOO?
YEP! I'M SHOWIN' ALL THE SYMPTOMS!
WANNA DANCE WITH ME?!

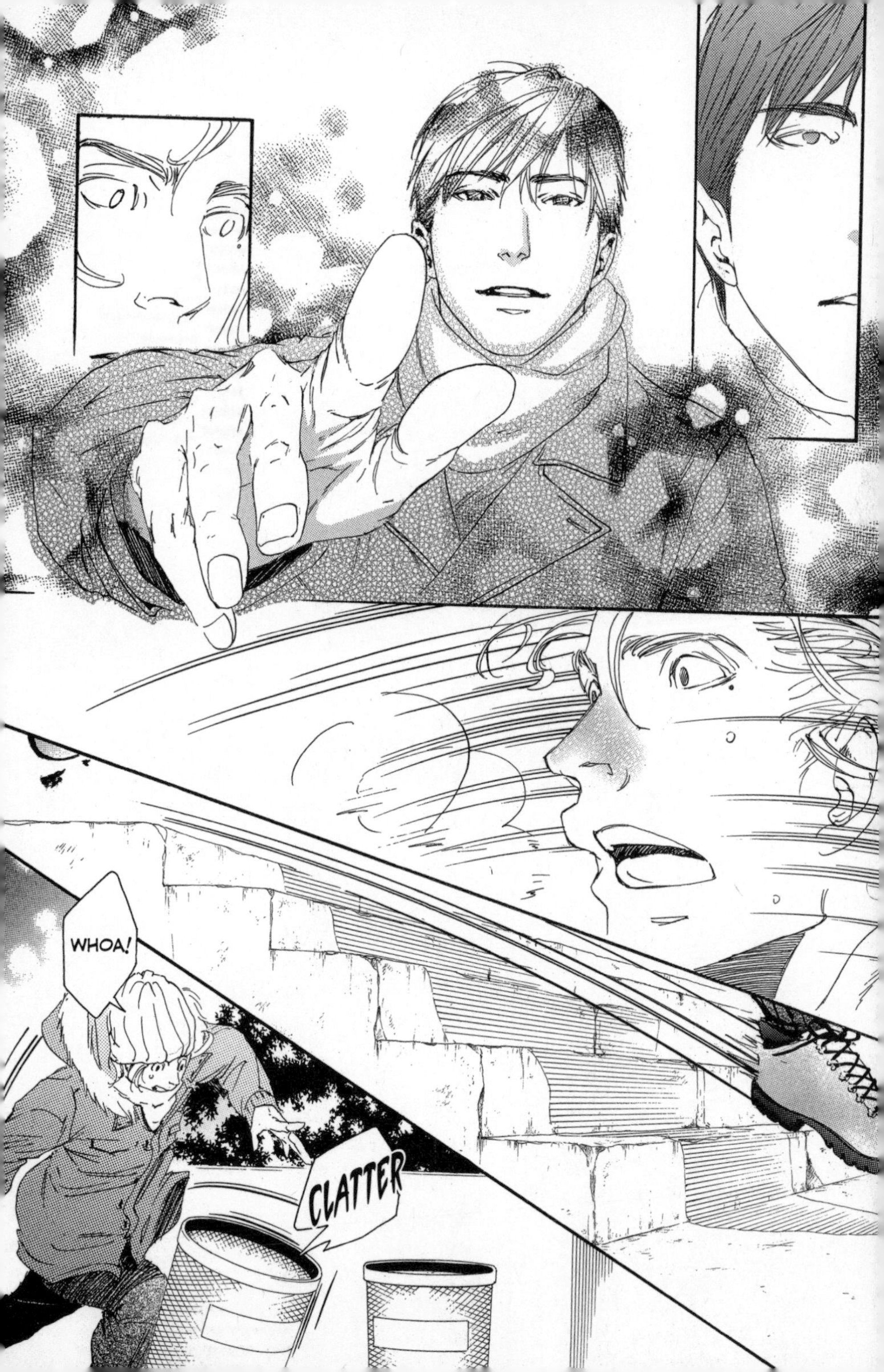
WHOA!
CLATTER

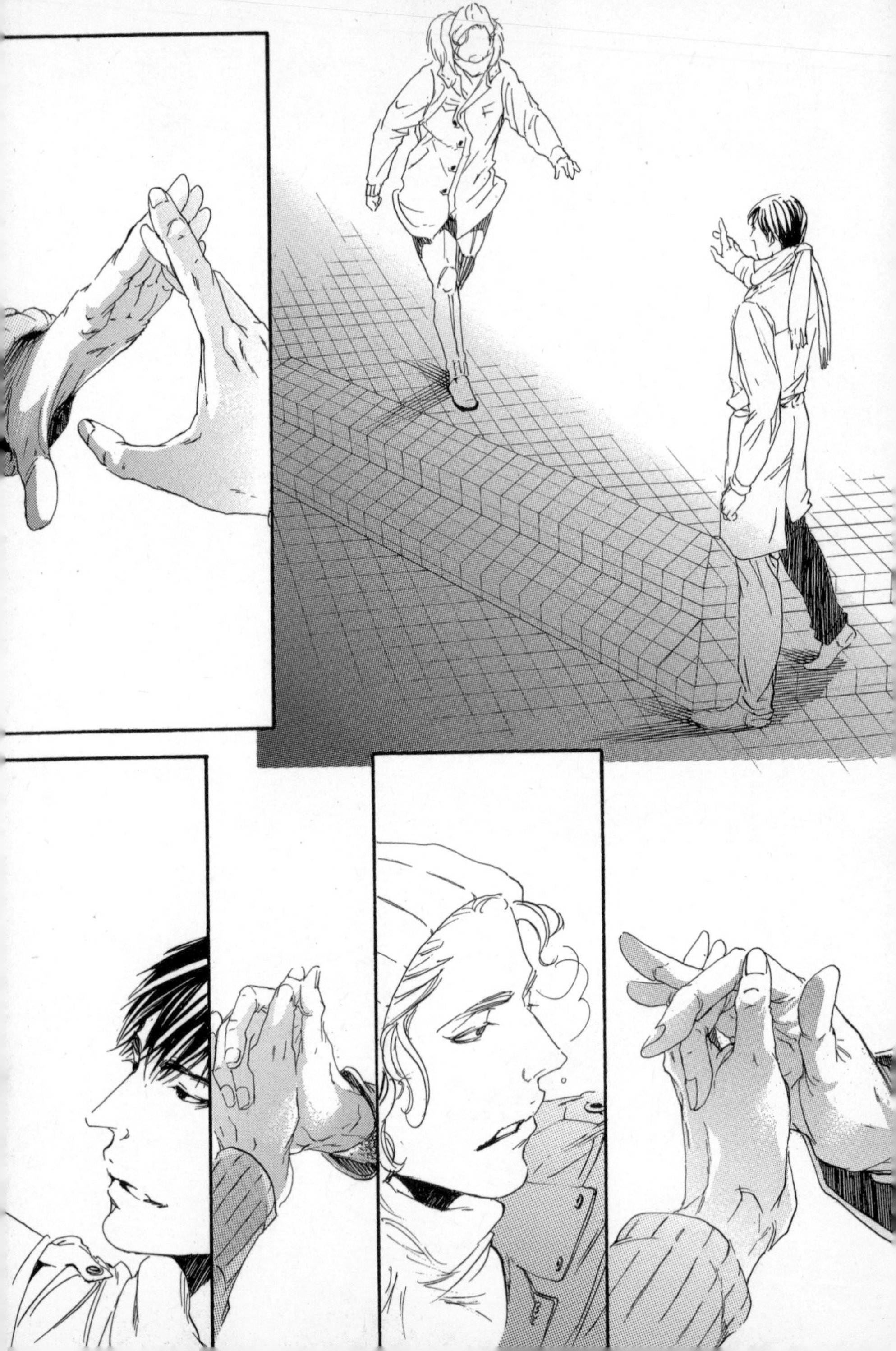

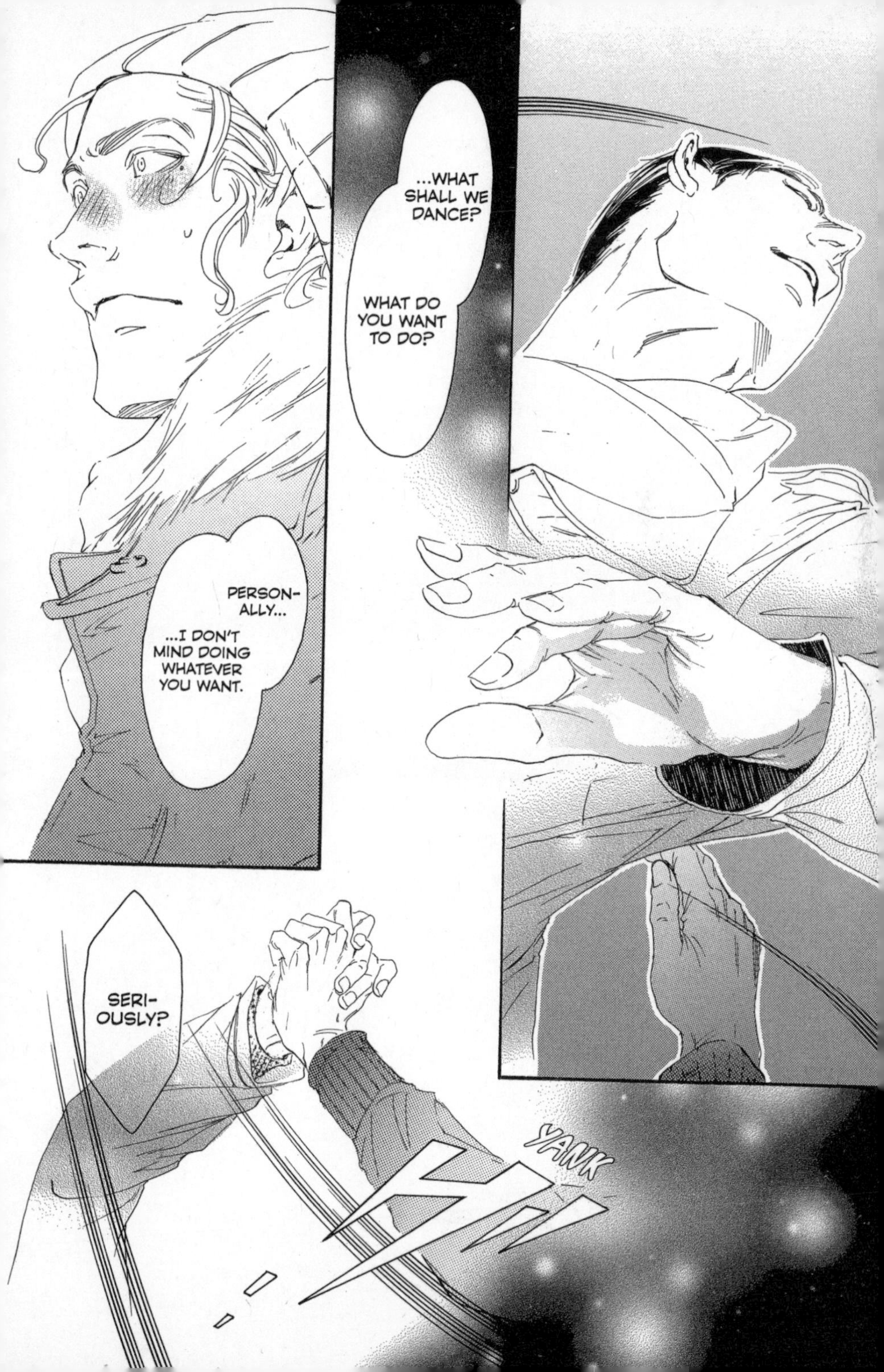
...WHAT SHALL WE DANCE?
WHAT DO YOU WANT TO DO?
PERSON-ALLY...
...I DON'T MIND DOING WHATEVER YOU WANT.
SERI-OUSLY?
YANK

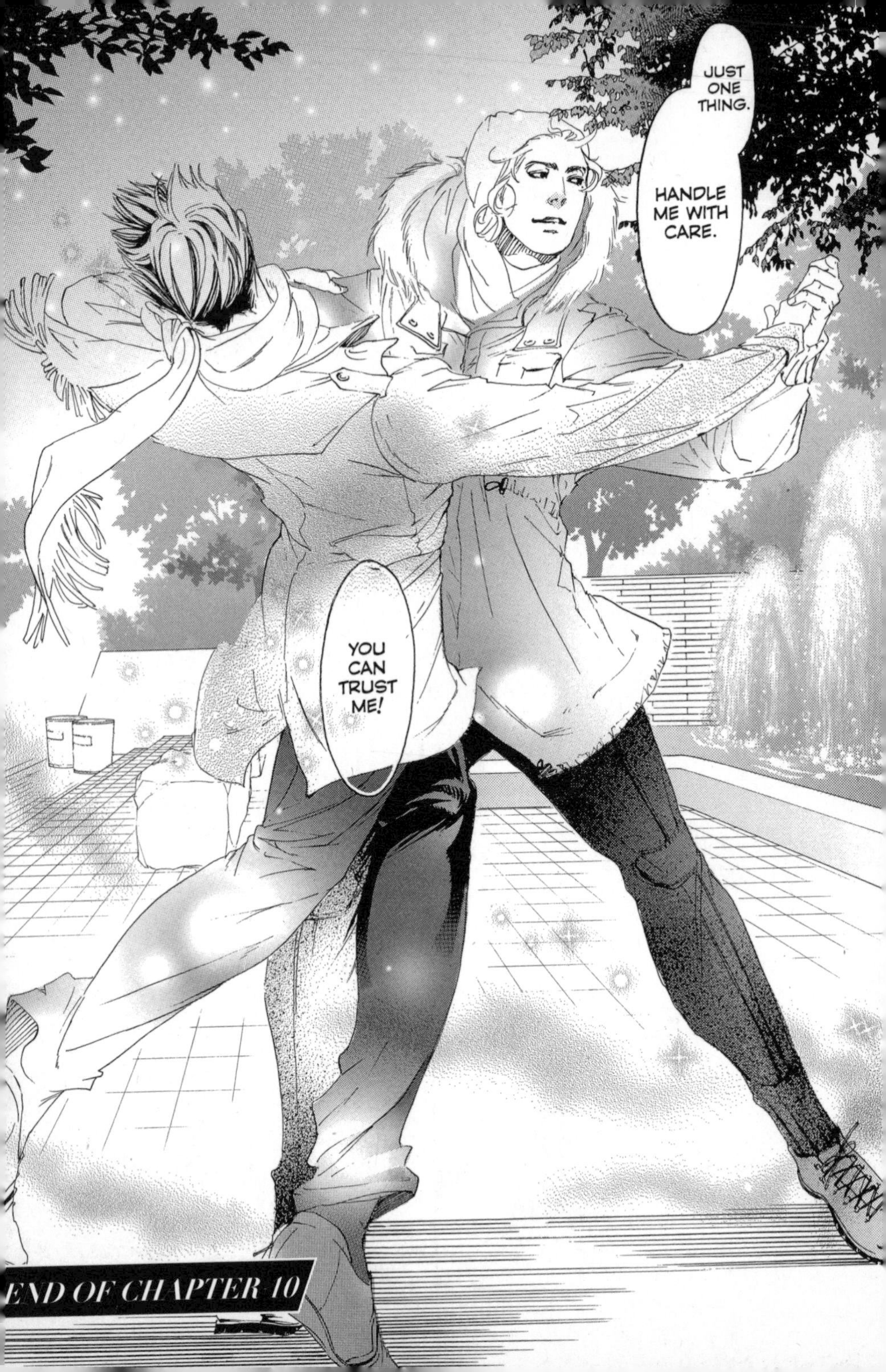
JUST ONE THING.
HANDLE ME WITH CARE.
YOU CAN TRUST ME!
END OF CHAPTER 10

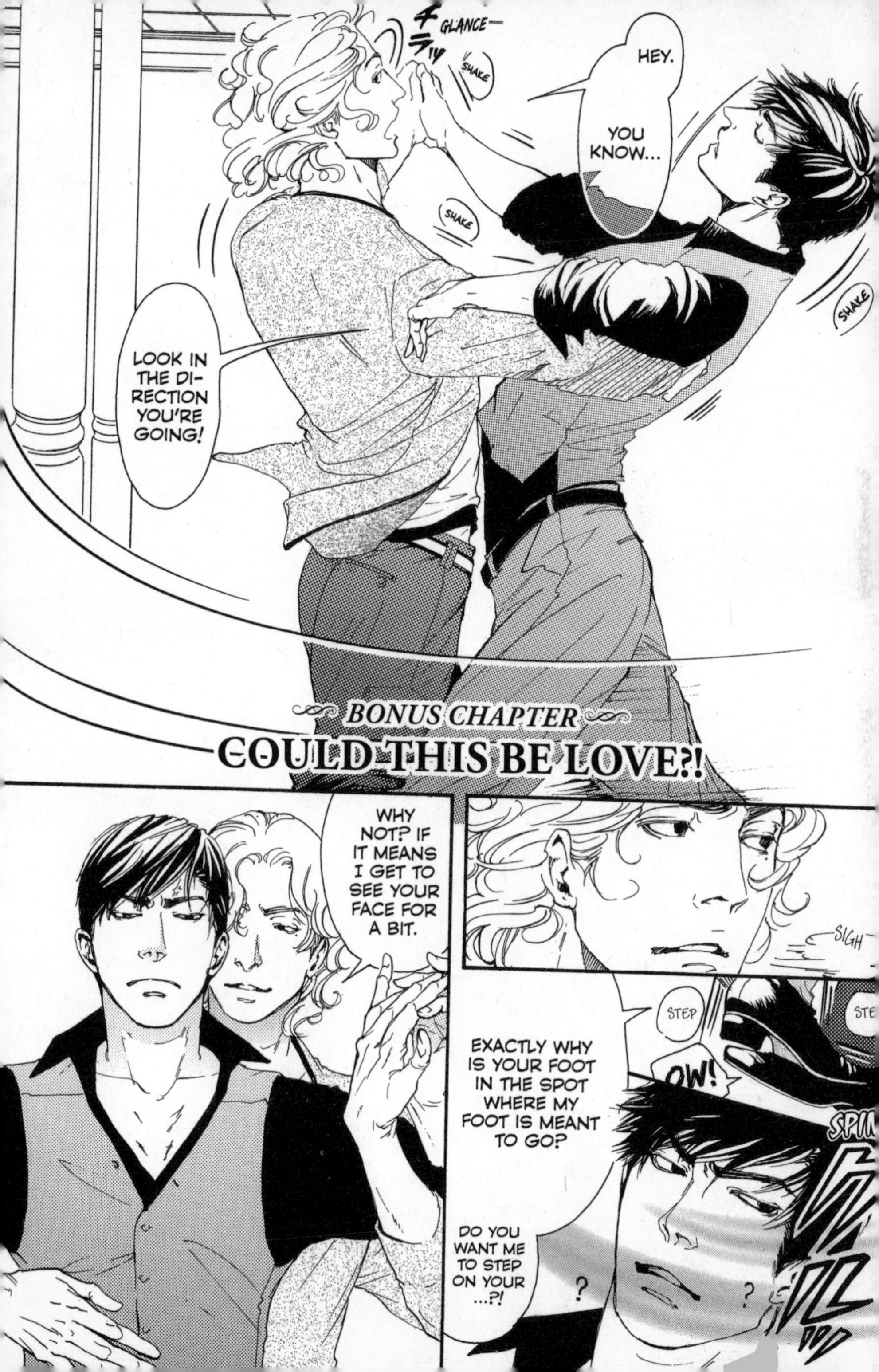
GLANCE
SHAKE
HEY.
YOU KNOW...
SHAKE
SHAKE
LOOK IN THE DI- RECTION YOU'RE GOING!
BONUS CHAPTER
COULD THIS BE LOVE?!
WHY NOT? IF IT MEANS I GET TO SEE YOUR FACE FOR A BIT.
SIGH
STEP
STE
OW!
EXACTLY WHY IS YOUR FOOT IN THE SPOT WHERE MY FOOT IS MEANT TO GO?
SPIN
DO YOU WANT ME TO STEP ON YOUR ...?!
?
?

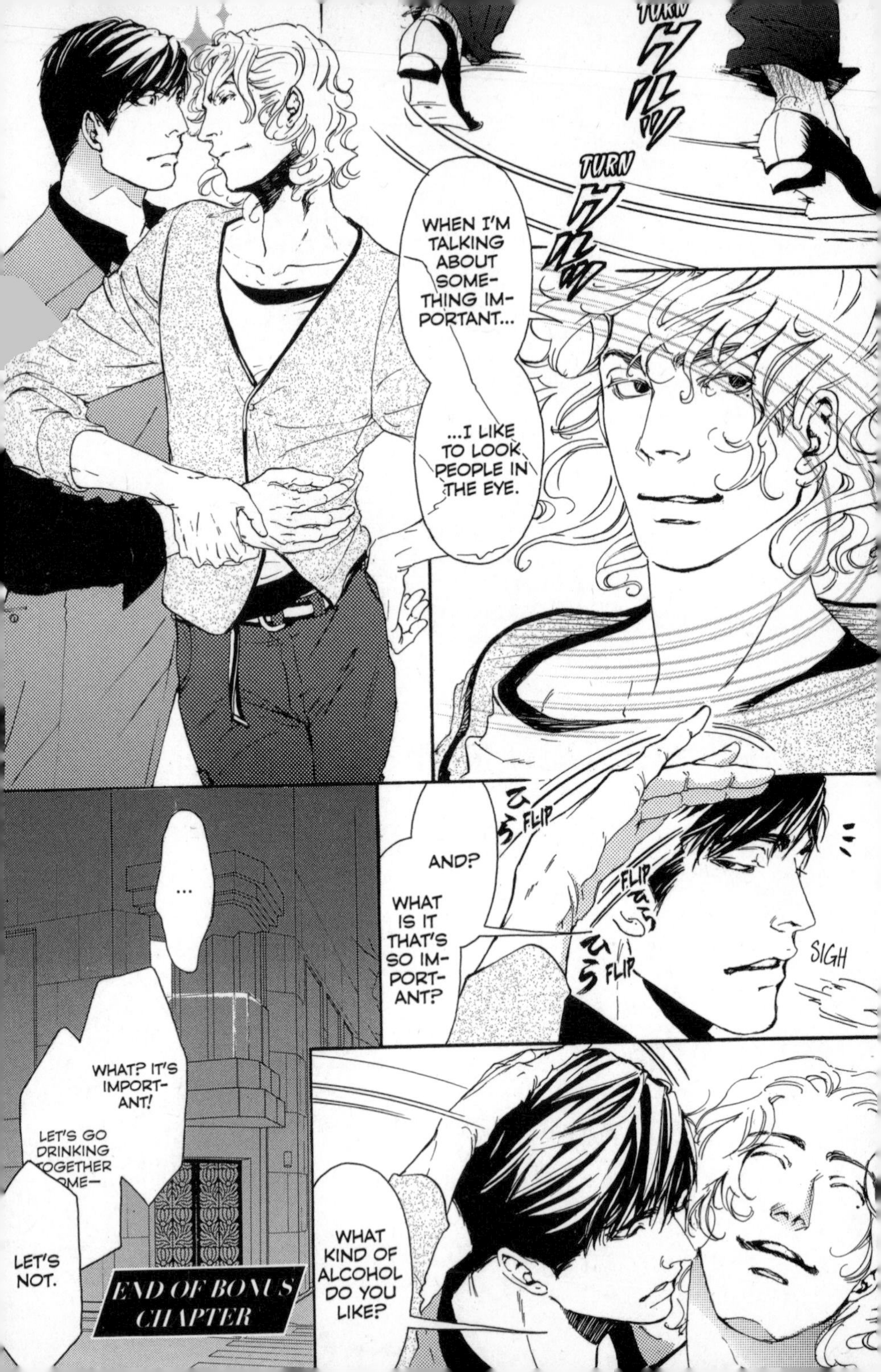
TURN
TURN
WHEN I'M TALKING ABOUT SOME-THING IM-PORTANT...
...I LIKE TO LOOK PEOPLE IN THE EYE.
FLIP
AND?
WHAT IS IT THAT'S SO IM-PORT-ANT?
FLIP
FLIP
SIGH
WHAT KIND OF ALCOHOL DO YOU LIKE?
...
WHAT? IT'S IMPORT-ANT!
LET'S GO DRINKING TOGETHER OME—
LET'S NOT.
END OF BONUS CHAPTER

Afterword

Here we are at volume 2, where the sweetness has increased.

The chapter titles I've included since volume 1 were chosen—and at times modified—from tunes often heard at ballroom dancing or competitive dancing conventions or schools (and they sometimes appear in the stories as well).

While studying the actual 10 Dance, I couldn't initially differentiate between the ten types of dance, but my Inouesatoh Breakthrough Solution was to differentiate them by music. I think you'd know most of them if you heard them, but you may not recognize them from their titles. Because of this, I tried as much as possible to pick well-known tunes. If you know the tune, I'd be delighted if you felt a little more familiar with it as you realize "this is a slow foxtrot, this is a cha-cha-cha tune." I'd like to describe for you the titles of the tunes that were the basis for each chapter title, as well as their categories (just one category).

Chapter 6: Fly Me to The Competition

Originally *Fly Me to The Moon* / Slow Foxtrot

The version sung by Sarah Vaughan is famous, isn't it?

Chapter 7: From Giulio With Love

Originally *From Russia With Love* / Rumba
Ahh, when it was published in the magazine I accidentally wrote 'Giulio' as 'Giorgio,' and nobody realized it, so he spent some time as Giorgio, but his name is Giulio.

Chapter 8: Can't Take My Eyes Off You

Originally the same name / Jive
It really shines, doesn't it? The Blackpool section as a whole shines, but I was writhing in pain over the portrayal of the love story, which I find difficult.

Chapter 9: Love Is A Wish Your Heart Makes

Originally *A Dream Is A Wish Your Heart Makes* (from Cinderella) / Waltz
I was quite relieved while drawing this, thinking "finally they can return to Japan." That said, volume 2 really is the kissing volume, huh?

Chapter 9.5: Shall We Dance?

Originally the same name / Waltz
I was going to call this *The Emperor And I*, but then I realized that's not a song name. Personally, I'm extremely woman-focused. In BL, I've always been advised to de-emphasize the women, so although I felt guilty for drawing the women, I drew the two men from Fusako's and Aki's points of view.

Chapter 10: Light My Fire

Originally the same name / Waltz
Every time I draw the two Shinyas in an enticing hold, I always experience anguish, as if my mind is being tortured.

...Special Thank Yous...

Ariga-sama, Kobato Uchida-sama, Yoko Tadano-sama, everyone in the *Young Magazine* Editorial Department, designer Fukumura-sama, Ota-sama, my teacher Inoue, my own U-chan, Yuki Uewaki-sama, Ran Shimoda-sama, Koichi Nishio-sama, Yumi Kojima-sama, the business people, the people at the printing office, the many bookstores, coordinator T-sama, and all my dear readers.

Inouesatoh

In addition to volume 2, some CDs have been released.

Translation Notes

Inspiration, page 22

When Sugiki says "you are my inspiration," the Japanese word he uses, *akogare*, also has other connotations, including "I yearn for you," or "I desire you." This ambiguity in meaning is why Suzuki is especially confused!

Ribbit, page 26

The frog here says "*kero*" in Japanese, which does mean "ribbit" in English, but is a play on words: the word *kero* can also mean feigning nonchalance, or pretending nothing has happened, so the frog here is a joking indicator of Sugiki's attempts to play it cool.

World Championships, page 40

Although Sugiki mentions the *World Championships* here, the competition they attend is held at the Winter Gardens at Blackpool, which is actually where the *Blackpool Dance Festival* is held. However the timing is also wrong, as the *Blackpool Dance Festival* is held in May, not January, and the event is clearly played out as the *World Championships*. This was probably done for dramatic effect, as Blackpool is familiar to readers, and Sugiki is known as the "Blackpool Monster."

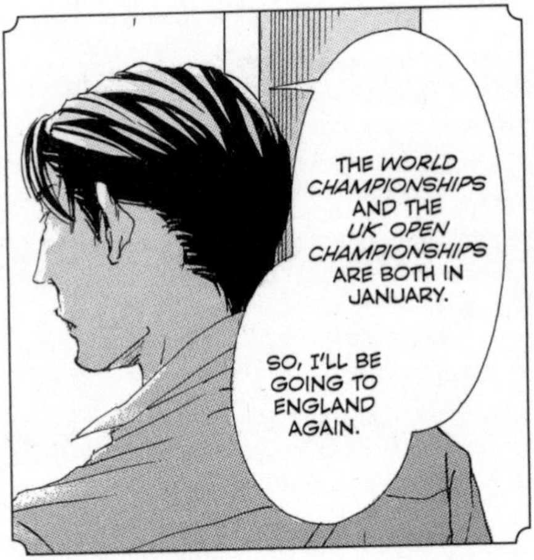
THE WORLD CHAMPIONSHIPS AND THE UK OPEN CHAMPIONSHIPS ARE BOTH IN JANUARY.
SO, I'LL BE GOING TO ENGLAND AGAIN.

Winter Gardens, page 73

The Winter Gardens is an entertainment complex in Blackpool, England, and houses the Empress Ballroom, where several high-profile dance competitions are held every year.

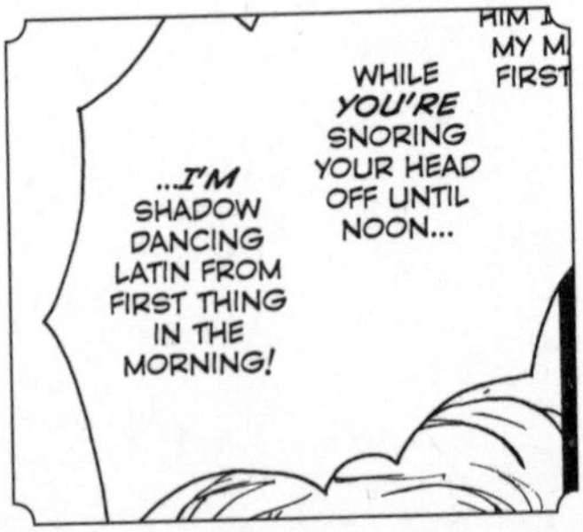
WHILE YOU'RE SNORING YOUR HEAD OFF UNTIL NOON...
...I'M SHADOW DANCING LATIN FROM FIRST THING IN THE MORNING!

Shadow dancing, page 163

Shadow dancing is practicing the dance steps by yourself, but as if you were dancing with a partner.

10 DANCE

Volume 2 Cover Flap
Bonus Comic

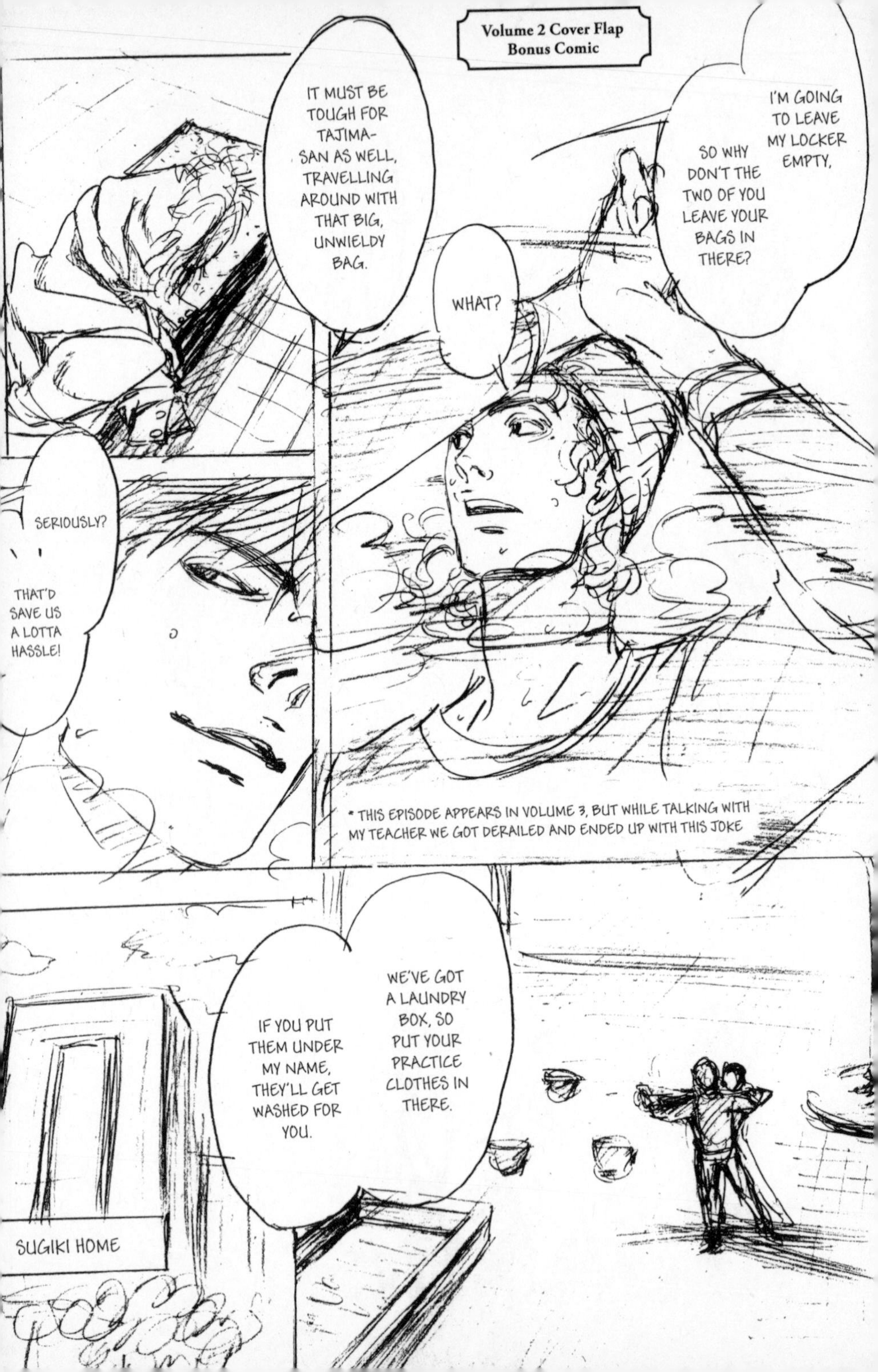
I'M GOING TO LEAVE MY LOCKER EMPTY,
SO WHY DON'T THE TWO OF YOU LEAVE YOUR BAGS IN THERE?
IT MUST BE TOUGH FOR TAJIMA-SAN AS WELL, TRAVELLING AROUND WITH THAT BIG, UNWIELDY BAG.
WHAT?
SERIOUSLY?
THAT'D SAVE US A LOTTA HASSLE!
* THIS EPISODE APPEARS IN VOLUME 3, BUT WHILE TALKING WITH MY TEACHER WE GOT DERAILED AND ENDED UP WITH THIS JOKE
WE'VE GOT A LAUNDRY BOX, SO PUT YOUR PRACTICE CLOTHES IN THERE.
IF YOU PUT THEM UNDER MY NAME, THEY'LL GET WASHED FOR YOU.
SUGIKI HOME

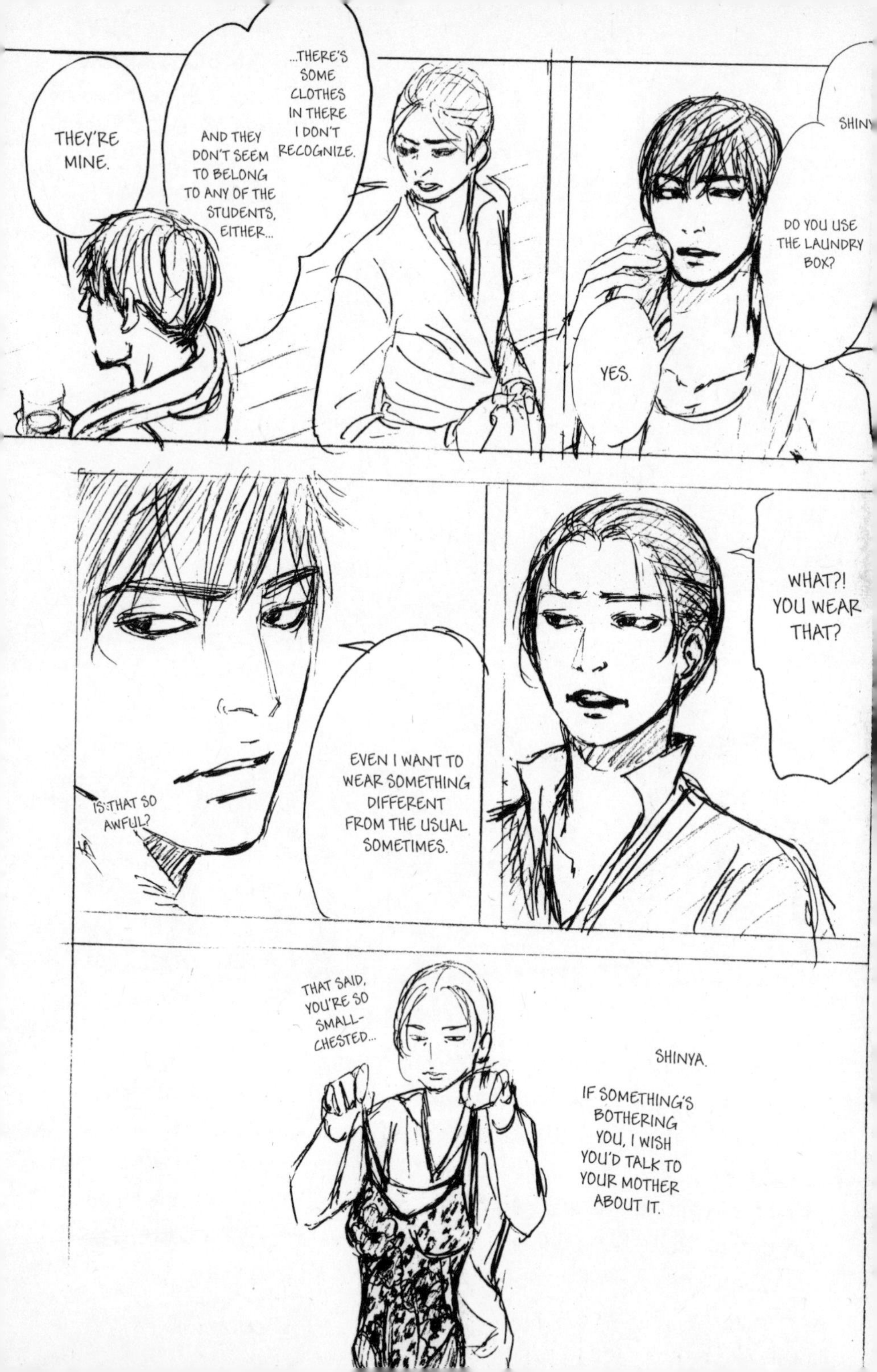
SHIN
DO YOU USE THE LAUNDRY BOX?
YES.
...THERE'S SOME CLOTHES IN THERE I DON'T RECOGNIZE.
AND THEY DON'T SEEM TO BELONG TO ANY OF THE STUDENTS, EITHER...
THEY'RE MINE.
WHAT?! YOU WEAR THAT?
EVEN I WANT TO WEAR SOMETHING DIFFERENT FROM THE USUAL SOMETIMES.
IS THAT SO AWFUL?
THAT SAID, YOU'RE SO SMALL-CHESTED...
SHINYA.
IF SOMETHING'S BOTHERING YOU, I WISH YOU'D TALK TO YOUR MOTHER ABOUT IT.

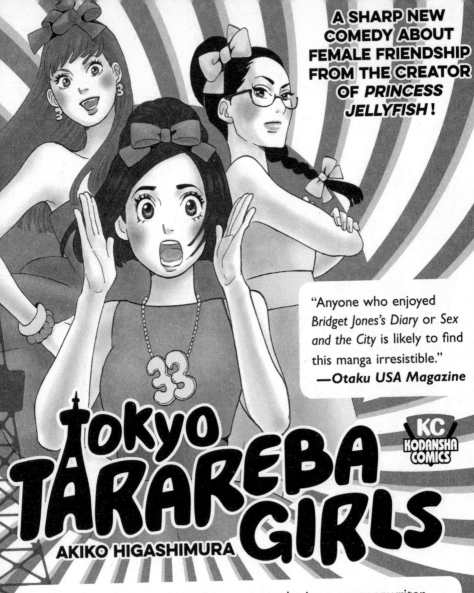

A SHARP NEW COMEDY ABOUT FEMALE FRIENDSHIP FROM THE CREATOR OF *PRINCESS JELLYFISH*!

"Anyone who enjoyed *Bridget Jones's Diary* or *Sex and the City* is likely to find this manga irresistible."
—*Otaku USA Magazine*

Tokyo TARAREBA GIRLS

AKIKO HIGASHIMURA

KC KODANSHA COMICS

Rinko has done everything she can to make it as a screenwriter. So at 33, she can't help but lament over the fact that her career's plateaued, she's still painfully single, and spends most of her nights drinking with her two best friends. One night, drunk and delusional, Rinko swears to get married by the time the Tokyo Olympics roll around in 2020. But finding a man—or love—may be a cutthroat, dirty job for a romantic at heart!

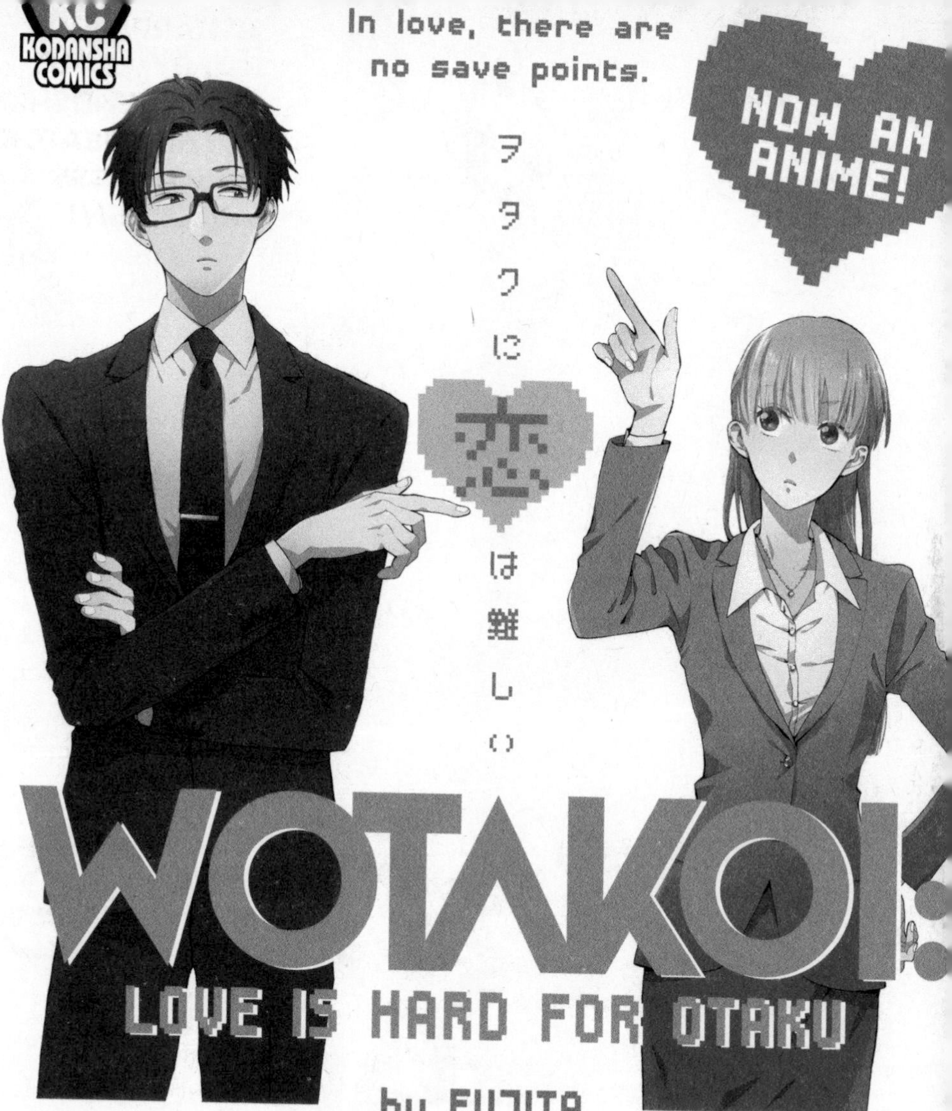
KC KODANSHA COMICS
In love, there are no save points.
NOW AN ANIME!
ヲタクに恋は難しい
WOTAKOI:
LOVE IS HARD FOR OTAKU
by FUJITA

Narumi has had it rough: Every boyfriend she's had dumped her once they found out she was an otaku, so she's gone to great lengths to hide it. At her new job, she bumps into Hirotaka, her childhood friend and fellow otaku. When Hirotaka almost gets her secret outed at work, she comes up with a plan to keep him quiet. But he comes up with a counter-proposal: Why doesn't she just date him instead?

KC
DANSHA
OMICS

complex age
yui sakuma

26-year-old Nagisa Kataura has a secret. Transforming into her favorite anime and manga characters is her passion in life, and she's earned great respect amongst her fellow cospayers. But to the rest of society, her hobby is a silly fantasy. As demands from both her office job and cosplaying begin to increase, she may one day have to make a tough choice— what's more important to her, cosplay or being "normal"?

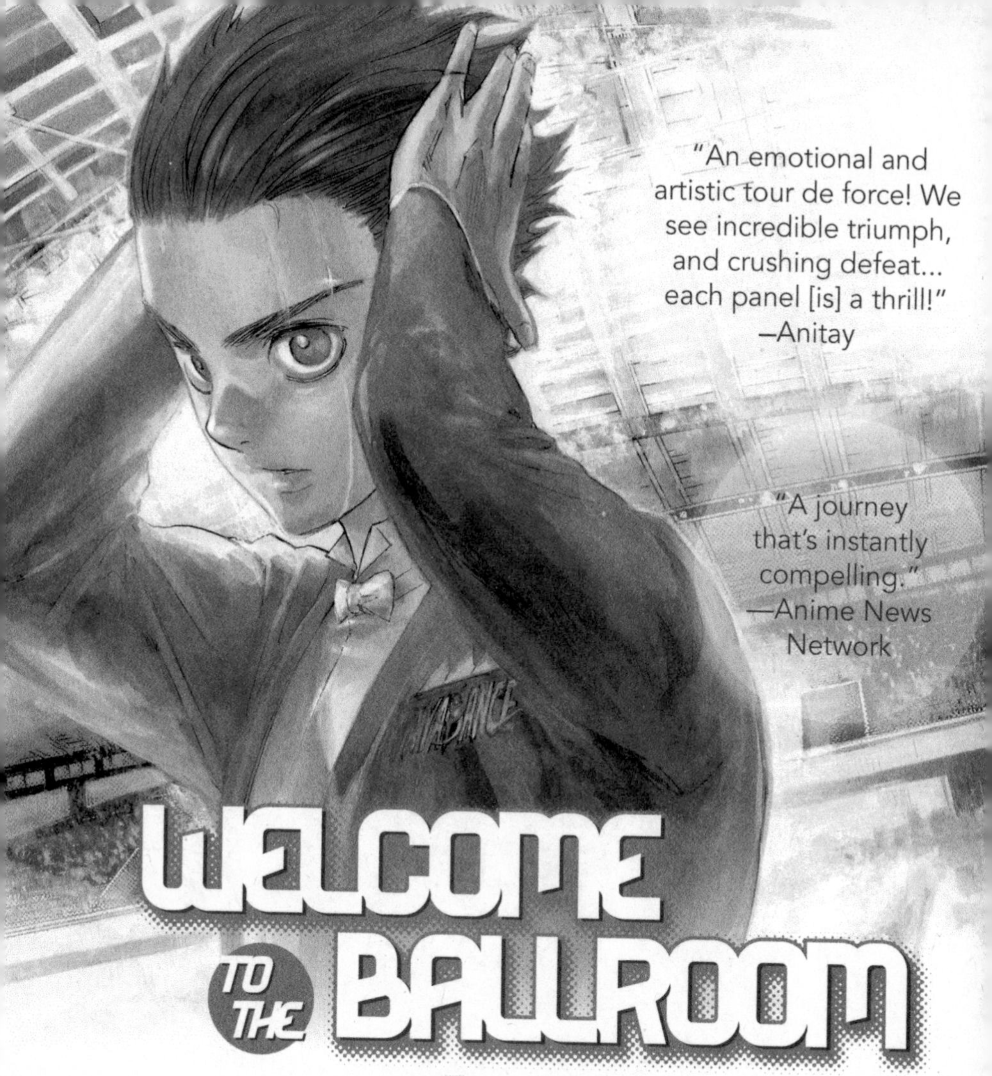
"An emotional and artistic tour de force! We see incredible triumph, and crushing defeat... each panel [is] a thrill!"
–Anitay
"A journey that's instantly compelling."
—Anime News Network

WELCOME TO THE BALLROOM

By Tomo Takeuchi

Feckless high school student Tatara Fujita wants to be good at something—anything. Unfortunately, he's about as average as a slouchy teen can be. The local bullies know this, and make it a habit to hit him up for cash, but all that changes when the debonair Kaname Sengoku sends them packing. Sengoku's not the neighborhood watch, though. He's a professional ballroom dancer. And once Tatara Fujita gets pulled into the world of ballroom, his life will never be the same.

KC KODANSHA COMICS

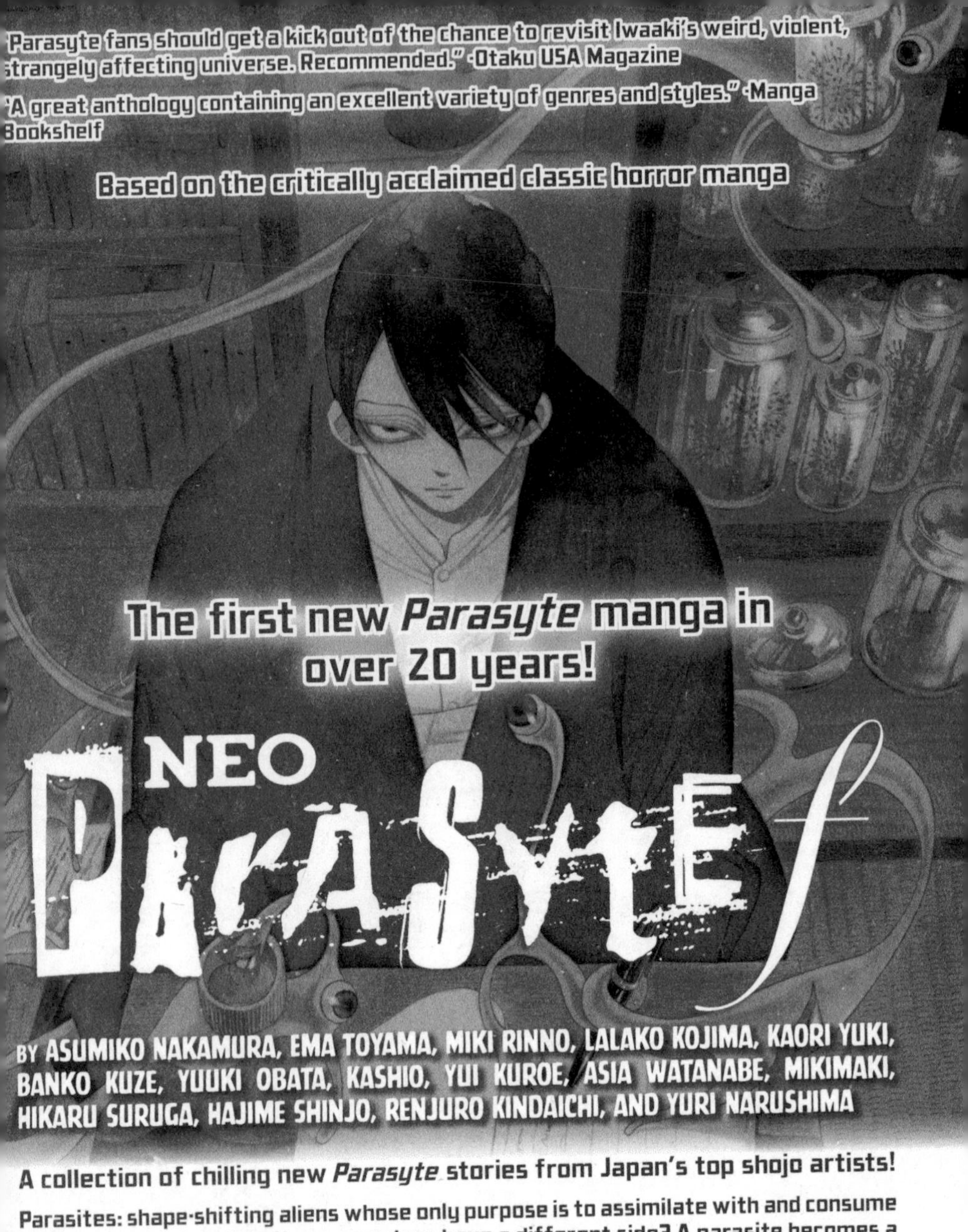
"Parasyte fans should get a kick out of the chance to revisit Iwaaki's weird, violent, strangely affecting universe. Recommended." -Otaku USA Magazine
"A great anthology containing an excellent variety of genres and styles." -Manga Bookshelf
Based on the critically acclaimed classic horror manga
The first new *Parasyte* manga in over 20 years!
NEO
PARASYTE f
BY ASUMIKO NAKAMURA, EMA TOYAMA, MIKI RINNO, LALAKO KOJIMA, KAORI YUKI, BANKO KUZE, YUUKI OBATA, KASHIO, YUI KUROE, ASIA WATANABE, MIKIMAKI, HIKARU SURUGA, HAJIME SHINJO, RENJURO KINDAICHI, AND YURI NARUSHIMA

A collection of chilling new *Parasyte* stories from Japan's top shojo artists!

Parasites: shape-shifting aliens whose only purpose is to assimilate with and consume the human race... but do these monsters have a different side? A parasite becomes a prince to save his romance-obsessed female host from a dangerous stalker. Another hosts a cooking show, in which the real monsters are revealed. These and 13 more stories, from some of the greatest shojo manga artists alive today, together make up a chilling, funny, and entertaining tribute to one of manga's horror classics!

KC KODANSHA COMICS

The Black Museum The Ghost and the Lady

By Kazuhiro Fujita

Deep in Scotland Yard in London sits an evidence room dedicated to the greatest mysteries of British history. In this "Black Museum" sits a misshapen hunk of lead—two bullets fused together—the key to a wartime encounter between Florence Nightingale, the mother of modern nursing, and a supernatural Man in Grey. This story is unknown to most scholars of history, but a special guest of the museum will tell the tale of The Ghost and the Lady...

Praise for Kazuhiro Fujita's *Ushio and Tora*

"A charming revival that combines a classic look with modern depth and pacing... **Essential viewing both for curmudgeons and new fans alike.**" — Anime News Network

"**GREAT!** The first episode of Ushio and Tora captures the essence of '90s anime." — IGN

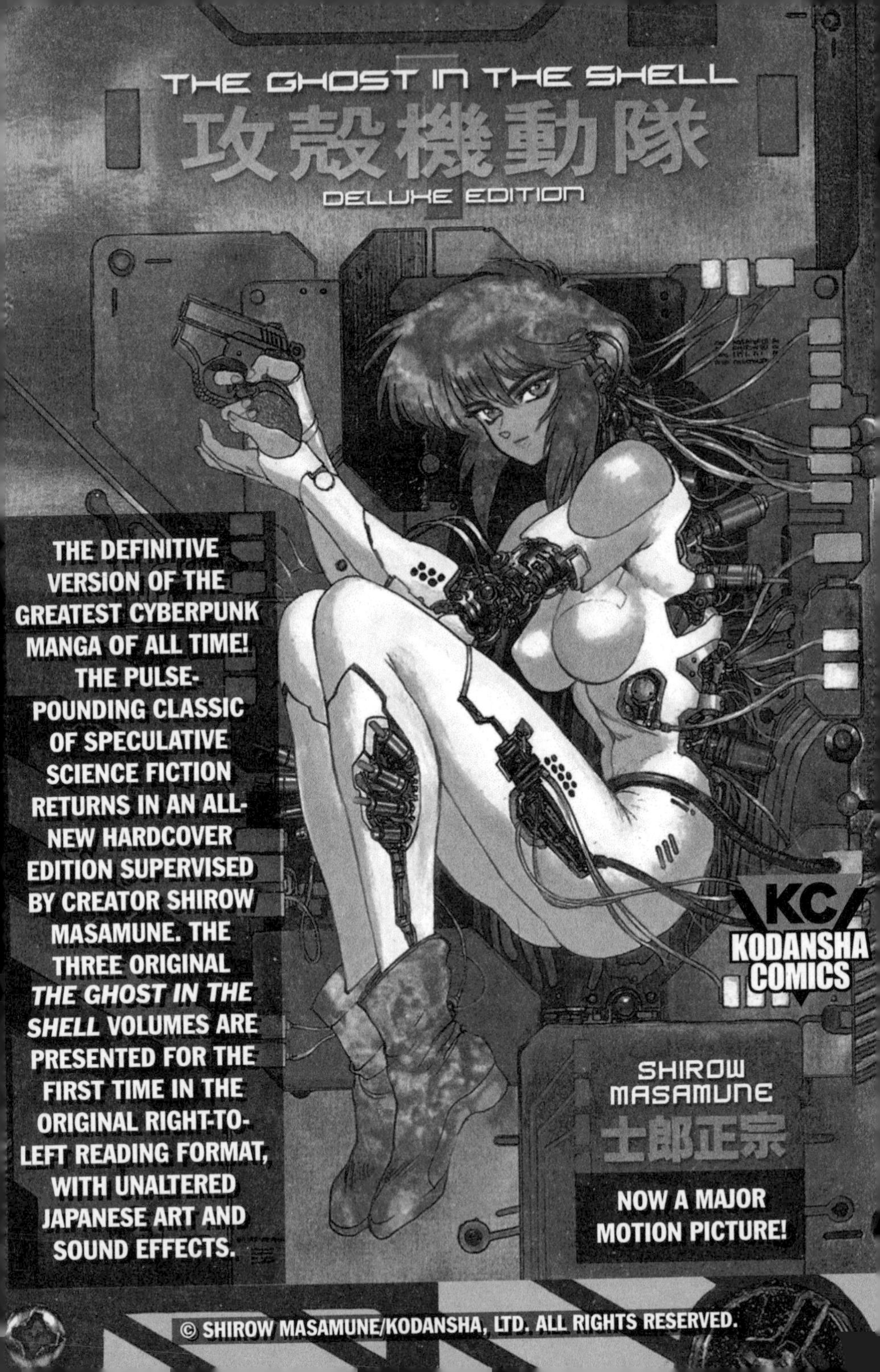
THE GHOST IN THE SHELL
攻殻機動隊
DELUXE EDITION
THE DEFINITIVE VERSION OF THE GREATEST CYBERPUNK MANGA OF ALL TIME! THE PULSE-POUNDING CLASSIC OF SPECULATIVE SCIENCE FICTION RETURNS IN AN ALL-NEW HARDCOVER EDITION SUPERVISED BY CREATOR SHIROW MASAMUNE. THE THREE ORIGINAL *THE GHOST IN THE SHELL* VOLUMES ARE PRESENTED FOR THE FIRST TIME IN THE ORIGINAL RIGHT-TO-LEFT READING FORMAT, WITH UNALTERED JAPANESE ART AND SOUND EFFECTS.
KC
KODANSHA COMICS
SHIROW MASAMUNE
士郎正宗
NOW A MAJOR MOTION PICTURE!
© SHIROW MASAMUNE/KODANSHA, LTD. ALL RIGHTS RESERVED.

THE SPACE OPERA
MASTERPIECE FROM
MANGA LEGEND
LEIJI MATSUMOTO
AVAILABLE FOR THE
FIRST TIME IN
ENGLISH!

LEIJI MATSUMOTO'S

Queen Emeraldas

KC
KODANSHA COMICS

"If you like space cowboys and pirates or simply want to get lost in a strange dreamlike story, Kodansha's beautiful hardcover is worth checking out."
- *Anime News Network*

"It's not so much a manga as it is a song. But you'll want to listen to it again and again."
- *A Case for Suitable Treatment*

"I'm pleasantly
surprised to find
modern shojo using
cross-dressing as a
dramatic device to deliver
social commentary...
Recommended."

-Otaku USA
Magazine

The prince in his dark days

By **Hico Yamanaka**

A drunkard for a father, a household of poverty... For 17-year-old Atsuko, misfortune is all she knows and believes in. Until one day, a chance encounter with Itaru—the wealthy heir of a huge corporation—changes everything. The two look identical, uncannily so. When Itaru curiously goes missing, Atsuko is roped into being his stand-in. There, in his shoes, Atsuko must parade like a prince in a palace. She encounters many new experiences, but at what cost...?

Japan's most powerful spirit medium delves into the ghost world's greatest mysteries!

Story by Kyo Shirodaira, famed author of mystery fiction and creator of *Spiral*, *Blast of Tempest*, and *The Record of a Fallen Vampire*.

Both touched by spirits called yôkai, Kotoko and Kurô have gained unique superhuman powers. But to gain her powers Kotoko has given up an eye and a leg, and Kurô's personal life is in shambles. So when Kotoko suggests they team up to deal with renegades from the spirit world, Kurô doesn't have many other choices, but Kotoko might just have a few ulterior motives...

IN/SPECTRE

STORY BY **KYO SHIRODAIRA**
ART BY **CHASHIBA KATASE**

Princess Jellyfish

Akiko Higashimura

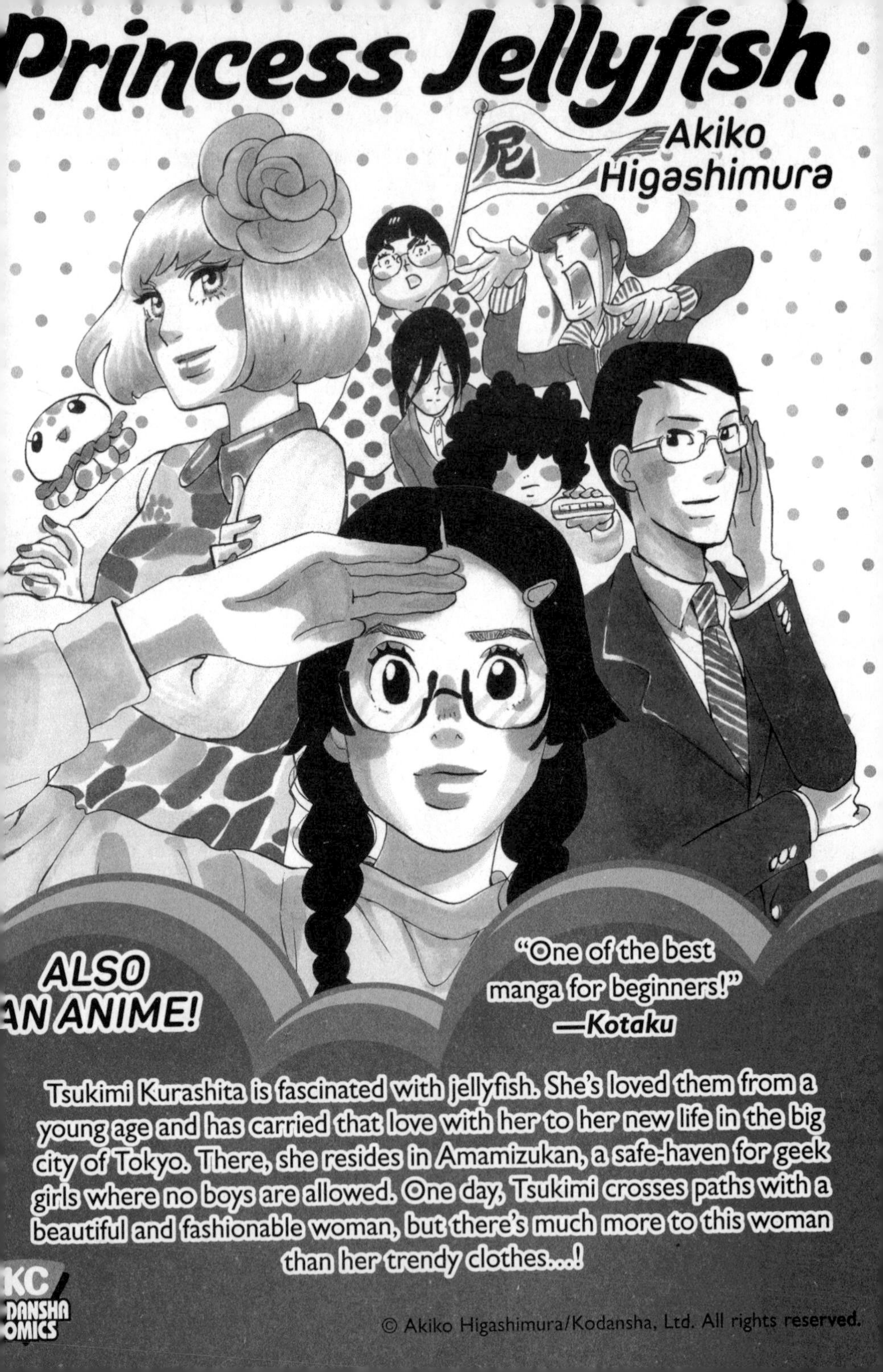

ALSO AN ANIME!

"One of the best manga for beginners!"
—*Kotaku*

Tsukimi Kurashita is fascinated with jellyfish. She's loved them from a young age and has carried that love with her to her new life in the big city of Tokyo. There, she resides in Amamizukan, a safe-haven for geek girls where no boys are allowed. One day, Tsukimi crosses paths with a beautiful and fashionable woman, but there's much more to this woman than her trendy clothes...!

KC DANSHA OMICS

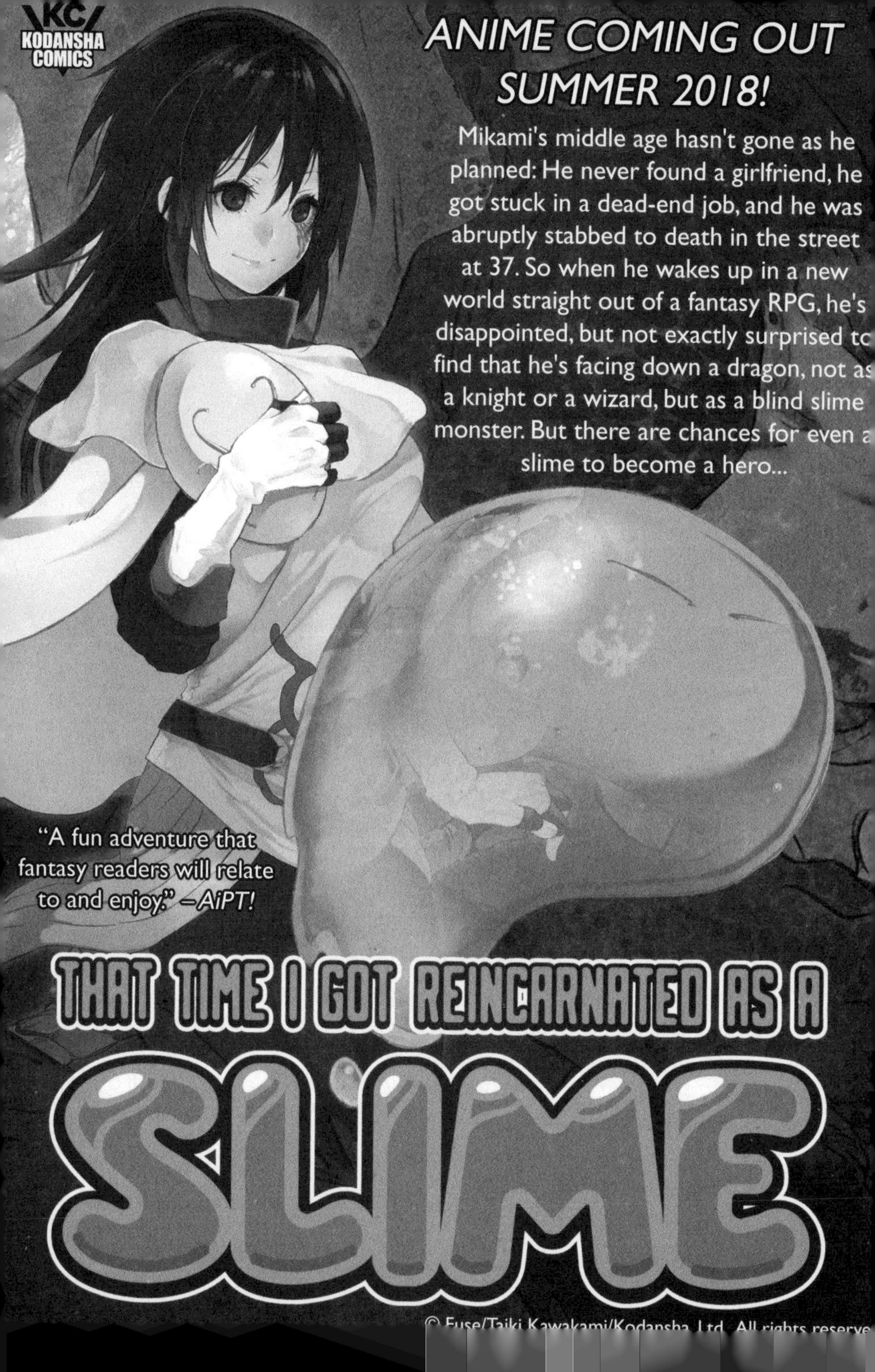
KC KODANSHA COMICS
ANIME COMING OUT SUMMER 2018!
Mikami's middle age hasn't gone as he planned: He never found a girlfriend, he got stuck in a dead-end job, and he was abruptly stabbed to death in the street at 37. So when he wakes up in a new world straight out of a fantasy RPG, he's disappointed, but not exactly surprised to find that he's facing down a dragon, not as a knight or a wizard, but as a blind slime monster. But there are chances for even a slime to become a hero...
"A fun adventure that fantasy readers will relate to and enjoy." –AiPT!
THAT TIME I GOT REINCARNATED AS A
SLIME
© Fuse/Taiki Kawakami/Kodansha Ltd. All rights reserved.

10 Dance volume 2 is a work of fiction. Names, characters, places, and incidents are the products of the author's imagination or are used fictitiously. Any resemblance to actual events, locales, or persons, living or dead, is entirely coincidental.

A Kodansha Comics Trade Paperback Original.

Published in the United States by Kodansha Comics, an imprint of Kodansha USA Publishing, LLC, New York.

Publication rights for this English edition arranged through Kodansha Ltd., Tokyo.

First published in Japan in 2017 by Kodansha Ltd., Tokyo.

ISBN 978-1-63236-766-2

Printed in the United States of America.

www.kodanshacomics.com

9 8 7 6 5 4 3 2 1

Translation: Karhys
Lettering: Brndn Blakeslee
Editing: Lauren Scanlan
Kodansha Comics Edition Cover Design: Phil Balsman